Modern Spanish Women as Agents of Change

Modern Spanish Women as Agents of Change

Essays in Honor of Maryellen Bieder

EDITED BY
JENNIFER SMITH

Bucknell University | Bucknell University Press

Lewisburg, Pennsylvania

Library of Congress Cataloging in Publication Control Number: 2018030070

A British Cataloging-in-Publication record for this book is available from the British Library.

∞ The paper used in this publication meets the requirements of the American National Standard for Information Sciences—Permanence of Paper for Printed Library Materials, ANSI Z39.48-1992.

www.bucknell.edu/UniversityPress

Manufactured in the United States of America

In loving memory

Maryellen Bieder passed away on January 31, 2018. While we wish she could have lived to see the book come out, she did indeed read every single one of the essays included here. This is how much she loved what she did—and what her colleagues in the field do.

She was incredibly sharp and productive until the very end, despite the many physical hardships she had to endure. Emerging from a coma, she had someone reach out to us on her behalf to let us know her predicament and why she had not responded to email. She passed away the next day. She clearly knew the end was near and wanted to say good-bye.

This volume is our way of saying good-bye to her and thanking her for the many ways she touched our lives. We will never forget you, Maryellen.

Contents

A Note on Translations

Unless otherwise noted, all translations are by the contributors.

In chapter 5, translations of the periodicals are by Jennifer Smith; in chapter 7, where noted, a quote by Emilia Pardo Bazán was translated by Walter Borenstein in his introduction to his translation of *La Tribuna* (*The Tribune of the People*); in chapter 9, all translations from Catalan to English, except where indicated otherwise, are by Maryellen Bieder, and the translation of "Caterina Albert i Paradís: Writing, Solitude, and Woman's *Jouissance*" by Neus Carbonell from Spanish to English is by Lourdes Albuixech; and in chapter 11, translations for Leopoldo Alas's *La Regenta* are taken from John Rutherford unless otherwise noted.

Modern Spanish Women as Agents of Change

Introduction

Jennifer Smith

Donald J. Trump secured the U.S. presidency in 2016 with 53 percent of white women's vote despite his explicitly sexist and hostile comments about women during the campaign. What followed was a great deal of speculation about why so many women, in twenty-first-century America, would vote for a man who exhibited such behavior. In an article in the *Nation*, Kathleen Geier argued that it was because feminism had failed to address the economic situation of white working-class women.[1] In an article in *Quartz*, Marcie Bianco related it to many white women's decisions to ally themselves with white men rather than women of color.[2] Citing what she sees as a "toxic cocktail of . . . internalized misogyny, and not-so-subtle racism," Bianco argued that this strategy always has, and always will, "impede women's political and economic progress."[3] Building on Bianco's idea of internalized misogyny, I would like to stress a point that is germane to the purpose of the volume at hand: it is not only men but many women who have rejected and continue to reject basic feminist principles, and this is the reason feminist scholarship and activism is still needed today.

Inspired by Maryellen Bieder's work as a teacher and scholar, I have dedicated most of my own research to the life and works of Emilia Pardo Bazán (1851–1921), one of Spain's first feminists. She was a prolific and talented author at a time when women who dared to take up the pen were dismissed in Spain as *literatas* (a term akin to the derogatory English word *bluestockings*). Frequently describing her own writing style as "manly" and "virile" so that it would garner the serious consideration it deserved, she rejected her subordinate status in society by boldly asserting that she had chosen to live by the same rights and freedoms that men enjoyed (and she did to the extent possible). Indeed, she was no big fan of political liberalism, which, she argued, had converted women into second-class citizens by giving rights and privileges to only one half of the population.[4]

Two things about Pardo Bazán's feminist beliefs and activism have haunted me in light of the recent U.S. presidential election results and many women's rejection of the 2017 Women's March on Washington, which occurred the day after Trump's inauguration. First is Pardo Bazán's assertion that women were actually a bigger obstacle to the success of feminism than men. In an article for the Buenos Aires newspaper *La Nación*, she wrote, "Mientras que los hombres españoles se burlaban del feminismo, las mujeres se crispaban, se escandalizaban se deshacían en protestas de sumisión a la autoridad viril. . . . Eran las peores enemigas de las que pensábamos reivindicarnos de derechos"[5] (While Spanish men made fun of feminism, women cringed, they were scandalized, they broke down in protests in favor of submission to masculine authority. . . . They were the worst enemies of feminism to those of us who were trying to earn our rights). Similar to Bianco's reference to female Trump supporters' "internalized misogyny," Pardo Bazán attributed women's opposition to feminism to a long cultural tradition of exalting men and masculinity and women's consequent lack of belief that they could find the same qualities they admired within themselves: "El inmemorial predominio del hombre en la ley y en la costumbre, ha afirmado en él carácteres que a la Mujer le ha ido perdiendo . . . la mujer hará bien en desechar lo que, a mi modo de ver, la tiene anquilosada: la timidez, la desconfianza en sus propias fuerzas, el amilanamiento fatal, fruto de tantos años de servidumbre"[6] (Men's immemorial legal and cultural dominance have created in men characteristics that women have lost . . . women would do well to disregard that which, in my opinion, keeps them stagnant: timidity, lack of confidence in their own strengths, a terrifying sense of being threatened, the fruit of so many years of servitude).

Unlike Anglophone suffragettes of the time, Emilia Pardo Bazán was not part of a much larger group; she challenged sexism mostly by herself and mainly through her writing. In her lifetime, however, she never saw most of fruits of her efforts: she was never allowed entrance into the Royal Academy of the Spanish Language, and when she finally was allowed to teach a course at the University of Madrid in 1916, near the end of her life, the course was boycotted by students and faculty alike and eventually canceled; they did not want a woman teaching at the university.

The second curiosity about Pardo Bazán's feminism that has come to mind these days was that she never spoke about female suffrage. There is nothing on record to explain this silence. However, those Spanish feminists who followed in her footsteps in the early twentieth century give us some insight. Many early twentieth-century Spanish feminists feared that because women were uneducated and strongly influenced by the Catholic Church and its traditional values, they would vote against a feminist agenda.[7] And indeed, when women were finally given the right to vote by the liberal government of the Second Republic (1933), the party that had given them the right to vote was swiftly voted out of office.[8] The degree to which women were responsible is still under debate,[9] but they were most definitely not overwhelmingly thankful to the party that had granted them suffrage, and this seems to confirm Pardo Bazán's assertion that women themselves were, at the time at least, an obstacle to their own liberation.

Returning to my initial point, then, I think Pardo Bazán understood something that we contemporary feminist women might sometimes forget: a lot of women are not feminists. Even today there are still women who subscribe to traditional values and are attracted to the idea of a strong man who will take care of them—maybe for the same reason that so many people of both sexes are attracted to the idea of a religious savior who will save them—more than to the idea that they are just as capable of fending for themselves.[10] Many conservative American women's disassociation from, and even condemnation of, the Women's March on January 21, 2017, is further evidence of this mind-set. Thus Pardo Bazán's view of women as impediments to their own emancipation seems to still hold today. However, unlike in Pardo Bazán's time, ideas that were once considered radical are now embraced by millions of women and men across the globe. Indeed, the 2017 Women's March has been estimated to be the biggest march in world history.[11] And for that, we are indebted to women like Pardo Bazán and many of the other women writers studied here, who were a small minority of defiant women who had to fight these battles with much smaller numbers.

Although things surely improved for women by the 1970s in the United States (Spain, of course, did not firmly establish full voting rights for women until 1977),[12] there still was a lot of work to be done, a fact attested to by the emergence of second-wave feminism. An important part of this battle was an increase in the number of women entering the world of academia, still very much a field dominated by men. One of these women was Maryellen Bieder. Bieder completed her PhD at the University of Minnesota in 1973 with a dissertation on narrative technique in the post–Civil War novels of Francisco Ayala. Wayne C. Booth's *The Rhetoric of Fiction* (1966) introduced "theory" and the reading of "texts" (a new word) through theory to the academic world of the time. Booth's eminently readable handling of narrative, perspective, irony, and unreliable narration came at just the right time for analyzing contemporary fiction and informed Bieder's dissertation, and soon-to-be book, *Narrative Perspective in the Post–Civil War Novels of Francisco Ayala*.[13] The book, which undertook a theoretical reading of two of Ayala's novels through Booth's categories, especially perspective and unreliability, was revolutionary in Bieder's career and linked her to the "theory" revolution in literary studies. It broke with a long tradition of plot analyses, thematic studies, and biographical approaches that linked the characters, places, and action of the novel to real people and places in the author's life.

While Bieder continued to study male writers—her work on Benito Pérez Galdós and Juan Goytisolo immediately comes to mind—it is mostly her groundbreaking work on Emilia Pardo Bazán and other women writers that has earned her a lasting reputation as a leading scholar of international stature in the field of Spanish literature. Bieder's interest in women writers came after the completion of her degree in the early 1970s. Bieder revolutionized the extant criticism on Pardo Bazán by bringing the question of gender more explicitly into the fold. Her early work on Pardo Bazán dealt largely with how this author sought to garner respect and authority as a novelist at a time when most male novelists refused to take a woman's work seriously.[14] She also explored Pardo Bazán's relationships with other women writers of the time,[15] a theme she had taken on again recently in her research on Pardo Bazán's relationship to the English author Gabriela Cunninghame Graham.[16] Moreover, Bieder helped define Pardo Bazán as one of Spain's first feminists by studying her essays on women,[17] her role in shaping an emerging feminist discourse in Spain,[18] and her ingenious narrative strategies that subverted conventional understandings of gender.[19] One of the first to give serious attention to Pardo Bazán's interest in the French literary movement of decadence, Bieder also studied how Pardo Bazán used it for feminist objectives in her last novel, *Dulce dueño* (*Sweet Master*).[20] In addition to studying the novels, essays, short stories, and theater of Pardo Bazán,[21] Bieder had recently turned her attention to visual portrayals of Pardo Bazán in the periodical press[22] and had begun to explore Pardo Bazán's views on race, religion, and class in relation to gender.[23]

Bieder was also pivotal in raising awareness of female authors who had yet to garner much critical attention when she entered the field. In the 1990s, she began to publish essays on the life, writings, and works of Concepción Gimeno de Flaquer (1850–1990)[24] and Carmen de Burgos (1867–1932).[25] And as early as the mid-1970s, she began researching contemporary women writers, particularly those who lived through and wrote about the Spanish Civil War. Her work on Mercè Rodoreda (1908–1983) focused largely on the role of language in shaping female identity in the novels and short stories by the Catalan author,[26] and her work on Carme Riera (1948–) investigated the interplay of gender and nationality and gender and literary consumption as well as the question of historical memory.[27] Bieder's recent coedited volume *Spanish Women Writers and Spain's Civil War* brings together cutting-edge research precisely in this field. Bieder also explored questions of nationality and historical memory in relation to gender in articles written on works by Marina Mayoral,[28] Neus Carbonell,[29] and Cristina Fernández Cubas.[30]

By the time I arrived at Indiana University as a graduate student in 1996, Maryellen Bieder was well established as a full professor teaching a wide range of courses on topics related to nineteenth- through twenty-first-century Spanish literature. She had rightfully garnered the reputation among the graduate students as one of the most intellectually engaging professors in the department. It was, of course, as my professor and mentor that Bieder had the greatest impact on my life and career. Her genuine interest in my ideas gave me confidence in myself and an enthusiasm for my work that is still with me today. In one of our discussions in her office on teaching, Bieder said to me, "If you really reach one or two students in a class, your class has been a huge success." I ponder these words several times a semester when not all my students' faces mirror my own enthusiasm for the works I am teaching, and it makes me feel better. But more importantly, I mention it here because Bieder, through her teaching, not only reached me but helped bring meaning and direction to my life. So I would now like to modify Bieder's statement to say that if in the course of one's career a professor can affect a student's life as profoundly as Bieder affected mine, that professor has had a successful career.

As a sign of my appreciation, I have put this volume together as a testament to the various ways that Bieder has inspired me and so many of the other fine contributors here who are all former students or colleagues of Bieder. These essays seek to honor Maryellen Bieder's influence and invaluable scholarly contributions by bringing together innovative research on modern Spanish women as writers, activists, and embodiments of cultural change.[31] It also seeks to remind us all of the importance of the work we do and of the lives and efforts of the many brave, dedicated women who came before us. This collection of essays is innovative in its focus on women as political activists, its inclusion of lesser-known women writers, and its incorporation of recent theoretical approaches such as postcolonialism, intersectionality, Lacanian psychoanalysis, affect theory, spatial theory, and queer theory. Moreover, the authors included here study women as agents and representations of social change in a variety of literary and nonliterary genres—namely, short stories, novellas, novels, plays, essays, and journalistic pieces. The essays cover canonical authors such as Emilia Pardo Bazán, Leopoldo Alas "Clarín," Gertrudis Gómez de Avellaneda, and Carmen de Burgos as well as lesser-known writers and activists such as María Rosa Gálvez, Faustina Sáez de Melgar, Sofía Tartilán, and Caterina Albert i Paradís.

Part I: Modern Spanish Women Writers as Activists

This section looks at nineteenth- and early twentieth-century women authors whose writings were specifically tied to their political activism. These women writers embraced causes ranging from the opposition to slavery, colonialism, and discrimination based on race, sex, and class to the support of female suffrage, freemasonry, and freethinking. Their activism, sometimes unconventional and even paradoxical, is long overdue for the critical attention it receives here. In the first essay in this section, "Gender, Race, and Subalternity in the Antislavery Plays of María Rosa Gálvez and Faustina Sáez de Melgar," Akiko Tsuchiya examines the intersections of these three categories in two abolitionist works: María

Rosa Gálvez's *Zinda* (1804) and Faustina Sáez de Melgar's *La cadena rota* (*The Broken Chain*; c. 1876). While *Zinda* and *La cadena rota* were written during different periods of the nineteenth century, both works highlight the struggle for the affirmation and autonomy of the female subject through the denunciation of slavery, which stood as a metaphor for woman's condition. In both Gálvez and Sáez de Melgar's dramatic works, the female subaltern subject—representing the racial other—must negotiate between the Enlightenment values identified with the masculine, metropolitan subject and the dominant discourses of race and gender that inscribe the colonized woman in a position of (double) subalternity. Departing from Gayatri Spivak's famous question "Can the subaltern speak?" this essay interrogates the notion that antislavery discourse, rooted in the Enlightenment project, necessarily leads to the decolonization of the subaltern subject, or a questioning of colonial discourse. At the same time, it argues that while Gálvez's work asserts female agency within the limits of the colonial order, subsuming the question of race under gender, Sáez de Melgar goes further in destabilizing metropolitan discourse through a recognition of the female subaltern subject's embodied personhood and her emergence as a political subject. Thus Sáez de Melgar is able to forge a space of discursive resistance that was not yet possible earlier in the century.

In the next essay in this section, "Forging Progressive Futures for Spain's Women and People: Sofía Tartilán (Palencia 1829–Madrid 1888)," Christine Arkinstall examines how Tartilán, from the 1860s until her death in 1888, carved out a prominent name for herself in fin-de-siècle letters. Associated with freemasonry, Tartilán contributed to Spanish and Portuguese periodicals, corresponded with leading contemporary male writers and critics, and hosted literary *tertulias* (gatherings) in Madrid in the late 1870s. On receiving her calling card, which identified her as an *escritora* (writer), Clarín admiringly described her as a *monstruo* (monster). First and foremost an essayist, she wrote critical works on Arab literature in Spain, historical studies, and a history of literary criticism. However, she also translated from Portuguese and Catalan, and her *Costumbres populares* (*Popular Customs*; 1880) enjoyed the distinction of a prologue by Mesonero Romanos. Her staunch advocacy and activism for the education of women and the working classes are evident in her *Páginas para la educación popular* (*Pages for the People's Education*; 1877), essays that previously appeared in the periodical *La Ilustración de la Mujer* (*The Enlightenment of Women*; Madrid). In fact, she replaced Concepción Gimeno as the director of this periodical and served in that role from approximately 1875 to her death. There Tartilán worked closely with other major female writers such as Matilde Cherner and Josefa Pujol de Collado. To date, the few articles that address Tartilán's works have focused on *Costumbres* and *Páginas*. Seeking a greater approximation to this figure and her place within fin de siècle Spanish culture, Arkinstall proposes to analyze a selection of

Tartilán's essays and several of her forgotten novellas: *Una deuda de veinte años* (*A Twenty-Year Debt*; 1875), *La caja de hierro* (*The Iron Box*; 1874), and *Borrascas del corazón* (*Storms of the Heart*; 1884).

The last essay in the section explores Carmen de Burgos's connection of fashion with feminism. In "Fashion as Feminism: Carmen de Burgos's Ideas on Fashion in Context," Roberta Johnson analyzes Burgos's ideas on fashion, makeup, and gesture as feminist strategies within the context of ideas put forth by Emilia Pardo Bazán somewhat earlier and the implementation of reforms in women's dress initiated by designers such as Mariano Fortuny, whose special pleated fabric allowed women to eschew the rigid corsets that kept their bodies literally and symbolically restrained. In her 1927 *La mujer moderna y sus derechos* (*The Modern Woman and Her Rights*), Carmen de Burgos devoted an entire chapter to *la moda* (fashion), along with chapters on more orthodox feminist subjects such as marriage and work. Burgos argues that fashion, rather than a frivolous pursuit, is one area in which women have been able to give free reign to their imaginations. She also points out that fashion provides women with a means of connecting internationally. Underlying her arguments about fashion is a running dialogue with Gregorio Marañón's ideas on the difference between the sexes that she carries on not only in *La mujer moderna y sus derechos* but in her last novel, *Quiero vivir mi vida* (*I Want to Live My Life*; 1931). If Marañón thought women and men should maintain sharply differentiated spheres, Burgos argues for absolute equality in all areas of life, an equality she believed fashion could help attain. Burgos's theories about fashion build not only on those of her predecessors; they point toward how feminists of the Franco era covertly manifested their rebellion (Carmen Laforet's hairstyle, for example), and they presciently coincide with the postfeminist ideas and practices of writers such as Carmen Alborch and Lucía Etxebarria.

Part II: Emilia Pardo Bazán as Literary Theorist and Cultural Critic

This section takes on the inimitable figure of Emilia Pardo Bazán. She was one of the first woman writers to secure a place for herself in the literary canon alongside the best male authors of her day, despite the many obstacles she had to surmount. Nevertheless, it has been the groundbreaking research by Bieder that has helped make Pardo Bazán's work relevant and alive for contemporary readers and scholars. The essays in this section make novel contributions to the extant criticism on Pardo Bazán by exploring how her narrative theories and cultural beliefs inform her literary works. More specifically, we see their application in the short story, in her hagiographical texts, and in a novella about the question of theatrical women. In the first essay in this section, "Emilia Pardo Bazán's

'Apuntes autobiográficos' and 'El baile del Querubín': A Theoretical Reexamination," Susan M. McKenna examines the autobiographical prologue that the Galician author penned in 1886 for the first edition of her novel *Los pazos de Ulloa* (*The House of Ulloa*). McKenna argues that "Apuntes" is a hybrid text, at once a brief summary of her literary trajectory and an imaginative synthesis of narrative theories and practices. Prominent among these pages is the significance of the storytelling act and the reader's response to said act: a mutually creative and reinforcing collaboration of originators. While "Apuntes" has received much less critical attention compared to its sister essay, *La cuestión palpitante* (*The Burning Question*), it received vehement commentary—mostly negative—in its own time from many of the leading authors of the day, including Menéndez y Pelayo, Clarín, and Pereda. Such criticism registered Pardo Bazán's use of "Apuntes" to hone her theoretical practices and to construct an autobiographical narrative that ranked her with her male contemporary authors. Part theory, part story, part synthesis, "Apuntes" circumscribes the author in both, and yet in neither, of the masculine and feminine traditions in which she was bound. Deploying the framework she identifies in "Apuntes autobiográficos," McKenna subsequently examines Pardo Bazán's little-studied short story "El baile del Querubín."

Emilia Pardo Bazán's application of narrative technique in the short story is also the subject of the next chapter in this section. In "The Twice-Told and the Unsaid in Emilia Pardo Bazán's 'Presentido,' 'En coche-cama,' 'Confidencia,' and 'Madre,'" Linda M. Willem examines individual stories within the Galician author's vast canon of short fiction that echo each other and constitute a retelling of the same idea but in a different manner. Willem specifically focuses on two such pairs of stories: (1) "Presentido" (1910) and "En coche-cama" (1914), about jewel robberies aboard trains from Paris to Madrid, and (2) "Confidencia" (1892) and "Madre" (1893), about mothers who are burned in house fires. The progression from the earlier stories to their subsequent counterparts is indicative of Pardo Bazán's stylistic experimentation and demonstrates her skillful handling of sophisticated narrative strategies that carefully control the reader's participation within the individual fictional worlds she creates. Willem draws on James Phelan's theories of narrative positioning and unreliable character narration, along with Armine Kotin Mortimer's concept of the "second story," to show how Pardo Bazán revisited her previously published material in ways that made the latter story of each pair more narratively complex, interpretively challenging, and ethically nuanced. These reworked stories exemplify her facility for devising innovative and effective strategies for the brief narratives of the newly forming short story genre that she helped create.

Pardo Bazán's attraction to both decadent literature and hagiography is the subject of the next essay in this section. In "Emilia Pardo Bazán, Joris-Karl Huysmans, and Stories of Conversion," Denise DuPont develops Bieder's identification of Pardo Bazán as a creative reader and interpreter of Huysmans, the French iconoclast who shares with his fictional characters a trajectory that runs from decadent aestheticism to Catholic asceticism. Huysmans's Des Esseintes, the typical decadent hero, blends with the spiritual seeker Durtal, the main character of *Là-bas* (*Down There*; 1891), *En route* (*En route*; 1895), *La cathédrale* (*The Cathedral*; 1898), and *L'oblat* (*The Oblate*; 1903), in a representation of this journey. Huysmans's two notorious protagonists strive for happiness by searching within as well as changing their physical locations. They flee from and reject society, but ultimately Durtal, the second major protagonist, learns to atone for his own sins and those of others. Thus following Bieder's lead, DuPont argues that in *Dulce dueño*, Pardo Bazán effectively recapitulates with the single story of her female hero, Lina, the spiritual trajectory that Huysmans's male characters traverse over the course of several novels.

The last essay in this section looks at Pardo Bazán's engagement with the condition of female actors in the theater. In "'A Most Promising Girl': Gender and Artistic Future in Emilia Pardo Bazán's 'La dama joven,'" Margot Versteeg reads Pardo's novella in the context of a group of nineteenth-century texts in which the actress represents a growing preoccupation/fascination with the female subject who defies stereotypical gender roles. Versteeg argues that this fascination with the figure of the actress in the nineteenth-century imaginary responds to a double sociohistorical reality. The expansion of the theater industry in nineteenth-century Spain had produced a notable female presence on stage, and women stage actors were a source of both attraction and anxiety. On the one hand, female performers served as aesthetic objects of desire. On the other, they were autonomous subjects and therefore a dangerous subversion of the model wife and mother. In the context of the traditional angel/prostitute binary, a woman on stage personified the process of the redefinition of gender categories that was taking place at the time. While male authors tended to construct actresses as dangerous forces that must be contained, for women who pursued a career in letters, such as Emilia Pardo Bazán, they were actually models to emulate. Versteeg's essay specifically analyzes the problematic resolution of "La dama joven" in the light of the discourses on gender and theater and dialogues with some of the most suggestive intertexts in the story: the romantic *folletín* (serialized novel) of the so-called virtuous woman, the play *Consuelo* (1878) by Adelardo López de Ayala, and George Sand's novel by the same name, *Consuelo* (1842). Versteeg concludes that in "La dama joven," Pardo Bazán distances herself as much from the women writers of the previous generation as from contemporary male realist authors in order to express a unique opinion on the future of artistic women—and of women in general.

Part III: Representations of Female Deviance

This final section explores representations of female deviance in both female- and male-authored texts in the light of spatial theory, Lacanian psychoanalysis, affect theory, and queer theory. In "A Woman's Search for a Space of Her Own in Gertrudis Gómez de Avellaneda's *Dos mujeres*," Rogelia Lily Ibarra argues that in this lesser-studied novel, Avellaneda takes what appears to be a typical love-triangle story and transforms it into an allegory of the fragmented state of the Spanish nation in the nineteenth century and a feminist critique. Through her representations of space, the author first highlights the cultural and ideological tensions resulting from the conflict between the preservation of traditional, autochthonous customs and the advancement of progressive French cultural influences. Avellaneda then challenges gender divisions embraced by liberals and conservatives alike, in which men were allowed to move freely in the public sphere while women were restricted to a domestic, private existence. Ibarra argues that Avellaneda does this by introducing female characters who blur the boundaries of these spaces by failing to fit into any of the roles available to the female subject at the time. Through female characters unable to find satisfactorily inhabitable spaces within the public/private, modern/traditional, masculine/feminine, social/natural binary spheres, Avellaneda underscores the inadequacy of such divisions and of the meaning given to these spaces and advocates a transcendence of these spatial divisions altogether.

In the next essay, "Caterina Albert i Paradís: Writing, Solitude, and Woman's *Jouissance*" (translation by Lourdes Albuixech), Neus Carbonell explores the works of Caterina Albert i Paradís, whose pen name was Víctor Català. Albert was born in 1869 within a family of rural proprietors who had a penchant for the arts. Caterina Albert led an unconventional life judging by the standards of nineteenth-century Catalonian society. She was, however, suspicious of her true inclinations and kept her pleasures as far from the public eye as possible. For this reason, her public image of a well-bred, rural, upper-class woman contrasts sharply with what she wrote and probably lived. The writings of Caterina Albert are actually an incursion into the unexplored area of feminine *jouissance*. The theatrical piece with which she initiated her literary trajectory and whose success was intolerable for the author, *La infanticida* (*Infanticide*), is in fact a monologue by an insane young woman who is abandoned and left alone with the remains of her lost love. This essay takes as its point of departure the idea that Albert wrote in order to capture something of a unique female *jouissance*, a pleasure always distinct from discourse, which forces the female subject to confront her own solitude, as is seen in the novel most acclaimed by critics, *Solitud*. Caterina Albert made her writing her *sinthome*, to use the term Jacques Lacan employs to refer to how James Joyce escaped the precipice of insanity. Nevertheless, what is radically unique about the Catalan author is how she was able to avoid solitude in the face of the *jouissance* of the Other.

In the next chapter, "The Obstinate Negativity of Ana Ozores," Jo Labanyi employs affect theory to analyze the eponymous protagonist of Clarín's *La Regenta.* Recent affect theory has questioned the sovereignty of the individual subject by breaking with the notion that emotion resides within the individual and that it forms the basis of the authentic self. As an energetic disturbance occurring at the interface of the self and world, affect is a form of emotion that is without a subject and without an object. Labanyi refers to Sianne Ngai's *Ugly Feelings*, which explores negative affects that lack any transcendental quality: feelings that are intransitive, noncathartic, related to inertia, obstructed agency and inaction, and fundamentally nonnarrative. The chapter explores the literary problem produced by the attempt to narrate nonnarrative emotions, using as a case study Leopoldo Alas's classic novel *La Regenta* (1884–1885). It aims to show how the novel anticipates certain aspects of the contemporary theorization of affect in its representation of a female protagonist who seems to have no identity, who does not progress or learn anything, but who yet succeeds in interesting the reader over the book's nearly one thousand pages—in most of which, nothing happens.

In the last essay in this volume, "Female Masculinity in *La Regenta* (1884–1885)," I deconstruct the link between men and masculinity in *La Regenta* through the lens of J. Halberstam's ideas in his/her book *Female Masculinity.* Halberstam argues that masculinity is actually most visible, and most threatening, when it leaves the male body and asserts that one of his/her aims is precisely to pry apart masculinity, maleness, power, and domination.[32] In order to deconstruct such linkages, s/he employs terms such as *hegemonic masculinity* and *heroic masculinities* to refer to conventional ideas that link masculinity to power, strength, and dominance. This concept of hegemonic masculinity is particularly useful in analyzing *La Regenta*, as the question of power and dominance in a decaying feudal and imperial society threatened by social and economic change is intimately intertwined with questions of gender or, more specifically, with the degree to which various characters perform or defy their respective gender roles. Consequently, my approach to the discussion of female masculinity is two-pronged. First, I deconstruct the connection between the male body and masculinity by examining the ways the male characters' inability to perform masculinity undermines their claim to it. Then I turn to the masculine women that populate the text. However, in contradiction to Halberstam's assertion that "female masculinity seems to be at its most threatening when coupled with lesbian desire,"[33] in *La Regenta*, it is not same-sex female desire that poses the most threat to society but rather masculine heterosexual women with raw ambition and a strong capitalist sense who turn Vetustan society on its head.

Thus together, the essays in this collection build on Bieder's work by studying how women (real and fictional) forged new paths in their day. These essays speak not only to their respective historical times periods but also to the present and the recently heightened divisions between reaction and progress. The chapters simultaneously remind us of how far we have come and how far we still have to go. Yet it is also my hope that the essays here remind us of the satisfactions to be found in women's intellectual and artistic struggles for personal autonomy and of the continued importance of the work all of us do as scholars and teachers of women's writing.

NOTES

1. Kathleen Geier, "Inequality among Women Is Crucial to Understanding Hillary's Loss," *Nation*, November 11, 2016, https://www.thenation.com/article/inequality-between-women-is-crucial-to-understanding-hillarys-loss/.

2. Marcie Bianco, "What Sisterhood? White Women Voted for Trump in 2016 because They Still Believe White Men Are Their Saviors," *Quartz*, November 14, 2016, https://qz.com/835567/election-2016-white-women-voted-for-donald-trump-in-2016-because-they-still-believe-white-men-are-their-saviors/.

3. Bianco.

4. Emilia Pardo Bazán, "La mujer española," in *La mujer española y otros escritos*, ed. and intro. by Guadalupe Gómez Ferrer (Madrid: Cátedra, 1999), 87.

5. Emilia Pardo Bazán, *La obra periodística completa en* La Nación *de Buenos Aires*, vol. 2, ed. Juliana Sínovas Maté (A Coruña: Diputación Provincial de A Coruña, 1999), 1322.

6. Quoted in Ángeles Quesada Novás, *El amor en los cuentos de Emilia Pardo Bazán* (Alicante: Publicaciones de la Universidad de Alicante, 2005), 32.

7. Geraldine Scanlon, *La polémica feminista en la España contemporánea (1868–1974)* (Madrid: Siglo XXI, 1976), 274–275, 279–280.

8. Scanlon, 274–275, 279–280.

9. Scanlon, 274–275, 279–280.

10. The title of Bianco's article suggests that many white women still look for white men to be their saviors (Bianco, "What Sisterhood?"). And of course, the idea that women are raised to believe that it is preferable to find a man who will shelter them from the hardships of the world rather than learn to fend for oneself was expressed most famously by Simone de Beauvoir in *The Second Sex*, trans. and ed. H. M. Parshley (New York: Vintage, 1989), 645–646.

11. Jason Easley, "Women's March Is the Biggest Protest in US History as an Estimated 2.9 Million March," *Politicus USA*, February 17, 2017, http://www.politicususa.com/2017/01/21/womens-march-biggest-protest-history-estimated-2-4-million-march.html.

12. Javier Dale, "El voto femenino en España cumple 80 años," *La Vanguardia*, November 13, 2013, http://www.lavanguardia.com/vida/20131119/54393615758/voto-femenino-espana-cumple-80-anos.html.

13. Maryellen Bieder, *Narrative Perspective in the Post–Civil War Novels of Francisco Ayala* (Chapel Hill: University of North Carolina Press, 1979).

14. Maryellen Bieder, "En-gendering Strategies of Authority: Emilia Pardo Bazán and the Novel," in *Cultural and Historical Grounding for Hispanic and Luso-Brazilian Feminist Literary Criticism*, ed. Hernán Vidal (Minneapolis: Institute for Study of Ideologies &

momentum in the 1860s in response to the U.S. Civil War, women of letters increasingly asserted their presence in this movement through their antislavery activism and writings. Among the members of the women's chapter of the Spanish Abolitionist Society were many prominent women of letters, including Coronado and Faustina Sáez de Melgar, who, in addition to her play *La cadena rota*, published columns denouncing slavery in her own periodical, *La Violeta* (*The Violet*). In sum, significant numbers of women were engaged in the antislavery cause in Spain throughout the nineteenth century.[10]

Returning to the female dramatists who are the subjects of this study, Gálvez, adopted and raised by an Andalusian family with military and political connections, was one of the most successful of the very small number of women dramatists of the late eighteenth century who tried to make a living through their writing. While she embraced many of the same Enlightenment values as her male contemporaries, she was unique in highlighting controversial gender issues such as rape, incest, and domestic violence.[11] Sáez de Melgar, for her part, was commonly known to be a neo-Catholic writer and editor of women's magazines in the mid-nineteenth century. Yet she played a crucial role in generating spheres of female action in nineteenth-century Spanish society through her participation in women's organizations, such as the women's chapter of the Abolitionist Society and the Ateneo de Señoras (Women's Athenaeum), of which she was named president in 1869. She was quite vocal in her abolitionist views, as evinced in her uncompromising denunciation of slavery as "el crimen más nefando de los tiempos de la civilización"[12] (the most nefarious crime of civilized times). In addition, the periodical *La Violeta*, founded and directed by Sáez de Melgar in the 1860s, had an important cultural impact among women's circles, and in spite of what Íñigo Sánchez Llama has called its "feminine format,"[13] it served as a forum for expressing antislavery sentiments.

That both Gálvez and Sáez de Melgar's plays present an implicit analogy between women's condition and chattel slavery is not surprising given the tradition of abolitionist literature by (white) women for whom slavery became a metaphor for their own subaltern status in a patriarchal society. Yet such an analogy must be rendered problematic precisely because of the Eurocentric, colonial discourse that frames the antislavery narrative. Avellaneda's *Sab* exemplifies this problem, as the Creole author's preoccupation with women's oppression and social marginalization overshadows the novel's denunciation of slavery, as several critics have noted.[14] In both Gálvez and Sáez de Melgar's dramatic works, the female subaltern subject—represented by the racial other—must negotiate between the Enlightenment values identified with the masculine, metropolitan subject and the dominant discourses of race and gender that inscribe the colonized woman in a position of subalternity. Departing from Gayatri Spivak's famous question "Can the subaltern speak?"[15] this study will interrogate the notion that antislavery discourse, rooted in the Enlightenment project, necessarily leads to the decolonization of the subaltern subject, or a questioning of colonial discourse.

Zinda is a fictional work that bears the name of the female protagonist, who is the queen of the Portuguese colony of Congo. According to Julia Bordiga Greinstein, Zinda was modeled on Nzinga Mbandi (1583–1663), the legendary queen of the West African kingdom of Matamba (part of present-day Angola) under Portuguese colonial rule in the seventeenth century.[16] Nzinga was considered to be the mother of African nationalism, having mobilized the slaves in her kingdom to join the war against the Portuguese slave traders.[17] Gálvez's drama gives center stage to the problems of slavery and colonialism during a historical period when the major European empires were beginning to establish the slave trade, an institution that would, by the eighteenth century, become firmly entrenched and fundamental to the economy of the empires.[18] Despite the Portuguese setting of Gálvez's work, the events clearly serve as an allegory of Spanish colonialism, responsible for the maintenance of the slave trade and slavery until well into the nineteenth century. (The Cuban slave trade was declared illegal in 1867, but slavery itself was not abolished until 1886.)

In both *Zinda* and *La cadena rota*, gender, race, and colonialism intersect in complex and oftentimes contradictory ways. The opening scene of the play shows the (black) African warrior Alcaypa ready to execute the Christian (Portuguese) commander, Pereyra, by setting him on fire, thus seeking to take revenge on the white colonizers responsible for the slavery of the black Africans. The queen, Zinda, who enters the scene, intervenes and saves Pereyra from this violent death, affirming that it was the commander himself who has taught her to be merciful.[19] In other words, he is cast from the beginning as the enlightened (Christian) European subject who brings reason and civilization to her land, where "reinaban las costumbres sanguinarias de la ferocidad"[20] (bloodthirsty and ferocious customs reigned). Thus the work reproduces the racialized opposition, constructed by the European imaginary, between civilization and barbarism, whereby the male European subject represents civilization, enlightenment, and reason while the African subject represents barbarism, ignorance, and uncontained passion. The stage directions reinforce this dichotomy, as the scene is set in a "bosque sombrío"[21] (somber forest), representing the darkness that contrasts with the enlightenment of the male European subject who is about to be thrown to his death. Death by bonfire is yet another symbol that evokes the primitivism of the Africans in the European's eyes. In response to Zinda's words of reason, the black warrior urges her to conserve "las costumbres de tu patria"[22] (customs of your homeland), implying that barbarism is the law of the African land. That is to say, the author has Zinda choose European reason over African barbarism from the very beginning of the play.

At the same time, Zinda, as a black African woman and a colonized subject, cannot by definition occupy the position of the white European man, even though she shares his Enlightenment values. In this case, while it is apparently the brown woman who saves the white man from the brown man, to play with Spivak's famous sentence,[23] the colonialist subtext of the play is such that, in reality, it is the white man (Pereyra) who is ultimately saving the brown woman (Zinda) from the savagery of brown men (Alcaypa and his African warriors). That is to say, the message conveyed by the work is that Pereyra, as the embodiment of (masculine) European reason, saves the black queen from the barbarism of the African warrior and the rest of the natives of the African kingdom by enlightening her.[24] He is cast as the benevolent colonizer who is set in contrast with both the "savage" African who resists European colonialism and the malevolent Dutch slave trader Vinter, who comes to Congo only to usurp, in Pereyra's absence, the latter's position as the commander of Congo's armies. One could argue that the play presents an apology of colonialism by granting protagonism to the "benevolent" Portuguese colonizer who brings civilization and enlightenment to the African nation as well as to the virtuous queen who agrees to negotiate a pact with him.[25]

How, then, does gender enter into the equation? Does Gálvez really give voice to the female subaltern subject in the work? If she is a "black African woman who has adopted white ways,"[26] as Elizabeth Franklin Lewis has argued, does Zinda's aspiration to emulate the (male) European subject's Enlightenment values grant her agency as a woman, if not necessarily freedom from colonialist ideology? If, as Julia Grinstein suggests, Gálvez modeled Zinda on the West African queen Nzinga, whose father raised her in the art or war, it would be to highlight her agency as a political leader—and, above all, as a warrior (the myth of the Amazon comes to mind)[27]—who led the resistance of the native (colonized) Africans against the Portuguese colonizers, major players in the transatlantic slave trade since in the seventeenth century. In Gálvez's play, it is Zinda who takes charge as political leader and military commander, asserting her authority not only over her subordinates but also over her husband, Nelzir, of whom she acts independently. On discovering her son's imprisonment by the Dutch colonizers, she exclaims to Pereyra, "Deja a mi brío el esplendor del triunfo"[28] (Leave the splendor of triumph to my courage), letting him know of her plan to seek revenge for her son. She orders Alcaypa to keep the incidents of the day hidden from her husband, acting on her own accord in the latter's absence. While the enlightened Pereyra seeks to tame "el furor atroz de una africana"[29] (the atrocious fury of an African woman) through his reason, attributing Zinda's plan of revenge—through an act of military aggression—to her "maternal cariño [que] te conduce a un extremo funesto"[30] (maternal love [that] leads you to this terrible extreme), she makes clear that she prioritizes her public role as a monarch and political leader as much as her maternal role in the private sphere. In fact, her refusal to betray her nation in exchange for her son's freedom, and even life, undermines societal expectations of woman's primary role as a guardian of the family within the private sphere. At the same time, in the context of this play, Gálvez politicizes the desire for justice that arises from Zinda's "maternal love," thus reconciling the private and the public—her obligations to the family and to the nation. As Virginia Trueba Mira has suggested, one of the transgressions in Gálvez's work is "la compatibilidad entre el mundo privado de los sentimientos y el mundo público de la política"[31] (compatibility between the private world of feelings and the public world of politics).

Zinda must, however, constantly negotiate between the identity that she has modeled on the male European paradigm of the Enlightenment and her "female volition, desire and agency," which, in one postcolonial critic's words, "are literally pushed to the margins of the civilized world."[32] In the first act, when the female protagonist urges her husband, Nelzir, to enter into negotiation with the Dutch slave trader (Vinter) rather than giving into his violent passions and desire for revenge, she is cast as the Enlightenment subject par excellence, upholding honor, virtue, and reason *in spite of* her African origin.[33] Yet as soon as the freedom of her nation—and its future, embodied in the figure of her imprisoned son—is threatened, she reclaims a much more radical subjectivity: her female agency becomes inextricably tied to her struggle as a colonized black woman fighting for the liberation of her nation from colonialism and slavery. Finding herself imprisoned by Vinter, she voices her refusal to submit to slavery and to sacrifice her freedom: "Yo espero / no ser jamás esclava de los blancos / . . . Mi hijo Zelido y yo libres nacimos; / infelices, mas libres moriremos"[34] (I wish / never to be a slave of the white people / . . . My son Zelido and I were born free; / we will die wretched but free). In the third act, she is willing to take the life of her own son before allowing him to be sold as a slave in Portugal. That is to say, *Zinda*, at the turn of the nineteenth century, already anticipates the "representation of female subjectivity as Romantic consciousness—a sense of outrage, the Promethean impulse toward revolt," which, according to Susan Kirkpatrick,[35] Gómez de Avellaneda reclaims in *Sab* (1841) nearly four decades later through the identification of the male slave with the Creole woman. In Gálvez's play, in fact, the female protagonist asserts her subjectivity by voicing her protest directly on stage; she does not need a male subaltern subject to speak for her, contrary to the case of Avellaneda's novel.

The female black warrior, who puts up a heroic resistance to Vinter's forces to fight for freedom and justice for her nation, is set in contrast with Pereyra's daughter Ángela (her name, of course, evokes the archetype of the white angel in the house), who passively resigns herself to marriage with Vinter, thus upholding the patriarchal norms on which colonialism is founded. Believing that her honor obligates her to wed Vinter, Ángela becomes objectified as war booty, an object of exchange, to be sacrificed to the male victor. Yet Zinda does not allow Pereyra's daughter to remain a victim. It is Zinda who gives back to Ángela the agency that has been taken away from her, involving her in a plan to deceive the slave trader by soliciting the help of the queen's warriors. That is to say, it is the brown woman who takes action to rescue the white woman from the white man.

Yet Pereyra's return at the end of the drama and the ensuing agreement the colonizer negotiates with the queen of the colonized nation complicates the problem of agency of the female and subaltern subjects. As in the beginning of the play, Pereyra reassumes the role of the benevolent and enlightened European. Rather than taking vengeance on the slave trader who has usurped his political position, murdered his son, and tried to coerce his daughter into a marriage she did not want, Pereyra, governed by a sense of justice, agrees to pardon his enemy from death; instead, he orders the slave trader's exile to Lisbon. On hearing Pereyra's verdict, Zinda not only holds up the Portuguese commander as the model of virtue and enlightened reason (she orders her warriors, "Respetemos las virtudes de este héroe portugués"[36] [Let us respect the virtues of this Portuguese hero]) but also agrees to accept the colonizers' religion (Christianity) in exchange for the end of the slave trade. That the final lines of the play leave us with the Portuguese commander's words praising Zinda for overcoming her barbarism to embrace the virtue of Christianity ("En ti se ha visto / que la ferocidad cede, y se rinde / a la santa virtud y al heroismo"[37] [In you we see / that ferocity gives way, and surrenders / to sacred virtue and to heroism]) suggests that the subaltern woman is no more than a medium through which colonialist discourse reinforces its own assumptions about its relation to the colonized other.

For Gálvez, the progressive values of the Enlightenment—reason, virtue, and freedom—originate in the metropolis, and it is precisely Zinda's "Europeanization," her adoption of "white ways"[38] through the influence of the male metropolitan subject, that grants authority to the female subaltern subject. That is to say, female agency can only be asserted within the limits of the colonial order; decolonization cannot truly be achieved while the discursive structures of imperial domination and hegemony remain largely intact within the framework of the work. Yet the fissures that Gálvez's heroine has introduced within metropolitan discourse, through her active and passionate resistance to slavery, are not insignificant given the historical and cultural context in which the actions of this drama take place. While the metropolitan subject cannot speak for the subaltern other without colonizing him or her, the rhetorical identification between the woman and the colonial other as a potential site of resistance to power allowed a strategic space from which the female writer could participate in a public debate that was dominated by male intellectuals.

While Gálvez, a writer formed in the Enlightenment tradition, anticipates—through her representation of the Queen Zinda—the new Romantic paradigms of feminine subjectivity that would emerge in the 1830s and 1840s,[39] Sáez de Melgar's *La cadena rota*, composed in the 1870s, reflects the influence of the melodramas of José Echegaray, who prolonged the Romantic legacy in theater. If, as for Peter Brooks, the melodrama seeks to articulate ethical imperatives through the expression of "pure and excessive" sentiments, often making morality and emotions indistinguishable,[40] it is also true that the genre played a major role in trying to resolve the ideological conflicts and contradictions that characterized the cultural dynamics of the nineteenth century.[41] In the works of Gálvez and Sáez de Melgar, the sentimental discourse of the melodramatic genre allows for the elevation of the subaltern subject—woman and the racial other—to the status of a hero who confronts the ethical problems arising from colonialism and slavery.

The first act of *La cadena rota* introduces the figure of the metropolitan subject, Horacio, who travels to Havana from Spain to marry his cousin Rosa, owner of a plantation and heiress to her father's fortune. The marriage, as was customary in those days among members of the social elite, has been arranged by the two families since the children's infancy. Horacio's arrival on the island coincides with the acquisition by his fiancée of two slaves, Ruderico and Azella, who are siblings and whose mother was brutally murdered by the slave trader Pedro Antonio. When Horacio meets Azella, he becomes increasingly attracted to her, while his relationship to his fiancée becomes ever more distant as he discovers her capricious and cruel character. From there, as one would expect in a melodrama, a series of sentimental conflicts involving this love triangle unfold, and the tragic denouement is rather predictable. When Rosa arranges to sell the slaves to Pedro Antonio without Horacio's knowledge, Azella chooses to die at her own brother's hands rather than face this cruel destiny.

Like the Europe/Africa dichotomy in Gálvez's *Zinda*, Sáez de Melgar's melodrama sets up the opposition between civilization and barbarism, identified, respectively, with the metropolis (Spain) and the colonies (Cuba). The discourse of colonialism intersects with that of gender, as the male metropolitan subject is cast as one who presumably brings Enlightenment values to colonial society, challenging the social order founded on the institution of slavery. The Creole woman (his fiancée), in contrast, embodies the barbarism of the colonies, driven by her economic interest in preserving this institution. While the gendered opposition between the terms *civilization/man/metropolis* and *barbarism/woman/colony* echoes and reinforces a common paradigm in abolitionist texts written by men, Sáez de Melgar's work also exposes the contradictions in colonial discourse: while presenting Horacio as the enlightened metropolitan subject, it glosses over the Spanish Empire's role in upholding the institution of slavery. We must recall, furthermore, that what originally brings the male protagonist to the Americas is to consolidate, through the marriage of the European man and the Creole woman, the economic relationship between the two families and, symbolically, imperial relations between the metropolis and the colony.

Yet Horacio's outrage on witnessing the treatment of the slaves by his Creole cousin and his desire for the racial and colonial other (the slave Azella) undermine the imperial romance, threatening to transform it into a miscegenation narrative. One critic has argued that the enlightened male character serves as a spokesperson for the female author who is unable to voice her political views directly;[42] however, the European male represents a far more complex point of convergence of discourses on gender and race. While other women's antislavery works—and Gómez de Avellaneda's *Sab* is a classic example—often establish an identification between the subalternity of (white/European or Creole) women and that of (African) slaves, how does Sáez de Melgar situate the racialized and gendered subaltern subject (woman of African descent) in relation to the masculine hero (the European man)? Can the subaltern speak in this play? What does it mean for the author to adopt the conventions of the sentimental heterosexual romance to represent the European man's (failed) fantasy of interracial desire?

Sáez de Melgar's play, at first sight, appears to be more subversive than that of Gálvez in positing the possibility of interracial desire. However, it becomes evident that interracial desire is only possible through the whitening of the racial other. While the slaves, Azella and her brother Ruderico, are of African descent, they themselves and others constantly call attention to the lighter complexion of their skin. The overseer considers Azella to be a "mestiza"[43] (woman of mixed blood), and the slaves refer to themselves as "cuarterones" (quadroons): "Nacimos . . . de una mestiza y un blanco y se nos dio educación muy esmerada"[44] (We were born . . . of a *mestiza* and a white person and we were given a very thorough education). For Karen Sánchez-Eppler, miscegenation provides an essential motif of virtually all antislavery literature, and she notes that "the light-skinned body is valued . . . precisely because of its ability to mask the alien African blackness that the fictional mulatto is nevertheless purported to represent."[45] In Sáez de Melgar's play, the siblings' blackness is also disguised by their literacy and love of letters and the arts ("Saben de letra y escriben" [They are literate and know how to write])[46]—that is, their resemblance to their presumably enlightened white brothers and sisters makes their redemption possible. Upon first meeting Azella's brother, Horacio exclaims, "Pero esa fisonomía revela un hombre de genio . . . Que este hombre sea un esclavo es cosa que no me explico"[47] (But those facial features reveal a very intelligent man . . . I can't explain how this man can be a slave). In fact, the slaves' erudition is their greatest crime in Rosa's eyes, as it grants them a subjectivity of their own that eludes the control of the Creole woman.

In Sáez de Melgar's work, as in that of Gálvez, the subaltern subject becomes a symbolic site where various struggles—on the basis of gender, race, and class—are articulated in very complex ways, evincing "multiple intersections of structures of power."[48] Even within the melodramatic conventions, where stock characters representing facile dichotomies (e.g., good vs. evil, oppressor vs. oppressed) are expected, Sáez de Melgar undermines clearly delineated power relationships and hierarchies. In fact, the work highlights various shifting relationships between the center and the margin. Horacio, in spite of his position as a male metropolitan subject, remains marginal to the social structure that maintains the system of slavery and is implicitly feminized, while the Creole woman Rosa, who upholds the institution and assumes the role of the oppressor, is masculinized. Curiously, his role, until the final scene of the first act, is limited to that of passive witness to the injustices committed against the slaves, in spite of the Enlightenment values of reason, progress, and freedom that he believes he has brought to the colony. In this scene, Rosa demands that the slave Ruderico cut off his sister's hair when Azella disobeys her mistress's order to dress without adornment. Assuming the role of the oppressive master, Rosa is masculinized as she attempts to strip the slave of her identity and agency over her own body, castrating her symbolically through this form of torture. Only on witnessing this scene does Horacio intervene, imposing his masculine authority over his fiancée to save the slaves from her wrath.

This emblematic scene marks the beginning of the slave's act of resistance, not only to physical enslavement, but also to rhetorical enclosure and circumscription. As Karen Sánchez-Eppler has suggested, an embodied definition of identity is central to reclaiming personhood for the slave's body, even as antislavery writers come up against the rhetorical limits of doing so. Citing Elaine Scarry's work on the body in pain, Sánchez-Eppler notes that "the inexpressible and undeniable nature of bodily experience, especially pain" and "the body's desperate resistance to the enclosure of its experience" drive language.[49] In Sáez de Melgar's scene, the slave's body is a site of both control and resistance. Azella's resistance to having her body clothed according to her mistress's wishes is also about the subaltern subject's rhetorical control over how she wants to be perceived and represented. Rosa's response to Azella's disobedience is an attempt to subjugate and violate the slave's body further, threatening to have Ruderico cut off his sister's hair. Rosa's threats of physical punishment and imprisonment against him in response to his refusal to obey her represent a rhetorical attempt to regain authority over the subaltern subject. It is, of course, only the metropolitan man's intervention that saves both of the slaves from punishment.

While the perspective of Horacio, the male metropolitan subject, has predominated up to this point of the drama, the beginning of the second act shifts to the subjectivity of the slaves themselves. At first, the image of the female slave (e.g., "pobre cautiva, / avecilla prisionera"[50] [poor captive, / an imprisoned little bird]) appears to suggest a lack of subjectivity and agency that so frequently characterizes representations of women in Romantic works authored by men. In contrast, the first half of the melodrama sets up the role of the masculine hero—driven by his Enlightenment principles and sense of justice—as that of a savior, not only of the slave he desires, but also of every slave on the island of Cuba. In his dialogue with Azella, Horacio combines the discourse of freedom (repeatedly affirming his intention to "romper vuestra cadena"[51] [break your chain]) with that of redemption ("Trabajo por lograr redimiros"[52] [I'm working to be able to redeem you]). Yet the Romantic paradigm of selfhood identified with the active male desiring subject in "its struggle against a resistant world" makes way,[53] in Sáez de Melgar's work, for possible new spaces of desire and subjectivity for the subaltern other—slaves in general, but the female slave in particular—affirming their struggle to reclaim not only their freedom and fundamental human rights but also their agency as desiring subjects. What most infuriates the female slave is the prohibition of desire, to which she believes she has a right despite her social marginality. Ruderico's words, "Si el amor / se prohíbe a nuestra raza, / somos máquinas"[54] (If love / is forbidden for our race, / we are machines), capture this sentiment. That a female slave be allowed openly to articulate her desire—and for a European man, no less—would undoubtedly have been subversive for the period in which the work was written.

In the third and final act of the play, Sáez de Melgar gives even greater voice to Azella, as she is granted increasing space in her dialogues and even a long monologue. Echoing the well-worn clichés of Romanticism in passages of exaggerated passion and sentimentality ("¡La vida es la libertad!"[55] [Life is freedom!]), Azella openly protests her condition of servitude and proclaims her right to love and freedom. Her choice to die at the hands of her own brother rather than to live enslaved by her mother's murderer comes to represent an act of agency, as evinced in her affirmation: "Siendo libre viviré, / si tal lo quiere mi suerte, / pero, si no, con la muerte / mi cadena romperé"[56] (Being free I will live, / if such is my destiny, / but, if not, with death / I will break my chains). In her discussion of antislavery writings that adopted the conventions of sentimental fiction, Sánchez-Eppler shows how the political efficacy of these works often depended on the ability of their authors to rearrange the real into sentimental format.[57] For Sánchez-Eppler, sentimental fiction (about slavery) is "an intensely bodily genre," both in identifying the body of the slave as a site of political struggle and in the emotional response (and literal tears) that the slave's story provokes in its readers.[58] It can be argued that the genre of the neo-Romantic melodrama adopted by Sáez de Melgar serves a similar function by calling attention to the power of sentiments—if not to literally change the condition of the body then to at least symbolically alter how that condition is perceived.[59]

Azella's body takes center stage in the final scenes of the play as a site of both material-economic and discursive struggle. By actively resisting commodification and subordination of her body by the slave owners, she fights for the recognition of ownership of her own body and, by extension, of her personhood. Repeated allusions to the fact that her body is beautiful and light skinned (for a woman of African descent) rhetorically mask her African identity and undoubtedly facilitated contemporary (European) readers' empathetic response to her struggles. Moreover, Sáez de Melgar does not represent Azella's violent death directly on stage; we only discover the slave's fate in the final scene of the drama, when the stage lighting focuses on her corpse, illuminated by the moonlight. In her brother Ruderico's words, she is "pura y hermosa . . . / mártir del dolor, / la madre de nuestro amor"[60] (pure and beautiful . . . / martyr of suffering, / mother of our love)—words that appear to echo nineteenth-century (European) bourgeois discourses on gender that exalted domesticity and self-sacrifice as the feminine ideal. Yet within the conventions of melodrama, such a representation of Azella's body would allow her to be recognized as a Romantic heroine who struggles to affirm her subjectivity, in spite of her subaltern status as a female African slave.

We need to question, as Spivak has done, whether there can ever be a pure form of subaltern consciousness in the context of colonial production.[61] On the surface, it might appear that Azella' self-sacrifice in *La cadena rota* only reenacts yet again the annihilation of the black body in a colonial context. Yet Sánchez-Eppler's observation with regard to North American antislavery fiction could also apply here to Sáez de Melgar's play: paradoxically, antislavery literature's "recourse to the obliteration of black bodies as the only solution to the problem of slavery actually confirms the ways in which feminist-abolitionist projects of liberation forced a recognition of the bodiliness of personhood."[62] That is, by allowing Azella the choice to die a Romantic heroine, representing her death as an act of emancipation, Sáez's drama transforms the body from a site of oppression into a site of resistance.[63] Within the structure of melodrama, the desiring female subject becomes a political subject who seeks to reclaim personhood through her body. Thus it would be possible to argue that Azella's radical and uncompromising stance in rejecting the enslavement of her body and even the possibility of life within the colonial order that upholds this institution goes further than Gálvez's work in destabilizing metropolitan discourse. As we have seen, Gálvez allows Zinda to negotiate her agency (to a certain extent) as a female subject, but only within the limits of colonialism. By disguising colonialism as enlightenment, *Zinda* forecloses the possibility of decolonization for the subaltern subject.

The differences in the representations of the male metropolitan subject in the two works are also significant. In *Zinda*, the "enlightenment" brought by the Portuguese commander Pereyra allows the queen to negotiate the end of slavery—but, it is important to add, on the colonizer's terms. In other words, Gálvez represents the metropolitan perspective, whereby the subaltern woman can be civilized and enlightened through religious colonization. In *La cadena rota*, in contrast, Horacio, who presumably occupies the dominant cultural position and is at first presented as a potential savior of the slaves, turns out to be incapable of either rescuing Azella or imposing his masculine will on his cousin, who insists on selling her property to the slave trader. Rather than rejecting the institution that commodifies the enslaved woman's body, he participates in it: he attempts to rescue Azella by offering his entire fortune to the slave trader in exchange for her. In other words, for the metropolitan subject, the enslaved woman whom he desires still remains a commodity that needs to be purchased within a colonial economy. In this context, her refusal to remain enslaved, both literally as well as symbolically, to the metropolitan economy of representation is, indeed, an act of agency, even if it means choosing her own death.

Ultimately, Sáez de Melgar's play undermines metropolitan masculinity, even as the concluding scenes shift back to Horacio's subjectivity. The final scene of the play, where we find him on his knees beside Azella's corpse, having failed to save her, emblematizes his impotence—and symbolically heralds the decadence of empire. Not only have his desire and his political idealism been frustrated; the arranged marriage with the Creole woman, which would have led to the restoration of the social order, does not take place. The identification between masculinity, on the one hand, and Enlightenment reason and progress, on the other, has all but been dismantled through the emasculation of the hero. In contrast, the subaltern woman, in the tradition of Romanticism, has drawn on the authority of her own subjectivity to pursue her desire and gain liberation from the chains of slavery and colonialism. It is no coincidence that the words uttered by Ruderico to the spirit of his dead sister, "Está tu cadena rota"[64] (Your chain is broken), are those that conclude the drama. Immediately before the curtain falls at the end of the play, the lights of the candelabra and the torches borne by the black people illuminate the scene. The heavy-handed symbolism of the lights, as well as that of the moon that penetrates into the garden, leave the spectators with hope for the future.

A comparative reading of these two antislavery plays may not offer definitive (or generalizable) conclusions about the changing representations of slavery and colonialism in the course of the three-quarters of a century that elapsed between the composition of the two works. Yet the Romantic concept of subjectivity and agency that Gálvez's drama anticipates through the figure of the subaltern woman Zinda emerges with full force in Sáez de Melgar's play. The later work forges a greater space of resistance for the female subaltern subject, albeit within the limits of the conventions of neo-Romantic melodrama. Ironically, it was the famous melodramatist José Echegaray who, upon reading Sáez's work, criticized it for its lack of verisimilitude, especially in its representation of the slaves as if they were white and educated—and of the female slave, in particular, as if she could actually inspire the love of a white man.[65] Echegaray's response not only reflects the typical attitude toward race of the Spanish readers of the times but also suggests that the melodramatic form allowed for a certain poetic license that would make it possible to disguise the subversive subtext of the antislavery work, such as the interracial romance and the transformation of the slave into a desiring subject.[66] Ultimately, however, the strategic use of melodrama in Gálvez and

Sáez de Melgar's plays had the potential to undermine, to a different degree, the dominant narratives of gender, race, and colonialism.

NOTES

1. Sáez de Melgar's play was published in 1879; however, it is believed to have been composed in 1875 or 1876 based on the fact that José Echegaray read the manuscript in March of 1876. Eduardo Pérez-Rasilla, introduction to *La cadena rota*, by Faustina Sáez de Melgar, ed. Eduardo Pérez-Rasilla (Madrid: Publicaciones de la Asociación de Directores de Escena de España, 1998), 20.

2. According to Elizabeth Franklin Lewis, *Zinda* was published in the third volume of María Rosa Gálvez's *Obras poéticas* (Madrid: Imprenta Real, 1804), 100–168, but never produced for the stage. See Lewis, "Breaking the Chains: Language and the Bonds of Slavery in María Rosa Gálvez's *Zinda*," Biblioteca Virtual Miguel de Cervantes, http://www.cervantesvirtual.com/obra-visor-din/breaking-the-chains-language-and-the-bonds-of-slavery-in-maria-rosa-galvezs-zinda-1804/html/b0e06e38-0bce-11e2-b1fb-00163ebf5e63_3.html#I_0_. References to *Zinda* in this essay are from the online text available through the Biblioteca Virtual Miguel de Cervantes.

3. I capitalize the word *Enlightenment* when referring to the eighteenth-century philosophical movement. Otherwise, I leave it in lowercase.

4. For an examination of the antislavery movement in the Spanish Empire prior to the independence of the colonies, see Emily Berquist, "Early Anti-slavery Sentiment in the Spanish Atlantic World, 1765–1817," *Slavery and Abolition* 31, no. 2 (2010): 181–205. However, it should be noted that many of the intellectuals who formed a part of this movement during its early stages denounced the slave trade rather than slavery itself.

5. Berquist, 189.

6. Theresa Ann Smith, *The Emerging Female Citizen: Gender and Enlightenment in Spain* (Berkeley: University of California Press, 1993), 11–12.

7. Susan Kirkpatrick, *Las Románticas: Women Writers and Subjectivity in Spain, 1835–1850* (Berkeley: University of California Press, 1989), 61.

8. Smith, *Emerging Female Citizen*, 11–12; Mónica Burguera, *Las damas del liberalismo respetable: Los imaginarios sociales del feminismo liberal en España (1834–1850)* (Madrid: Cátedra, 2012), 24.

9. In Carolina Coronado, *Obra poética*, ed. Gregorio Torres Nebrera, vol. 2 (Mérida: Editora Regional de Extremadura, 1993), 731–733, 839. Other nineteenth-century women who embraced the antislavery cause include the Romantic poet Rogelia León, who published two antislavery poems in her anthology *Auras de la Alhambra* (Granada: Imprenta y Librería de D. José María Zamora, 1857): "El negro Plácido" ("The Black Plácido"; 129–134), an elegy to the Cuban poet Gabriel de la Concepción Valdés, who was executed after being accused of instigating the slave uprisings of the 1840s, and "Canción del esclavo" ("Song of the Slave"; 205–210), a rewriting of Espronceda's famous Romantic poem "La canción del pirata" ("Song of the Pirate"). Echoing the lyric speaker of Espronceda's poet who, in the pirate's voice, proclaims freedom from social laws, the speaker of León's poem adopts the voice of a slave to affirm his right to freedom. Joaquina García Balmaseda (1837–1893), dramatist, actress, translator, journalist, and director of *El Correo de la Moda* (*Fashion Post*) composed a poem, "¡Caridad en favor del esclavo!" ("Charity on Behalf of the Slave!"), which appeared in *El cancionero del esclavo* (Madrid: Publicaciones

Populares de la Sociedad Abolicionista Española), 77–85, along with Concepción Arenal's prize-winning poem.

10. See Lisa Surwillo, "Poetic Diplomacy: Carolina Coronado and the American Civil War," *Comparative American Studies: An International Journal* 5, no. 4 (2007): 409–422, for an account of how the personal and the political intersected in Coronado's antislavery writings in the context of the U.S. Civil War.

11. Lewis, "Breaking the Chains."

12. "Variedades" ("Varieties"), *La Violeta* 3, no. 159 (December 17, 1865): 610.

13. Íñigo Sánchez Llama, *Galería de escritoras isabelinas: La prensa periódica entre 1833 y 1895* (Madrid: Cátedra, 2000), 194.

14. Kirkpatrick, *Las Románticas*, 156–157; Nina Scott, introduction to *Sab*, by Gertrudis Gómez de Avellaneda (Austin: University of Texas Press, 1993), xxiv.

15. Gayatri Chakravorty Spivak, "Can the Subaltern Speak?," in *Marxism and the Interpretation of Culture*, ed. Cary Nelson and Lawrence Grossberg (Urbana: University of Illinois Press, 1988), 271–313.

16. Julia Bordiga Grinstein, "Nzinga-Nbandi / Zinda Njinga, heroína del nacionalismo africano," Biblioteca Virtual Miguel de Cervantes, http://www.cervantesvirtual.com/obra-visor-din/nzinga-nbandi-zinda-njinga-heroina-del-nacionalismo-africano/html/325122fe-1dd2-11e2-b1fb-00163ebf5e63_2.html#I_0_.

17. For a detailed account of the historical figure on whom the character Zinda is based, see Grinstein.

18. Lewis, "Breaking the Chains"; Virginia Trueba Mira, "Paradojas de la alteridad en *Zinda* de Rosa Gálvez," Biblioteca Virtual Miguel de Cervantes, http://www.cervantesvirtual.com/obra-visor-din/paradojas-de-la-alteridad-en-zinda-de-rosa-galvez/html/a36ef558-0bce-11e2-b1fb-00163ebf5e63_3.html#I_0_.

19. María Rosa Gálvez, *Zinda*, Biblioteca Virtual Miguel de Cervantes, http://www.cervantesvirtual.com/obra-visor/zinda--drama-tragico-en-tres-actos/html/dcd228aa-2dc6-11e2-b417-000475f5bda5_2.html#I_0_, act 1, line 57. References to this text will be cited by act and line number, as page numbers are unavailable in the web edition.

20. Gálvez, act 1, lines 60–61.

21. Gálvez, act 1.

22. Gálvez, act 1, line 72.

23. Spivak's original sentence is "White men are saving brown women from brown men," by which she refers to the collective fantasy of the imperial enterprise ("Can the Subaltern Speak?," 296–297).

24. Pereyra's own words to Alcaypa reflect the colonialist mind-set that reduces the African warrior to the status of the barbarian: "No insultes, africano, mi desgracia. / Tú no sabes el hombre a quien ofendes; / mas Zinda, tu gloriosa soberana, / bien conoce a Pereyra, y tu barbarie / será por su justicia castigada" (Gálvez, *Zinda*, act 1, lines 30–34; African, do not insult my misfortune. / You don't know the man whom you offend / but Zinda, your glorious sovereign, / knows Pereyra well, and your barbarism / will be punished by her justice). Alcaypa urges the other black warriors to burn him, responding to Pereyra with the following words: "Eres un blanco; / para ser un tirano esto te basta" (act 1, lines 37–38; You're a white person; / that's enough to be a tyrant).

25. Trueba Mira, in "Paradojas de la alteridad," notes, "Lejos de cuestionar la política europea colonialista, *Zinda* es una defensa de esa política" (Far from questioning the European colonialist politics, *Zinda* is a defense of this politics).

26. Lewis, "Breaking the Chains."

27. Grinstein, "Nzinga-Nbardi." Arturo Morgado García cites the sources on which Gálvez has presumably drawn to construct the literary figure of Zinda. Historical and travel narratives in the seventeenth century referred to her as "la amazona de los negros" (the Amazon of the blacks), whose monstrosity was reflected in her masculine dress and in her gender ambiguity (Morgado García, "*Zinda* [1804], de María Rosa Gálvez de Cabrera, y las reflexiones sobre la esclavitud en la España finidieciochesca," in *Mujeres esclavas y abolicionistas en la España de los siglos XVI al XIX*, ed. Aurelia Martín Casares and Rocío Periáñez Gómez [Madrid: Iberoamericana-Vervuert, 2014], 188–189).

28. Gálvez, *Zinda*, act 1, lines 265–266.

29. Gálvez, act 1, lines 283.

30. Gálvez, act 1, lines 233–234.

31. Trueba Mira, "Paradojas de la alteridad."

32. Ania Loomba, *Colonialism/Postcolonialism*, 3rd ed. (New York: Routledge, 2015), 156. Loomba is referring not to Gálvez's work but to representations of Amazonian femininity in colonial writings of the non-European world. As noted previously, Gálvez's Zinda similarly evokes the myth of the Amazon.

33. Lewis, "Breaking the Chains."

34. Gálvez, *Zinda*, act 2, lines 90–96.

35. Kirkpatrick, *Las Románticas*, 153.

36. Gálvez, *Zinda*, act 3, lines 381–382.

37. Gálvez, act 3, lines 416–418.

38. Lewis, "Breaking the Chains."

39. Kirkpatrick, *Las Románticas*, 2.

40. Peter Brooks, *The Melodramatic Imagination: Balzac, Henry James, Melodrama, and the Mode of Excess* (New Haven, Conn.: Yale University Press, 1976), 42.

41. Michael Hays and Anastasia Nikolopoulou, introduction to *Melodrama: The Cultural Emergence of a Genre* (New York: St. Martin's Press, 1996), viii–x.

42. Pérez-Rasilla, introduction to *La cadena rota*, 31.

43. *Mestiza* refers to a woman of mixed European and indigenous descent.

44. Sáez de Melgar, *La cadena rota*, 65, 70.

45. Karen Sánchez-Eppler, *Touching Liberty: Abolition, Feminism, and the Politics of the Body* (Berkeley: University of California Press, 1993), 33.

46. Sáez de Melgar, *La cadena rota*, 69.

47. Sáez de Melgar, 76–77. The trope of racial hybridity is reminiscent of Avellaneda's protagonist Sab, a light-skinned *mulato*. The narrator of the novel emphasizes his "culture"; he is well read and endowed with "talento natural" (natural talent; Gertrudis Gómez de Avellaneda, *Sab*, ed. José Servera [Madrid: Cátedra, 2004], 128). It is evident, from both Avellaneda and Sáez de Melgar's works, that the more the African subject resembles the European's own concept of the self, the more the former is deemed worthy of sympathy or admiration. Spivak's critique of what she calls "third worldist criticism" applies to all metropolitan discourse about the colonized subject: "The other must always be constructed by way of consolidating the self" (Gayatri Chakravorty Spivak, "Imperialism and Sexual Difference," *Oxford Literary Review* 8, nos. 1/2 [1986]: 229). Outside of the Hispanic context, Sánchez-Eppler discusses the significance of the "light-skinned slave" in the context of antislavery fiction's fascination with miscegenation (*Touching Liberty*, 33).

48. Chandra Talpade Mohanty, "Cartographies of Struggle: Third World Women and the Politics of Feminism," in *Third World Women and the Politics of Feminism*, ed. Chandra Talpade Mohanty et al. (Bloomington: Indiana University Press, 1991), 14.

49. Sánchez-Eppler, *Touching Liberty*, 8.

50. Sáez de Melgar, *La cadena rota*, 103.

51. Sáez de Melgar, 108.

52. Sáez de Melgar, 109.

53. Kirkpatrick, *Las Románticas*, 14, 23.

54. Sáez de Melgar, *La cadena rota*, 105.

55. Sáez de Melgar, 154.

56. Sáez de Melgar, 161.

57. Sánchez-Eppler, *Touching Liberty*, 26.

58. Sánchez-Eppler, 26.

59. Sánchez-Eppler, 26.

60. Sáez de Melgar, *La cadena rota*, 194–195.

61. Spivak, "Can the Subaltern Speak?," 295.

62. Sánchez-Eppler, *Touching Liberty*, 48.

63. Sánchez-Eppler thus characterizes the project of feminist-abolitionist discourse in antebellum United States (49).

64. Sáez de Melgar, *La cadena rota*, 196.

65. I quote from José Echegaray's text: "Comprendo perfectamente que en V. ha dominado el poeta, que ha procurado V. hacer el drama simpático y bello y que *una negra*, con su desdichada inferioridad física, acrecentada por su horrible estado, no podía ser en la escena un tipo romántico, ni inspirar amor a Horacio. *Creo que ha hecho V. bien*; pero esto probará que el argumento es más propio de la edad clásica que de la época presente, en cuanto se refiere a la esclavitud. En suma, el drama del *esclavo americano* considero que es otro" (Eduardo Pérez-Rasilla, epilogue to *La cadena rota*, 198, emphasis in the original; I understand perfectly that the poet has ruled in you, that you have tried to write a likeable and beautiful drama and that a black woman, with her sad physical inferiority, made greater by her horrible state, could not be a Romantic type on stage, nor inspire Horacio's love. I think you did the right thing; but this will prove that the plot is more appropriate for the classical age than the present, in so far as its reference to slavery. In sum, I consider the drama of the American slave to be different).

66. Although the play was never performed on stage, it was well received, as at least three editions of the work were published, according to David Gies, "La mujer vista por la mujer: El personaje femenino en el teatro escrito por mujeres en la segunda mitad del siglo XIX," in *Lectora, heroína, autora (La mujer en la literatura española del siglo XIX)*, ed. Virginia Trueba Mira et al. (Barcelona: Promociones y Publicaciones Universitarias, 2005), 155.

CHAPTER 2

Forging Progressive Futures for Spain's Women and People

SOFÍA TARTILÁN (PALENCIA 1829–MADRID 1888)

Christine Arkinstall

From the 1860s until her death in 1888, Sofía Tartilán carved out a prominent name for herself in nineteenth-century letters. First and foremost an essayist, she also translated from Portuguese and Catalan, and her *Costumbres populares: Colección de cuadros tomados del natural* (*Popular Customs: A Collection of Scenes Taken from Real Life*; 1880) enjoyed the distinction of a prologue by Ramón de Mesonero Romanos, who described Tartilán as "una dama cuyo innegable talento le permite manejar la pluma con el mismo desembarazo y destreza con que, la inmensa mayoría de su sexo, sabe manejar el abanico"[1] (a lady whose undeniable talent allows her to wield the pen as easily and skillfully as most of her sex does the fan). Her relentless advocacy and activism for the education of women and the working classes are evident in her editorship of the Madrid periodical *La Ilustración de la Mujer* (*The Enlightenment of Women*)—which, according to José Luis Sánchez Carrera, she directed from 1875 to 1888[2]—and her *Páginas para la educación popular* (*Pages for the People's Education*; 1877), published in instalments in *La Ilustración* and in book form. In short, Tartilán was no second-ranked writer but, on the contrary, as one review of *Costumbres populares* affirmed, "figura en primera fila entre los escritores de la época"[3] (one of the leading writers of our day). Why, then, the dearth of scholarship on her? Spanish scholars have chiefly focused on her educational endeavors, while outside Spain the few references to Tartilán center on her feminist thought.[4] Seeking a greater approximation to this figure and her place within fin de siècle Spanish culture, this chapter proposes to examine a selection of Tartilán's essays and the following novellas: *Una deuda de veinte años* (*A*

Twenty-Year Debt; 1875), *La caja de hierro* (*The Iron Box*; 1874), and *Borrascas del corazón* (*Storms of the Heart*; 1884).[5]

Born in Palencia in 1829, where she lived until the age of ten,[6] Tartilán would begin her residence in Madrid with her first marriage in 1851 and remained there until her death. Widowed from her first husband, she remarried Manuel Eduardo Delgado in the late 1860s or early 1870s, later separating from him.[7] The fact that Tartilán's literary production increases from 1874 onward may be partly attributable to her separation around then and the resulting need for her own source of income. As 1883 records reveal, Tartilán's Madrid address for some years was number 7, Jesús del Valle Street, where she lived with her widowed elder brother, Manuel Tartilán.[8] Also living there for several years, as attested to by Tartilán's letters (1877–1879) to composer Francisco Asenjo Barbieri, was Tartilán's close friend Matilde Cherner, who published under the pseudonym Rafael Luna.[9]

Tartilán was one of an emerging breed of professional female journalists. Reputedly her earliest-known press contributions were to the Madrid periodical *La Caza* (*The Hunt*) between 1865 and 1868.[10] However, she produced the bulk of her writings in the 1870s and 1880s, forging such a reputation for herself that Clarín called her a *monstruo*[11] (monster). Publishing poems, short stories, novels, essays, literary criticism, and historical pieces, Tartilán's most influential works were *Historia de la crítica* (*History of Literary Criticism*; 1875), *Páginas para la educación popular*, and *Costumbres populares*, dedicated to Juan Eugenio Hartzenbusch, mentor and close friend.[12] Tartilán's work was also featured in the new second part of the 1879 edition of Teodoro Guerrero y Pallarés's and Ricardo Sepúlveda's best-selling *Pleito del matrimonio* (*Matrimonial Disputes*; 1873), alongside pieces by such established writers as Gaspar Núñez de Arce, Hartzenbusch, Pedro Antonio de Alarcón, Mariano José de Larra, Ángela Grassi, Concepción Arenal, Concepción Gimeno de Flaquer, María del Pilar Sinués (a close friend), Patrocinio de Biedma, Faustina Sáez de Melgar, and Joaquina Balsameda.[13] Another work in which she was included with just one other female writer, Sáez de Melgar, was the *Novísimo romancero español* (*Latest Spanish Poetry*; 1879), while she was singled out for special acclamation with Emilia Pardo Bazán for her contribution to an *Álbum calderoniano* (*Album in Homage to Calderón*; 1883).[14] Furthermore, Tartilán contributed to *Las mujeres españolas, americanas y lusitanas, pintadas por sí mismas* (*Spanish, American, and Portuguese Women, Portrayed by Themselves*; 1885), a volume that bore pieces by such leading contemporary female writers as Rosario de Acuña, Gimeno de Flaquer, Josefa Pujol de Collado, and Pardo Bazán.[15]

Much of Tartilán's prolific work first appeared in periodicals across the nation in the 1870s and 1880s. Among them figured Madrid's *La Ilustración de la Mujer*, *El Correo de la Moda* (*Fashion Post*), *Flores y Perlas* (*Flowers and Pearls*), *El Ramillete* (*The Bouquet*), and *La Enciclopedia* (*The Encyclopedia*).[16] She also frequently contributed to Málaga's *El Mediodía* (*The Midday Paper*) and translated from the Portuguese António Duarte Gómes Leal's *La peste negra* (*The Black Plague*) and from Catalan Víctor Balaguer's poetry.[17] Indeed, in 1881 Tartilán was the only female writer to be mentioned with Sinués as translators of Portuguese literary works into Castilian.[18] Enjoying lengthy associations with *El Correo de la Moda*, which Grassi directed for many years; *Cádiz*, directed by Patrocinio de Biedma; and Málaga's *Revista de Andalucía* (*Magazine of Andalusia*), Tartilán also contributed to Madrid's progressive liberal periodical *La Iberia* (*Iberia*; where Arenal published and Arenal's husband worked), Salamanca's *El Eco del Tormes* (*The Echo of the Tormes*), and Madrid's *La Ilustración de la Infancia* (*Children's Education*).[19] As well as her directorship of *La Ilustración de la Mujer*, Tartilán is mentioned as having headed the 1872 periodical of the Masonic lodge of the same name, *Las Hijas del Sol* (*Daughters of the Sun*), to which Arenal also contributed.[20] Emilia Serrano effected a longer stewardship of this periodical, while Gimeno de Flaquer also participated in the lodge.[21]

Well connected, Tartilán participated in Palencia's Ateneo Científico, Literario y Artístico (Scientific, Literary, and Artistic Athenaeum) and Madrid's Ateneo de Bellas Letras (Literary Athenaeum) and Fomento de las Artes (Promotion of the Arts).[22] At one event at the Fomento de las Artes in November 1879, Tartilán read poetry alongside José Zorrilla, who attended her literary soirées, together with Sinués.[23] Tartilán also likely participated, with Sinués and Arenal, in Sáez de Melgar's Ateneo Artístico y Literario de Señoras (Women's Artistic and Literary Athenaeum), established by the Krausist Fernando de Castro.[24] In 1880, Barcelona's *La Ilustración* included Tartilán as a contender for a Spanish "academia femenina" (feminine academy) with Carolina Coronado, Grassi, Rosalía de Castro, Sinués, Arenal, Balsameda, Gimeno de Flaquer, and Sáez de Melgar, while in 1883, Tartilán was disparagingly cited with Sinués as part of an "invasión de mujeres literatas" (invasion of female scribblers) and "poetisas de jardín" (flowery poetesses).[25]

Tartilán died from a stroke in Madrid on July 2, 1888.[26] A posthumous article in *La Ilustración Ibérica* (*The Iberian Enlightenment*) notes that Tartilán's works were read in some Spanish schools alongside works by Harriet Beecher Stowe and Arenal.[27] In 1905, Carmen de Burgos, in her address "Misión educadora de la mujer en el periodismo" ("Women's Educational Mission through Journalism"), delivered in Madrid on June 15, acknowledged Tartilán's leadership in Spanish journalism at the helm of periodicals for women.[28] Today Tartilán's association with Palencia is honored through the Colegio Público Sofía Tartilán (Sofía Tartilán Public School).

Chronologically, Sofía Tartilán belonged to the same generation, the "1843 Generation," as those influential female authors acclaimed during Isabel II's reign: Grassi, Sinués, and Sáez de Melgar, whose writings formed the Isabelline canon.[29] However, whereas these writers began their literary careers in the 1850s, according to extant archival documents, Tartilán's commenced in the late 1860s.

Nonetheless, Tartilán contributed to the periodicals that these women directed, moved in their circles, and participated in cultural functions with them. Like them, she too belonged to the Spanish middle class, was shaped by the Romantic and costumbrist literature of Coronado and Cecilia Böhl de Faber (Fernán Caballero), directed periodicals, and lived in Madrid.[30]

Grassi, Sinués, and Sáez de Melgar subscribed to a "high culture" that premised a Christian idealism, associated artistic beauty with moralizing works that produced virtue, and exhibited nostalgia for old traditional structures and modes of being.[31] Although, as I discuss later on, aspects of Tartilán's novellas capture these aspirations, in essays like *Páginas para la educación popular* she seeks to replace traditional structures and practices with more progressive ones. Tartilán's works, then, are emblematic of what she herself called a "siglo de transición"[32] (century of transition). They mirror a society in transition from a former aristocratic order informed by the static values of the Catholic Church to a capitalist world in which class mobility and demands were reshaping old structures and ways of living.[33]

Politically of Republican persuasion, a Christian feminist, and associated with freemasonry, Tartilán also embraced the philosophy of Karl Christian Friedrich Krause. As Mary Lee Bretz notes, the Krausist movement, which Julián Sanz del Río championed in Spain from 1857 until 1869, stressed reason, progression toward perfection through social action, and the "harmonious synthesis" of opposing differences.[34] Krausist principles inform Tartilán's activism for better education and conditions for women and the working classes, leading her initiatives to be compared to Arenal's.[35] Instances are Tartilán's efforts as a member and protector of Barcelona's La Laboriosa (The Industrious One) and as the secretary of the society La Estrella de los Pobres (The Star of the Poor), established in October 1873 to aid the poor in times of death.[36] Her social conscience can be inferred from her donation of books to popular libraries and her participation in a compilation of works, *La redención de un quinto* (*The Redemption of a Reservist*), with José Echegaray, Ramón de Campoamor, Blanca de los Ríos, Sinués, and others to redeem a medical student from military service.[37]

In the 1860s and early 1870s, the period when Tartilán began to publish, Krausist ideals also helped shape a transitional discourse, which, Bretz affirms, "moves away from romanticism towards realism without accepting many of the tenets of either."[38] As reflected in her novellas, Tartilán's own discourse challenges the Romantic emphasis on desire and fantasy in favor of order and reason, confirming Bretz's premise that liberal aesthetics cannot be easily distinguished from more conservative models. Didacticism, then, was a feature of both the moralizing literature of the "1843 Generation" and, paradoxically, more progressive writers, whose work demonstrates "an increasing didacticism . . . as a means of hastening the demise of traditional authority."[39]

Similar to Grassi, Sinués, and Sáez de Melgar, Tartilán produced a didactic, domestic literature that sought to instruct and produce virtuous mothers, who, as family educators, would create the future citizens of the liberal nation. As Mónica Burguera elucidates, from the mid-1830s onward, the formation of the Spanish liberal state was premised on a conceivably inalterable sexual order amid an ever-changing social order. Essential to sustaining the new liberal order organized around the family was women's education—but always within the framework of the complementarity of the sexes. In this elaboration of a liberal middle-class model of a moral maternity at the service of the nation and progress, the female members of the Spanish Institute (1839–1853) played an important role.[40] To a certain extent, Tartilán's writings and initiatives, therefore, intersect with the work undertaken between 1834 and 1850 by these "damas del liberalismo respetable" (ladies of respectable liberalism), as Burguera calls them, with which she would have been more than familiar.[41] At the same time, however, Tartilán contributes more daring nuances, especially through her *Páginas para la educación popular*.

Tartilán's didactic pretensions see her privilege realism over fantasy, as evident in her costumbrist writings and her predilection for history. Appropriately, costumbrism and realism are both genres that seek to forge an authentic Spanish novel.[42] This emphasis on realism and the teachings of history is palpable in the novellas that I now discuss: *Una deuda de veinte años*, *La caja de hierro*, and *Borrascas del corazón*. Tartilán also wrote a short story, "Las puertas del cielo" ("The Gates of Heaven"), and a later novella, *La loca de las olas* (*The Madwoman of the Sea*; 1884), which I have been unable to locate.[43]

Published in 1875 in *El Correo de la Moda*, *Una deuda de veinte años* captures the essence of Tartilán's fiction.[44] Presented as a fictional piece, it is a biographical sketch of the Italian Baroque painter Salvator Rosa de Arenella (1615–1673), whose brooding landscapes with characteristics of the sublime brought him acclaim from Romantic artists. Features of Rosa's life that Tartilán's novella includes are his making of powerful enemies such as Gian Lorenzo Bernini because of his satirical plays and his participation in 1648 in Masaniello's uprising against the rule of Habsburg Spain in Naples. By framing her biography as a work of fiction that only clearly reveals itself as a historical study in the third and final part, Tartilán authorizes herself to write on a "virile" subject under cover of the sentimental morality tale characteristic of the Isabelline canon. At the same time, she displays her considerable knowledge of art not only through Rosa but also through reference to Francisco de Zurbarán, to whose paintings the idyllic family scene that opens the novella is compared. In this sense, Tartilán draws on an erudite communal sociolect that bestows authority on her writing.[45]

Tartilán couches Rosa's life as a morality tale of charity, restitution, and redemption that exalts the generosity of the poor. Taken in by a peasant family near Naples in 1628 when Rosa is destitute, he expresses his gratitude to the family members by painting them. Twenty years later, when fleeing from his enemies in Rome, Rosa finds himself for a second time in the family's home. In the interval, their young daughter has died, and her memory, preserved in Rosa's painting, has inspired the sole surviving son, Pablo, to paint himself. Rosa advises Pablo to sell the painting for his parents' benefit and takes him on as his disciple. Depicted as a source of moral regeneration, the peasant family embodies a generosity of spirit and Christian acceptance that provide a troubled Rosa with a certain peace and contentment: "Contribuyendo a calmar su agitado espíritu la cristiana conformidad de aquellos padres que tan rudos golpes habían sufrido"[46] (With the Christian conformity of those parents who had suffered such cruel blows contributing to calm his agitated spirit). The novella thus nostalgically exalts a mode of living that in nineteenth-century Spain is well under threat in a capitalist economy.

Tartilán's emphasis on the intermingling of fiction and real life acquires greater prominence in *La caja de hierro* and *Borrascas del corazón*, which both appeared in 1874 in a volume edited by José Rodríguez Seoane.[47] *La caja de hierro* reveals itself as a carefully crafted novella of nested stories. Presented initially as a moralistic tale of love for female bourgeois readers—"Quizá encontraréis una lección provechosa, que pudiera serviros en los asuntos del corazón"[48] (You will perhaps find here a beneficial lesson that may help you in affairs of the heart)—the novella is unusual in its self-reflexive, metaliterary features, foregrounded from the start. It commences by distinguishing itself from the Gothic novel exemplified by Ann Radcliffe: "No esperen mis amables lectores, que detrás del título . . . se escondan misteriosas aventuras, ni espeluznantes escenas, a manera de las que, en sus misterios de Olofernes, presenta *una Radclife*, ni . . . ha de aparecer indispensablemente en su trama algún descompuesto cadáver, algún puñal"[49] (Don't expect, kind readers, that this title . . . conceals mysterious adventures or horrifying scenes such as those that *a Radcliffe* . . . might present in her mysteries of Holofernes, nor that its plot must contain a decomposed corpse or dagger). Rather, Tartilán insists that the novella is a true story that her aristocratic female mentor encouraged her to write.

The novella also differs from a typical love story, as its first six pages are framed by a metaphysical discussion between Tartilán and her mentor, mysteriously called "la señora de G."[50] (Mrs. G.), on how to write the story itself. The mentor justifies their discussion of the love life of their mutual friend, Amelia de Sandoval, by affirming that she speaks to Tartilán as a writer, not as a woman, and that professional motivations justify what could otherwise be seen as an invasion of someone's private life. The writer, she reminds Tartilán, has dual identities that cannot be mapped one on to the other: "No es la mujer quien está delante de nosotras en este momento. Harto sabido es que el poeta y el escritor tienen un doble ser, que algunas veces difiere bastante entre sí"[51] (It is not the woman who is here before us at present. It is well known that the poet and the writer have dual identities, which are sometimes quite different). Real life and fiction are further intertwined when Tartilán suggests beginning the story with their dialogue on how to represent it. Moreover, the friends' conversation stresses the fact that Tartilán is a professional writer with literary commitments, underlining the novella's autobiographical content: "Tengo un grave compromiso con cierta amiga, a quien he prometido una anécdota para su semanario"[52] (I have an important commission from a certain friend, to whom I have promised a tale for her weekly).[53] Consequently, as Hazel Gold declares in her discussion of Realism, "the act of framing, thus fictionalized and incorporated . . . is engulfed by the very fictional content it was meant to frame. Outside becomes inside, referentiality becomes self-referential."[54]

The novella continues to insist on its alleged real-life content in that its protagonist, Amelia, relates her story to Tartilán in a metadiegetic narrative. She stresses that far from being a work of fiction—"Ni un drama, ni una novela"[55] (Neither a drama nor a novel)—her tale is typical of a young, upper-class woman married to a man with whom she is not passionately in love. Now thirty years old and mother of a daughter, Amelia narrates events that occurred ten years previously. Removed from her husband's activities in the public sphere, Amelia blames the tedium of her daily life, in turn due to women's inadequate education, for the inappropriately close relationship that developed then between herself and a young, handsome marine lieutenant, Carlos Alfieri. She maintains that it is not so much a lack of liberty that led to her sentimental liaison but rather an excessive freedom that arises when married bourgeois women, trophy wives, are unable to spend their time more usefully: "La mujer . . . se queja de no ser libre, cuando lo que le pesa es esa misma inoportuna libertad que le otorga aquel a quien ella ha hecho su dueño y señor"[56] (Women . . . complain that they are not free, when what weighs on them is that inopportune freedom that those whom they have made their lord and master have given them). Her downfall, Amelia comments, would have been inevitable had it not been for her "exquisita sensibilidad"[57] (exquisite sensitivity) and her timely recovery of her reason. Comprehending how ridiculous her sentimental dream was, Amelia now keeps, as a medical prescription and cure, a withered rose from her hair that Carlos had once kissed in the eponymous iron box of the novella's title. The narrative ends at this point, as Tartilán states that she wishes to let her readers draw their own conclusions.

Not only does the novella expose the mechanisms of fashioning stories and reject the melodramatic sensationalism of Gothic and Romantic literature to favor a didactic writing indebted to reason and Realism; it also dismisses the myths that accompany the sociocultural construction of Woman, here encompassed in the box, a proxy for Pandora's box. As the first woman in Greek mythology, Pandora released the evils of humanity on yielding to her curiosity and opening a jar, often depicted as a box. If the box's contents, as Laura

Mulvey argues, signify a "displaced representation of female sexuality as mystery and threat," then Pandora's curiosity is "a self-reflexive desire to investigate femininity itself"[58] and thus test the basis for such representations. In Tartilán's novella, there are multiple Pandoras: the main narrator who desires to know Amelia's secret; the readers whose curiosity invites them to solve the tale's mystery, likened to a closed box; and Amelia herself, whose sexual desire for Carlos is symbolized through the rose.

Tartilán's initial description of the box, compared to a crime victim, underscores its sinister dissonance: "Formando un conjunto bastante inarmónico, apercibí el cuerpo del delito, o lo que es lo mismo, *la caja* guardadora de la anécdota que yo ansiaba conocer"[59] (I observed the dead body, which formed a rather inharmonious picture, or rather, *the box* that guarded the tale that I yearned to know). The box's association with death, however, and its illegible foreignness, denoted through Arabian or Egyptian markings, are transformed in Tartilán's rendition of the fable. Amelia's opening of the box, a metaphor of her opening her heart, becomes a vehicle for humanity's good rather than its downfall precisely because she has chosen not to open her body, symbolized in the contained rose, so as not to endanger her marriage and family. Lifting the lid off the box, Mulvey declares, opens "domestic space into a complex terrain of social and sexual significance" and undoes the dialectic of inside/outside on which Pandora's myth relies,[60] thus undermining the domestic/public divide on which nineteenth-century femininity rests. Tartilán's re-presentation of this myth dismisses the cultural identification of Woman with a suspect duplicity to vindicate women's ability to make reasoned decisions and potentially participate in the public sphere. Just as Amelia's transparency and openness are intended to provide readers with judicious insights into the female psyche, so too do realist narratives seek to produce an apparently mimetic, transparent window on society.

The narrative formula that Tartilán uses in *La caja de hierro* is duplicated in *Borrascas del corazón*. Again constructed as a series of embedded stories, it opens by affirming its grounding in reality despite its melodramatic, sentimental title: "Lo que os voy a referir, lectores míos, no es una novela, ni un cuento: conozco a los personajes que van a figurar en mi relato, y hasta yo misma he tenido parte en este pequeño drama"[61] (What I am about to tell you, my readers, is not a novel or a story: I know the characters in my tale, and I myself have played a part in this little drama). Convalescing from an illness in Seville, the narrator becomes acquainted with a young seamstress, Felicia, who works in her humble, rural Seville dwelling. Felicia is distinguished by not only her beauty but also her uncommon air of refinement: "Me dijo con exquisita finura"[62] (She told me with exquisite refinement) and "Tenía en toda su persona un tinte de distinción que no podia confundirse con el vulgo de las mujeres del pueblo"[63] (Her whole being exuded an air of nobility not present in the majority of the village women). Tartilán's portrayal of the seamstress thus parallels Sinués's statement in her 1857 novel *Premio y castigo* (*Reward and Punishment*): "La distinción de modales es innata en la aristocracia verdadera y en vano se pretende aprender o imitar"[64] (Distinction in manners is innate to true aristocracy and cannot be acquired or imitated). The aristocracy to which Tartilán's novella alludes, however, is the new social order of the self-made, upper-middle class from which Felicia originates and to which she will return: a fact that recalls Gold's argument that rendering common characters noble through representation enabled the middle class to validate itself and mitigated its "anxieties of origin."[65]

Chapters 5 and 6 constitute Felicia's story, which she relates to the narrator. Born to an entrepreneurial English father and a Spanish mother who was the daughter of a rich merchant, Felicia suffered the consequences of her family's unexpected loss of fortune. From being one of the richest heiresses in Andalusia, she is plunged into poverty, and as such, her mother tells her, she must be a model of virtue and adjust her expectations to avoid future unhappiness. Tartilán's novella thus deals with one of the greatest fears that confronts the middle class in an emerging capitalist society: becoming declassed.[66]

Faced with the family's misfortune, Felicia's mother is portrayed as the loving spouse and maternal educator idealized in the domestic discourse of the Isabelline writers, demonstrating a "paciencia angelical"[67] (angelical patience) toward her withdrawn husband and educating Felicia through good books, music, and her own knowledge. When, however, fire engulfs their home, Felicia's father becomes blind; her mother, mad; and their economic situation even more precarious. To sustain the family, Felicia embroiders for Sevillan nobility. One year later, Felicia aids a young man, Enrique de Zea, thrown from his horse outside her home, following the advice of her father who tells her, echoing the tenets of the Isabelline canon, that charity is the most important virtue. Falling in love with Enrique, the eighteen-year-old Felicia is divided between her passion and her filial duty. Hence when Enrique asks Felicia to marry him and accompany him to Rome, where he will study painting sponsored by the Spanish government, Felicia refuses. A week after Enrique's departure, Felicia's father commits suicide so as not to stand in the way of her happiness, followed soon after by her mother's demise. Like Enrique, then, Felicia is now an orphan: a common Romantic trope that allows for the re-creation of characters unfettered by their pasts.

Moved by Felicia's story, the narrator resolves to find Enrique when visiting Italy. In Rome, she asks an old family friend to visit Enrique's studio to ascertain his character and see if he has reproduced Felicia's image in his paintings. Again, as in *La caja de hierro*, Tartilán self-consciously privileges metaliterary issues to lay bare the process of artistic creation. The friend responds that her idea is "novelesca" (like something out of a novel) but that life itself constitutes a complicated narrative plot: "¿Qué es la vida sino una novela complicada?"[68] (Isn't life itself a complicated novel?). The narrator's character, he remarks, is "observador y algo romántico"[69] (observant and somewhat romantic). Felicia's story, he summarizes, is as moving as a chapter in Eugène Sue's socially motivated feuilletons *The Mysteries of Paris* (1842–1843) and *The Wandering Jew* (1844), a comparison that the narrator finds flattering,[70] revealing Tartilán's cosmopolitan literary tastes and her deliberate remodeling of elements from foreign literatures. When the friend effectively ascertains that all Enrique's paintings reproduce Felicia's image, the narrator confronts Enrique with her discovery. Tongue in cheek, the narrator declares, "Si yo no quisiera tanto a Felicia, dejaría mi novela sin desenlace por ahora, pues temo que el amante mate al artista"[71] (Were I not so fond of Felicia, I would leave my novella without an ending, because I fear that the lover will kill the artist). Unhappiness, she explains, produces great works more than happiness.

Back in Madrid, the narrator sends for Felicia from Seville. Meanwhile, Enrique's rich uncle dies, "ni más ni menos que un tío de novella"[72] (just like an uncle in a novella), bequeathing him his fortune and enabling him—now rich, independent, and established as an artist—to marry Felicia. One of Enrique's paintings, which depicts Isabel I rescuing the Christians captive in Granada's dungeons, accompanied by a lady-in-waiting in Felicia's likeness, is among the finest historical paintings held in the Museo Nacional (National Museum). Nowadays, Felicia Kimpar de Zea, whose real name cannot be revealed, is "el más bello ornato de los salones de la buena sociedad"[73] (the most beautiful ornament in high society's salons). In general, Felicia conforms to a traditional model of femininity in which filial duty comes before passion, Woman is muse and beautiful object rather than creating subject, and domestic virtue, hard work, and feminine abnegation triumph over adversity. As for Enrique, like Rosa, he is a self-made man who embodies middle-class virtues and recognized artistic worth.

In her 1878 essay "Estudio del natural" ("Study of Real Life"), Tartilán elucidates the reasons for her focus on real-life cases and history and highlights again the influence of Krausism. The study of the human heart, the most difficult of all, enables humanity to progress toward perfection and encompasses the philosophical truths of all schools, just as the human soul represents variety within unity.[74] This stress on the reconciliation of differences in a transcendental unity is one of the main theses of Krausist thought.[75] Furthermore, Tartilán continues, the study of the human heart provides the science of life, which affords greater knowledge than all other sciences[76]—a statement that mirrors the idealism of Krausism compared with a more "scientific," positivistic perspective.

Finally, the study of passions, vices, and virtues provides an infinite variety of psychological studies, recorded by the observer, which help combat humanity's many evils. The observer, Tartilán remarks, does not need to be a learned man or philosopher; she herself has spent the most rewarding moments of her life dedicated to such observation, admiring humankind's variety within its most perfect unity.[77] By privileging the study of the heart, Tartilán conforms to a normative sociocultural framework that aligns femininity with the emotions. However, by denying the need for specialized training, she also gives women permission to write without requiring the sanction of external authorities. Moreover, Tartilán's literary *cuadros* (pictures) concur with a vision of writing that presents the writer, as Charles Baudelaire stated in 1863, as the "painter of modern life" and, in Mesonero Romanos's terms, as an observer and painter of society.[78] Hence as a subject of the gaze rather than its object, Tartilán appropriates a position traditionally reserved for men and legitimates women's participation in the liberal enterprise of literature at the service of progress.

Many of Tartilán's essays were first published in Madrid's *La Ilustración de la Mujer*, which José María Dalmau founded in mid-1873 as the mouthpiece for the aforementioned society, La Estrella de los Pobres.[79] At first, Gimeno de Flaquer directed the periodical until Tartilán took it over in 1875.[80] In keeping with Tartilán's affirmation that "la misión de nuestro sexo en la tierra no es otra que el amor, la paz y la caridad"[81] (our sex's mission on earth is love, peace, and charity), the periodical dedicated its proceeds from subscriptions to establishing free schools for poor girls. The periodical was published fortnightly in eight-page issues with consecutive pagination. More conservative than its Barcelona counterpart led by Pujol de Collado, the content came from male and female contributors, especially Pujol de Collado and Cherner, while Tartilán wrote most of the lead articles.[82] Essays on education for the people and women's issues dominated, interspersed with poems, a bibliographic section, and the odd theater review. In 1877, with the periodical entering its fifth year of publication, Tartilán's lead article, "Nuestro programa" ("Our Mission"), reaffirmed the periodical's objective of educating women for humanity's good: "¿Queréis el bien de la humanidad? Pues educad, instruid, e ilustrad a la mujer"[83] (Do you want humanity's good? Well, educate, instruct, and enlighten women). Urging women, the foundation of the happiness of nations and societies, to do everything possible to educate themselves, Tartilán maintains that an enlightened education produces morality and virtue. Hence she seeks to educate not only women's hearts but also their minds in accordance with Enlightenment principles, given that, as Pilar Ballarín notes, "educación" (education) was aimed at the heart, while "instrucción"[84] (instruction) was directed at the mind.

La Ilustración de la Mujer was where Tartilán first published in essay form what would appear in 1877 as a 271-page volume: *Páginas para la educación popular*.[85] Among the many reviews in the press of the day was the glowing appraisal from Francisco Flores García, director of *La Enciclopedia* to which Tartilán contributed, who highlighted its "brillantes páginas" (brilliant pages), "eclecticismo ilustrado"[86] (enlightened eclecticism), and the chapters dedicated to women's education. Likewise, Víctor Cuende described Tartilán's book as "bellísimo" (very beautiful) and its writer as endowed with a "fijeza de pensamiento" (intellectual focus) and "severidad de ideas"[87] (seriousness of ideas) that distinguish her from other female writers.

As indicated in its title, *Páginas* ostensibly deals with the need to educate the working classes and eradicate poverty.[88] This mission, which Tartilán claims is the great problem of her age (*Páginas*, 5), nonetheless cloaks a more pressing concern that dominates three of the work's four parts: the improvement of women's education. As Geraldine Scanlon explains, despite the 1857 Ley Moyano de Instrucción Pública (Moyano Law for Public Education) and the establishment in 1858 of the inadequate Escuela Normal de Maestras (Normal School for Female Teachers), little was done over the next decade to improve the education of women, who still could not study science or classics. It was not until 1870 that the Krausists provided greater impetus for improving women's education, when Fernando de Castro founded the Asociación para la Enseñanza de la Mujer (Association for Women's Education), which generated a raft of professional schools for women. For Scanlon, Tartilán's *Páginas*, together with Arenal's *La mujer del porvenir* (*The Woman of the Future*; 1868) and *La mujer de su casa* (*The Woman of Her House*; 1883), constituted for those times the most forceful denunciation of women's traditional education.[89] Consequently, Tartilán emphasizes that the age that exalts progress has failed women, the most important part of society, by not educating them.[90]

Part 1 stresses that the regeneration of Spain depends on the education of its people, "esa gran palanca"[91] (that great lever). Nations such as France, Germany, and England, Tartilán insists, are a century more advanced than Spain in educating their working classes. The education of the Spanish people should be effected through popular literature, workers' athenaeums and places of work, and an orally based education.[92] Tartilán's familiarity with socialist ideology stands out in her epigraph from Víctor Hugo[93] and her use of the word *proletariado*.[94] She defends equality of education,[95] coeducation,[96] and the duty of a bourgeois minority to educate the masses.[97] She authorizes her argument for equality of education through the principle of the complementarity of the sexes, visible in her citing of Rousseau's thoughts on the mother as the family's moral arbiter and natural educator.[98] Tartilán also wants free, compulsory education for children[99] and girls' working hours to be given special attention.[100] Indeed, she prioritizes girls' education because later, as mothers, they will educate future generations.[101] Women's sanctioned mission as mothers and angels in the house, then, as Mary Nash indicates, was not restricted to the bourgeoisie but also governed working-class women's conduct.[102]

Women's education comes to the fore from part 2 onward. Tartilán negates women's alleged intellectual incapacity and their cultural limitation to reproduction, blaming men's egotism for the laws that restrict women.[103] Women's education must be serious and informed by reason so as to provide a solid foundation for public and private virtues.[104] Although nowadays women are not denied a soul, Tartilán states that their current education annuls their souls[105] and merely serves to "barnizar a la joven, charolarla"[106] (varnish the girl, give her a superficial gloss). Maintaining that "woman" is a cultural construction—"La confección de esa entidad social que se llama mujer"[107] (The confection of that social body called woman)—and therefore repudiating essentialist premises regarding women, Tartilán affirms that their education is essential to the perfect society to which men of progress and science aspire.[108]

Fundamental to women's education, Tartilán states, are reading, writing, arithmetic, sewing that produces useful items (Tartilán criticizes embroidery), and even economy.[109] Hence the imperative to focus on what is useful rather than superfluous so that, contrary to Felicia's destiny in *Borrascas*, women can be more than a "mueble de adorno en un salón"[110] (ornamental piece of salon furniture). Consequently, Tartilán stresses what Ballarín calls a culture of domestic usefulness rather than the upper-class culture of adornment.[111] Indeed, Tartilán observes that middle-class women's inadequate education and the ensuing distortion of their natural reason make them more ignorant than peasant women.[112]

Tartilán stresses that mothers, as ordained by reason and divine and natural law, are best suited to undertake their daughters' education, for which they should assume full responsibility.[113] In this aspect, she follows reformists like Mesonero Romanos, Pablo Montesino, and Ramón de la Sagra, who also insisted that as mothers, women were naturally best suited to educate their children and thus sustain the liberal moral order within the family and society. It was the allegedly natural connection between femininity, charity, and Christianity, la Sagra argued, that placed women at the forefront of society's moral regeneration.[114]

In part 3, and founding her argument on nature and logic, Tartilán advocates teaching women history so that, as mothers, they can draw on its lessons to educate future citizens for their contributions to the nation.[115] Tartilán sees history as the "madre natural de todas las ciencias"[116] (natural mother of all the sciences) and a chaste matron, keeper of truth. In contrast, she opines, entering into the fraught debates regarding the merits of realism and naturalism, the novel is a "cortesana impúdica"[117] (wanton courtesan) that inflames passions, with the naturalist novel the worst of all. Later she insists that women of all classes must receive a solid education, because the well-educated mother who instils in her family principles of compassion and patriotism and a love of order, work, and study makes an immense contribution to her nation, regardless of her class. Correspondingly, citizens who are useful to their nation will bring the country material prosperity, the foundation of peace.[118]

Tartilán also lambasts great male thinkers for identifying Woman with the realm of the emotions, thus proscribing her access to reason and a socially useful role and thereby allowing Man to dominate her more easily. Such an approach breeds fanaticism and superstition, obstacles for progress.[119] Especially interesting is Tartilán's remark that her ideas are her own and not a mere reflection of what is in vogue. Hence, she stresses, she does not vindicate concepts that have been bandied about, such as women's emancipation, their complete freedom and equality, and their right to intervene directly in public affairs. Rights will follow when the educated woman knows how to use them prudently.[120]

Evidently, Tartilán's vision for women concurs with the discourse of domesticity that defined women's primary roles as mothers and wives. However, by stressing the political implications of women's domestic roles as educators of future citizens and makers of national well-being, Tartilán's stance brings a feminism of difference into play with a feminism of equality premised on rationality. As Cristina Enríquez de Salamanca explains, nineteenth-century "Spanish bourgeois culture detected in the epitome of the maternal model, the domestic angel, a kind of rationality which made her inclusion in the political system logically unavoidable"—a shift that the female writers of domesticity between 1850 and 1880 exploited.[121] Enríquez de Salamanca continues, "What could have initially been just a 'private' practice of 'private' individuals, went beyond the boundaries of family life, since it was precisely in their maternal functions that women were proposed as political subjects in 1877, 1878, 1907, and 1908 Parliamentary debates on women's suffrage."[122] Therefore, the model of feminism that Tartilán espouses shows features of relational feminism, which, by foregrounding women's roles as daughters, wives, and mothers, did not tie women's emancipation to their autonomy.[123]

Constant in Tartilán's argument is her oscillation between proposing that women might play a greater part in public affairs and advocating their strict adhesion to the domestic sphere. Thus she posits that for the well-educated woman, "quizás llegara un día que hasta se creyera con derecho a intervenir en los asuntos de su patria, empleando la justa influencia que naturalmente la hubieran conquistado su ilustración y sus luces"[124] (there may perhaps arrive the day when she might even believe that she has the right to intervene in the affairs of her nation, employing the just influence that her enlightenment and intelligence have naturally earned her). Why this has not yet happened is due to men's arrogance. Yet later she remarks, "No se crea que nosotros abogamos por esa instrucción que ha de llevar a nuestro sexo a la vida pública. Nuestra verdadera emancipación está dentro del hogar"[125] (Don't think that we support an education that takes our sex into public life. Our true emancipation lies in the home). Moreover, Tartilán insists, women themselves must take responsibility for their own education.[126]

In her final chapter in part 4, Tartilán addresses women's physical education. Embracing the axiom of mens sana in corpore sano[127] (a healthy mind in a healthy body), she acknowledges the positivistic reasons for this premise but states that her advocation of women's physical education concerns the loftier objectives of society's health and progress, which depend on the mother's physical health: "Todo cuanto pueda servir de eje y de palanca a la marcha del progreso humano, está supeditado a la organización débil o robusta, de donde toma sus principios vitales"[128] (Everything that acts as axis and lever for humanity's progress is dependent on whether the organism in which it begins life is weak or robust). Hence Tartilán expresses the Krausist and liberal avowal of the inseparability of body and mind/soul, which challenges the conservative binary that affirms the superiority of a "masculine" mind over a "feminine" body.[129] Tartilán stresses that her argument applies to all social classes and that intellectual wealth has the power to erase social distinctions: "No nos dirigimos a ninguna clase de la sociedad exclusivamente . . . todas las clases sociales se confunden en una cuando se trata de la ilustración intelectual y sus efectos"[130] (We do not address any one social class exclusively . . . all social classes are one when the benefits of an enlightened education are concerned). Nonetheless, Tartilán's closing words offset the more advanced viewpoints contained in her essay to mirror conservative discourses that position women in essentialist terms as a "rayo de sol" (ray of sunshine), as a "flor de esencia pura y delicada, [que] embalsamará con la fragancia de sus virtudes . . . el templo sagrado de la familia" (pure and delicate flower [that] will perfume with the fragrance of her virtues . . . the sacred temple of the family), and as an "ángel de paz y de amor"[131] (angel of peace and love).

Sofía Tartilán was an important presence in Spanish cultural and literary life during the decades that witnessed Spain's Glorious Revolution (1868), First Republic (1873–1874) and early Restoration period. Bearing the legacy of the Isabelline canon that would ideally confine women's writings and actions to the domestic sphere but also shaped by powerful progressive movements such as Krausism, freemasonry, and republicanism, Tartilán's significant body of work channels the premises of maternal Christian virtue to engage with the political subjects of education for the working classes and women and increased rights for both. Indeed, Tartilán's reputation as a staunch feminist is clear from a posthumous reference to her in 1894 in the progressive Republican periodical *El País*, which compared her to the seventeenth-century Madrid writer María de Zayas (1590–c. 1647) and the contemporary French feminist María Deraismes (1828–1894).[132] The emphasis in Tartilán's fictional pieces on history, realism, and the artificiality of narrative frames are necessary components in an overall didactic mission committed to exposing cultural myths harmful to women, cultivating reason, and forging a liberal Spanish nation founded on the principles of intellectual equality, order, industriousness, and usefulness.

NOTES

1. Ramón de Mesonero Romanos, "Carta prólogo de Ramón de Mesonero Romanos," in *Costumbres populares: Colección de cuadros tomados del natural*, by Sofía Tartilán, ed. José Luis Sánchez García (Madrid: Miraguano, 2004), 29.

2. José Luis Sánchez García, prologue to *Costumbres populares*, 14. According to María Lafitte, Tartilán was still directing Madrid's *La Ilustración de la Mujer* in 1882 and 1883. See María Lafitte, *La mujer en España: Cien años de su historia, 1860–1960* (Madrid: Aguilar, 1964), 88–89.

3. Review of Tartilán's *Costumbres populares* in the periodical *El Imparcial* 4838 (November 22, 1880): 2.

4. Lou Charnon-Deutsch, *Fictions of the Feminine in the Nineteenth-Century Spanish Press* (University Park: Pennsylvania State University Press, 2000), 278; Alba González Sanz, *Contra la destrucción teórica: Teorías feministas en la España de la Modernidad* (Oviedo: KRK, 2018), 549–552; Catherine Jagoe, *Ambiguous Angels: Gender in the Novels of Galdós* (Berkeley: University of California Press, 1994), 13, 16.

5. Sofía Tartilán, *Una deuda de veinte años*, *El Correo de la Moda* 2 (January 10, 1875): 10; no. 3 (January 18, 1875): 18–19; no. 4 (January 26, 1875): 26–27; Sofía Tartilán, *La caja de hierro*, in *La lengua larga*, ed. José R. Seoane (Madrid: Juan Iniesta, 1874), 219–240; Sofía Tartilán, *Borrascas del corazón* (Madrid, 1884).

6. Sánchez García, prologue to *Costumbres populares*, 11–12; Carmen García Colmenares and José Luis Sánchez García, "Sofía Tartilán: Autobiografía de una educadora desconocida," in *Actas VI Coloquio de Historia de la Educación: Mujer y educación en España, 1868–1975* (Santiago de Compostela: Universidad de Santiago, 1990), 153. Ángeles Carmona González erroneously gives Tartilán's birthplace as Málaga in "Tartilán, Sofía," in *Escritoras andaluzas en la prensa de Andalucía del siglo XIX* (Cádiz: Universidad de Cádiz, Instituto Andaluz de la Mujer, 1999), 253.

7. In the early 1880s, Manuel Eduardo Delgado became the director of Madrid's satirical Republican newspaper, *El Motín* (*The Uprising*). See references to his imprisonment in Madrid's *Cárcel Modelo* for not paying press fines (*El Motín* 32 [August 10, 1884]: 1; *El Motín* 33 [August 17, 1884]: 1; *El Motín* 35 [August 31, 1884]: 3; and *El Motín* 23 [June 7, 1885]: 1; as well as *La Época* [*The Epoch*] 12 [January 17, 1888]: 3). Tartilán was not the only contemporary female writer to separate from her husband: others were María del Pilar Sinués and Rosario de Acuña.

8. Carlos Bailley-Bailliere, ed., *Anuario del comercio, de la industria, de la magistratura y de la administración* (Madrid: Bailley-Bailliere, 1883), 236, 408. Other addresses were Jacometrezzo St. and Manuela Malasaña St. (Sánchez García, prologue to *Costumbres populares*, 13).

9. Sofía Tartilán, "Cartas de Tartilán a Barbieri, 1877–1879," in *Apuntes biográficos de diversas personas, cartas y otros documentos*, ed. Francisco A. Barbieri, MSS/14045/70-77, National Library of Spain. In 1875, Cherner contributed to *La Ilustración de la Mujer*, "Las mujeres pintadas por sí mismas," which were epistolary essays addressed to Tartilán. On Cherner, who committed suicide on August 15, 1880, see González Sanz, *Contra la destrucción teórica*, 400–402, 555–568; María de los Ángeles Rodríguez Sánchez, "Matilde Cherner: Una voz femenina y crítica ante la prostitución en la España de 1880," in *Actas XIII Congreso Asociación Internacional de Hispanistas* (1998), vol. 2, 370–378, Centro Virtual Cervantes, http://cvc.cervantes.es/literatura/aih/pdf/13/aih_13_2_046.pdf.

10. Carmona González, "Tartilán, Sofía," 254.

11. Clarín, quoted in Andrés Zamora Juárez, *El doble silencio del Eunuco: Poéticas sexuales de la novela realista según Clarín* (Madrid: Fundamentos, 1998), 90n14.

12. The following poems are available online in the Digital Press Library, National Library of Spain: "Mi deseo" (*Revista de Andalucía* 7 [January 1, 1877]: 28); "A Martínez

Monroy" (*Revista de Andalucía* 10 [January 4, 1877]: 32); "El mar" (*Cádiz* 4 [June 10, 1878]: 27–28); "La flor de otoño" (*Revista de Andalucía* 16 [January 1, 1879]: 64); "¡Quién! . . ." (*Cádiz* 30 [October 30, 1879]: 237); and "¡Quid divinum!" (*Las Dominicales del Libre Pensamiento* 99 [January 4, 1885]: 4). Regarding *Historia de la critica*, published by the Sevillan printer Salvador Acuña, see *El Globo: Diario Ilustrado* 52 (May 22, 1875): 207; and *El Solfeo* 30 (September 26, 1875): 4. On Tartilán's friendship with Juan Eugenio Hartzenbusch, see her correspondence with him between 1875 and 1877. She addresses him as "mi respetado y querido amigo" (my dear, respected friend) and seeks his advice on literary pieces that she and Cherner, her "amiguita" (little friend), have written (Sofía Tartilán, "Cartas 1875–1877, Madrid, a Juan Eugenio Hartzenbusch," MSS/20809/17-22, National Library of Spain).

13. See *El Correo de la Moda* 48 (December 26, 1879): 379; *El Nuevo Régimen* 177 (May 26, 1894): 4. On Tartilán's friendship with Sinués, see Sánchez García's note to Tartilán's *Costumbres populares*, 51.

14. On the *Novísimo romancero español*, see *El Correo de la Moda* 22 (June 10, 1879): 175; and *El Semanario Murciano* 68 (June 1, 1879): 8. Regarding the *Álbum*, see *Revista de España* 91 (March–April 1883): 510.

15. This text was perhaps a contestation of the conservative costumbrist volume *Las mujeres españolas, portuguesas y americanas* (1872–1873), to which Geraldine Scanlon refers in *La polémica feminista en la España contemporánea, 1868–1974*, trans. Rafael Mazarrasa (Madrid: Akal, 1986), 20.

16. Diego Ignacio Parada, "Sofía Tartilán," in *Escritoras y eruditas españolas*, vol. 1 (Madrid: M. Minuesa, 1881), 265–266. Tartilán's contributions to *Flores y Perlas*, which Sinués directed, were in March 1888. There she contributed poems (one dedicated to Sofía Casanova) and a short piece, "Fantasía," alongside writers such as Carolina Coronado, Casanova, Salomé Núñez y Topete, and Joaquina Balsameda.

17. Juan P. Criado Domínguez, "Tartilán, Doña Sofía," in *Literatas españolas del siglo XIX: Apuntes bibliográficos* (Madrid: Imprenta de Antonio Pérez Dubrull, 1889), 156–158. Tartilán's translation of Gómez Leal's work appeared in Madrid's *Revista Contemporánea* 16 (July 1878): 129–144. For lists of the periodicals to which Tartilán contributed, see Carmona González, "Tartilán, Sofía"; and José Luis Sánchez García, "Bibliografía," in *Costumbres populares*, 23–25.

18. "El iberismo en la literatura moderna de España y de Portugal," *Revista de España* 83 (November–December): 389. Tartilán was well versed in Victorian and fantastic literature as well as art, as evident in her allusions to Charles Dickens, E. T. A. Hoffmann, and Goya, among others, in *Costumbres populares* and her metaliterary and meta-artistic references in her novellas.

19. In *Cádiz*, Tartilán wrote in the late 1870s a cultural column, "Revista de Madrid," which incorporated sections approximating literary criticism. In *Revista de Andalucía*, she published the following substantial pieces: "La Edad Media" (no. 6 [October 10, 1876]: 13–21); "Belisario" (no. 7 [January 1, 1877]: 71–76); "La Roma del Imperio y la Francia moderna" (no. 7 [January 1, 1877]: 230–238; no. 8 [January 2, 1877]: 111–114; no. 9 [January 3, 1877]: 71–77); "Estudio del natural" (no. 11 [January 1, 1878]: 263–267); "La casa de paso" (no. 13 [January 3, 1878]: 69–74); "Las plagas de Madrid" (no. 15 [January 1, 1879]: 54–59); and "No es cierto" (no. 16 [January 1, 1879]: 129–133). On *La Iberia*, see García Colmenares and Sánchez García, "Sofía Tartilán," 154. In *El Eco del Tormes*, Tartilán published her essay "El tedio," while "Los niños" appeared in *La Ilustración de la Infancia* 101 (January 12, 1879): 260–262.

20. María Teresa Díez de los Ríos San Juan, "Catálogo de publicaciones periódicas masónicas (siglo XIX)," in *Fuentes y documentos para la historia de la educación en su relación con la masonería española*, ed. Pedro Álvarez Lázaro, https://dialnet.unirioja.es/descarga/articulo/1154999.pdf, 767 and "Tartilán, Sofía," www.mcnbiografias.com. The Hijas del Sol lodge was founded in Madrid in 1872 as an association within the lodge Hijos del Trabajo. Its principal objectives were to counter fanaticism through women's education and undertake charitable initiatives. Natividad Ortiz Albear, *Las mujeres en la masonería* (Málaga: Universidad de Málaga, 2005), 94–95.

21. On Emilia Serrano's and Gimeno de Flaquer's links, see Carmen Simón Palmer, "Puntos de encuentro de las mujeres en el Madrid del siglo XIX," *RDTP* 56, no. 1 (2001): 195, http://rdtp.revistas.csic.es; and Simón Palmer, *Actividades públicas de las madrileñas en la I República* (Madrid: Artes Gráficas Municipales / Área de Régimen Interior y Patrimonio, 2002), 25–26.

22. On Tartilán's involvement with Palencia's *Ateneo*, see José Luis Sánchez García, *El ateneo científico, literario y artístico de Palencia (1876–1926)* (Palencia: Merino Artes Gráficas, 1989), 126, 129, 147, 195. On her participation in Madrid's *Ateneo de Bellas Letras* and *Fomento de las Artes*, see *La Época* 10090 (August 2, 1880): 4. For Simon Palmer, the *Fomento de las Artes* showed the first signs of feminist initiatives in Spain. One of its objectives was to contribute to the education of the working classes (*Actividades públicas*, 25–26).

23. See *La Época* 9833 (November 10, 1879): 2; and *La Época* 9850 (November 27, 1879): 3.

24. Regarding the Ateneo Artístico y Literario de Señoras, see Sánchez García, prologue to *Costumbres populares*, 15–16; Íñigo Sánchez Llama, *Galería de escritoras isabelinas: La prensa periódica entre 1833 y 1895* (Madrid: Cátedra, 2000), 315. As Scanlon notes, it later became the Sociedad de Conferencias y Lecturas (*Polémica feminista*, 34).

25. *La Ilustración* 6 (December 12, 1880): 47; *El Pabellón Nacional* 3418 (August 19, 1883): 2.

26. *La España Artística* 5 (July 8, 1888): 2.

27. *La Ilustración Ibérica* 309 (December 1, 1888): 767. Sánchez Llama notes that Sáez de Melgar's 1881 *Páginas para las niñas* also became an official text in Spanish schools (*Galería de escritoras isabelinas*, 321–322).

28. Carmen de Burgos, "Misión educadora de la mujer en el periodismo," *Unión Ibero Americana*, December 1905, 87.

29. On these three writers, see Sánchez Llama, *Galería de escritoras isabelinas*. He defines the Isabelline canon as "prácticas culturales que privilegian el contenido virtuoso en la definición de la belleza estética fusionando una lectura conservadora y aristocrática del neoclasicismo con las propuestas más tradicionales del movimiento romántico. . . . defensa de las instituciones monárquicas y eclesiásticas, intenso nacionalismo antirrevolucionario y hostilidad a la cultura impresa de origen francés traducida en España desde 1833" (65–66; cultural practices that privilege virtuous content as defining aesthetic beauty, fusing a conservative, aristocratic Neoclassicism with the most traditional premises of Romanticism. . . . defense of the monarchy and Catholic Church, intense antirevolutionary nationalism, and hostility to translations of French works since 1833).

30. Sánchez Llama, 29–30.

31. Sánchez Llama, 30, 33, 39.

32. Tartilán, "Roma del Imperio," 230.

33. Sánchez Llama, *Galería de escritoras isabelinas*, 40.

34. Mary Lee Bretz, *Voices, Silences and Echoes: A Theory of the Essay and the Critical Reception of Naturalism in Spain* (London: Tamesis, 1992), 35.

35. Sánchez García, *Ateneo científico*, 126.

36. Criado Domínguez, "Tartilán," 156–158.

37. See *La Correspondencia de España* 8268 (November 10, 1880): 3; and *El Día: Suplemento Literario* 878 (October 23, 1882): 7.

38. Bretz, *Voices, Silences and Echoes*, 42.

39. Bretz, 43, 47.

40. Mónica Burguera, *Las damas del liberalismo respetable: Los imaginarios sociales del feminismo liberal en España (1834–1850)* (Madrid: Cátedra, 2012), 19, 165, 224–229.

41. From the early 1840s, progressive women's magazines, such as Gertrudis Gómez de Avellaneda's *La Ilustración: Álbum de las Damas* (1845), took up the debates around women's roles. On these periodicals, see Burguera, *Damas del liberalismo respetable*, 322–371. See also Christine Arkinstall, "A Feminist Press Gains Ground in Spain, 1822–1876," 111–125; and "Forging a Nation for the Female Sex: Equality, Natural Law and Citizenship in Spanish Feminist Essays, 1879–1920," 147–157, both in *A New History of Iberian Feminisms*, ed. Silvia Bermúdez and Roberta Johnson (Toronto: University of Toronto Press, 2018).

42. Tartilán's work was influenced by costumbrist writers such as Fernán Caballero and Mesonero Romanos, as well as by Grassi, Sinués, and Sáez de Melgar, who all cultivated this genre (see Sánchez Llama, *Galería de escritoras isabelinas*, 260–261, 297, 339–340).

43. "Las puertas del cielo," *El Correo de la Moda* 36 (September 26, 1879): 287; and no. 37 (October 2, 1879): 294–295. Mention is made of the publication of *La loca de las olas* in *El Motín* 38 (September 25, 1884): 4. Simon Palmer also refers to another novella, *Rosa del corazón* (1873), published in *El Correo de la Moda* (*Actividades públicas*, 31).

44. Tartilán, *Una deuda de veinte años*, in *El Correo de la Moda* 2 (January 10, 1875): 10; no. 3 (January 18, 1875): 18–19; and no. 4 (January 26, 1875): 26–27.

45. I here draw on Bretz's development of Roger Fowler's concept of sociolect, which Mikhail Bakhtin in turn sees as "authoritative utterances that set the tone—artistic, scientific, and journalistic works on which one relies, to which one refers, which are cited, imitated, and followed" (quoted by Bretz, *Voices, Silences and Echoes*, 24).

46. Tartilán, *Una deuda de veinte años*, in *El Correo de la Moda* 4 (January 26, 1875): 26.

47. Tartilán, *La caja de hierro*, in *La lengua larga*, ed. Seoane (Madrid: Juan Iniesta, 1874), 219–240. The original title of *Borrascas del corazón*, titled thus in the 1884 version available online, National Library of Spain, and that I use in this study, was *La lucha del corazón* (1874). However, it seems that there was a still earlier version, *Luchas del corazón*. See *La Época* 7632 (August 28, 1873): 4.

48. Tartilán, *Caja de hierro*, 220.

49. Tartilán, 219.

50. Tartilán, 225.

51. Tartilán, 226.

52. Tartilán, 224.

53. Several of Tartilán's works are semiautobiographical. In "La casa de paso," she narrates that she left Palencia at the age of ten, while in *Borrascas del corazón*, she alludes to a stay in Seville for health reasons (Sánchez García, prologue to *Costumbres populares*, 11–12).

54. Hazel Gold, *The Reframing of Realism: Galdós and the Discourses of the Nineteenth-Century Spanish Novel* (Durham, N.C.: Duke University Press, 1993), 15.

55. Tartilán, *Caja de hierro*, 228.

56. Tartilán, 229.

57. Tartilán, 232.

58. Laura Mulvey, "Pandora: Topographies of the Mask and Curiosity," in *Sexuality and Space*, ed. Beatriz Colomina (New York: Princeton Architectural Press, 1992), 66.

59. Tartilán, *Caja de hierro*, 225–226.

60. Mulvey, "Pandora," 55, 58.

61. Tartilán, *Borrascas*, 3.

62. Tartilán, 9.

63. Tartilán, 10.

64. María del Pilar Sinués, *Premio y castigo* (Madrid: Julián Peña, 1857), quoted by Sánchez Llama, *Galería de escritoras isabelinas*, 338.

65. Gold, *Reframing of Realism*, 12.

66. On the promise of social mobility and fear of social descent that accompany capitalism, see Sánchez Llama, *Galería de escritoras isabelinas*, 109–110.

67. Tartilán, *Borrascas*, 15.

68. Tartilán, 26.

69. Tartilán, 26.

70. Tartilán, 27.

71. Tartilán, 29.

72. Tartilán, 31.

73. Tartilán, 32.

74. Tartilán, "Estudio del natural," 264.

75. Bretz, *Voices, Silences and Echoes*, 35.

76. Tartilán, "Estudio del natural," 265, 267.

77. Tartilán, 265–266.

78. Regarding Charles Baudelaire, see *The Painter of Modern Life, and Other Essays* (London: Phaidon, 1964). For Mesonero Romanos, see Bretz, *Voices, Silences and Echoes*, 16; Enrique Rubio Cremades, "Costumbrismo: Definición, cronología y su relación con la novela," Biblioteca Virtual Miguel de Cervantes, http://www.cervantesvirtual.com/obra/costumbrismo-definicin-cronologa-y-su-relacin-con-la-novela-0/.

79. Extant issues of this periodical are nos. 52–89, National Library of Spain (May 31, 1875–December 15, 1876); and nos. 91–100, in Madrid's Hemeroteca Municipal (City Press Library; December 30, 1876–June 1, 1877).

80. Ana I. Simón Alegre, "Diez cartas y una escritora: Concepción Gimeno," Universidad de Zaragoza, https://siem.unizar.es/sites/siem.unizar.es/files/users/siem/Premio/xiv_premio_investigacion-ana_simon.pdf. Gimeno de Flaquer had previously directed Barcelona's *La Ilustración de la Mujer* in 1872. Luz Sanfeliu, "Del laicismo al sufragismo: Marcos conceptuales y estrategias de actuación del feminismo republicano entre los siglos XIX y XX," *Pasado y Memoria: Revista de Historia Contemporánea* 7 (2008): 60.

81. Quoted by Simón Palmer, "Puntos de encuentro," 191.

82. Cherner contributed "Las mujeres pintadas por sí mismas: Cartas a Sofía." The continuation of the fifth letter, on what Cherner calls intuitive science and derived from mysticism, magnetism, and spiritism, maintains that women will be the priestesses and

legislators of this new science that will perfect existing beliefs, sciences, and laws to make them worthy of women's intelligence (no. 55 [July 15, 1875]: 436–437). For historical overviews of nineteenth-century Spanish women's periodicals, see Inmaculada Jiménez Morell, *La prensa femenina en España (desde sus orígenes a 1868)* (Madrid: Ediciones de la Torre, 1992); Adolfo Perinat and María Isabel Marrades, *Mujer, prensa y sociedad en España 1800–1939* (Madrid: Centro de Investigaciones Sociológicas, 1980); and María del Carmen Simón Palmer, "Revistas españolas femeninas del siglo XIX," in *Homenaje a don Agustín Millares Carlo*, vol. 1, ed. Fondo para la Investigación Económica y Social de la Confederación Española de Cajas de Ahorros (Las Palmas de Gran Canaria: Caja Insular de Ahorros de Gran Canaria, 1975), 401–446.

83. *La Ilustración de la Mujer* 91 (January 15, 1877): 413.

84. Pilar Ballarín, "La construcción de un modelo educativo de 'utilidad doméstica,'" in *Historia de las mujeres en Occidente*, vol. 4, *El siglo XIX*, ed. Georges Duby and Michelle Perrot (Madrid: Taurus, 1993), 601.

85. These essays were already appearing in the earliest extant issue of *La Ilustración de la Mujer* (May 31, 1875).

86. *El Globo: Diario Ilustrado* 713 (September 23, 1877): 3.

87. *El Correo de la Moda* 2 (January 10, 1878): 15. Other substantial reviews appeared in the *Revista de Andalucía* 10 (January 4, 1877): 48; and *Revista Contemporánea* 11 (September–October 1877): 372–374.

88. María del Carmen Sánchez Carrera, "El pensamiento de Sofía Tartilán y el krausismo," in *Actas de las VII Jornadas de Investigación Interdisciplinaria: Mujeres y hombres en la formación del pensamiento occidental*, vol. 2, ed. Virginia Maquieira d'Angelo (Madrid: Universidad Autónoma de Madrid, 1989), 267–275; Margarita Nieto Bedoya and Carmen García Colmenares, "El pensamiento educativo de Sofía Tartilán," in *Actas VI Coloquio*, 254–260.

89. Scanlon, *Polémica feminista*, 17–18, 30–42, 22–23. Tartilán's mentors, Hartzenbusch and Mesonero Romanos, supported social reform and women's education, the former through the Spanish Institute and the latter through articles in his *Semanario Pintoresco Español* (1836–1858); Burguera, *Damas del liberalismo respetable*, 67, 73, 173–178.

90. Sofia Tartilán, *Páginas para la educación popular* (Madrid: Enrique Vicente, 1877), 253.

91. Tartilán, 69.

92. Tartilán, 38–40, 68.

93. Tartilán, 5.

94. Tartilán, 6. See also Sánchez Carrera, "Pensamiento de Sofía Tartilán," 272.

95. Tartilán, *Páginas*, 41.

96. Tartilán, 73.

97. Tartilán, 45.

98. Tartilán, 9–10.

99. Tartilán, 87.

100. Tartilán, 86.

101. Tartilán, 76.

102. Mary Nash, "Identidad cultural de género, discurso de la domesticidad y la definición del trabajo de las mujeres en la España del siglo XIX," in *Historia de las mujeres*, 589.

103. Tartilán, *Páginas*, 96–97.

104. Tartilán, 98.

105. Tartilán, 108.

106. Tartilán, 150.
107. Tartilán, 102.
108. Tartilán, 105. Pardo Bazán makes similar observations in "La mujer española" (1890; Scanlon, *Polémica feminista*, 28).
109. Tartilán, *Páginas*, 113–115, 118.
110. Tartilán, 124.
111. Ballarín, "Construcción de un modelo educativo," 603. Tartilán critiques such a culture of adornment in her essay "Roma del Imperio," 230–238.
112. Tartilán, *Páginas*, 179.
113. Tartilán, 135–136, 170.
114. Burguera, *Damas del liberalismo respetable*, 169–182, 215.
115. Tartilán, *Páginas*, 149.
116. Tartilán, 153.
117. Tartilán, 156.
118. Tartilán, 176–178.
119. Tartilán, 162–164.
120. Tartilán, 172–173.
121. Cristina Enríquez de Salamanca, "The Question of the Political Subject in Nineteenth-Century Spanish Domestic Discourse," in *Spain Today: Essays on Literature, Culture, Society*, ed. José Colmeiro et al. (Hanover, N.H.: Dartmouth College, Department of Spanish and Portuguese, 1995), 104–105.
122. Enríquez de Salamanca, 108–109.
123. Alda Blanco, "Teóricas de la conciencia feminista," in *La mujer en los discursos de género: Textos y contextos en el siglo XIX*, ed. Catherine Jagoe et al. (Barcelona: Icaria, 1998), 453, 464.
124. Tartilán, *Páginas*, 207.
125. Tartilán, 205.
126. Tartilán, 242, 246, 249.
127. Tartilán, 261.
128. Tartilán, 263.
129. Bretz, *Voices, Silences and Echoes*, 36.
130. Tartilán, *Páginas*, 263.
131. Tartilán, 271.
132. "La mujer se emancipa," *El País* 2437 (February 24, 1884): 2.

CHAPTER 3

Fashion as Feminism

CARMEN DE BURGOS'S IDEAS ON FASHION IN CONTEXT

Roberta Johnson

Today it is widely accepted that fashion and style in clothes have political and social impact.[1] Even as early as the Hoover administration, "when the cotton industry was spiraling, Lou Hoover [first lady from 1929 to 1933] was asked to pose for photographs wearing cotton dresses."[2] Presidential candidate Hillary Clinton's color-coded pantsuits and "kitten" heels are taken as a barometer of her standing in the poles (she has come a long way since she was criticized for her "schoolgirlish . . . penchant for headbands").[3] In a July 28, 2016, *New York Times* article titled "Changing the Rules of Power Dressing: Hillary Clinton and Theresa May Help Herald a New Age, Redefining Fashion at the Helm," Vanessa Friedman points out that "most of us don't have to decide on sanctions against Syria, or whether to try to reinstate the Glass-Steagall Act, but we all have to get dressed in the morning. That's the sweet spot where public politician and private person meet. . . . And right now it is an enormous opportunity: to redefine what being a female leader means, on every level. There is finally a critical mass to seize it."[4] The new conservative British prime minister Theresa May believes that fashion may be a political advantage, calling her shoes an "icebreaker."[5] Queen Elizabeth II of Britain is especially noted for wearing timeless clothes and accessories (her perennial handled handbags draped over her arm) that reassure the British public that despite economic ups and downs (and Brexits), the realm is calm and secure.[6] And of course, we recall Princess Diana's ability to capture attention for her charitable causes with her stunning, fashion-forward clothes. Her successor, Kate, duchess of Cambridge, and her Spanish counterpart Queen Letizia of Spain, likewise garner attention and favor for their respective royal families with interesting and well-chosen clothing styles that consistently show up in popular magazines. First Lady Michelle Obama's clothes (and now those of her daughters) place the spotlight on the role of presidential families in harnessing goodwill among the public.[7] Booth Moore remarked at the time of the 2009 inauguration that "Michelle Obama may be a trained lawyer with an Ivy League education, but on Tuesday night she will be America's Top Model. What she wears to the inaugural balls will set the style agenda for the administration and hold a mirror up to what it means to be a woman in America right now, which still includes being judged by your appearance."[8]

Despite these recent testimonials in the press to the impact of fashion in politics, the dearth of interest in fashion among twentieth-century American feminist thinkers makes Carmen de Burgos's chapter on *la moda* (fashion) in her *La mujer moderna y sus derechos* (*The Modern Woman and Her Rights*; 1927) all the more striking. Carmen de Burgos (1867–1932) was a truly modern woman. Married at an early age, she left her alcoholic, philandering husband to move to Madrid with her only surviving child to make her own way in the world by teaching, public speaking, and writing. She was an imposing physical presence—large, one might say—and she was unmistakably modern in her hairstyle and her dress, although she clearly understood that the new flapper style did not suit her ample body. In her attention to physical appearance, Burgos was very much in tune with her times, and in her major feminist essay *La mujer moderna y sus derechos*, she wrote about the importance of physical appearance, especially fashion, for women's liberation. One of the fourteen chapters of that book is devoted entirely to *la moda*. The table of contents lists the following subjects for chapter 12: "El derecho a la moda; Razones de la existencia de la moda; Su influencia en la vida de la mujer; Influencia que ejerce la literatura; Emancipación de la mujer por la moda; Costumbres modernas; Clubs y deportes; La uniformidad de la belleza" (The right to fashion; Reason for the existence of fashion; Its influence on women's lives; The influence it exerts; Women's emancipation via fashion; Modern customs; Clubs and sports; The uniformity of beauty).[9]

Burgos was not alone at the turn of the twentieth century in taking note of fashion's importance in foregrounding and promoting the "new woman" image, a woman who worked outside the home, supported herself financially, and went out unaccompanied. Ilya Parkins especially points to Charles Baudelaire, German sociologist and philosopher Georg Simmel, and Walter Benjamin, who, in seeking "to understand the unique character of modern life frequently turned to fashionable dress as a material embodiment of the spirit of modernity."[10] These thinkers found parallels between fashion and modernity in the fact that fashion changed rapidly; thus "its tempo was understood to reflect the accelerated pace of modern life."[11] Parkins additionally remarks that fashion straddled

> the poles of industrial and consumer capitalism, it had a long reach—and it called attention to the importance of *both* aesthetics and commerce as mediating factors in modernity rather than privileging one or the other . . . fashion made visually and materially apparent the instability of many of the

> ideological boundaries that were central to modern culture. Mythical modernity was structured by a series of dualisms: 'man' and nature, subject and other, art and industry, east and west, black and white, masculinity and femininity, among many others. . . . Fashion called into question binary oppositions that had a strong hold in modernity's picture of itself. In this sense, fashion dramatized the underside of modern life, the alternative narratives that structured every day, lived experiences of modernity, highlighting the gap between ideals and representations.[12]

Carmen de Burgos's ideas on fashion likewise "call into question" a number of myths of her age, especially that fashion was a frivolous occupation (recall Galdós's menacing message about women's spending too much time and money on clothes in *La de Bringas* [*Bringas's Wife*]; an obsession with fashion leads the protagonist of his novel to moral and material ruin).

In chapter 12 of her *La mujer moderna y sus derechos*, Burgos includes eating, speaking, behavior, and dress in the category of *la moda*. However, she adds that "generalmente se restringe el sentido para limitarla al traje, y a lo sumo, a los usos sociales"[13] (generally the meaning of fashion is limited to dress, or at most, to social practices). In her definition and understanding of how fashion functions, Burgos contradicted Simmel's statement that we can almost never find a material, aesthetic, or any other reason that can explain variations in fashion. For Burgos, "la moda muere gastada y vuelve a renacer, sustituyendo a cada una de sus fases otra nueva y distinta, que en el fondo es siempre la misma. Pero la moda no es una cosa caprichosa y arbitraria como cree Simmel"[14] (fashion dies worn out and is reborn, substituting each one of its phases with a new and different one, which in essence is always the same. But fashion is not capricious and arbitrary as Simmel believes). However, if we were wondering where fashion fits into a book on the rights modern women could expect to enjoy or obtain, Simmel provides a clue. For Simmel, "the only motivations with which fashion is concerned are formal social ones."[15] Toward the end of his essay on fashion from 1904, Simmel asserts that "fashion is . . . a social form of marvelous expediency, because, like the law, it affects only the externals of life, only those sides of life which are turned to society. It provides us with a formula by means of which we can unequivocally attest our dependence upon what is generally adopted, our obedience to the standards established by our time, our class, and our narrower circle, and enables us to withdraw the freedom given us in life from externals and concentrate it more and more in our innermost natures."[16] Burgos's friend, the medical doctor Gregorio Marañón, however, interpreted fashion's changes as originating in the constant need for renewal in sexual attraction. Here, I argue that Burgos's ideas about fashion draw on Simmel's social interpretation and Gregorio Marañón's biological understanding to forge a unique position that combines both the sociological and the biological.

Pilar Ballarín, editor of the 2007 Biblioteca Nueva edition of *La mujer moderna y sus derechos*, comments in her introduction that "Frente a Simmel, [Burgos] niega que la moda sea algo caprichoso y arbitrario y se apoya en Marañón para explicar los motivos de utilidad, económicos y sexuales que la fundamentan, aspectos que intentará demostrar"[17] (Contradicting Simmel, [Burgos] denies that fashion is capricious and arbitrary and relies on Marañón to help her explain the utilitarian, economic, and sexual motives at its heart, aspects that she attempts to demonstrate). However, we need to read Simmel a little more carefully than did Ballarín; he did not portray fashion as capricious and arbitrary; rather, he tied fashion closely to social class and how the classes view themselves. Thus he noted that fashion is constantly in motion. Like Simmel, Burgos believed that fashion registers something important about the social body that adopts it. Early in her essay on fashion, she writes, "Se puede comprobar cómo la *utilidad* y la *necesidad* han influido en la moda. En ella hay siempre algo muy importante, muy recóndito, capaz de revelar por sí sólo el alma de una época y el espíritu de un pueblo"[18] (One can show how *utility* and *necessity* have influenced fashion. In fashion there is always something important, very recondite, capable of revealing all by itself the soul of an epoch and the spirit of a people).

Significantly, Burgos was writing her essay on fashion on the eve of the Second Spanish Republic, which would take the figure of a woman dressed in classical garb as its symbol. Recall that Mariano Fortuny invented a new form of dress—the Delphos gown—likewise based on the classical pleated column that liberated women from the corset and the need to maintain a waspish waistline. For Burgos, there is a strong identification between feminism and fashion. She avers that "el feminismo ha venido a salvar la moda porque ha emancipado a la mujer"[19] (feminism has come to save fashion, because it has emancipated women). As Simmel pointed out, a seminal feature of fashion is its expendability; fashion requires constant change, and for Burgos, feminism provided women's freedom, an important means for changes to be introduced. Without freedom, change would be much more difficult to effect. And in fact, radical changes in fashion were possible thanks to women's liberation from the social norm of not displaying too much of the body—the ankles, the breast, the arms, and so on. Both Simmel and Marañón attempted to understand why fashions change so rapidly and so often. For Marañón, the dynamic involving fashion can be traced to the need to be sexually attractive; for Simmel, changes in fashion are related to the dynamics among the social classes.

Burgos followed Marañón in finding a biological basis for fashion's changes. Marañón points out that couples need constant changes in order to maintain sexual attraction, and Burgos notes fashion as a way of introducing innovation into a relationship:

> Nunca la mujer es más brillante y más visible que cuando la moda varía mucho. Sus variaciones traen una constante renovación de la figura, es como

> si se colocase delante de un foco de luz que la iluminase e hiciese valer ya el brazo, ya la mano, ya el descote o ya la cabellera, y esto trae una exaltación de las pasiones aunque, como el mismo Marañón reconoce, hay veces en que la vida sentimental y psíquica de la pareja es lo bastante frondosa para encontrar en ella misma motivos de renovada curiosidad.[20]
>
> Women are never more brilliant and more visible than when fashion is highly varied. Its variations bring constant renovation to her figure; it is as if she placed herself before a spotlight that singled out an arm here, a hand, a neckline, or the hair there, and this brings about an exaltation of the passions, which although as Marañón himself recognizes, there are times when the sentimental and psychic life of a couple is dense enough to find motives for renewed curiosity within it.

Marañón may have been influenced by Simmel, who, among other things, focused on the individualizing feature of fashion. Burgos explains Marañón's ideas as follows: "Marañón lo explica, porque el hombre ama en la mujer el *género*, y ella tiene que hacer esfuerzos para destacarse, individualizarse, atraerlo y retenerlo. La mujer, en cambio, ama en el hombre al *individuo*. Asegura que durante unos años, el hombre desea a la mujer, bajo una forma determinada. Al cabo la atracción se debilita y siente el deseo de cambiar"[21] (Marañón explains it, because what the man loves in the woman is *gender*, and she has to make an effort to stand out, to be an *individual*, attract him and retain him. Woman, on the other hand, loves the individual in a man. He assures that for a few years, the man desires the woman, in a certain form. Then the attraction weakens and he feels the need for change). Simmel, however, finds that individuals imitate in order not to feel alone in their actions. According to Simmel, "Whenever we imitate, we transfer not only the demand for creative activity, but also the responsibility for the action from ourselves to another. Thus the individual is freed from the worry of choosing and appears simply as a creature of the group, as a vessel of the social contents."[22]

Simmel notes that the imitator is the passive individual who believes in social similarity and adapts him- or herself to existing elements, whereas the teleological individual constantly experiments and restlessly strives, relying on his or her own personal conviction. According to Simmel, fashion satisfies several fundamental human drives: the need for differentiation, "the tendency toward dissimilarity," and "the desire for change and contrast."[23] Simmel interjects the notion of social class into his argument about how fashions change, asserting that "fashions differ for different classes—the fashions of the upper stratum of society are never identical with those of the lower; in fact, they are abandoned by the former as soon as the latter prepares to appropriate them."[24] (Simmel overlooks the fact that in eighteenth-century Spain, the upper classes imitated the lower classes in their jaunty *majo* and *maja* modes, as a number of Goya's paintings of the Duquesa de Alba attest. Goya, in some self-portraits, portrayed himself either in court clothing, reaching for the highest level of the social strata, or as a bullfighter, imitating a class beneath his true middle-brow status).[25] Thus for Simmel, fashion represents nothing more than one of the many ways we seek to combine in uniform spheres of activity the tendency toward social equalization with the desire for individual differentiation and change.

Simmel's essay on fashion is framed by his view of the relationship between the individual and society: "Fashion is merely a product of social demands, even though the individual object which it creates or recreates may represent a more or less individual need."[26] For Simmel, there is a close connection between the consciousness of individual personality and that of the material forms of life, a connection that runs all through history. The social regulation of inner and outer life is a sort of embryo condition, in which the contrasts of the purely personal and the purely objective are differentiated, the action being synchronous and reciprocal. Therefore, whenever man appears essentially as a social being, we observe neither strict objectivity in the view of life nor absorption and independence in the consciousness of personality. For Simmel, this process is top down: "Social forms, apparel, aesthetic judgment, the whole style of human expression, are constantly transformed by fashion, in such a way, however, that fashion—*i.e.* the latest fashion—in all these things affects only the upper classes. Just as soon as the lower classes begin to copy their style, thereby crossing the line of demarcation the upper classes have drawn and destroying the uniformity of the coherence, the upper classes turn away from this style and adopt a new one, which in turn differentiates them from the masses; and thus the game goes merrily on."[27] Simmel further refines this dynamic by identifying two separate social tendencies as "essential to the establishment of fashion, namely, the need of union and the need of isolation on the other."[28] He avers that both tendencies are absolutely necessary to the formation of fashion, and again relating this principle to social class, he finds that "the lower classes possess very few modes and those they have are seldom specific; for this reason the modes of primitive races are more stable than ours."[29]

Carmen de Burgos upends Simmel's idea that changes in fashion are driven by social class—styles originating in the upper classes, filtering down to the middle and lower classes, and then beginning all over again when the upper classes realize that the classes below them are now dressing like they are. Burgos believes that fashion, rather than enforcing class distinctions, is the great equalizer.[30] At the end of her chapter "La moda," Burgos boldly declares, "La moda tiende a igualarlo todo. Esa diferencia que existía en el aspecto exterior de la gran dama, la burguesa y la mujer de *conducta* dudosa, ha desaparecido. Todas visten lo mismo. No se diferencia de una simple señora, una Princesa o una Reina. Está todo permitido. Hasta las prendas que no usaba la mujer del pueblo son ya de su dominio. Una doncella lleva sombrero como una dama"[31] (Fashion tends to equalize everything. The differences that used to be evident in the appearances of a great lady, a bourgeois woman, and a woman of ill repute have disappeared. Everyone dresses alike. A princess or a queen cannot be distinguished from a common woman. Everything is permitted. Even the clothing items that a peasant woman did not use are now in her domain. A maid wears a hat just like her mistress). This last statement reminds us of Burgos's well-studied novelette *La flor de la playa* (*The Beach Flower*; 1920), in which a working-class seamstress and a lower-middle-class office clerk vacation in Portugal as a married couple, and the woman wears a hat to simulate middle-class respectability.[32] However, Burgos turns to the Marañón-like biological arguments in the following paragraph of *La mujer moderna y sus derechos*:

> Pero lo más raro es que se aproxima también la indumentaria de los dos sexos. Cuesta a veces trabajo distinguir a la primera mirada a una mujer peinada *a lo garçon*, con blusa camisero, levita o smoking de corte inglés, sombrero masculino y falda estrecha, de un hombre barbilampiño, con gran cuello de sport y pantalón ancho. Gómez de la Serna ha pintado la mujer *andrógina*, que busca ese subterfugio para contrarrestar la influencia masculina en "La mujer vestida de hombre." Sólo cuando aún llevan aretes se distingue el niño de la niña.[33]

> But even more strange is that the dress of the two sexes has grown closer together, At first glance, it is sometimes difficult to distinguish a woman with a *boyish haircut*, with a shirt-like blouse, an English-cut jacket, a masculine hat and a tight skirt from a shaven man, with a high sports collar and wide pants. Gómez de la Serna has painted the *androgynous* woman who seeks out this subterfuge in order to counter masculine influence in "The Woman Dressed as a Man." Only when the girl child wears earrings can she be distinguished from a boy.

We recall that Marañón was particularly concerned about women's assuming masculine characteristics.

Burgos's final observation about women's fashion becoming more masculine is that women had not yet begun to wear pants, a practice that was, in fact, just around the corner. And she ends her essay on a biological (racist) note: "La uniformidad de la belleza no favorece a la mujer. Un ilustre artista explicaba el triunfo de una bailarina negra en París, por ser la única que se distinguía en la monotonía de las mujeres, con una misma silueta y una misma máscara"[34] (Uniform beauty does not favor women. An illustrious artist explained the triumph of a black dancer in Paris, because she was the only one who stood out among the monotonous women, all with the same silhouette and the same mask). Thus in her essay on fashion, Burgos situates herself at the crossroads between social and biological explanations for changes in human practices. She finds that fashion changes can be effected both by social factors external to biology and via predetermined biological impulses. Burgos's finely tuned dance between the sociological and the biological—between Simmel's and Marañón's approaches—makes Burgos's essay on fashion an important contribution to the theoretical discussions of the subject in early twentieth-century Europe and reveals that Burgos should be included in any consideration of Spanish thought of the period.

Significantly, Burgos's feminist position on fashion can be compared to that of so-called postfeminist thinkers in Spain and elsewhere.[35] Had Carmen de Burgos's works and those of other pre–Civil War feminists not been completely erased from the public consciousness during the long Franco regime (1939–1975), the feminism in Spain that arose upon the dictator's death in 1975 would have saved itself a lot of work. For example, Maruja Mallo's dress and public behavior in the 1920s and 1930s were a flagrant rejection of traditional Spanish norms for women. María Martínez Sierra and Carmen de Burgos held feminist positions that were very similar to those of postfeminists Carmen Alborch and Lucía Etxebarria in the 1990s. External manifestations of feminist positions have a long history in Spanish feminism, beginning with the public personae of the two pillars of nineteenth-century Spanish feminism—Concepción Arenal and Emilia Pardo Bazán. Arenal had a sober, retiring personality and look, while Doña Emilia was outgoing, less discrete, and more polemic. Arenal's feminist thought centers on women's social role, while Pardo Bazán's focuses on women as individuals.

During the Franco regime, the smoldering embers of the pre-Republican and Republican-era feminism of which Carmen de Burgos formed an important part were kept alive via appearances and certain novelistic characters, such as the "odd girl." In 1944, only five years into the Franco regime's attempt to fashion the perfect Spanish society in which the traditional family unit was the model for individual life as well as for the state, Carmen Laforet broke the patriarchal model by winning the first Nadal Prize at twenty-two years of age. Although she married the following year and began to bear what would eventually be five children, she was a famous writer who was recognized everywhere. Her struggle to maintain her writer's vocation while attending to her obligations as a wife and mother is a hidden story revealed in more than four hundred letters amassed by Israel Rolón-Barada for his doctoral dissertation and partially published as *Puedo contar contigo* (*I Can Count on You*), Laforet's correspondence with Ramón Sender. Little of this part of Laforet's life has ever been made public until recently, but she had a feminist effect on some people through her physical presence. During a time when women's appearance was socially prescribed and even institutionally dictated through the Sección Femenina (Women's Section), Carmen Laforet went her own way and appeared in all the many photos of her with a completely natural, even unkempt, look, especially exemplified by her hair. Carmen Martín Gaite comments on the enormous importance Laforet's physical appearance had for her when she was growing up with the dictates of rigorous and often tortuous grooming, replete with permanent waves, curlers, and nightly beauty rituals: "Recuerdo que cuando le dieron el primer premio Nadal a una mujer, lo que más revolucionario me pareció, aparte del tono desesperanzado y nihilista que inauguraba con su novela, fue verla retratada a ella en la portada del libro, con aquellas greñas cortas y lisas"[36] (I remember when they gave the first Nadal Prize to a woman, what seemed most revolutionary to me, aside from the nihilistic and desperate tone that she ushered in with her novel, was to see her portrayed on the cover of the book with that short, straight hair). Carmen Laforet's friend Emilio Sanz de Soto remembers that many young people had newspaper clippings with Laforet's image pinned on their walls as a representation of youthful rebellion, like posters of rap stars on teenagers' walls today.[37]

These covert feminist gestures gave way to public conferences and more overt publications after 1975, but sartorial feminism once again surfaced with the splintering of organized feminism in the 1980s and feminism's institutionalization in 1982 with the Instituto de la Mujer (Woman's Institute). Emphasis on the physical from the mid-1980s to the present links current Spanish feminism with feminist approaches of the early Franco years. In the more recent climate of fragmentation and dispersion, Spanish feminists continue to rely on the corporal feminism of the 1940s and 1950s: "Otra constante en la valuación de las políticas son las alusiones a su aspecto físico o su vestuario. Como señala Amelia Valcárcel: 'Mientras los cuerpos de las mujeres sigan sobre-significados e hipernormalizadas existirá un sobreesfuerzo de presentación del yo correspondiéndose con una marca de genericidad potencialmente ahogadora de ese yo'"[38] (Another constant in the evaluation of the female politicians are the allusions to their physical appearance or their clothes. As Amelia Valcárcel points out: "While women's bodies continue to be over-signified and hypernormalized there will exist an exaggerated effort to present a self that corresponds to a generative point that can potentially drown out that self").

Jacqueline Cruz, for example, assigns Carmen Alborch, minister of culture under the first socialist government and later a socialist congresswoman, and Rosa Díez, also a socialist congresswoman, the distinction of having moved Spanish women in politics away from masculine models, which they signaled in their habits of dress; Carmen Alborch "demostró un desparpajo 'a la hora de vestirse, maquillarse y pintarse el pelo, que rompía con la estética timorata del traje de chaqueta,' mientras que . . . 'su [la de Rosa Díez] forma de hablar, de vestirse, de peinarse, de moverse, sus propuestas, la presentaban como una mujer joven, desenvuelta la estética de una 'teen'"[39] (demonstrated an impudence "in her dress, make-up, and hair color that broke with the timid aesthetic of the jacketed suit," while . . . "her [Rosa Díez's] way of speaking, dressing, wearing her hair, of moving, her proposals presented her as a young woman in the bold style of a 'teen'"). In many newspaper reports, Alborch was singled out for her red hair and red lipstick.

The statements women politicians and writers make with their clothes and appearance are often a point of attack for the opposition. Cruz summarizes that "en cualquier caso, las mujeres políticas se encuentran siempre bajo la lupa del juicio indumentario. No es fácil olvidar las burlas concitadas por Loyola de Palacio y por Isabel Tocino en relación con su vestuario y aspecto físico"[40] (in any case, women in politics always find themselves under the microscope of wardrobe judgment. One cannot forget the jokes that the clothes and physical appearance that Loyola de Palacio and Isabel Tocina inspired). She goes on to point out that often, it is female newspaper columnists who engage in unflattering observations about female politician's physical appearances. She quotes the politically charged comments of Karmentxu Marín on Isabel Tocino, Partido Popular (Popular Party)[41] minister of the environment: "'Con qué nos sorprenderá, tras haberla visto disfrazada de pastorcilla y de motera?', '¿Los fabricantes de laca están desolados por sus cambios capilares?'"[42] ("So she will surprise us after we have seen her disguised as a shepherdess and a *motera*?", "Are the nail polish manufacturers unhappy because she has changed her hair color?"). Maruja Torres comments about Ana Palacio, the Partido Popular minister of foreign affairs: "'Ha mejorado mucho desde que ha decidido prescindir de la asesoría en abalorios Tudor con que nos torturaba, y planea del orbe por sus confines con el *set* de complementos justo'"[43] ("She has improved since she decided to leave behind the counsel of Tudor beads with which she tortured us and glides around the confines of the globe with the appropriate set of accessories").

In defining feminism, Lucía Etxebarria emphasizes the importance of dress and appearance: "Ser feminista no . . . implica renunciar al sujetador, el lápiz de labios, los tacones de aguja y los pendientes. Se trata de reclamar el poder de las mujeres y el derecho de cada una de nosotras a utilizar ese poder según nuestros propios términos"[44] (To be a feminist does not . . . imply renouncing the bra, lipstick, stiletto high heels, and earrings. It is a matter of reclaiming women's power and the right of each one of us to utilize this power on our own terms). Like Carmen Laforet (whom she has imitated in other things as well, although in a much more extravagant fashion), Etxebarria uses her own body as a formidable sign of her independence from any reigning norms for female corporality. She flatly refuses to conform to fashion dictates and to the slender norms for women's figures, taking her support for such refusal from Annie Sprinkle, conceptual artist, ex–porn star, ex-dancer, and ex-prostitute, "una mujer que reinvindica el uso del cuerpo como vehículo de comunicación política y cultural, contraponiéndolo a la cosificación del cuerpo como icono que nos ofrecen cada día los medios de comunicación"[45] (a woman who reinstates the use of the body as a vehicle for political and cultural communication, pitting it against the reification of the body as an icon that the media offer us every day). Etxebarria knows the importance of dress in political figures when commenting on the Partido Popular's prominent political figure Loyola de Palacio, who she claims "integra la contradicción de liderar una lista conservadora simbolizando casi un icono feminista de mujer fuerte y autogestionada cuyas acciones importan más que su físico (al contrario que el resto de las mujeres de su partido, todas oros, mechas y perlas, el atuendo y las maneras de Loyola siempre se han caracterizado por su sobriedad)"[46] (incorporates the contradiction of leading a conservative list by almost symbolizing a feminist icon of a strong and self-made woman whose actions are more important than her physical appearance [in contrast to the other women of her party, who are all gold, highlighted hair and pearls, Loyola's dress and manners have always been characterized by their sobriety]). When Etxebarria won the Premio Nadal for *Beatriz y los cuerpos celestes* (*Beatriz and the Celestial Bodies*) in 1998, she could hardly be characterized by her *sobriedad*. In choosing her clothes and accessories, she seemed to sense that she would win the prize and receive media attention: "Lucía Etxebarria se vistió la noche del martes para ganar. Vestido rojo. Bolso en forma de corazón, guantes a lo Gilda en rojo, tatuaje acorazonado y pendientes a juego"[47] (Lucía Etxebarria dressed to win on Tuesday. Red dress. Purse in the shape of a heart, Gilda-style gloves, a heart-shaped tattoo and earrings to match). As a further testament to the fact that women's physical appearance has a deep relationship with politics in Spain, when the Socialist Party won the elections in 2004, the women who formed part of the new government, including the incoming vice president, put on a fashion show. Surely, Carmen de Burgos would have approved. Burgos's ideas about fashion as a feminist statement have become more overt in the current U.S. fashion scene. In a recent collection of clothes for spring 2017, a "black silk georgette T-shirt was embroidered with Susan B. Anthony's words, 'They threw things then but they were not roses.'"[48]

NOTES

1. Carmen de Burgos was nowhere to be found in my undergraduate or graduate education in Spanish literature (1960s and 1970s) or in any of the books and articles I read over the years about the Generation of '98 or the Spanish vanguard writers, even though her life and activities were contemporaneous with theirs. It was MLA, December 1989 in Washington, DC, when I was chair of the Twentieth-Century Spanish Division and had the responsibility of organizing three sessions. I chose the topic of "New Literary History for Twentieth-Century Spain," and I invited Maryellen Bieder to participate. Maryellen gave her now landmark paper "Woman and the Twentieth-Century Spanish Literary Canon: The Lady Vanishes." What a revelation! There were women writing during the male-bastioned Generation of '98, and Carmen de Burgos was chief among them. Franco's censors' edict that Burgos's work (along with that of Voltaire and Rousseau, among others) not be republished or sold in Spain had effectively erased Burgos from Spanish literary and intellectual history. I hastily finished the book I was working on at the time, the all-male *Crossfire: Philosophy and the Novel in Spain 1900–1936*, in order to start another book, *Gender and Nation in the Spanish Modernist Novel*, that included

the women writers of the same period. There were few republications of Burgos's writing even then—Concepción Nuñez Reyes's anthology was and continues to be a precious resource. When I decided to include Burgos in the book I was working on about Spanish women who were writing at the same time as the hallowed Generation of '98, Maryellen generously sent me photocopies of the Burgos novelettes she had unearthed in Madrid's Biblioteca Nacional. Thus I was introduced to the subtle ambiguities of novelettes like *La entrometida* (*The Meddler*) and *El hombre negro* (*The Black Man*). Since Maryellen's mind-blowing revelation twenty-five years ago, I have never taught a course on early twentieth-century Spain that does not include Carmen de Burgos; invariably, several students in each class pass over the opportunity to write their seminar papers on hallowed figures like Unamuno, Azorín, Baroja, or Lorca to address Carmen de Burgos. My University of Kansas graduate students Paqui Paredes, Mark Harpring, and José Ballesteros included Burgos in their textbook anthology of Spanish literature *Voces de España* (*Voices of Spain*), and Paqui published an article on Burgos's novelette *La flor de la playa* (*The Beach Flower*). Recently, my UCLA graduate student Zeke Trautenberg's seminar paper on Burgos for my course on "Contextualizing Twentieth-Century Spanish Literature" was published in *Hispanic Review*. I want to thank Maryellen Bieder for getting me into the Carmen de Burgos industry; Maryellen's legacy has had legs. Maryellen essentially initiated what would become a major scholarly interest in early twentieth-century Spanish studies, especially emphasizing Burgos's role as an early Spanish feminist when being a feminist in Spain was a difficult and lonely task.

2. Booth Moore, "A National Pastime: Ever since Martha Washington, We've Fixated on First Lady Fashion and the Messages It Conveys," *Los Angeles Times*, January 18, 2009. Moore goes on to point out that "although there's no written rule that first ladies must wear American-made clothing, the tradition started with Martha Washington (1789–1797), who was encouraged to wear 'homespun' clothing instead of British fashions in the aftermath of the Revolutionary War" (P4). Oddly, little has been written from a feminist point of view on the connection between fashion and feminism. As Annette Messager notes, "What is interesting is that if one goes through the iconic works of the first, second and third waves of feminist writers, there is so little that actually addresses fashion. Rereading Simone de Beauvoir, Kate Millet, Shulamith Firestone, Germaine Greer, Lucy Lippard, Linda Nochlin and so many others, I was struck by the dearth of attention to the subject, which after all has everything to do with how identity is constructed for the outside world" ("Body Politic," Excerpt from *Voluntary Tortures*, first published in 1972; repr., *New York Times Style Magazine*, February 25, 2007).

3. "Dressed to Impress," *Los Angeles Times*, January 18, 2009, P5. It is hard to imagine that Hillary Clinton, today having firmly settled into the color-coordinated pantsuit, would receive the kind of criticism for her appearance that she did when she first ran for president in 2007: "Why hasn't she landed upon a signature style other than her fallback position of mix-and-match jackets or trousers? There is a discernible discomfort with who she wants to present herself as being at any particular moment. One could argue that women everywhere would readily identify with that. Her sartorial floundering, her casting around for an outfit that works for her, should engender sympathy" (Daphne Merkin, "The Politics of Appearance: In a Realm Where Simulation Is All Authenticity May Lie in the Details," *New York Times Style Magazine*, August 26, 2007, 309). Criticism of Hillary's appearance continued to dog her campaign in 2007. The *Washington Post* ran an article that remarked on the cleavage evident when Hillary gave a speech run on C-SPAN.

The *Post* article and its aftermath is summarized by Sarah Wheaten in the *New York Times*: "Ms. Lewis also lamented a moment during Monday's Democratic presidential debate when John Edwards asked to critique Mrs. Clinton, jokingly expressed reservations about her coral jacket, which Senator Barack Obama defended" ("Latest Campaign Issue? One Candidate's Neckline," *New York Times*, July 28, 2007, A13). Hillary Clinton seems finally to have found her fashion comfort level, settling into Ralph Lauren pantsuits, which she has worn at key moments in the 2016 presidential campaign: the campaign kickoff rally, her Democratic Convention acceptance speech, and the first two debates with Republican nominee Donald Trump. Vanessa Friedman notes of Clinton's designer choice: "Mr. Lauren is, perhaps, the most ur-American of American designers: a man who built an empire on the mythology of the untrammeled West, where cowboys roamed free among herds of bison, along with a kind of 'Brideshead Revisited' Anglo past" ("Ralph Lauren May Have Found a New Muse in Clinton," *New York Times*, October 11, 2016, A16).

4. Vanessa Friedman, "Changing the Rules of Power Dressing," *New York Times*, July 28, 2016, D1. In another piece on a similar topic, Friedman notes that "although they [clothes] are often seen as handicapping women in positions of authority, acting as a distraction from her achievements and substance, they can also be a strategic communication tool. One that is, ironically, more accessible to women than to men, who are stuck in the never-ending generic suit loop, forced to rely on the distinguishing characteristics of hair and tie color" ("The Power That Comes from Clothes," *New York Times*, October 30, 2014, E5)

5. Friedman, D2. Theresa May was wearing leopard-print pumps at her first meeting with German Chancellor Angela Merkel in July 2016, reminding us of Jo Weldon's conclusion that "in the last few centuries spotted-cat motifs attract attention and exude power, ferocity, independence, sophistication" (quoted in Eve M. Kahn, "Dressed to Kill, in Leopard Prints," *New York Times*, April 29, 2016, C29). The meaning of such a fashion statement on May's part is all the more poignant in light of her support for the United Kingdoms's Brexit vote, which favored Britain's leaving the European Union much to the chagrin of leading European Union countries, Germany chief among them.

6. Elizabeth Paton remarks on Queen Elizabeth's coronation gown, which incorporated symbols from countries of her far-flung commonwealth: "It was wearing this dress, with her nation's history stitched atop her hemline, that Queen Elizabeth II took to the British throne in 1953, sending a message from the monarchy via her appearance that was broadcast to millions all over the world watching the moment on TV" ("More Than Pearls, a Bag and a Crown: A Peek inside the Wardrobe of Queen Elizabeth II," *New York Times*, August 11, 2016, D7).

7. See Cathy Horyn, "First in Fashion," *New York Times*, December 30, 2012, D1, D7; and Bee Shapiro, "Malia Obama's Look, like Mom's, Sells Clothes," *New York Times*, August 27, 2015, D1, D8. Cathy Horyn remarked after Barack Obama was reelected in 2012 that "Michelle Obama has used celebrity and style to redefine the role of first lady. Now, with four more years in the White House, can she step off the glamour pedestal and broaden the reach of her powerful voice? . . . In hindsight, her decision to shift from mom and busy professional to glamour figure was a brilliant one. It effectively protected her" ("First in Fashion," D1). Horyn earlier noted about Michelle Obama's striking lemon-colored outfit for the 2009 inauguration, "Here is a bolder woman, a serious woman from Chicago and Harvard who is not afraid to express herself with fashion, and it is the kind of confidence that many women will recognize in themselves. Her clothes tell us that she has an adventurous spirit, as well as a sense of humor, and if some of these garments have almost

an old-fashioned womanly quality, then they tell us that she is indeed not your average fashionista" ("The First Lady Tells a Story with Fashion," *New York Times*, January 21, 2009, P16). And Jeannine Stein attributes "femininity and strength" to Michelle Obama's penchant for bare arms ("Arms and the Woman," *Los Angeles Times*, March 29, 2009, P4).

8. Booth Moore, "Can She Stay 'Everywoman'?," *Los Angeles Times*, January 18, 2009, P5. Booth goes on to point out that the clothes Michelle Obama wore in public and on television (often from middle-brow stores such as the Gap and J. Crew) "did more to convince voters that she is 'one of us' than almost anything else. It's no wonder, after years of being inundated with paparazzi and red carpet photos of stars wearing millions of dollars of free designer duds, that Obama's real-world style would captivate us. She is a fashion icon for the everywoman."

9. Carmen de Burgos, *La mujer moderna y sus derechos*, ed. Pilar Ballarín (Madrid. Biblioteca Nueva, 2007), 259.

10. Ilya Parkins, "Fashion," in *The Cambridge Companion to Modernist Culture*, ed. Celiz Marshik (Cambridge: Cambridge University Press, 2015), 96.

11. Parkins, 96.

12. Parkins, 96.

13. Burgos, *La mujer moderna*, 248.

14. Burgos, 248.

15. Georg Simmel, "Fashion," *International Quarterly*, October 1, 1904, 135, http://www.modetheorie.de/fileadmin/Texte/s/Simmel-Fashion_1904.pdf.

16. Simmel, 148.

17. Pilar Ballarín, introduction to *La mujer moderna*, 47.

18. Burgos, *La mujer moderna*, 249. In this statement, one hears echoes of the Generation of '98 notion of *intrahistoria* (soul or essence—*volksgeist*—inner history [everyday life, as opposed to external history of changes in government, wars, etc.]), but I leave the tantalizing possibility of the coincidence of Burgos's philosophical ideas with those of her male counterparts for another occasion.

19. Burgos, 253.

20. Burgos, 254.

21. Burgos, 255.

22. Simmel, "Fashion," 133.

23. Simmel, 134.

24. Simmel, 134.

25. Something similar has occurred today with upper-middle-class youths' imitating lower-class black youths' baggy, low-slung jeans.

26. Simmel, 134.

27. Simmel, 135.

28. Simmel, 137.

29. Simmel, 137.

30. Joshua Zeitz makes a similar argument in his 2006 book *A Madcap Story of Sex, Style, Celebrity, and the Women Who Made America Modern* (see Liesl Schilinger: "After Channel's design revolution, women who wanted to look stylish no longer needed to buy expensive clothing. 'Thanks to me,' she once said, working women 'can walk around like millionaires.' But his liberalizing of female dress could bewilder hidebound citizens. In a study published in 1929, an Indiana businessman complained, 'I used to be able to tell something about the background of a girl applying for a job as a stenographer by her

clothes . . . but today I often have to wait till she speaks, shows a gold tooth, or otherwise gives me a second clue" [18]).

31. Burgos, *La mujer moderna*, 270.

32. See Francisca Paredes and Ezequiel Trautenberg for discussions of the meaning of dress in this novelette.

33. Burgos, *La mujer moderna*, 262.

34. Burgos, 263.

35. By *postfeminism*, I refer to the reaction on the part of some women to what they consider an extreme attempt by feminists to erase all feminine markers, such as makeup and very feminine clothing.

36. Carmen Martín Gaite, *El cuarto de atrás*, 3rd ed. (Barcelona: Destino, 1980), 66.

37. I met Emilio several times in the company of Carmen Laforet, and on one of those occasions, he mentioned this to me.

38. Jacqueline Cruz and Barbara Zecchi, *La mujer en la España actual* (Madrid: Icaria, 2004), 89.

39. Cruz and Zecchi, 90.

40. Cruz and Zecchi, 90.

41. The Partido Popular is Spain's conservative political party.

42. Karmentxu Marín, quoted in Cruz and Zecchi, *La mujer en la España*, 90.

43. Maruja Torres, quoted in Cruz and Zecchi, 90.

44. Lucía Etxebarria, *La Eva futura: Cómo seremos las mujeres del siglo XXI, y en qué mundo nos tocará vivir* (Barcelona: Destino, 2000), 15.

45. Etxebarria, 98.

46. Etxebarria, 153–154.

47. Lucía Etxebarria, "Me presenté al Nadal para suavizar la reacción de mis padres a mi novela," *El País*, January 8, 1998.

48. Vanessa Friedman, "What's Daring These Days? Try a Political Manifesto," *New York Times*, September 13, 2016, A18.

PART II

Emilia Pardo Bazán as Literary Theorist and Cultural Critic

CHAPTER 4

Emilia Pardo Bazán's "Apuntes autobiográficos" and "El baile del Querubín"

A THEORETICAL REEXAMINATION

Susan M. McKenna

In 1886, at the behest of her editor, Emilia Pardo Bazán penned an autobiographical prologue that served to introduce the first edition of her novel *Los pazos de Ulloa* (*The House of Ulloa*). A hybrid text, "Apuntes autobiográficos" ("Autobiographical Notes") is at once a brief summary of her literary trajectory and an imaginative synthesis of narrative theories and practices. Prominent among these pages is the significance of the storytelling act itself and the reader's response to said act—a mutually creative and reinforcing collaboration of originators.

With the exception of studies by Federico Sáinz de Robles (1947), Carmen Bravo-Villasante (1962), Elvira Martín (1962), Robert Osborne (1964), and more recently, Nelly Clèmessy (1982), Marina Mayoral (1986), María de los Ángeles Ayala (1997), Elizabeth J. Ordóñez (2002), Cristina Patiño Eirín (1995), and Carmen Pereira-Muro (2010),[1] "Apuntes autobiográficos" has received little critical attention compared to its sister essay, *La cuestión palpitante* (*The Burning Question*; 1882–1883). Yet in its own time, it received vehement commentary—mostly negative—from many of the leading authors of the day, including Pereda, Menéndez Pelayo, and Clarín, to name a few. Writing to Galdós in 1886, Pereda, for example, first praises *Los pazos* as her best novel to date: "*Los pazos* me han parecido la mejor novela de la Pardo, con capítulos de una belleza indiscutible, sin que parezca por toda la novela señal alguna de ese pujo de sectaria artificiosa del naturalismo convencional al uso, que tanto la perjudica en otras. Así se lo he dicho, o dado de entender, al escribirla"[2] (It seems to me that *Los pazos* is her best novel yet, with chapters of unquestionable beauty; a novel without a trace of yearning for that artificial confidentiality of conventional naturalism so in vogue today that is so detrimental to others. I told her so, or let it be known, when I wrote to her). Nonetheless, he continues, "Lo que reputo por insoportable e indigerible, es la autobiografía del principio; aquello, salvo la forma y el 'argumento' es de una cursilería semi estúpida que tumba de espaldas. Sobre estas páginas del libro no le he dicho ni una palabra por temor de soltar una vergüenza"[3] (What I deem insufferable is the autobiography that precedes it. Except for, perhaps, its form and "argument," I am struck by its silly pretension. I have not said a word about these pages for fear of saying something rude).

Likewise, Menéndez Pelayo, who has read the prologue but not the novel, writes to Valera, "Doña Emilia Pardo Bazán ha publicado el primer tomo de una novela que no he leído. Pero sí he leído unos apuntes autobiográficos con que la encabeza y que, a mi entender rayan en los últimos términos de la pedantería. Dice entre otras cosas, que cuando era niña la Biblia y Homero eran sus libros predilectos y los que nunca se le caían de las manos"[4] (Doña Emilia Pardo Bazán has written the first volume of a novel I have not read. But I have read the autobiographical notes that precede it and, to me, they ultimately border on pedantry. She says, among other things, that when she was a child, the Bible and Homer were her favorite books and that they never left her hands). He continues, "Parece increíble y es para mí muestra patente de la inferioridad intelectual de las mujeres—bien compensada con otras excelencias—, el que teniendo doña Emilia condiciones de estilo y tanta aptitud para estudiar y comprender las cosas, tenga al mismo tiempo un gusto tan rematado y una total ausencia de tacto y discernimiento"[5] (It seems incredible, and it is for me a patent example of the intellectual inferiority of all women—well compensated with other virtues—that Doña Emilia, having the temperament and so much aptitude for studying and understanding the world, also has such bad taste and a total lack of tact and discernment). Such negative reactions may be explained by the fact that "Apuntes" is more than just a prologue; it is the means by which Pardo Bazán continued not only to hone her theoretical practices but also to construct an autobiographical narrative that defined her as a serious author on a par with her male contemporaries,[6] which was clearly threatening to many male authors of the time. Part theory, part story, part synthesis, "Apuntes" circumscribes the author in both, and yet in neither, of the masculine and feminine traditions in which she was bound.

"El baile del Querubín" ("The Cherub's Dance"), published in the second issue of Pardo Bazán's *Nuevo Teatro Critico*[7] (*New Critical Theater*) five years later in 1891, may not be the first story to come to mind when considering narrative theory, but it is a story that exhibits well four of the predominant theoretical themes developed in Pardo Bazán's autobiographical notes. These subjects include the effect of childhood and early education on her writing, the prescription of societal roles for men and women, the significance of intertextuality and cross-cultural pollination in literary construction, and the pleasure(s) of the text, both readerly and writerly. This essay examines one of Pardo Bazán's more seemingly lighthearted texts, "El baile del Querubín," through the critical lens of her own narrative theories, which she elaborated in her "Apuntes."

Throughout the centuries, autobiography has been the means by which women writers have attempted to write themselves into history. In the most minimalist of terms, the definition of *autobiografía* (autobiography), according to the *Diccionario de la Real Academia Española* (*DRAE*; *Dictionary of the Royal Academy*), is "la vida de una persona escrita por ella misma"[8] (the life of an individual written by him- or herself). Equally relevant are the words *prologue* and *notes*. The *DRAE* defines *prólogo* (prologue) as "un discurso antepuesto al cuerpo de la obra en un libro de cualquier clase, para dar noticia al lector del fin de la misma obra o para hacerle alguna advertencia"[9] (an essay at the beginning of any kind of work that serves to either introduce the reader to or warn the reader about that work); and the word *apunte* (note) as "un asiento o nota que se hace por escrito de algo"[10] (a written entry or note). As is evident in "Apuntes," all three intentions are integral to the author's design. Moreover, Pardo Bazán utilizes the text's first sentence to refashion her title and thus her purpose by using the hyphenated term "apuntes autobiográfico-literarios"[11] (literary-autobiographical notes). This slight, yet significant, modification in terminology allows for an expansion of the parameters of the traditional prologue and also serves to communicate to the reader, from the onset, both the author's predilection for rewriting the script and the artificial construct inherit in all texts. A wordsmith in several European languages, Pardo Bazán self-consciously chose the language and the subject matter for this prologue with intelligence and care as she presents herself to an audience in autobiographical form for the first and only time in her career.

The explosion of theoretical work advanced over the past few decades on women's autobiography since Sidonie Smith's groundbreaking study in 1987 reinforces the significance of the form even as we continue to redefine the language used and the texts analyzed.[12] In the wake of all the 1990s "post-isms" (postcolonialism, postfeminism, and postmodernism), the openness of such newly minted categories as "women's autobiographical practices," "women's personal narratives," and "women's life-writing," for example, all speak to a shift away from uncritical, mostly Western understandings of the subject of autobiography toward those that are much more inclusive. This broader conceptualization of texts includes diaries, letters, memoirs, travel narratives, meditations, cookbooks, family histories, spiritual records, collages, and art books—and perhaps, today, even emails, blogs, and tweets. Contemporary historians, literary and cultural critics, narratologists, and linguists now consider it standard practice to consider the processes of subject formation and agency as functions of writing. So too is the attention paid to the audience of these texts, both real and/or implied. For this reason, in the case of an author such as Pardo Bazán, one cannot ignore the historical specificity—demarcated within the confines of late nineteenth-century Spain—in which she constructs her autobiography, for it plays a fundamental role in the national, gendered, and linguistic arguments that she seeks to make.

Sidonie Smith and Julia Watson have argued that in an "androcentric tradition," authorization was unavailable to most women.[13] Historically absent from both the public sphere and the modes of written narrative, women were compelled to tell their stories differently from men but, nonetheless, had effectively done so throughout the centuries. Any theory of female textuality, they maintain, must recognize how the dominant culture fictionalized women and, consequently, how women autobiographers challenged these prevailing gender ideologies to write their own life narratives.[14] They propose several key questions for reading a woman's autobiography pertinent to this analysis of Pardo Bazán's "Apuntes." First, how does the woman autobiographer "authorize her claim to writing"?[15] Second, how does she "negotiate the gendered fictions of self-representation"?[16] Third, how does either the presence or the absence of sexuality as subject in the story mark her literary authority?[17] The "double-voiced structure"[18] inherent in women's autobiographical narratives, they suggest, reveals the continuing negotiation between women's "desire for narrative authority and their concern about excessive self-exposure."[19] This is the fine line that Pardo Bazán had to traverse throughout her long and often tumultuous career.

In her study of Pardo Bazán's prologues, Cristina Patiño Eirín calculates that over her lifetime, the author wrote at least fifty-seven prologues: twenty-six for herself and another thirty-one for her contemporaries.[20] For her own books, she begins in 1879 with the prologue to *Pascual López, autobiografía de un estudiante de medicina* (*Pascual López, Autobiography of a Medical Student*) and concludes in 1905 with the one she writes for *La quimera* (*The Chimera*). These twenty-seven in particular, Patiño Eirín maintains, underscore the diverse theoretical precepts and doctrines developed within each individual work.[21] Similarly, the thirty-one prologues written for friends, editors, and authors attempting to make a place in the profession introduce a great variety of genres and literary styles including poetry, novels, short stories, and translations. In addition to presenting the author and his or her work to the public, the prologues also address some of the social, political, cultural, and philosophical conversations and controversies in which they were conceived. A writer very much attuned to the pulse of her century, Pardo Bazán used every medium available, including her prologues, to express often controversial attitudes and ideas on ongoing debates and subjects.

The use of a literary prologue to introduce either a novel or a collection of poems or short stories was a customary practice in Spain, as well as most other European countries, not only during the nineteenth century but also in those that preceded and followed it. One classic example, and one on which she readily could have modeled her "Apuntes," is Cervantes's 1605 prologue to *El ingenioso hidalgo don Quijote de la Mancha* (*Don Quixote: The Ingenious Gentleman of la Mancha*).

The Cervantine references in the text itself are numerous, and she makes a point of telling her reader several times, much to Menéndez Pelayo's chagrin, that the *Quijote*, along with the Bible and Homer's *Iliad*, were the three most influential books in her early reading career: "Hoy cometo la tontería de ponerme muy hueca recordando que los tres libros predilectos de mi niñez y esto sin que nadie me encareciese de propósito su valor, fueron la *Biblia*, el *Quijote*, y la *Iliada*"[22] (Today I feel rather chuffed to remember that my three favorite childhood books, without anyone having pointed out to me their worth, were the Bible, *Don Quixote*, and the *Iliad*). Consequently, she boasts of being able to recite entire chapters of the knight's adventures without omitting a period or tilde—"capítulos enteros, que recitaba sin omitir punto ni tilde"[23] (entire chapters, which I would recite without omitting a period or accent). Moreover, she justifies the writing of her autobiography, what Smith terms "authorizing her claim to writing," with a pointed comparison, asking her reader, "¿A quién no regocijaría hoy el hallazgo de algún apunte autobiográfico de Cervantes que aclarase puntos oscuros en su vida y hechos?"[24] (Who wouldn't be delighted today to find some autobiographical sketch from Cervantes that would clarify some of the more unknown facts of his life and his works?). Reminiscent in her structure, style, tone, and tradition, the narrator of Pardo Bazán's "Apuntes" likewise assumes the time-honored pose of the humble author seeking recognition from a discerning public. As with her predecessor's text, every instance of feigned humility is met with an even stronger affirmation of the author's talent and genius. Like Cervantes, Pardo Bazán is conscious of her role in creating and defending a new genre—that of the modern novel in Cervantes's case and that of the realist/naturalist novel in Pardo Bazán's case—and both make use of the birthing metaphor to introduce their progeny to the public.[25] Yet "Apuntes autobiográficos" is also a direct response to Valera's *Apuntes sobre el nuevo arte de escribir novelas*[26] (*Notes on the New Art of Writing Novels*; 1887), which, in turn, is a direct response to Pardo Bazán's *La cuestión palpitante* (1883–1884).[27] Hence the palimpsestic layers of narrative construction are many and transgress both gender and genre.

"Apuntes" opens with an immediate address to her "lector amigo" (friendly reader), directly underscoring the intimate relationship that exists between the author/narrator and her public. The confidential discourse is repeated several times with strategic modifications that include "piadoso lector" (pious reader), "discreto y benigno lector" (discreet and kind reader), and "lector pacientícismo" (patient reader). Thus piety, discretion, kindness, and patience are the characteristics of choice bestowed upon the sympathetic reader of her autobiographical prologue and the novel it precedes. This implied understanding between author and reader comes full circle when she concludes the essay by invoking her "lector, amigo incognito" (unknown friendly reader) one final time, emphatically employing forms of the familiar *tú* (you) twice in the last sentence. Pardo Bazán deploys the conversational tone of an epistolary dialogue to uphold and promote her aesthetic theories and to reaffirm her position as an important author. After all, she contends, "bien mirado, el arte no es otra cosa sino la comunión del alma individual con el alma colectiva" (all things considered, art is none other than the communion of the individual soul with the collective soul).[28] Constituting a special case among her prologues, these "Apuntes," argues Patiño-Eirín, fulfill a function that is at once "introductorio-presentativa y programático-publicitaria"[29] (introductory presentation and programmatic publicity). "Apuntes autobiográficos," she concludes, "suministran información valiosísima para conocer el pensamiento literario de Pardo Bazán, y el progresivo conocimiento que adquiere de la novela y del movimiento literario español y europeo en la segunda mitad del XIX"[30] (offer valuable information for understanding the trajectory of Pardo Bazán's literary thought and the knowledge she acquired of the novel and of the Spanish and European literary movements during the second half of the nineteenth century).

Pardo Bazán's first literary memory corresponds to the end of the war in Africa in 1860—a series of verses composed by a nine-year-old child to honor the returning soldiers, some of whom, she recounts, were very handsome in their uniforms. This early memory, nonetheless, is meant to signify so much more. Pardo Bazán links this initial foray into the world of literature with both an awareness of herself as a desiring female subject and intense feelings of patriotism for "the Nation." Additionally, she continues, "de mí sé decir que ese sentimiento es uno de los que no han modificado ni lecturas, ni estudios, ni azares de la vida, ni ciertos sofismas que hoy corren disfrazados de última palabra del desengaño filosófico, cuando no son más que atrofia del alma y signo infausto de decadencia de las naciones"[31] (I can rightly say that for me this sentiment is one that has not been altered over the years by my reading, studies, or life events nor by certain sophisms that today are masked as the last word of philosophical disillusion when they are really no more than the atrophy of the soul and the unfortunate sign of a nation's decadence). She concludes, "Me encuentro en ese particular—lo digo con orgullo—a la altura de una mujer del pueblo"[32] (In this matter, I find myself—and I say it with pride—equal to the common woman). Throughout the essay, Pardo Bazán will defend herself against the accusation that she is an *afrancesada* (Francophile). She may admire the French Romantics; appreciate the realism of Flaubert, Zola, or Balzac; and even praise the waters of Vichy or Parisian culture, but she is first and foremost a patriot, a nationalist, and a Spaniard. Two particular anecdotes underscore this sentiment. She recounts that going head-to-head one night with her esteemed Victor Hugo, she first defended the Spanish Golden Age tradition and then educated him and his French *tertulia* (literary gathering) on the works of contemporary Spanish writers about whom, she relates, "no sabía media palabra"[33] (he knew nothing). In another section, she acknowledges the superiority of the French realists but then counters the praise by accentuating her own preference for, and loyalty to, the Spanish realists. Moreover, as Carmen Pereira-Muro asserts, Pardo Bazán defiantly sought to reconcile this embrace of the masculine projects of nationalism and the realist novel with her own womanhood and feminism.[34] At once conciliatory and provocative, she uses this approach to gain recognition as a woman writing in a man's world. Notable for their integral connection to her first literary memories, the reaffirmations of her patriotism and her gender are two significant motifs she develops throughout the text.

The next several sections outline the eclectic reading patterns of "una niña curiosa"[35] (a curious child) whose early book choices were governed by the private libraries she encountered along the way. By the time she was fourteen, she was allowed to read everything except the works of Alexandre Dumas, Eugène Sue, George Sand, Victor Hugo, and the other French romantics.[36] When she finally read Hugo for the first time, she imagined all works of fiction to be "extraordinario, desmesurado y fatídico"[37] (marvelous, excessive, and dangerous). She herself could never write a novel, she says, because it would require an extraordinary imagination, something she did not possess.[38] Not until she encounters the Spanish realist novelists—Valera, Alarcón, Pereda, and Galdós—and makes the connection between their work and the tradition of Spanish realism does she even consider the possibility of writing a novel of her own. She explains, "Si la novela se reduce a describir lugares y costumbres que nos son familiares, y carácteres que podemos estudiar en la gente que nos rodea, entonces (pensé yo) puedo atreverme; y puse manos a la obra"[39] (If writing a novel means describing familiar places, customs, and characters that can be studied in the people around us [I thought to myself], then I might dare to try, and so I did). Pardo Bazán thus justifies her decision to write fiction by drawing a direct link between the contemporary Spanish realists and her "antiguos conocidos"[40] (old friends)—that is, Cervantes, Hurtado, and Espinal. The strategic significance of this correlation cannot be overstated. By establishing a line of continuity vis-à-vis the tradition of Spanish realism, one that begins with Cervantes and the picaresque novels and runs through the present, Pardo Bazán legitimizes at once both the genre itself and her own cultural nationalism.

Pereira-Muro takes up this theme in an essay contrasting Pardo Bazán's "Apuntes" to Galdós's *Trafalgar*, written in 1873. Examining a series of textual coincidences between the two works, Pereira-Muro maintains that with "Apuntes," Pardo Bazán "aspiraba a consagrarse como miembro de pleno derecho en la esfera pública de la alta cultura Española"[41] (sought to prove she belonged in the public sphere of Spanish high culture) at the same time that she defended her patriotism, which critics questioned because of her association with French literature. Most importantly, Pardo Bazán's allusions to Galdós's *Episodios Nacionales* (*National Episodes*) and, more specifically, to *Trafalgar*, she argues, constituted another subtle tactic with which the author tried to construct a new space inside the literary establishment in which being a woman "no es tan solo detrimento, sino una aportación fundamental a la construcción literario-nacional"[42] (was not a deterrent but rather a fundamental contribution to the construction of a national literary consciousness). Although Pardo Bazán never completely breaks with the masculine cultural paradigms of her times, she nonetheless succeeds in creating a place for the woman author as a cocreator of "esa nación imaginaria proyectada por la novela realista"[43] (the imaginary nation projected by the realist novel) and as an active subject "de esa nación deseada" (of this desired nation).

The emergence of the modern Spanish nation and its representation in the late nineteenth-century novel developed concomitantly with the construction of contemporary notions of masculinity and femininity. "Apuntes" evinces this relationship through its intentional yet understated amalgamation of national identity formation and female autobiographical narration. Furthermore, in tracing the evolution of her narrative theories and strategies, Pardo Bazán emphasizes their link not only to the Spanish tradition by directly citing Cervantes, Santa Teresa, Fray Luis, Iriarte, Zorrilla, Galdós, and so on but also to a transnational cross-pollination that began with the Romans. Every country, she admits, should endeavor to cultivate its own novelistic tradition—and in Spain even more so, considering its illustrious past—without fear of embracing the modern methods as long as they are based on rational principles, suitable for a contemporary understanding of what constitutes art. She continues, "Y me pareció que no se debían rechazar los progresos en el arte de hacer novelas por su procedencia traspirenáica, atendido que basta saludar la historia de la literatura para saber que las tres naciones latinas, Italia, Francia, y la Península Ibérica, tienen de tiempo inmemorial establecido el cambio de ideas estéticas y la reciprocidad de influjo literario"[44] (We should not reject advancements in the art of writing novels because they come from the other side of the Pyrenees. One only needs to look at history to know that the three Latin nations, Italy, France and the Iberian Peninsula have exchanged aesthetic ideas and maintained a reciprocal flow of literary influences since time immemorial). The Romans influenced our law, she affirms, and we sent them our orators and poets; the French troubadours taught us their songs, and in return, we lent them our dramatists. The list, she concludes, is interminable, the results both productive and rich.[45] She leaves it now in the hands of her "benigno lector" (benevolent reader), who knows better than anyone else what he prefers, appreciates, and delights in: "El sano manjar nacional, servido en fina loza"[46] (A healthy national cuisine, served in select earthenware).

The defense of her literary theories is peppered with culinary metaphors and domestic images of cooking. Indeed, Ordóñez maintains that the rhetoric of domesticity employed in "Apuntes" is yet another narrative strategy that allows Pardo Bazán to buffer her feminine intrusion into the masculine literary world.[47]

Furthermore, by "putting her own slant on those timeworn tropes," Ordóñez continues, "she implicitly casts herself, as author, into the role of good (non-gendered) cook."[48] Several times throughout the text, Pardo Bazán draws our attention to the difficulties she encountered as a writer simply because she was a woman. Beginning with her education, she writes, "Apenas pueden los hombres formarse idea de lo difíçil que es para adquirir cultura autodidáctica y llenar los claros de su educación"[49] (Men can hardly form an idea of how difficult it is for a woman to acquire culture and to fill in her education by teaching herself). Men are handed their education, attend university, write and publish without thinking twice about their privileged position. Women, on the other hand, have no access to this world and are discriminated against when they, even gingerly, try to place one toe inside. For men, she writes, "todas ventajas; y para la mujer, obstáculos todos"[50] (all advantages; and for women, all obstacles). From here, the argument becomes more personal as she recounts her own situation: "Viendo lo mal fundado de mi instrucción, mi erudición a la violeta y el desorden de mis lecturas, me impuse el trabajo de enlazarlas y escalonarlas, llenando los huecos de mis conocimientos a modo de cantero que tapa grietas de pared"[51] (Seeing my ill-founded instruction, false erudition, and the disorder of my studies, I began the task of ordering and connecting the dots, filling in the gaps of my knowledge just like a mason fills in the cracks in the wall). Having emphasized the dearth of a formal education, she now turns the model on its head to outline the authority of her self-made edification. She knows the Spanish and classical literature inside and out; has read, and even met, all the major French Romantics and realists; and has mastered Krause, Kant, and Hegel.[52] She translates Byron and Shakespeare; reads Schiller, Goethe, and Heine in German; and makes sure to mention here her knowledge of Plato, Aristotle, St. Thomas, and Descartes.[53] Having fully established the breadth and the depth of her erudition, she casually throws in, almost as if it were an aside, the fact that she is also a mother: "Jaime, mi primogénito, nació en junio de 1876, y apenas expiró la cuarentena, a pesar de mis padecimientos y fatigas de nodriza y madre, realicé el proyecto que traía formado desde Madrid, de optar al premio del Certamen que se celebraba en Orense para honrar la memoria de Padre Feijóo"[54] (My firstborn, Jaime, was born in July 1876, and with my quarantine scarcely ended and in spite of my ailments and fatigues as a nursing mother, I carried out the plan formulated in Madrid to compete in Orense for the prize of best essay written to honor the memory of Father Feijóo). The essay takes twenty days to write. She wins not only first prize for "Ensayo crítico de las obras de Padre Feijóo" ("Critical Essay on the Works of Father Feijóo") but also a golden rose for her poem "Oda a Feijóo" ("Ode to Feijóo"). "Me calificó," she writes, "diciendo que tenía un cerebro de hombre encerrado en cabeza femenina"[55] (They assessed me, saying that I had the brain of a man enclosed within the head of a woman). Her response to these critics is evident in that she refuses to be delimited by anachronistic categories that just don't fit. Motherhood, ambition, accolades, and success all go hand in hand for Pardo Bazán.

Feijóo's influence on Pardo Bazán's feminist development is significant. Second only to her father, Feijóo, writes Bravo-Villasante, "será siempre su maestro de feminismo" (will be the most important source of inspiration for her feminism).[56] Feeling "capaz de todo" (capable of anything) after reading his "Defensa de la mujer" ("Defense of Women"), she would often recite from memory the first few sentences of this essay for inspiration: "En grave empeño me pongo. No es ya sólo un vulgo ignorante con quien entro en la contienda. Defender a todas las mujeres, viene a ser lo mismo como ofender a todos los hombres superficiales . . . El más corto lógico sabe, que de la carencia del acto a la carencia de la potencia no vale la ilación; y así de que las mujeres no sepan más, no se infiere que no tengan talento para más"[57] (I place myself in an immense imbroglio. It is not only against the ignorant commoner with whom I enter into battle. To defend all women is the same as to offend all superficial men . . . Simple logic dictates that a lack of action does not necessarily translate to a lack of potential; so if women don't know about something, one should not infer that they don't have the ability to learn more). Her greatest tribute to the Galician Benedictine is her *Nuevo Teatro Crítico*, suitably named in honor of his grand Enlightenment encyclopedia *Teatro Crítico Universal* (*Universal Critical Theater*; 1726–1739). From January 1891 to December 1893, Pardo Bazán wrote, produced, and financed thirty issues of this monthly periodical containing short stories, essays, reviews, and historical and biographical pieces. With complete control of the publication, she could and did write on anything that she wanted. The range, depth, and consequence of the topics addressed continue to astound even today's seasoned scholars. In her biography of Pardo Bazán, Pilar Faus, for example, describes her own response to *Nuevo Teatro Crítico* as one of "asombro y admiración"[58] (amazement and admiration) for what is, without doubt, the pinnacle of Pardo Bazán's journalistic career. Indeed, some of Pardo Bazán's most critical condemnations of the state of women's affairs in late nineteenth-century Spain are found in these pages, especially in her essays on women's education.

In October 1892, Pardo Bazán, along with 528 other women from Spain, Portugal, and the Americas, including Concepción Arenal, Carmen Rojo, and Concepción Sainz, attended an international congress on education and pedagogy, participating in sessions that addressed both women's aptitudes for the professions and the limits imposed on women's education. As the chair of a session, she presented in writing the conclusions her session reached and gave a synopsis of the speeches. That same month, she published her speech, some memories, and some of the findings in her journal.[59] In one essay, "La educación del hombre y la de la mujer, sus relaciones y diferencias" ("Men and Women's Education: Similarities and Differences"), she compares the types and levels of instruction provided to each, citing many more differences than similarities. To ameliorate the disparities and, ultimately, for all of society to progress, she argues, a fundamental change in perspective must occur—namely, a woman's education must not be based on her reproductive functions. Rather, she states, "la instrucción y cultura racional que la mujer adquiera, adquiéralas en primer término para sí, para desarrollo de su razón y natural entendimiento, porque el ser racional necesita ejercitar las facultades intelectivas lo mismo que necesita no atrofiarse sus demás órganos"[60] (a woman acquires an education and cultural reasoning, in the first place, for her own good, for the development of her own reason and understanding. Rational human beings need to use their intellectual faculties in the same manner that they exercise the other organs to prevent atrophy). Moth erhood, if and when it occurs, is a temporary function, not a constant state of being.[61] The development of one's mind and, subsequently, the opportunity to utilize this knowledge in one's desired vocation are incontestable rights that must be afforded to all humanity.[62] Change is never easy, she argues, yet in this case, it is not only possible but necessary. Women must be granted equal access to secondary and university education alongside men as well as the opportunity to utilize their education in a way that best benefits both them and society.[63] Despite the fact that she received considerable criticism, both during the congress and afterward upon publishing her speech, she concludes here somewhat optimistically, hopeful that the proposals initiated in the congress will produce something "práctico, concreto y fructuoso"[64] (practical, concrete, and useful) for the immediate and long-desired reform of women's education.

The focus of "Apuntes" on the topic of women's education and its concomitant theme, the societal roles for men and women, predominates as well in much of Pardo Bazán's fiction. So too do her explorations of intertextuality, cross-cultural pollination, the artifice of literary construction, and the pleasures of the text. To explore briefly the synchronic relationship between theory and practice, this analysis draws a parallel between "Apuntes" and a little-known story of hers, "El baile del Querubín." Seemingly simple and straightforward, the story's plot involves a first-person narrator who recounts an event from his past. Growing up in a large, wealthy family in Santiago, Ramón and his cousins enjoy the privileges of their class and spend their evening hours learning all the newest dances as well as the traditional and regional ones. The vicar of the Bernadine nuns (el padre vicario de las monjas Bernardas) gets wind of this and confronts Ramón in the street one day, demanding that the youth confess to the lascivious activities taking place at his home. Provoked by the vicar's misreading of the dances, Ramón invents all kinds of stories, titillating the old man's imagination into such a fever that he nearly falls down the steps. That afternoon, the vicar contacts the parents, the dances are canceled, and the devastated children now sit listlessly around the patio, fondly remembering their innocent pastime. Later that night, the vicar shows up at the house, explains that he didn't mean for them to stop dancing entirely, and then proceeds to teach them the more "danzas honestas" (modest dances) like the "baile del querubín." Flapping his arms like an angel in flight, shouting for the children to keep in step, he circles the patio like an old magpie, repeating all the while to keep "a compás, a compás, a compás"[65] (in time, in time, in time). Soon the children and their parents can barely contain their laughter. And so, the narrator concludes, "ahí tienen ustedes cómo nunca nos divertimos más que la noche en que pensamos aburrirnos mortalmente"[66] (there you have it how we never had more fun than on that one night when we thought we would all die from boredom). End of inner story.

The framing device, however, is where Pardo Bazán tells the real story—a narrative technique she successfully employs throughout her career. His hair now gray, Ramón looks back with nostalgia at "aquellas doradas horas"[67] (those golden hours) of his youth. Life has kicked him around a bit, he says, affording him "a pena por día, y algunas veces ración doble"[68] (daily hardships and sometimes a double dose). Having felt that sublime tug toward glory, he became a writer and scribbled down a few pages, though he's not sure that they will outlast him. Over the years, he confides, he encountered various critics who, inspired by the vicar's tradition, "quisieron obligarme a que sólo bailase *el baile del Querubín* . . . con muchísimo compás!"[69] (wanted him to stay in step, keep time, and only dance *el baile del Querubín*). End of the real story. Like those critics who neither read "Apuntes autobiográficos" nor *Los pazos* but were happy to disparage them, the vicar in "El baile del Querubín" never sets eyes on the children's dances yet nonetheless feels completely justified in censuring them. His soliloquy wherein he works himself up into a frenzy of sexual conjectures is manifested through a series of unanswered questions and ellipses, allowing Ramón and the reader to fill in the blanks for themselves: "No ha habido . . . , quiero decirlo con toda limpieza posible . . . , no ha habido algún . . . , vamos, algún roce . . . , en fin, algún contacto . . . , indiscreto . . . , alguna aproximación excesiva . . . , imprudente . . . , entre personas de distinto sexo . . . , algún . . . , alguna . . . posición . . . , que . . ."[70] (There was not . . . , I mean to say it as innocently as possible . . . , was there never once . . . , well now, some brush . . . , some contact . . . , indiscreet . . . , some excessive closeness . . . , imprudent . . . , between people of the opposite sex . . . , some . . . , position that . . .). This is also the case for some of the more vociferous critics of naturalism who, contends Pardo Bazán, "no fueron los menos indignados por confesión propia, ni habían leído ni pensaban leer una sola de las vitandas novelas discutidas, y hablaban de las malas doctrinas defendidas en *La cuestión palpitante* sin hojear el libro"[71] (by their own confession had not read, nor even thought about reading, one page of the works they disparaged and then also criticized the evil doctrines endorsed in *La cuestión palpitante* without having opened the book). As rendered in the autobiography and the short story, then, the guardians of good taste and acceptable behavior projected misconduct where there was none and condemned what was new, modern, uncommon, or unseen. Those who transgress, our two narrators included, run the risk of misinterpretation, censorship, and ultimately exclusion. This was a risk, it seems, that both Pardo Bazán and Ramón were willing to take.

The prescription of societal roles is a second theme that intersects and links the two works. "Apuntes" and "El baile del Querubín" evince a gendered pattern of socialization for Spain's upper classes at the same time that they undermine it with narrative irony. Most children, Ramón reports, learn at an early age to play games that reinforce their future roles in society: boys act out certain professions while girls prepare for courtship, motherhood, and running the household. Later, as they grow into adults, boys are encouraged to embrace their independence and attend university while girls remain at home to hone their domestic skills. This rigid model of education, the narrator maintains, reflects a "curioso panorama infantil de la existencia futura, teatro de inocentes marionetas, en quienes la *mimesia* o parodia se adelanta al conocimiento reflexivo y la comprobación de la vanidad universal"[72] (odd childhood panorama of a future existence, a theater of innocent marionettes, in whom *mimesis* or parody gets ahead of the reflexive knowledge and the confirmation of universal vanity). Likewise, Pardo Bazán's account of the tedium she endured as a student in a girl's finishing school in Madrid, though humorous, points to the lack of a rigorous curriculum for young women. Alongside a smattering of grammar, the fables of La Fontaine, much mythology, and a bit of geography, she recalls, the girls garnered enough French so that even "las menos lerdas salimos de allí hechas unos loritos, parlando francés a destajo" (the least dull among us left there like little parrots, speaking French in excess). More notable in its mockery, perhaps, is the experience of "ver un eclipse de sol por vidrios ahumados, experimento que me pareció el colmo de la ciencia astronómica"[73] (watching a solar eclipse through smoked panes of glass, an experiment that seemed to me the pinnacle of astronomical science). With a light hand, she deploys a concrete instance in her own life to portray the deplorable conditions of women's education.

The two works converge, as well, in their foregrounding of narrative construction, intertextuality, and the pleasures of the text. "Apuntes" reads like a real "who's who" of literature with its profusion of titles, authors, genres, schools, movements, and citations that intersect and interconnect continents and generations. Throughout the essay, Pardo Bazán consciously constructs an identity that affirms her position as an author of rank, touting both her qualifications and her innate talents. In the closing paragraphs, writing from a room she likens to a cell in her rural home the Granja de Meirás, she softens this bravado slightly, situating herself in the serene haven of her native Galicia. Tucked away in an edenic, natural setting reminiscent of Fray Luis de León's garden, this final section evokes a sense of continuity with the past, mysticism, tradition, shared legacy, and the harmonious blend of the old and the new. She writes, "Si yo pudiese jactarme de haber contribuido, de cualquier modo y en cualquier grado que fuese, a esta prosperidad relativa de la novela española, tendría por muy bien empleadas las horas que paso, pluma en riste, y cuartilla enfrente, en este rincón de Mariñas, en esta celda de la vieja Granja de Meirás—el lugar donde siento más de continuo la ligera fiebre que acompaña a la creación artistica"[74] (Were I able to boast that I had contributed in some way to the relative success of the Spanish novel, I would say that the hours I spend pen in hand, sheet of paper in front of me, in this corner of Mariñas, in this cell in the ancient Granja de Meirás—the place where I feel more continuously the slight fever that accompanies artistic creativity—then I would say they were hours well spent). Invoking literature, art, music, poetry, and the natural sciences, she finds herself at peace with them all, sovereign in her domain. Ramón too concludes his story with a self-conscious awareness of his own literary identity and with a nostalgic yearning for the past. He, however, finds no solace in the tranquil night, no harmony in nature. Having danced to his own music, Ramón must now pay the price. The critics have not been kind to him, and yet he does not give in. Rather, he muses, the pleasure is in the dancing—that is, in the writing itself—and that is a joyous act that they cannot take away from him, for it is, after all, Ramón's dance we observe, his story we read, and neither one will stay in step.

In sum, both of the works addressed here evince themes that repeat themselves throughout Pardo Bazán's complicated and, at times, turbulent career: misreadings and misrepresentations, censorship, the function of art, nostalgia for the past, prescriptive roles for men and for women, the harmonious blend of the old and the new, the significance of literary construction, the thirst for recognition, the pain incurred when not following in step. Ramón and our author have ruffled a few feathers, learned a few tricks, seen a few sunsets. And their ironic wink cautions the reader once again to beware of those critics who seek to condemn what they do not understand. Ramón insists, "Así es que bailábamos, si con total inocencia, con poderosa ilusión"[75] (Thus it was that we danced, with complete innocence and with powerful illusion). Usually one step ahead and always to her own tune, Pardo Bazán will continue to write her own music and choreograph her own dance despite, and perhaps because of, the choir of critics who fault her notes and censure her steps. A prologue that is more than a prologue, a story that is more than a story, "Apuntes" and "El baile del Querubín" are works that depend on the well-crafted persona of their narrators—witty, critical, inventive, and adventurous. "We like to imagine that facts are found, not made," writes author Eula Biss, "and if the story of a life is true, then we have trouble accepting that it might also be crafted. But plots don't just happen to us, we invent them for ourselves."[76] Could not the same be said of Emilia Pardo Bazán?

NOTES

1. Federico Sáinz de Robles, introduction to *Obras completas de Emilia Pardo Bazán*, vol. 1, 4th ed. (Madrid: Gráficas Halas, 1973), 9–37; Carmen Bravo-Villasante, *Vida y obra de Emilia Pardo Bazán* (Madrid: Revista de Occidente, 1962); Elvira Martín, *Tres mujeres gallegas del siglo XIX: Concepción Arenal, Rosalía de Castro, Emilia Pardo Bazán*, 2nd ed. (Barcelona: Aedos, 1962); Robert E. Osborne, *Emilia Pardo Bazán: Su vida y sus obras* (Mexico City: Ediciones de Andrea, 1964); Nelly Clèmessy, *Emilia Pardo Bazán como novelista* (Madrid: Fundación Universitaria Española, 1981); Marina Mayoral, ed., *Estudios sobre "Los pazos de Ulloa"* (Madrid: Cátedra, 1989); María de los Ángeles Ayala, introduction to *Los pazos de Ulloa*, by Emilia Pardo Bazán (Madrid: Cátedra, 1997); Elizabeth J. Ordóñez, "Passing Notes: Theory and Self-Representation in Pardo Bazán's 'Apuntes autobiográficos,'" *Crítica Hispánica* 24, nos. 1/2 (2002): 145–156; Cristina Patiño Eirín, "Aproximación a los prólogos de Emilia Pardo Bazán," *Boletín de la Biblioteca de Menéndez Pelayo* 71 (1995): 137–167; Carmen Pereira-Muro, "Maravillosas supercherías: Género sexual y nacionalismo en los 'Apuntes Autobiográficos' de Pardo Bazán y *Trafalgar* de Galdós," *Hispanic Review* 78, no. 1 (2010): 71–100.

2. Letter from Pereda to Galdós, 1886, quoted in Carmen Bravo-Villasante, *Vida y obra*, 134.

3. Letter from Pereda to Galdós, 1886, quoted in Bravo-Villasante, 134.

4. Letter from Menéndez Pelayo to Valera, quoted in Bravo-Villasante, 134.

5. Bravo-Villasante, 134–135.

6. Ordóñez, "Passing Notes," 145.

7. Emilia Pardo Bazán, *Nuevo Teatro Crítico* 2, no. 16 (April 1892). Pardo Bazán penned the entire volume, along with volumes 1 and 3, by herself. No additional volumes were published.

8. *Diccionario de la lengua española*, s.v. "autobiografía," Real Academia Española, http://dle.rae.es/?id=4R6lwKL.

9. *Diccionario de la lengua española*, s.v. "prólogo," Real Academia Española, http://dle.rae.es/?id=UL4CigL.

10. *Diccionario de la lengua española*, s.v. "apunte," Real Academia Española, http://dle.rae.es/?id=3LHgZeu.

11. Emilia Pardo Bazán, "Apuntes autobiográficos," in *Obras completas*, vol. 7, ed. Dario Villanueva and José Manuel González Herrán (Madrid: Ediciones de Fundación José Antonio Castro, 1999), 5.

12. See Sidonie Smith, *A Poetics of Women's Autobiography: Marginality and the Fictions of Self-Representation* (Bloomington: Indiana University Press, 1987). For an excellent compendium of different theoretical approaches, see Sidonie Smith and Julia Watson, eds., *Women, Autobiography, Theory: A Reader* (Madison: University of Wisconsin Press, 1998).

13. Smith and Watson, introduction to *Women, Autobiography, Theory*, 12.

14. Smith and Watson, 12.

15. Smith and Watson, 12.

16. Smith and Watson, 12.

17. Smith and Watson, 12.

18. The term *double-voiced* is used here to explain how women autobiographers, especially those in the nineteenth century, simultaneously employed conventional language

and form while confronting, resisting, and subverting that very same language and form to create something new.

19. Smith and Watson, introduction to *Women, Autobiography, Theory*, 12.
20. Patiño Eirín, "Aproximación a los prólogos," 141.
21. Patiño Eirín, 141.
22. Pardo Bazán, "Apuntes autobiográficos," 15.
23. Pardo Bazán, 11.
24. Pardo Bazán, 6.
25. For more on this topic, see Susan M. McKenna, "Images of Paternity in the *Quijote*," *Hispanófila* 132 (2001): 28–33.
26. Juan Valera, *Apuntes sobre el nuevo arte de escribir novelas* (Madrid: M. Tello, 1887).
27. Emilia Pardo Bazán, *La cuestión palpitante*, ed. José Manuel González Herrán (Barcelona: Anthropos, 1989).
28. Pardo Bazán, "Apuntes autobiográficos," 7.
29. Patiño Eirín, "Aproximación a los prólogos," 147–148.
30. Patiño Eirín, 148.
31. Pardo Bazán, "Apuntes autobiográficos," 10.
32. Pardo Bazán, 10.
33. Pardo Bazán, 40.
34. Pereira-Muro, "Maravillosas supercherías," 84.
35. Pardo Bazán, "Apuntes autobiográficos," 11.
36. Pardo Bazán, 17.
37. Pardo Bazán, 18.
38. Pardo Bazán, 17–18.
39. Pardo Bazán, 33.
40. Pardo Bazán, 33.
41. Pereira-Muro, "Maravillosas supercherías," 82.
42. Pereira-Muro, 82.
43. Pereira-Muro, 82.
44. Pardo Bazán, "Apuntes autobiográficos," 38.
45. Pardo Bazán, 38.
46. Pardo Bazán, 55.
47. For a thought-provoking analysis of the many levels of discourse in Pardo Bazán's two cookbooks, including culinary tropes, see Hazel Gold, "Del foro al fogón: Narrativas culturales en el discurso culinario de Emilia Pardo Bazán," in *La literatura de Emilia Pardo Bazán*, ed. José Manuel González Herrán (A Coruña: Real Academia Galega, 2009), 313–323.
48. Ordóñez, "Passing Notes," 153–154.
49. Pardo Bazán, "Apuntes autobiográficos," 25.
50. Pardo Bazán, 25.
51. Pardo Bazán, 26.
52. Pardo Bazán, 24–26.
53. Pardo Bazán, 24–26.
54. Pardo Bazán, 30.
55. Ana María Freire López, "La primera redacción, autógrafa e inédita de los 'Apuntes autobiográficos' de Emilia Pardo Bazán," *Cuadernos para Investigación de la Literatura Hispánica* 26 (2001): 305–336.

56. Bravo-Villasante, *Vida y obra*, 51.

57. Bravo-Villasante, 51.

58. Pilar Faus, *Emilia Pardo Bazán: Su época, su vida, su obra*, vol. 1 (A Coruña: Fundación Pedro Barrié de la Maza, Conde de Fenosa, 2003), 499.

59. Rocío Charques Gámez, *Los artículos femenistas en el* Nuevo Teatro Crítico *de Emilia Pardo Bazán*, Cuadernos de trabajos de investigación 5 (Sant Vicente del Raspeig: Centro de Estudios sobre la Mujer, 2003), 70–72, http://pmayobre.webs.uvigo.es/pdf/emilia_pardo_bazan/nuevoteatrocritico.pdf.

60. Emilia Pardo Bazán, "La educación del hombre y la de la mujer: Sus relaciones y diferencias," in *La mujer española y otros escritos*, ed. Guadalupe Gómez-Ferrer (Madrid: Cátedra, 1999), 162.

61. Pardo Bazán, 162.

62. Pardo Bazán, 165.

63. Pardo Bazán, 169.

64. Pardo Bazán, 177.

65. Emilia Pardo Bazán, "El baile del Querubín," in *Cuentos completos*, vol. 1, ed. Juan Paredes Núñez (A Coruña: Fundación Pedro Barrié de la Maza, Conde de Fenosa, 1990), 232.

66. Pardo Bazán, 233.

67. Pardo Bazán, 233.

68. Pardo Bazán, 233.

69. Pardo Bazán, 233.

70. Pardo Bazán, 229–230.

71. Pardo Bazán, "Apuntes autobiográficos," 43.

72. Pardo Bazán, "El baile del Querubín," 226–227.

73. Pardo Bazán, "Apuntes autobiográficos," 12.

74. Pardo Bazán, 56.

75. Pardo Bazán, "El baile del Querubín," 228.

76. Eula Biss, "Layers of Time," *New York Times Book Review*, March 29, 2015, 1.

CHAPTER 5

The Twice-Told and the Unsaid in Emilia Pardo Bazán's "Presentido," "En coche-cama," "Confidencia," and "Madre"

Linda M. Willem

Emilia Pardo Bazán is by far the most prolific Spanish short story writer of her era and a key figure in the development of that genre within Spain. Throughout the entire last decade of the nineteenth century and the first two decades of the twentieth, her stories formed a mainstay of the literary offerings printed in such influential newspapers and periodicals as *Blanco y Negro* (*Black and White*), *El Imparcial* (*The Impartial*), *La Ilustración Española y Americana* (*The Spanish and American Illustrated Weekly*), *El Liberal* (*The Liberal*), *La Esfera* (*The Globe*), and her own *Nuevo Teatro Crítico* (*New Critical Theater*). Yet despite the volume and significance of these stories, scholars have traditionally preferred to focus on Pardo Bazán as a novelist. In 1990, however, Juan Paredes Nuñez's compilation of 580 of her stories in a single four-volume set, *Cuentos completos* (*Complete Stories*), set in motion an explosion of critical interest that has continued into the twenty-first century.[1] Among the many recent studies that have been published, several have brought to light the sophisticated narrative strategies contained within Pardo Bazán's brief fiction: Maryellen Bieder has discussed the subtleties of narrative plotting, Joyce Tolliver has explored the intricacies of narrative voice, Susan McKenna has examined the narrative structures of beginnings and ends, Susan Walter has focused on the interrelationship between narrative frames and their embedded stories, and my own work in this area has dealt with narrative strategies of indirection.[2] Together these studies demonstrate the vitality and innovation of Pardo Bazán's short fiction writing, marking her as a pioneer in employing narrative devices that set a standard of quality for Spain's emerging short story genre.

Pardo Bazán's vast corpus of short stories displays a wealth of stylistic and thematic variety as well as a dazzling array of plotlines and characterizations. Within the highly diversified content of these brief fictions, however, individual stories can be found that echo each other and constitute a retelling of the same idea but in a different manner. These are not mere variations on a theme; rather, they are fresh narrative approaches to concepts that Pardo Bazán had already presented to the public. As such, they exemplify her facility for narrative experimentation. I will focus on two pairs of stories—"Presentido" ("Premonition"; 1910) / "En coche-cama" ("In a Sleeping Car"; 1914) and "Confidencia" ("Confidence"; 1892) / "Madre" ("Mother"; 1893)[3]—to show how in each case, Pardo Bazán reworked her previously published material in ways that made the latter stories more narratively complex, interpretively challenging, and ethically nuanced.

Pardo Bazán's "Presentido" narrates in third person the robbery and murder of a man who is traveling by train from Paris to Madrid. Her frame tale, "En coche-cama," has a first-person narrator relate virtually the same story, except for the fatal outcome, to an internal narratee. Despite the similarity in the plot details of these two short stories, their different modes of narrative presentation create strikingly different effects, with the framing device in "En coche-cama" requiring a more active role by the reader, who must judge the reliability of what the internal narrator is saying. The presence of a frame, however, does not in itself define the participatory nature of a narrative, as is seen in "Confidencia" and "Madre." Both are frame stories and both center on a mother who is burned in a house fire, but it is the *manner* in which Pardo Bazán reconfigures the relationship among the frame, the embedded story, and the narrator from one story to the next that determines the greater degree of involvement and interpretation demanded of the reader in "Madre."

For each set of paired stories, the key issue concerns the different narrative techniques used to present the similar content and how those techniques affect the reader's role. As such, those techniques are directly tied to what rhetorical and ethical critic James Phelan views as the two main activities that narratives encourage—observing and judging—with the audience's observer role making the judgment role possible.[4] Phelan's approach studies how the textual phenomena of individual narratives "position" the audience engaged in its observing and judging activities and how that positioning affects our cognitive understanding (what we comprehend and how we comprehend it), emotional response (what we feel and how those feelings come about), and ethical engagement (what we are asked to value and how we respond to being invited to make judgments).[5] Phelan's concept of position is useful for my examination of the fundamentally different roles required of the reader in "Presentido" versus "En coche-cama" and in "Confidencia" versus "Madre."

The third-person narrator's opening paragraph of "Presentido" establishes the tone of violence and terror that will permeate the story from its first sentence to its last. After telling us that "corría el tren violentamente" (the train was violently running), the narrator equates the train with a "monstruo antidiluviano a quien persiguiesen enemigos invisibles y que huyese de ellos" (an antediluvian monster that is being pursued by invisible enemies and is fleeing from them) and states that "hay en la marcha . . . algo profundamente terrorífico, que no [*sic*] sólo no percibimos en fueza de la costumbre"[6] (in the movement there is . . . something profoundly terrifying, which we don't perceive simply due to force of habit). But one traveler, Julio Morales, does perceive it, and "notaba sin querer . . . la sensación obscura y angustiosa del miedo"[7] (he unintentionally noticed . . . the dark and harrowing sensation of fear). The story's title, "Presentido," arises from Julio's feelings: "Percibía la aproximación del peligro como se puede percibir, al entrar en una caverna, la presencia de los murciélagos colgados de sus paredes, de la cual avisan, no los sentidos corporales, sino algo que va más allá del sentido, un instinto indefinible, profundo, radicado en lo hondo del ser"[8] (He felt the nearness of danger as one can perceive, upon entering a cavern, the presence of bats hanging from the walls, a presence that is not communicated through the physical senses, but rather through something that goes beyond feeling, an indefinite, profound instinct from the depths of one's being). The narrator's verb constructions—the *nosotros* (we) conjugation and the impersonal *se puede* (one can)—position the reader within the train compartment alongside the traveler. The subsequent paragraphs legitimize Julio's fear and sense of danger by providing a logical reason for those feelings. We are told that he is going from Paris to Madrid to be reunited with the woman he loves, who is now free to marry him due to the death of her elderly husband. He is carrying with him a small suitcase containing a string of pearls and other expensive jewelry he had purchased as a gift for his beloved. In his haste to be with her, however, he had neglected to observe certain safety precautions. Rather than wait three days to get *coche-cama* accommodations, he settled for a regular compartment seat. He also forgot to check in his suitcase for safekeeping, and he failed to bring a revolver with him. Suddenly sensing his vulnerability, "la garra del miedo apretaba casi físicamente su corazón, no cobarde"[9] (the grip of fear almost physically squeezed his heart, which was not that of a coward).

The reader is then positioned within the mind of this character through a free indirect thought passage summarizing his attempts to control his emotions, first by telling himself that travelers often carry objects of value without incident, and then by convincing himself that he should try to get a good night's sleep. But as Julio slips into sleep, "la imaginación, en fantástico devaneo, surgía escenas trágicas"[10] (his imagination, in passing fantasies, issued forth tragic scenes), and the reader remains positioned within the inner world of the character through the narrator's account of those nightmares. First, a group of angry workers bursts into the compartment shouting insults against the rich and throwing the jewels in Julio's case onto the railroad tracks to be crushed. Then a solitary thief silently enters the compartment and steals the case while Julio is sleeping. Finally, two men open the door of the compartment during a station stop and attack Julio to rob him of his jewel case. At this point, we are told that

> esta parte del sueño, cuando realmente Julio había caído en el letargo hondo, tenía todo el relieve de la realidad.
>
> No era la visión confusa de un dormir plomizo, congestivo, como es siempre en el ferrocarril; era algo que participaba de lo obscuro del sueño y lo bien definido de las sensaciones que siguen al despertar. Julio se reconocía despierto. El peso de un cuerpo vigoroso gravitaba sobre su pecho con opresión violenta. Unas manos oprimían su garganta, impidiéndole pedir auxilio. Los dedos que se clavaban en su pescuezo estrechaban la presión.[11]

> this part of the dream, when Julio really had fallen into a deep lethargy, had all of the appearance of reality.
>
> It was not the confused vision of a heavily congestive sleep, as is usual on a train; it was something that combined the vagueness of a dream and the clarity of the sensations that follow upon awakening. Julio recognized that he was awake. The weight of a sturdy body violently pressed on his chest. Hands squeezed his throat, preventing him from calling out for help. The fingers that were fastened around his neck tightened their grip.

From our position within the consciousness of the character, we experience the same disorientation as he does upon awakening to find himself the victim of a real crime. Like him, we at first are not sure if this is really happening. But it is, and Julio's murder by strangulation is redundantly followed by a dagger plunged into his heart. The story ends with the escape of the assailants with the jewels, but not before one of them curses the other for having needlessly spilled blood that would stain their clothes if they searched Julio's body for more to steal.

"Presentido" draws on the conventions of what Laura Susan Spear calls "speed narratives": popular, widely circulated, and mass-produced short novels about crime and violence aboard trains.[12] Set within "the fastest vehicle in Belle Epoque pulp fiction,"[13] these were fictional extensions of the sensationalized newspaper accounts of actual crimes that the turn-of-the-century European public read daily, and they presented the train as a "new lawless space" that brought together members of the various social classes in close proximity while providing little protection from criminals who could enter and leave the space at each stop.[14] As such, these novels helped instill a "fear of travel, fear of assassins, and fear of *movement*" in their readers.[15] Furthermore, they used "powerful animal imagery" of "dangerous creatures" to represent "the train's deadly and catastrophic force."[16] Each novel typically "would integrate a high level of anxiety and fear into its attention-grabbing plot, thus reflecting the suspense felt by passengers of the train journey itself."[17] These emotions were doubly felt on the night train, which Spear calls "a factory of terror" because it "generates thoughts, stirs up the imagination, and churns nightmares."[18] The protagonist of "Presentido" acutely experiences this anxiety and fear as he travels through the night in an unguarded compartment of the speeding monster.

Throughout the narrative, our observation and judgment activities are exercised from positions that facilitate our identification with Julio. We feel both *with* him and *for* him. At no point do we doubt that this man, "ya probado en la vida" (already tested by life), experiences a profound fear in his "corazón, no cobarde"[19] (heart, which was not that of a coward) because we experience that fear—and the reasons for it—through being positioned within his mind. Furthermore, from that position, we drift in and out of sleep with him as his imagination fuses together a composite of railway crime scenarios, and we ultimately share with him the violent attack that results in his death. In "Presentido," Pardo Bazán utilizes the conventions of railway crime fiction to transform the banal act of riding a train into a cathartic Greek tragedy, not only eliciting our pity for Julio as we observe his fate being determined by dark forces that are seemingly beyond both human scale and human control, but also arousing our fear that such a fate could befall us during our next journey.

The peril of train travel returns as the subject of "En coche-cama," and pity is precisely the emotion that Braulio Romero hopes to receive from the friend to whom he tells his story. In this case, however, the reader's response to Braulio is strongly affected by his friend's unwillingness to provide that pity. In his book, *Living to Tell about It: A Rhetoric and Ethics of Character Narration*, Phelan studies the dynamics of embedded narratives and speaks of character narration as an art of indirection, where an implied author communicates to the ideal reader by means of a character narrator's communication to another character.[20] That art consists of a single text functioning effectively for its two audiences (the reader on the one hand and the internal narratee on the other) and its two purposes (the implied author's and the character narrator's). The framing device of "En coche-cama" positions the reader to observe and judge not only the character narrator who tells the embedded story but also the internal narratee who receives it and then relays it to us as the narrator of the frame.

Braulio prefaces his story by stating, "Hay una hora en que nadie deja de sentir el frío de terror. . . . Y lo peor es que nos quite la facultad de discurrir y de luchar; lo peor es que nos hace dudar de nosotros mismos para toda la vida. Desde aquel lance, yo he perdido la fe que tenía en un individuo para mí antes muy interesante, que se llama Braulio Romero, y a quien ya considero un fantoche"[21] (There is a point when no one fails to feel the coldness of terror. . . . And the worst thing is that it takes away from us the power to reflect and to fight; the worst thing is that it makes us doubt ourselves for all of our life. Since that event, I have lost the faith that I had in an individual named Braulio Romero, who had previously been very interesting to me, and whom I now consider to be a ridiculous person). By using the *nosotros* (we) form of reference and the *nadie deja de* (no one fails to) construction, Braulio presents his story as just one specific case of terror's all-pervasive influence on everyone.

After these preliminary remarks, Braulio recounts the details of his story. On one of his frequent trips between Paris and Madrid, while enjoying the solitude of his first-class *coche-cama* accommodations, he is surprised to see another passenger take the empty seat in his cabin several hours after the beginning of the journey. Braulio describes the passenger as a tall, stocky Englishman with fiery eyes who removes a small revolver from his case immediately upon entering the cabin, and after examining the weapon, he places it in the pocket of his overcoat. Although the steward assures Braulio that the passenger does indeed belong in that cabin and supplies a logical reason for his late arrival, Braulio experiences what he calls a "*shock* psíquico . . . que se me desquició el alma"[22] (a psychic shock . . . that unhinged my soul). He wonders if this silent stranger could be a thief and then suddenly remembers that his suitcase contains a fortune in jewels that he is transporting as a wedding gift from the marqués de R to his niece. Unlike the stranger, Braulio is not carrying a revolver, although he normally does so. He tells himself that there is no reason for the stranger to know about the jewels and that having a revolver is simply a common safety precaution of travelers, but terror still keeps Braulio from sleeping all night. With the dawn, however, sleep overcomes him. Upon waking, he finds himself alone with his suitcase. It is not until he opens it in Madrid that he realizes that the jewels are missing.

At this point in Braulio's story, his friend asks him, "¿De modo que era un ladrón?" (So he was a thief?), to which Braulio responds affirmatively but then goes on to say, "Lo que me robó aquel hombre era de más valía; la confianza en mí mismo, las mejores prendas de mi ánimo. . . . Me robó el espíritu"[23] (What that man robbed me of was of greater value: my self-confidence; the best qualities of my spirit. . . . He stole my courage), thereby echoing the self-doubt and loss of faith in himself that he mentioned in his opening remarks. Unlike Julio in "Presentido," Braulio is not dead, but he presents himself as having to suffer through a life no longer worth living. Braulio falls silent, but after a brief pause, the friend asks him "con intención" (with intention) the following question: "¿Se había usted . . . divirtido mucho . . . en Paris, antes de ese viaje?"[24] (Did you . . . have a really good time . . . in Paris, before that trip?). Indeed, if this question were not filled with intention, it would be a ridiculous response to Braulio's last statement. But what is that intention? No explanation is given, but Braulio "comprendió, y repuso, moviendo la cabeza: Puede ser, puede ser" (understood and answered, nodding his head: Perhaps, perhaps).[25] What is the reader to make of this brief final dialog?

Throughout Braulio's narration, the reader has been placed in the same listening position as the narratee friend, but once that friend begins his verbal interaction with Braulio, our position shifts to observing and judging them both. Faced with the narratee's unsympathetic response and seemingly inappropriate, but nevertheless meaningful, final question, along with Braulio's comprehending and evasive answer, the reader is obliged to reexamine both Braulio's embedded story and the frame that contains it in order to make sense of what is going on.

In so doing, the reader becomes positioned to formulate what Armine Kotin Mortimer has called a "second story," which is hidden but suggested through the unacknowledged clues in the text. Mortimer likens the second story construction to the submerged bulk of an iceberg that must be detected solely through the tip that can be seen. As with the second stories Mortimer has found in the short fiction of Guy de Maupassant, W. Somerset Maugham, Katherine Mansfield, and Edith Wharton,[26] the second story in "En coche-cama" "is not told outright but . . . constitutes a complete narrative that is *not secondary* in importance. In all such cases, the 'second story' is necessary to the intelligibility of the text."[27] Mortimer also notes that second stories are based on secrets and typically refer to illegal or immoral activities that are "better left unsaid."[28] It is the reader's task to articulate the unspoken.

The opening frame of "En coche-cama" is helpful to the reader undertaking that task. It begins with its narrator stating that "a pesar de lo que voy a referir, mi amigo Braulio Romero es hombre que tiene demostrado su valor. Ha dado de él pruebas reiteradas y púbicas"[29] (despite what I am about to relate, my friend Braulio is a man who has demonstrated his valor. He has proved it repeatedly and publicly), and he goes on to mention the many difficult situations that Braulio had successfully weathered in the past, including serving as a correspondent during the Cuban campaign. The frame narrator then states that "sin embargo, lo que me refirió . . . es de esos casos de insuperable miedo, que aniquilan momentáneamente la voluntad y hasta cohíben la inteligencia, por clara que nos la haya dado Díos. Y Romero la tenía despierta y brillante"[30] (nevertheless, what he related to me . . . is one of those cases of insurmountable fear, that momentarily annihilates the will and even limits intelligence, no matter how lucid it has been given us by God. And Braulio had a very lively and bright intelligence). The wording of this introduction undercuts the credibility of Braulio's story by juxtaposing Braulio's bravery and quick-wittedness against his claims of having experienced a fear that rendered him helpless. The frame narrator subsequently speaks of Braulio's current physical condition, caused in part by his "decadencias morales" (moral decline), and mentions his "bigote teñido" (dyed mustache) followed by the comment, "Debilidad también esto del tinte"[31] (That dye was also a weakness). Since the word *tinte* can refer to both the dye and the false appearances it creates, it suggests a weakness in Braulio's nature that is related to both vanity and deception. These details point to a licentious lifestyle and duplicitous nature that explains the question posed to Braulio about his activities in Paris before the train trip.

In this opening frame, the friend is signaling to the reader that he does not believe Braulio's story and that we shouldn't either. After all, we only have Braulio's word that the robbery had taken place. Whereas the crime in "Presentido" is told in reliable, third-person narration that includes free indirect thought passages that conventionally are accepted as true renderings of a character's mind, in "En coche-cama," both the crime and Braulio's thoughts are told in first-person narration, which cannot be so readily trusted. It is the reader's task to determine Braulio's degree of reliability as a character narrator.

When we reexamine Braulio's story, questions do arise about his actions and feelings, especially when we compare them to Julio's situation in "Presentido." Why isn't Braulio carrying a revolver on this particular occasion, as was his custom? Julio's failure to pack one was due to the haste with which he arranged his trip, but Braulio provides no explanation. Also, why is Braulio so overcome with fear during the journey? Unlike Julio, who is subject to the risks of traveling in an open compartment, Braulio spends the night in a first-class *coche-cama*, and since that is his customary accommodation, during his many previous trips between Paris and Madrid he presumably has shared cabins with other travelers, at least some of whom would have been armed. Finally, if Braulio suspected the stranger to be a thief, why did he wait until he arrived in Madrid to examine the contents of his suitcase to check if the jewels were still there? If he had seen that they were missing while still on the train, Braulio would have been able to report the robbery and make inquiries as to the movements of the stranger who had disappeared from his cabin.

These questions, combined with the information we receive from Braulio's friend—both in his capacity as narratee and frame narrator—allow us to guess Braulio's secret and formulate the text's second story. The marqués's jewels were indeed stolen, but the thief was Braulio himself, and his story is an elaborate ruse to cover up his own culpability. Unlike Julio, who was carrying jewels he had bought and paid for himself, Braulio was transporting a fortune in jewels owned by someone else, and as the frame narrator reminds us, "las circunstancias disponen"[32] (circumstances set things in motion). The second story we can construct features Braulio taking advantage of his sole authority over the jewels—as they were to pass from the hands of the marqués to his niece—in order to keep them for himself, possibly to present them as a gift to someone with whom he had an amorous affair in Paris or possibly to sell them to pay for any of the other pleasures he had enjoyed there before returning by rail to Madrid. To conceal his crime, Braulio then cast himself not only as the victim of a robbery by an anonymous stranger but also as the victim of a debilitating fear that sooner or later strikes the hearts of all men. But his friend's unsympathetic response and probing final question constitutes a refusal to be complicit in this lie, and Braulio's sly final response indirectly acknowledges that his friend has guessed his secret.

In Phelan's taxonomy of unreliable character narration, Braulio's narrative is an example of "misreporting" the facts.[33] He deliberately fabricated the story of the robbery for his own advantage, and the implied author guides the reader to come to that conclusion by placing Braulio's story within a frame whose narrator indirectly communicates his disbelief in what he has heard. At the close of the story, the truth remains unspoken, but Braulio's final words confirm the reliability of the frame narrator's suspicions and justify the second story that the reader has been led to construct.

The conventions of railroad crime drama are present in both "Presentido" and "En coche-cama," but they function differently in each story. Pardo Bazán's straightforward approach to the genre in "Presentido" elicits pity for Julio as we experience along with him the chilling terror and shocking brutality that he suffers. In contrast, Pardo Bazán subverts the emotional pull of railroad crime fiction in "En coche-cama" by having the plotline told by an unreliable character narrator who makes an unsuccessful and undeserved bid for the sympathetic response normally accorded the victims of that genre.

The second story concept also informs Pardo Bazán's 1893 frame story "Madre." The frame consists of two male friends who are strolling through a park and chance upon a disfigured woman, the condesa de Serená, who is watching over her grandchildren. The frame's narrator notices his friend's rather exaggerated manner of greeting her: "Se quitó el sombrero hasta los pies y saludó como únicamente se saluda a las reinas o a las santas"[34] (He removed his hat, lowering it down to his feet, and greeted her in a manner that only queens or saints are greeted). While they continue to walk, the reader is positioned with the frame narrator as he listens to his friend tell "la historia o leyenda de las cicatrices y de la perdida hermosura"[35] (the story or legend of the scars and lost beauty) of the countess. Widowed at the age of twenty-one and extraordinarily beautiful, the countess had many suitors, but she rejected them all in favor of dedicating herself to her sickly daughter, Irene, who as a result of being overindulged "salió antojadiza, voluntariosa, exigente, convencida de que su capricho y su gusto eran lo único importante en la tierra"[36] (turned out to be capricious, willful, demanding, and convinced that her every whim and wish were the only important things in world). Pale and thin, Irene grew up to become a young woman devoid of any physical charms. Despite the countess's efforts to play down her own natural good looks and artificially enhance her daughter's appearance by dressing her in finery, all eyes were on the elder of the two. As a result, "Irene, mortificada, ulcerado su amor propio, se mostraba desabrida con su madre y pasaba semanas enteras sin hablarle"[37] (Irene, annoyed and her self-pride wounded, acted surly to her mother and spent entire weeks without talking to her).

The countess's solution was to find a husband for Irene, settling on the handsome Enrique de Acuña, who "reunía prendas no comunes de talento y corazón"[38] (displayed an uncommon combination of talent and heart). Although Enrique had been one of the countess's many admirers, he and Irene soon were "amartelados prometidos"[39] (a love-struck engaged couple). When the newlyweds returned from their honeymoon, the affection, consideration, and familiarity with which Enrique treated the countess were "como de hermano"[40] (like that of a brother). Unfortunately, he had a tendency to repeat in jest that "sólo por tener tal suegra, cien veces volvería a casarse con Irene Serená"[41] (just to have such a mother-in-law, he would marry Irene Serená a hundred times over). As a consequence, "Irene reincidía en la antigua sequedad y dureza y en los desplantes y murrias. Delante de su marido conteníase; pero apenas él volvía la espalda, ella daba suelta al mal humor y a la acritud de su genio"[42] (Irene relapsed into her old curtness and harshness as well as her insolence and melancholy. In front of her husband, she contained herself, but as soon as he turned his back, she gave free rein to her temper and sour temperament).

One night, Enrique innocently mentioned at dinner that while he and the countess had been walking together that day, she received so much unwanted attention from strangers on the street that he told one particularly persistent man that he was her husband. Upon hearing this, Irene left the table in a rage and went to her room, slamming the door behind her. Enrique followed her, emerging a half hour later to tell the countess that Irene was adamant about no longer living in her mother's house. Later that evening, the lamp in the countess's room set fire to the curtains, enveloping the countess in flames and leaving her face severely disfigured. At this point, the character narrator tells his friend that he had been told about the accident by the countess's servants, who attributed the fire to the countess accidentally having left the lamp lit before going to sleep. He goes on to say that Irene and her mother now live in peace.

At the end of his story, the character narrator asks the frame narrator—and by extension, the reader positioned with him—the following question: "¿Qué opina usted de las quemaduras de la condesa?"[43] (What is your opinion on the countess's burns?). By specifically referring to the *quemaduras* (burns), the character narrator is calling into question the servants' explanation of how the countess received them and is indirectly indicating that he has composed a second story that posits the true explanation. But if this is not a simple case of an accident due to carelessness, what could it be? One possibility, as Walter has noted, is that the countess had started the fire on purpose to destroy her own beauty and thus end the jealousy and rivalry felt by her daughter.[44] We can infer that the character narrator does indeed believe that the countess had an intentional hand in her own disfigurement because of a comment he made earlier about the countess wishing she could pluck out her beautiful eyes, as did Santa Lucía, and present them to Irene on a tray. His belief in this second story also explains why he had greeted the countess with such an extreme display of respect when he encountered her in the park and why he referred to the story of her lost beauty as a *leyenda* (legend). The character narrator's actions, his allusion to Santa Lucía, and the question with which he ends his story were designed to require the frame narrator to guess his second story and to accept his interpretation of the events over the official explanation by the servants.

The frame narrator, in turn, indicates that he has indeed guessed the second story and concurs with his friend on its validity over the servants' explanation by providing a response to his friend's question that is both verbal and nonverbal: "Que esta María Coronel vale más que la otra, repondí, inclinándome a mi vez ante la madre de Irene"[45] (That this María Coronel is worth more than the other one, I responded, bowing in turn before Irene's mother). In so doing, he matches the character narrator's reference to Santa Lucía by citing yet another historical figure: the fourteenth-century pious widow Doña María Coronel, who according to legend had destroyed her beauty by throwing boiling oil on her face to discourage the persistent sexual advances of King Pedro I and consequently received the thanks and admiration of the queen, who placed a crown on her head. The frame narrator thereby specifically links the countess not only with an act of self-mutilation but also with one that resulted in disfiguring burns. In addition, his subsequent gesture of bowing to the countess duplicates that of his friend, implying that the countess does indeed warrant the type of bow usually given only to queens and saints because she is a modern-day equivalent to both Santa Lucía and the "coronated" María Coronel.

The reader, having observed this secret communication between the two friends, must now switch roles—no longer just observing but also judging—in order to validate or reject the credibility of this untold second story suggested by the character narrator. Is it plausible that the countess had resorted to such drastic measures to keep Irene from wanting to move out of her house? When we remember how difficult it had been for the countess to be apart from Irene even for the short span of the girl's honeymoon, which seemed like "un siglo de dolor para la condesa"[46] (a century of pain for the countess), it certainly is plausible. Indeed, this second story of the countess's self-disfigurement fits well within Mortimer's definition of a secret that is "better left unsaid."[47]

However, this second story also is strikingly atypical in not concealing an illegal or immoral act. On the contrary, it tells the secret of loving self-sacrifice. But a further examination of the text yields yet another possible second story that conforms more fully to the conventions outlined by Mortimer. This other second story is based on information in the embedded narrative, but it is constructed by the reader rather than by the character narrator. It also suggests an intertextual connection with another short story by Pardo Bazán, "Confidencia," which was published exactly one year prior to the publication of "Madre," and that also tells the tale of a mother who is burned when curtains in her room catch fire. Furthermore, "Confidencia" and "Madre" were republished together by the author in her 1894 collection of *Cuentos nuevos* (*New Stories*), thereby allowing them to enter into an implicit dialog with each other for the volume's contemporary audience.[48]

"Confidencia" opens with the following statement by the frame narrator: "Nunca me había sido posible adivinar qué oculto dolor consumía a Ricardo de Solís, imprimiendo en sus facciones una huella tan visible de siniestra amargura"[49] (It had never been possible for me to guess what dark pain was eating away at Ricardo de Solís, stamping onto his features such a visible mark of sinister bitterness). He then outlines the process he undertook to satisfy his "deseo de conocer el secreto"[50] (desire to know the secret), starting with extensive but futile inquiries into Ricardo's health, finances, and love life and ending with a plan to befriend the man in order to learn the truth firsthand. With time, Ricardo did indeed confide in the frame narrator, telling him about his loving but overprotective mother against whom he had rebelled as a young man by disobeying her and drinking to excess "sólo por mortificarla"[51] (just to vex her). Returning home drunk one night, he was chastised by his mother "con toda la energía de su amor"[52] (with all the power of her love), and when she tried to help him to bed, he swore that if she continued to treat him like a child, he would set fire to the house. He accompanied this threat by grabbing a candlestick from the table and throwing it at the curtains, which immediately went up in flames. He ran to get help, returning to find his mother on the floor in a faint and with her clothing ablaze from having been in contact with the curtains. She took the blame for the fire, telling everyone that "ella misma, con la bujía, se había prendido fuego a la ropa"[53] (she herself, with the candlestick, had set fire to her clothing). At this point in his narrative, Ricardo gave a detailed and gruesome description of the suffering that his mother had endured for eight days prior to succumbing to death. When the frame narrator assured Ricardo that his mother must have forgiven him before she died, Ricardo revealed the final and crucial element of his secret: that it is precisely his mother's forgiveness that he could not live with. The frame narrator concludes by saying that he never saw Ricardo again but heard that he left Spain to go to Tangiers, where he committed suicide.

The framing device of "Confidencia" places the reader as an observer alongside the frame narrator as he hears Ricardo's embedded narration, but this is done only after we previously have been placed in the position of listening to the frame narrator's own observations about Ricardo before that confession was made. Nothing in Ricardo's secret or the emotion with which he tells it runs counter to the frame narrator's description of him as "la tétrica imagen de la pena"[54] (the somber image of suffering), so we accept the frame narrator's assessment of it as the truth. There is no second story for us to construct.

The crime of a mother being burned by her own child, however, does return as a possible second story in "Madre," where it provides an alternate secret explanation to the one constructed by the character narrator. The key to formulating this other second story lies in the reader's understanding that all the information in the embedded story is filtered through the perspective of the character narrator. Therefore, it is necessary for us to separate what he says about the parties involved from what they actually said themselves. There is, for example, no evidence that he actually heard the countess say that "con vida y alma se hubiese quitado—a ser posible—aquella tez de alabastro y nácar, aquellos ojos de sol, y poniéndolos en una bandeja, como los de Santa Lucía, se los hubiese ofrecido a su niña, al ídolo de toda su honrada y noble existencia"[55] (with her life and soul she would have removed—if it were possible—that alabaster and mother-of-pearl complexion, those shining eyes, and placing them on a tray, like those of Santa Lucía, she would have offered them to her daughter, the idol of her entire honest and noble existence). This simply is his impression of the situation from his point of view as one of her many former admirers whom she kept at arm's length. The reference to Santa Lucía is his invention, which encapsulates the essence of his second story version of the events and that he uses as a clue for his friend to come to the "correct" conclusion about the countess's burns.

What, then, are the statements that can be attributed to the other characters? Within the embedded story, these are limited to the words that the countess's servants overheard and told to the character narrator. They include Enrique's dinner table story as well as what he told the countess after he returned from his discussion with Irene in their bedroom. It is this conversation with the countess that provides the reader with the building blocks to construct the alternate second story, which the character narrator has overlooked. It begins with Enrique's summary of what Irene had said to him, including an italicized duplication of her exact words: "Que Irene no quería vivir más en la casa materna, y que era tal su empeño de irse, que si no se realizaba la separación, amenazaba con hacer *cualquier disparate*"[56] (That Irene didn't want to live in her mother's house any longer and that she was so determined to go, if the separation did not take place, she threatened to do *something wild and foolish*). This is immediately followed by the quoted dialog between Enrique and the countess:

> —Pero tranquilícese usted—añadió en amargo tono de reconcentrada cólera—, he sabido imponerme y la he tratado con severidad, porque lo merece su locura.
>
> Y como la condesa, más pálida que un difunto, se apoyase en un mueble por no caer, exclamó Enrique:
>
> —¡Señora, el carácter de su hija de usted preveo que nos costará muchas penas a todos![57]

> "But keep calm," he added in a bitter tone of concealed anger, "I knew how to take control the situation and I treated her with severity, because that's what her madness deserved."
>
> And as the countess, paler than a corpse, was supporting herself on a piece of furniture so as not to fall, Enrique exclaimed:
>
> "Madame, I foresee that your daughter's character will cost all of us a lot of sorrow!"

Enrique's refusal to acquiesce to Irene's demands is implied in his assurance to the countess that he had taken control of the situation. It is possible, then, that the willful and petulant Irene decided to act on her threat by committing the *disparate* (wild foolishness) of burning down her mother's house, symbolically beginning with her mother's room, either in a fit of anger, as did Ricardo in "Confidencia," or as a ploy to force her husband to change residences. After all, no servants actually witnessed how the fire started, as their account of the events proves, because if any servant had been there to take care of the lamp, the supposed accident would not have occurred. Their explanation of the countess's carelessness was either conjecture on their part or what they had been told by the countess, who, like Ricardo's mother, pretended that she had caused the fire in order to protect her child. This second story is further supported by Enrique's prediction to the countess that Irene's temperament will be the cause of much sorrow for all of them.

Standing in contrast to the servants' story of the accidental cause of the countess's burns are two different second stories—one constructed by the character narrator and supported by the frame narrator and the other constructed by the reader without the knowledge of either narrator. In the first second story, the character narrator is a reliable guide who leads both the frame narrator and the reader to discover the unspoken truth of the countess's self-mutilation. In the alternate second story, the character narrator engages in an unreliable "misreading" of the situation that the frame narrator accepts but the reader must reject to find the hidden truth in the words of Irene's threat. Both second stories remain open as viable answers to the question about the countess's burns, with each transforming the incident of the fire from a simple act of carelessness into a profoundly moving act of either self-sacrifice or forgiveness on the part of a mother for her beloved daughter.

Both "Presentido" and "En coche-cama" are stores of train travel and jewel thieves. Both "Confidencia" and "Madre" tell of a tempestuous relationship between mother and child that ends with a fire. Within each pairing, however, the earlier story of the two requires a lesser degree of involvement by the reader than does the later one. In "Presentido" and "Confidencia," the reader is positioned to accept the facts of the stories, while in "En coche-cama" and "Madre," the reader is positioned to replace the presented facts with second stories that are necessary to complete the unwritten portion of each text. Through her interplay of reader positioning and narrator reliability/unreliability in "Presentido," "En coche-cama," "Confidencia," and "Madre," Pardo Bazán was able to experiment with various ways of eliciting reader participation in the cognitive, emotional, and ethical dimensions of her original and reworked material. Moreover, in the case of "Madre," she pushed the limits of the second story construction by allowing the reader to devise two different "second stories." This inventive doubling of the hidden possibilities in "Madre" anticipated the ambiguity and resistance to closure found in modernist narratives by providing the reader with a choice between two mutually exclusive alternatives to the official account of the events.

The progression from her earlier stories to their subsequent counterparts exhibits Pardo Bazán's ability to revisit her own work with renewed creativity and greater complexity. In addition, these reworked stories are indicative of her ingenious engagement with literary forms. Mortimer has stated that the second story construction "is particular to short stories" because if it were "translated to the scale of a novel," it "would lose some of its definition," and as such, it would not produce what she calls the "wow effect" experienced by readers when they suddenly decipher what has been left unsaid.[58] In "Madre" and "En coche-cama," Pardo Bazán subtly produces that "wow effect" by combining the second story concept with two other literary conventions—a framing device and unreliable narration—and by cultivating the indirect form of communication inherent in all three constructions. Together these strategies of indirection maximize the reader's participation in discovering what is merely suggested.

In the nineteenth century, the short story was still a fledgling genre, being nourished by the demand for fictional narratives to fill the pages of the proliferating number of newspapers and periodicals being published. Pardo Bazán responded to that demand and, in the process, was instrumental in developing and defining what the short story would become. Her sophisticated handling of the second story concept in "Madre" and "En coche-cama" exemplifies the experimental spirit and vitality that infuses her short story writing. As one of the great nineteenth-century practitioners of the short story genre, Pardo Bazán not only led the way in devising communicative strategies that worked effectively within brief narratives but also helped legitimize the new genre by demonstrating the capacity of imaginative fiction to provide a complex and challenging reading experience regardless of its length.

NOTES

1. Juan Paredes Nuñez, ed., *Cuentos completos*, 4 vols. (A Coruña: Fundación Pedro Barrié de la Maza, Conde de Fenosa, 1990).

2. Maryellen Bieder, "Plotting Gender / Replotting the Reader: Strategies of Subversion in Stories by Emilia Pardo Bazán," *Indiana Journal of Hispanic Literature* 2, no. 1 (1993): 137–157; Joyce Tolliver, *Cigar Smoke and Violet Water: Gendered Discourse in the Stories of Emilia Pardo Bazán* (Lewisburg, Pa.: Bucknell University Press, 1998); Susan McKenna, *Crafting the Female Subject: Narrative Innovations in the Short Fiction of Emilia Pardo Bazán* (Washington, D.C.: Catholic University of America Press, 2009); Susan Walter, *From the Outside Looking In: Narrative Frames and Narrative Spaces in the Short Stories of Emilia Pardo Bazán* (Newark, Del.: Juan de la Cuesta, 2010); and Linda M. Willem, "The Story Not Told: Sex and Marriage in Pardo Bazán's 'Los cirineos' and 'La argolla,'" *Hispania* 95, no. 4 (2012): 587–595.

3. Emilia Pardo Bazán's "Presentido" and "En coche-cama" were initially published in *La Ilustración Española y Americana*, "Confidencia" first appeared in *El Imparcial*, and "Madre" was published in Pardo Bazán's own *Nuevo Teatro Crítico* (Paredes Núñez, *Cuentos completos*, 1:481–482; 4:455–456).

4. James Phelan, "Narrative Judgments and the Rhetorical Theory of Narrative: Ian McEwen's *Atonement*," in *A Companion to Narrative Theory*, ed. James Phelan and Peter J. Rabinowitz (Malden, Mass.: Blackwell, 2005), 322–336.

5. James Phelan, *Living to Tell about It: A Rhetoric and Ethics of Character Narration* (Ithaca, N.Y.: Cornell University Press, 2005), ix, 22–23.

6. Emilia Pardo Bazán, "Presentido," in *Cuentos completos*, 4:104. The wording in the original text is "que sólo no percibimos."

7. Pardo Bazán, 4:104.

8. Pardo Bazán, 4:104.

9. Pardo Bazán, 4:105.

10. Pardo Bazán, 4:106.

11. Pardo Bazán, 4:106.

12. Lauren Susan Spear, "Vanishing Vectors: Trains and Speed in Modern French Crime Fiction and Film" (PhD diss., University of Illinois at Urbana-Champaign, 2007), 162.

13. Spear, 161.

14. Spear, 164.

15. Spear, 163, emphasis in the original.

16. Spear, 10.

17. Spear, 7.

18. Spear, 187.

19. Pardo Bazán, "Presentido," 4:105.

20. Phelan, *Living to Tell about It*, 1.

21. Emilia Pardo Bazán, "En coche-cama," in *Cuentos completos*, 4:308.

22. Pardo Bazán, 4:309.

23. Pardo Bazán, 4:310.

24. Pardo Bazán, 4:310.

25. Pardo Bazán, 4:310.

26. Armine Kotin Mortimer, "Second Stories," in *Short Story Theory at the Crossroads*, ed. Susan Lohafer and Jo Ellyn Clarey (Baton Rouge: Louisiana State University Press, 1989), 278–298; Mortimer, "Second Stories: The Example of 'Mr. Know-All,'" *Studies in Short Fiction* 25 (1998): 307–314; Mortimer, "Fortifications of Desire: Reading the Second Story in Katherine Mansfield's 'Bliss,'" *Narrative* 2, no. 1 (1994): 41–52; Mortimer, "Romantic Fever:

The Second Story as Illegitimate Daughter in Warton's 'Roman Fever,'" *Narrative* 6, no. 2 (1998): 188–198.

27. Mortimer, "Example of 'Mr. Know-All,'" 307–308, emphasis in the original.

28. Mortimer, "Second Stories," 282.

29. Pardo Bazán, "En coche-cama," 4:307.

30. Pardo Bazán, 4:307.

31. Pardo Bazán, 4:308.

32. Pardo Bazán, 4:307.

33. For Phelan, "there are six main types of unreliable narration: misreporting, misreading, and misregarding; underreporting, underreading, and underregarding . . . with the first group . . . the audience must reject the narrator's words and reconstruct an alternative; with the second group . . . the audience must supplement the narrator's view" (*Living to Tell about It*, 219). Greta Olson succinctly summarizes Phelan's distinctions as follows: "Regarding the first group, narrators may falsely report fictional events ('misreporting'), or make mistakes of perception ('misreading'), or falsely evaluate events ('misregarding'). In the second group, narrators may evidence unreliability in their not telling enough about what is happening ('underreporting'), their failing to grasp events completely ('underreading'), or their making incomplete value judgments ('underregarding')." See Olson, "Reconsidering Unreliability: Fallible and Untrustworthy Narrators," *Narrative* 11, no. 1 (2003): 100–101.

34. Emilia Pardo Bazán, "Madre," in *Cuentos completos*, 1:190.

35. Pardo Bazán, 1:190.

36. Pardo Bazán, 1:191.

37. Pardo Bazán, 1:192.

38. Pardo Bazán, 1:192.

39. Pardo Bazán, 1:192.

40. Pardo Bazán, 1:192.

41. Pardo Bazán, 1:192.

42. Pardo Bazán, 1:192.

43. Pardo Bazán, 1:193.

44. Walter, *From the Outside Looking In*, 99–100.

45. Pardo Bazán, "Madre," 1:193.

46. Pardo Bazán, 1:192.

47. Mortimer, "Second Stories," 282.

48. Emilia Pardo Bazán, *Cuentos nuevos*, in *Obras completas*, vol. 2, ed. Federico Carlos Sainz de Robles (Zaragoza: Aguilar, 1964), 1387–1473.

49. Emilia Pardo Bazán, "Confidencia," in *Cuentos completos*, 1:166.

50. Pardo Bazán, 1:166.

51. Pardo Bazán, 1:168.

52. Pardo Bazán, 1:168.

53. Pardo Bazán, 1:169.

54. Pardo Bazán, 1:166.

55. Pardo Bazán, "Madre," 1:192.

56. Pardo Bazán, 1:193, emphasis in the original.

57. Pardo Bazán, 1:193.

58. Mortimer, "Second Stories," 276–277.

CHAPTER 6

Emilia Pardo Bazán, Joris-Karl Huysmans, and Stories of Conversion

Denise DuPont

In her article "Divina y perversa: La mujer decadente en *Dulce dueño* de Emilia Pardo Bazán" ("Divine and Perverse: The Decadent Women in Emilia Pardo Bazán's *Sweet Master*"), Maryellen Bieder describes Pardo Bazán's Lina Mascareñas as a femme fatale "decadente . . . hedonista, burladora, perversa, satánica, mística, y posiblemente loca"[1] (decadent . . . hedonist, mocking, perverse, satanic, mystic, and possibly insane) who turns to the divine. The thesis of "Divina y perversa" is to demonstrate that Lina's conversion story does not clash with the decadentism, hagiography, and feminism of this novel, which resists reduction to one dominant discourse.[2] With this goal in mind, Bieder's insightful study traces the interweaving of the various stories told in *Dulce dueño* (1911) and reveals the richness of Pardo Bazán's work by highlighting the confluence and shared objectives of seemingly contradictory discourses.

And yet Bieder does hint at a hierarchy of influences by referring at one point to the works of Joris-Karl Huysmans as the "intertexto principal" (main intertext) for *Dulce dueño*, thereby identifying this French decadent writer as particularly decisive for Pardo Bazán's final novel.[3] Not only do I agree with this emphasis, but in my contribution here, I build on Bieder's designation of Huysmans as the primary intertext. Pardo Bazán was indeed a creative reader of the French iconoclast, who shares with his fictional characters a trajectory that runs from refined artistic indulgence and unconventional sexual experimentation to spiritual exaltation and a rejection of the bodily realm[4]—a journey from decadent aestheticism to Catholic asceticism. As Bieder notes, Huysmans's decadent hero Des Esseintes (*À rebours* [*Against Nature*]; 1884)—a superior, talented individual who attempts to create a selfishly guarded aesthetic space—blends with the spiritual seeker Durtal, the main character of *Là-bas* (*Down There*; 1891), *En route* (1895), *La cathédrale* (*The Cathedral*; 1898), and *L'oblat* (*The Oblate*; 1903).[5] Huysmans's two notorious protagonists strive for happiness by searching within as well as changing their physical locations. They flee from and reject society, but ultimately Durtal, the second major protagonist, learns to atone for his own sins and those of others.[6] Following Bieder's lead, I argue here that in *Dulce dueño*, Pardo Bazán effectively recapitulates with the single story of her female hero, Lina, the spiritual trajectory that Huysmans's male characters traverse over the course of several novels.

Lina's Spiritual Journey: Relief from the Burden of Self

As a prelude to my discussion of Lina's parallels with Des Esseintes/Durtal, I would like to briefly review her experiences, highlighting the aspects of her story that are most important for this reading.[7] The illegitimate daughter of Catalina Mascareñas, Lina grows up as Natalia, raised in seclusion and urged to enter a convent when she comes of age. When Catalina's legitimate heir, Lina's half-brother, dies (and their mother follows him soon after), Natalia becomes the rich heiress Lina, who devotes a good portion of her new wealth to cultivating a luxurious appearance and lifestyle. Pressured to choose a mate by older male advisers and friends (including her unacknowledged father, Farnesio, her mother's administrator) in the same way that she was earlier nudged toward the convent by two of these same paternal figures, Lina allows herself to be courted without much interest in the prospect of marriage. She searches for an ideal love, and the suitors she encounters do not live up to her expectations. She does experience a strong physical attraction to her cousin José María, her second suitor, but becomes disillusioned when she discovers his liaison with her maid and subsequently commits to celibacy after asking a doctor to teach her about sexual activity and its consequences. Her final suitor mocks her idealism and fails to embody the selfless love he has professed for Lina when she tests his loyalty in a dangerous adventure that leads to his death by drowning.

Although she is not blamed for her suitor's death, it is at this point that Lina attempts to confess her sins to her spiritual adviser, Carranza, author of the hagiography of St. Catherine of Alexandria, to which Lina has listened attentively in the novel's frame. She reveals her guilt to Carranza in her mother's prayer room, with a portrait of St. Catherine looking down on her from above the altar and in the presence of the small plaque of St. Catherine that she had taken to Alcalá the day Carranza read the hagiography. Lina remembers the song that the girls playing outside sang the day of the reading—"¡Levántate, Catalina, / levántate, Catalina, / que Jesucristo te llama!"[8] (Arise, Catherine, / arise, Catherine, / Jesus Christ is calling you!)—and seems to respond to that call for spiritual renewal. However, rather than absolving Lina of her failings, Carranza denounces her as a monster, a victim of "degeneraciones modernistas"[9] (modernist degenerations) culminating in perversion disguised as purity and chastity, and abandons her, leaving Lina responsible for her own penance and restitution.

She begins the penitential process by destroying an onyx clock, a symbol of her wealth, and paying a prostitute to disfigure her after explaining that she is making restitution for her sins.[10] She sees that true beauty is coming to her but realizes that there is more to be done: Lina plans to renounce her inheritance at the end of a year's time and begins to feel living water within her.[11] She makes another confession, this time in the church of Jesus, to a young Capuchin, sad and drawn, with a yellowish, blue-veined complexion—presumably as a result of his own ascetic practices.[12] Appalled at Carranza's lack of charity and mercy when Lina informs him of the results of her first confession, the Capuchin calls on Jesus Christ to help him understand the worldly atmosphere—so unfamiliar to him—that has been the stage for Lina's errant behavior. He reads in her actions an excessive pride, individualism, and misguided refinement inspired by a belief that she is superior to and independent of those around her.[13] The Capuchin friar recommends that she cultivate the natural, simple humility she has already strived for with the prostitute: he warns her that maintaining this modest attitude will be her greatest and most challenging penance but will lead her to the divine love she longs for.[14]

Traveling third class among people she identifies as *plebe* (rabble) and *gentuza* (riffraff), Lina has dressed as modestly as possible, but she realizes that inner reform will be difficult, because she sees only differences rather than similarities between herself and the other occupants of the train car.[15] They cannot possibly relate to the heaven that she now knows she must seek within herself.[16] And she wonders why St. Catherine was able to maintain her luxurious attire and preserve her beautiful outward appearance even as she suffered martyrdom.[17] This does not seem fair. Why should she, Lina, have to change her appearance when her patron saint did not?

Despite this internal resistance, Lina continues her spiritual journey: she arrives at the desert—the objective of her trip ("El desierto que me había atraído como objeto de mi viaje" [The desert that had attracted me as the reason for my journey])—where she will be close to a Carmelite convent as well as some "casuchas desparramadas"[18] (scattered huts). In heading to the desert as part of her conversion and also engaging in ascetic training (*askesis*, literally meaning "training") when she reaches her destination, Lina thus imitates both St. Catherine, of the novel's hagiographic frame, and Trifón, the anchorite modeled on St. Anthony of the Desert who converts the Egyptian princess, also in the frame. As Helen Waddell explains with respect to the desert fathers, of whom Anthony is the most famous, their objective was to free the soul from its enslavement by the passions: "Human passion, the passion of anger as well as of lust, entangled the life of the spirit: therefore passion must be dug out by the roots."[19] Lina's particular sins are pride and self-centeredness, and she fights them in the desert using Anthony's methods. Furthermore, following the example of the beguines, who so intrigued Huysmans, as is evident in chapter 12 of *L'oblat*, Lina chooses to live in one of the huts rather than the convent.[20] There, in a modern-day *béguinage*, she encounters a blind woman and the girl who accompanies her—both beekeepers—and Lina, the rich young woman who had come to depend on maids, now chooses to keep house in her own simple dwelling.[21]

Although Lina still lacks an emotional or spiritual connection to the impoverished women, she serves them while also frequenting the church at the convent ("Voy a la iglesia diariamente"[22] [I go to the church daily]). She learns the occupation of beekeeping and tends to her companions with such assiduity that they believe her a saint, despite the fact that Lina herself is acutely aware that she feels no love for her charges and laments this failing.[23] Recalling Santa Teresa and her entreaties, Lina cries for her "Sweet Master" and begs him to come in the form of love and spiritual renewal—until she senses the beginnings of an interior transformation. By practicing the virtues of docility and renunciation, she creates a space for the accumulation of spiritual honey just as the cells of the comb prepare to house the honey made by the bees.[24] Now thinking of San Juan de la Cruz and St. Catherine as well as Santa Teresa, Lina knows that she has yet to experience spiritual union, divine betrothal, and the piercing of her soul by the angel's dart: love remains absent from her heart, and she continues to see herself as radically different from the people around her.[25]

Her miracle comes in the form of an outbreak of smallpox, when Lina is at a low point, plagued by Santa Teresa's spiritual dryness and San Ignacio de Loyola's desolation. Caring for the afflicted adolescent girl Torcuata, who imagines her caretaker as the "Virgen del Carmen" (Our Lady of Mount Carmel), Lina feels a "cuchillo de la piedad" (Teresian knife of mercy), a "herida en lo secreto del ánima" (wound in the depths of her soul) when she finally realizes that she feels another's pain as her own.[26] Mirroring St. Francis's kissing a leper, Lina kisses her patient and feels the honey of her own charity drip onto the girl's face, livid with pox ("Sobre la faz de la niña . . . gotea la miel de mi caridad" [Over the face of the girl . . . drips the honey of my charity]). A nonconsuming fire penetrates her body, dissolving her heart and carrying her to the ecstasy of union with her "dueño"[27] (master). Lina's story ends with her report that she is happy in the asylum where she has been confined, abandoned, and attacked by all but her father, Farnesio, and the poor women she has nursed. Most likely, her father will drag her back into the world from which she has retreated.

From Des Esseintes to Durtal: Moving toward God

As Bieder has observed, Emilia Pardo Bazán covers in one novel the entire Huysmansian trajectory. Nevertheless, there are some interesting discrepancies. The unreformed Lina, decadent idealist and aesthete, clearly has much in common with Des Esseintes. If Lina imagines different lives for herself by trying out various suitors, Des Esseintes switches from one group of acquaintances to another, with the culmination of his social life and erotic excesses being the extravagant funeral feast for his virility.[28] In this way, Des Esseintes's sexual exploits come to an end as he begins his retreat to his "refined Thebaid,"[29] while Lina's are nonexistent, since she remains chaste at all times: she may disdain men in a fashion similar to Des Esseintes's renunciation of women, but in her case, the rejection does not stem from surfeit. Another intriguing difference is that while Des Esseintes makes an artwork of his surroundings (the infamous jeweled tortoise and the mouth organ of liqueurs being just two examples), Lina, both artistic subject and object, decorates herself, as has been noted by Susan Kirkpatrick and Carmen Pereira-Muro as well as Bieder.[30] Also, in the case of Huysmans's protagonist, the aesthetic experimentation continues and even escalates during the retreat, while Lina's arrival at the "desert" marks her definitive abandonment of refined excess: she truly imitates Anthony instead of aestheticizing his retreat, as Des Esseintes does.

Yet there are a number of indications that Des Esseintes is already on a path that will carry him toward the conversion of Durtal, even though Huysmans's biographer Robert Baldick cautions against exaggerating these anticipations of the spiritual turn: "The cry for faith that [Huysmans] put into Des Esseintes' mouth was . . . quite unconscious."[31] Des Esseintes's craving for a "refined Thebaid," his praise for the monasteries' preservation of Latin culture and of art in general,[32] his affection for Bresdin's *Comedy of Death* with its meditating hermit,[33] his bedroom modeled after "a monastery cell,"[34] his identification with eremites "ripe for solitude,"[35] his "fellow-feeling for those who were shut up in religious houses, persecuted by a vindictive society,"[36] his sense that the seeds planted in him by his Jesuit educators were "showing signs of germinating,"[37] his "taste . . . for religious objects,"[38] and his "ardent aspirations toward an ideal"[39] all point toward the eventual conversion of the Huysmansian protagonist(s).

In this transitional period, Des Esseintes continues to find Schopenhauer more convincing than Kempis,[40] but when his health falters, he focuses on the genius of contemporary Catholic literature, often tinged with sickness or sadism in the work of Baudelaire, Barbey d'Aurevilly, and Flaubert: "It was only among writers who had not been ordained, among secular authors who were devoted to the Catholic cause and had its interests at heart, that prosaists worthy of attention were to be found."[41] Des Esseintes's musings at this stage mirror Pardo Bazán's discussions of the same authors in *La literatura francesa moderna* (*Modern French Literature*), as described by John Kronik.[42] For Pardo Bazán, "Baudelaire, Barbey, Richepin, and Verlaine belonged to that exciting group . . . whose Catholicism came to light in their terrified attraction to sin and in their horror of and fascination with sacrilege but whose religious sentiment was no less palpable for having emerged from corruption"; she was "stirred by the emotion, virility, and suggestiveness of the confessions of the sinner who was conscious of his wrongdoing and had a sense of responsibility."[43]

The ailing Des Esseintes realizes that his favorite work by Flaubert is now *La Tentation de Saint Antoine* (*The Temptation of Saint Anthony*), inspiration for his ecstatic celebration of his ventriloquist lover's rendition of the dialogue of the sphinx and the chimera: Des Esseintes senses that the voice of the chimera is addressed to him, speaking to him of the "feverish desire for the unknown, the unsatisfied longing for an ideal."[44] Instead of simply fetishizing or trivializing Anthony's temptations, Des Esseintes begins to respond to the story of Anthony and the desert on a deeper level: perhaps the sphinx and the chimera mark the turning point of his spiritual journey. For Pardo Bazán, *La Tentation de Saint Antoine* is the story of the ultimate triumph of faith: "Es del dominio de la historia del pensamiento, y son las herejías, las sugestiones diabólicas, las creencias exaltadas por el ascetismo, lo que presta alma a tan singular creación"[45] (It is about the command of the history of thought, and it is the heresies, the diabolical proposals, and the beliefs exalted by ascetism that give this singular creation its soul). Flaubert's sphinx and chimera are featured in Pardo's *La quimera* (*The Chimera*; 1905), as has been documented by Francisca González Arias,[46] and the sphinxes as suitors and philosophical temptations figure in *Dulce dueño*, threatening St. Catherine when she seeks her "Sweet Master."

Bewitched by the same fantastic creatures that line Catherine's path to the desert of conversion and appear in Lina's and St. Anthony's spiritual tests, Des Esseintes embarks on a similar course. But as soon as he begins to take comfort in the memories of the Jesuit fathers who touched his early life with religious rites and the plainsong that is "the idiom of the ancient Church, the very soul of the Middle Ages"—"the diuturnal hymn which had risen for centuries past towards the Most High"[47]—Des Esseintes's doctor orders him back to Paris, echoing Farnesio's threats to remove Lina from her asylum. Des Esseintes faces this prospect with horror and indignation: remembering the Trappists who live in isolation from society and manage to maintain their health, he does not understand why he is not permitted the same option. Disgusted with the degraded world he will soon rejoin, Huysmans's protagonist grasps at Schopenhauer for comfort but then realizes he has nowhere else to turn but to prayer, and so he cries out the final words of the novel: "Lord, take pity on the Christian who doubts, on the unbeliever who would fain believe, on the galley-slave of life who puts out to sea alone, in the night, beneath a firmament no longer lit by the consoling beacon-fires of the ancient hope!"[48]

Forced from his Thebaid against his will, as Lina will most likely be as well, the Des Esseintes who cries to God to help his unbelief (as in Mark 9:24) is comparable to the Lina of a slightly earlier stage in her trajectory, when she remembers Saint Teresa's plaints and begs for attention from her "Sweet Master." Huysmans's decadent hero's desperate prayer anticipates the transition in the author's work from Des Esseintes to Durtal, the seeker of *Là-bas*, *En route*, *La cathédrale*, and *L'oblat*. In *En route*, Durtal visits a Trappist monastery and is enraptured by the liturgy and common life, but in the end, he knows he is "still too much the man of letters to make a monk, and yet . . . already too much a monk to remain among men of letters."[49] Nevertheless, Durtal has progressed from Des Esseintes's starting point: whereas Des Esseintes left his Thebaid merely lamenting the loss of his solitude, Durtal grieves the "ideal community" he can merely visit rather than making it his permanent home[50] and cries out, "Ah! Lord, that I might live, live in the shadow of the prayers of humble [swine-herd] Brother Simeon!"[51] This breach in his haughty misanthropy brings him one step closer to being charitable.

The next novel in the series, *La cathédrale*, is the story of Durtal's studies of the Chartres cathedral before he again visits a monastery—this time, that of the Benedictines at Solesmes. The third text of the trilogy, *L'oblat*, chronicles his solution to the challenge of living as both monk and man of letters when he becomes a Benedictine oblate: "In mystical parlance, *En route* had corresponded to the purgative life, *La cathédrale* was to represent the contemplative life, and *L'oblat* the unitive life."[52] At the end of *L'oblat*, Durtal continues to pray the divine office at the monastery after most of the monks retreat to Belgium as a result of the new legislation that threatens religious orders in France. He thus accepts the responsibility to tend charitably to his Benedictine brothers who have remained behind.[53] He questions God—again he will have to return to Paris, "into all that hubbub!"[54]—but this time, Durtal's attitude is different because he realizes that "there is much to atone for" and that faithful servants such as himself must take up this task without resistance: "If Divine chastisement is prepared for us," Durtal muses, "let us get our backs ready and show that at least we have the virtue of willingness."[55]

Using gendered imagery, he acknowledges that there are no female substitutes to perform the duties of faith on his behalf: "In the spiritual life we have not always the luck of the man who marries a washerwoman, or a midwife, who does all the work, while the husband can afford to look on and twiddle his thumbs!"[56] And then, finally, he prays, making the last words of this novel an echo of the entreaties that closed *À rebours* and *En route*, now with an additional emphasis on self-forgetting as providing greater access to the divine: "O, Dear Lord, grant that we may not barter our souls thus; grant that we may forget self once and for all. Grant that we may live, no matter where, so long as it be far from ourselves, and close unto Thee!"[57] In this way, in addition to anticipating Lina's calls to her "Sweet Master," Durtal accepts his physical relocation and reinsertion into society, asking only for protection from self-centeredness so that he too might draw closer to God.

The Question of Mystical Substitution: Who Will Expiate Sin?

Durtal's reference to the husband who can no longer rely on his wife/servant to do his spiritual work can also be related to Lina's trajectory and to a broader connection between Pardo Bazán and Huysmans. These characters and authors are linked to each other by way of the topic of mystical substitution, compensation, or reversibility—three names for the same phenomenon—which may be defined as how "Carmelites and Poor Clares in far-off convents could take upon themselves the greater part of [others'] trials and temptations."[58] Huysmans, creator of Des Esseintes and Durtal, experienced a spiritual evolution similar to that of his protagonists, traveling as they did the long road from aesthetic decadence, to occultism, to prolonged visits to monasteries, and finally to a Benedictine oblature that involved accepting responsibility to atone for himself rather than depending on cloistered monks or nuns to expiate for him. An essential stage in this complicated journey was Huysmans's 1901 hagiographical text *Sainte Lydwine de Schiedam* (*Saint Lydwine of Schiedam*), and given her comparison of her dear friend Blanca de los Ríos to the suffering saint, we know that Pardo Bazán was touched by Huysmans's story of the late fourteenth-century Dutch saint who spent her life in intense physical and spiritual trials.[59] Lydwine appears in the writings of the French author years before he devotes an entire book to her. In *En route*, the protagonist makes the acquaintance of his spiritual adviser, Abbé Gévresin, thanks to the fact that Durtal is investigating the life of Blessed Lydwine (or Lidwine) of Schiedam, "true patroness of the sick," whose illnesses, accidents, disfigurement, and inanition are described by the abbé in the third chapter of the novel.[60] While Lydwine herself was bedridden at home instead of cloistered, "we can verify [in her] that plan of substitution which was, and is, the glorious reason for the existence of convents," according to the abbé, who refers specifically to St. Teresa of Jesus in the following passage: "This substitution of a strong soul freeing one who is not strong from perils and fears is one of the great rules of mysticism."[61] Soon after this discussion with the abbé, Durtal's spiritual journey takes him down the Rue de la Santé, "bounded on the right by the Prison de la Santé and Sainte Anne's madhouse, and on the left by convents," "a kind of prison corridor, with cells on either side, where some were condemned to temporary sentences, and others, of their own free will, suffered lasting sorrows."[62]

Traversing the same figurative territory as Lina at the boundary of the convent, the prison, and the asylum, Durtal recalls a visit he made to a Carmelite convent to witness a postulant's profession of vows. He reviews the harsh rule the Carmelites observe and the humility they attain, concluding that "they must indeed pity us, and set themselves to expiate the imbecility of a world which treats them as hysterical fools, for it cannot even understand the joy in suffering of souls like these."[63] Despite the disrespect with which their sacrifices are received, the contemplatives do penance for the very world that disdains them. This is why, the abbé explains to Durtal, "a weak and honest soul" should choose a monk for his or her confessor, because monastics alone—"the lightning conductors of society"—"know the effects of the law of substitution, and if they see that in spite of their efforts the penitent succumbs, they end by freeing him by taking his trials on themselves."[64] Lina, then, takes a similar approach in turning to the Capuchin of her second confession after the failed attempt with Carranza. Already adept at the ascetic life, the haggard monk will compensate for the weaknesses of Lina's penitential program if she is not up to the task. The Durtal of *En route* is a vulnerable neophyte similar to Lina. He knows that he must cling to his monks, since he himself is no Lydwine and is unable even to maintain his resolve to write this saint's life: "Physical suffering breaks me down, drives me to despair," he exclaims.[65]

Having made a retreat with the Trappists at Notre-Dame d'Igny in 1892, visited Schiedam in 1893, resided at the Benedictine Abbey of Solesmes in 1896, taken the robes of an oblate novice at Ligugé in 1899, and professed final vows as an oblate in 1901, Huysmans himself eventually does tell the story of the Blessed Lydwine. In the text published in Paris in June 1901 as *Sainte Lydwine de Schiedam*, Huysmans outlines the "law of equilibrium between Good and Ill" in the context of mystical substitution: "When man becomes too ignoble and kings too impious, God allows epidemics to be unchained, earthquakes, famines, and wars; but His mercy is such that He then excites the devotion of His Saints, enhances their merits, even practices a little deception with Himself, that His wrath may be appeased and equilibrium re-established."[66] Lydwine, then, was one of these devoted saints who reestablished the balance between good and evil. Her afflictions were varied and overwhelming, as her hagiographer recounts: "Her cheeks became hollow and her flesh melted away; she became so thin that she was only skin and bone; the comeliness of her features disappeared in the protuberances and hollows of a face which, from pink and white, became of a greenish hue, and finally ashen. Her wishes had been granted; she was as ugly as a corpse. Her lovers rejoiced that they had been dismissed, and she no longer feared to show herself abroad."[67] The issue of showing herself abroad, though, quickly becomes irrelevant, as she is attacked by additional ills and confined to bed:

> Violent neuralgic pains assailed her. . . . Her forehead was cleft from the roots of the hair to the centre of the nose; her chin dropped under the lower lip, and her mouth swelled; her right eye was extinguished, and the other became so tender that the least light caused it to bleed. She suffered also from a violent toothache, which raged sometimes for weeks and rendered her half mad. . . . Her nose was filled first with a livid humour, then with inflamed sores. . . . Next the lungs and liver decayed; then a cancer devoured her flesh; and finally,

> when the pestilence ravaged Holland, she was the first victim, and was afflicted with two abscesses.[68]

She then willingly increased these two abscesses to three, wishing to honor the Trinity, and was blessed by the granting of her wish.[69]

However, as Huysmans reveals, even the exemplary Lydwine fell into desolation and was as at times as bewildered and unwilling as Durtal. The holy priest Jan Pot had to explain to her the significance of her mission in order for her to embrace it, and he did this by instructing Lydwine to increase her meditation on the Passion of Christ—to accompany him to the Garden—so that she might "supply by [her] sufferings what are still necessary to His."[70] When she continued to struggle and bemoan her fate, Jan Pot informed her that even her dryness and distraction were graces and that "prayer recited by compulsion may be the most agreeable that God can receive, seeing that it is the only one that costs the utterer dear": her vocation was the completion, in the words of St. Paul, of "the sufferings of Christ."[71] Jan Pot tells Lydwine that her savior "cannot suffer again Himself, because he has ascended to Heaven and his Father," and for that reason, "if He is still to suffer here below, it can only be in His Church, in the members of His mystic body."[72] Using a local metaphor to help Lydwine understand, Jan Pot explains that "if these souls, capable like their Creator of being chastised for the crimes of which they are not guilty, did not exist, it would be with the universe as it would be with our own country without the protection of the dykes. It would be engulfed by the tide of sins like Holland by the flow of waves."[73] As consolation for Lydwine, Jan Pot then predicts that her savior will eventually favor her to such an extent that she will feel overcompensated for her suffering. This reward does indeed come in the form of angelic and divine visitations and other attentions, although Lydwine continues to be afflicted with moments of weakness and doubt, as does Durtal.

Still, as mentioned previously, by the end of *L'oblat*, Durtal is at relative peace with his obligation to bear the burden of sacrifice and suffering himself rather than depending on others to do it for him. In this novel, Huysmans had added to the treatment of mystical substitution in *Saint Lydwine* a nuptial analogy that seems to convince even confirmed bachelors like Durtal (and Huysmans himself) to contemplate marriage: *L'oblat* locates the origins of mystical substitution in the crucifixion, "and in a memorable apotheosis of pain [Huysmans] personified Suffering as the betrothed of Christ."[74] Durtal is captivated by such imagery and convinced of the need to take over from Christ as "Spouse of Lady Suffering" because of the evil he sees around him and the vulnerability of the religious orders bearing the burden of prayer and atonement.

He must have had thoughts similar to those Huysmans expresses in the concluding pages of *Saint Lydwine*, where the author notes that "in the orders whose aim is mortification and penance, such as the Calvarians, Benedictines, Trappists,

Clarisses, Carmelites, to name only five, women, whose maladies defy doctors' diagnosis, suffer that they may neutralize the demoniacal abominations of our day, but we have to ask ourselves whether the convents are numerous enough," since there are tragedies such as the May 1897 fire at a benefit bazaar that claimed the lives of many devoted leaders in charitable efforts.[75] Huysmans wondered in a letter composed at the time of the catastrophe at the bazaar whether such events could be attributed to the insufficient numbers of contemplative monastics who might "expiate the sins of others every day in their monasteries."[76] And in *Saint Lydwine*, the author asks, "Would such a disaster have been avoided if there had been more monasteries of strict observance, more souls determined to inflict voluntary suffering on themselves and endure the chastisement which sin had made inevitable?"[77] Huysmans notes that his own times require more Lydwines because "God demands much of us."[78] While he exclaims, "I could never do it willingly, I am not a Saint like Lydwine," Huysmans also recognizes that just as Lydwine was only enlightened with respect to her mission once it was undertaken, "Jesus begins by making his followers suffer, and explains himself afterwards" so that "there is nothing to be done but to give to Him."[79]

We know that Pardo Bazán was familiar with this heartfelt hagiography of the Dutch saint because she mentions it in a 1910 article devoted to her friend Blanca de los Ríos, whom she portrays as a dedicated scholar/martyr who works through intense pain. Pardo Bazán compares De los Ríos to "el encantador" (the charming) Huysmans's Santa Lidovina de Schiedam, who "con un cuerpo más que crucificado no desmayó en su espíritu ni un instante"[80] (with a body that was beyond crucified, never fainted in spirit even for an instant). As Bieder has noted, Pardo Bazán was not particularly disturbed by Huysmans's early novels, nor was she worried about adding *Là-bas* to her library.[81] In *La literatura francesa moderna*, she grouped Huysmans with Verlaine as one of the "convertidos y místicos"[82] (converted and mystical ones) and with the Goncourts and Maupassant as "not normal" ("En esta etapa literaria nos vemos rodeados de gente más o menos anormal: no son normales los Goncourt, ni Huysmanns; Maupassant muere loco"[83] [In this literary period we are surrounded by people who are more or less abnormal: neither the Goncourts nor Huysmanns (*sic*) are normal; Maupassant died insane]). Still, his story of Saint Lydwine inspired her to refer to the author as charming, so it would seem that his later works increased Pardo's affection for the wide-ranging French author.

Having confirmed that she was acquainted with the text of *Saint Lydwine*, we can speculate about when she might have discovered Huysmans's saint's life. Published in France in June 1901, might she have read it during her journey to Belgium and Holland in August 1901, about which she wrote the essays that were later collected as *Por la Europa católica* (*Travels through Catholic Europe*)? Huysmans's text ends with a travel diary of his research trip for *Saint Lydwine*, and he comments on the same cities that Pardo visits and describes in her own collection of essays. In chapter 8 of the hagiography, when he outlines Lydwine's vision of paradise, Huysmans includes a detailed discussion of Van Eyck's "Adoration of the Lamb," the Ghent altarpiece featured in one of Pardo Bazán's articles in *Por la Europa católica* and in her novel *La quimera*. Could Huysmans have been her model for both of these texts? In any event, if we are inclined to keep score as to which of the two authors first covered a certain subject, it is helpful to remember that in *San Francisco de Asís* (*Saint Francis of Assisi*; 1882), Pardo Bazán wrote beautifully about the Gothic cathedral and the society that created it long before Huysmans addressed the same topic in *La cathédrale* (1898).

Returning to our comparison of the two authors' works, Lydwine calls to her "Sweet Master"[84] just as Lina Mascareñas does toward the end of *Dulce dueño*, and the lessons of mystical substitution learned by the Dutch saint provide a helpful lens for reading the conclusion of Pardo Bazán's novel. Lina, like Durtal, realizes that she herself must atone for extreme pride and individualism—the century's great affliction, according to the Capuchin. She atones for her own excesses, for the errors of her parents who abandoned her and lived dishonestly, and for the evils of her age in general. As she says to the prostitute who serves as an instrument for her penance, "Quiero expiar"[85] (I want to atone), and Bieder has highlighted this penitential aspect of the end of the novel: "Es de notar que *Dulce dueño* termina también con el reconocimiento, por parte de Lina, de la necesidad de expiar sus pecados—y los ajenos"[86] (It is noteworthy that *Dulce dueño* also [i.e., in addition to Huysmans's Catholic novels] ends with the recognition, by Lina, of the need to atone for her own sins and for those of others). Lina, the same woman whose fortune and talents have allowed her to make many changes in her environment and to have a significant impact on those around her, now knows she must abandon herself in order to achieve spiritual union with her divine spouse ("Lo primero que necesito es abandonarme").[87] Once she realizes that she has reached the limits of her agency to effect the results she desires and admits that she is powerless to achieve her redemption, God takes over as in San Juan's passive nights, and Lina receives an opportunity for spiritual growth with the outbreak of smallpox. The afflicted Torcuata acts as her mystical substitute, the innocent victim who suffers on Lina's behalf and dissolves her hardened heart.[88] Still, as we have seen, Lina does not expect Torcuata to bear this weight permanently.

Lina's subsequent happiness in the asylum is analogous to Durtal's acceptance of his own responsibility to atone, rather than relying on a Carmelite nun. He realizes he has made spiritual progress and is strong enough to carry the burden, just as Huysmans himself was forced to do. The French author protested that he was no Lydwine himself, but as noted previously, he also recognized that suffering often begins before the penitent is psychologically prepared. His own relationship with intense suffering started long before he finished *Saint Lydwine of Schiedam*, as his increasingly intense tooth and jaw pain coincided with the ominous political developments constraining the religious orders.[89] Given that the orders' spiritual work faced interruption, others would have to take the place of the monks and nuns. As his biographer observes, "with *L'oblat*, Huysmans had written *finis* to the memoirs of his spiritual life: it now only remained for him to put into effect the lessons of renunciation and resignation which he had learnt."[90]

This he did, echoing Lydwine's hollow cheeks, dropping chin, partial blindness, violent toothache, cancer, abscesses, and inability to eat.[91] By September 1906, he had given up on the possibility of being cured and admitted in a letter that he had been selected to follow a daunting path: "I am going to be taken above by a way which, for lack of courage, I would not have chosen myself."[92] In another letter from the fall of 1906, he noted that while suffering is "the token of divine love," it is also "a frightful thing," though it meant "all so much less on the account to be settled in purgatory."[93] As new tumors appeared on his neck and cheek, Huysmans wrote to a correspondent: "I have a vague intuition that henceforth I shall be led out of the paths of literature and into the expiatory ways of suffering until I come to die. The worst of it is that I haven't a very decided sense of vocation for that sort of life, but in the end I shall undoubtedly get into the way of it."[94] With all his teeth extracted, his tongue eroding, his doctor's official diagnosis of cancer, and the emergence of additional abscesses, Huysmans refused morphine in order to embrace the "sufferings of God," which he did with "wonderful peace of mind" and a wish "to continue to be purified," certain that "the most important thing is to obey. God's will be done."[95] Thus Huysmans prays as Lina does, in the final words of *Dulce dueño*: "Hágase en mí tu voluntad"[96] (Let your will be done in me)—the words from the Passion that Lydwine was instructed to consider as well: not my will but yours be done.[97]

For the next stage of Huysmans's spiritual journey, we have the testimony of his secretary, Jean de Caldain, who wrote in April 1907 that Huysmans's cancer had spread, that he had requested the sacrament of extreme unction, and that their daily routine involved tending to the perforated roof of Huysmans's mouth and the jaw that would soon collapse: "Scrap by scrap, I have to pull away pieces of putrefying flesh—and the stench is appalling!!! Our poor master has that frightful smell in his nostrils night and day!"[98] In this instance, Huysmans could not imitate Lydwine, whose rotting flesh produced a sweet odor that Schiedam's inhabitants sensed far beyond the limits of her home and attracted visitors to her bedside. But was Huysmans's situation—an increased mortification, reminder of imminent death, and trial in humility—perhaps an even greater blessing than hers? In any case, friends did in fact call on him in the final weeks. One of them, François Coppée, concluded that Huysmans had anticipated his own end when he described Lydwine's trials.[99]

Secretary Caldain then reported an important shift, noting that Huysmans, in the days after receiving extreme unction, wondered if he might be "the total of a sum," asking, "Who knows whether I am not expiating the sins of others?"[100] Thus his suffering had taken him from a point in which he saw himself as relieving only his own future burden in purgatory ("All so much less on the account to be settled in purgatory," quoted previously) to imagining that he too might be one of the innocents designated to atone for others. Remembering the other chosen sufferers of mystical substitution he had studied and adored, Huysmans finally felt confident enough to inquire whether he might, after all his trials, aspire to their ranks. As Lina Mascareñas treasured the image of St. Catherine of Alexandria, Huysmans died accompanied by a portrait of a different Catherine: his beloved mystic Catherine Emmerich, bedridden, with her head wrapped in bandages, as Huysmans's was when he was buried.[101]

Pardo Bazán on Huysmans: Last Words

Was Emilia Pardo Bazán aware of the drama of Huysmans's final days? We know that she kept up with him at least as far as *Saint Lydwine of Schiedam*—and found him charming. With the attention his long agony and death received in the French press, it is hard to imagine that she would have been oblivious, particularly given her ties to the French literary world. In 1916, on the occasion of the death of Remy de Gourmont, Pardo complimented Gourmont's descriptions of Huysmans's nervous character, sensitive stomach, and melancholy—indeed, she dined with Huysmans herself in 1886–1887 and was able to confirm Gourmont's characterization.[102] But Pardo did not approve of Gourmont's disloyalty to Huysmans—the two men had a falling out related to the fact that Gourmont suspected Huysmans of taking advantage of, or even feigning, his conversion in order to sell books and win fame[103]—and she used this example to lament the fact that writer friends tend to betray each other, even though they claim to be great mutual admirers.[104] Considering that the rest of the article emphasizes Gourmont's misogyny, it is easy to imagine that Pardo might have been speaking from personal experience when she made this observation. It would have been nice if she had written that projected fourth volume of her *La literatura francesa moderna*, which was to be titled *La decadencia* (*Decadence*), because she would certainly have had to deal in more detail with Huysmans and his spiritual evolution.

As it is, she does make this statement in the Gourmont necrology: "El mismo Gourmont lo afirma, Huysmans conservó siempre un resto de fe, y al final de su vida la recobró por completo. No se trataba de una farsa, ni de un reclamo literario: la llamada conversión del autor de *La Catedral* fue sincera"[105] (Gourmont himself affirmed that Huysmans always kept a remnant of faith, and that at the end of his life he recovered it completely. We are not talking about a farce or literary tactics: the so-called conversion of the author of *The Cathedral* was sincere). So-called conversion, Pardo Bazán writes, meaning that the faith Huysmans supposedly discovered later in life was in fact always part of his searching idealism, even from his earliest days. By the same logic, I perhaps should have put quotation marks around the word *conversion* in the title of this essay, because we could say the same about Des Esseintes, Durtal, and Lina. In place of the more extensive commentary Pardo Bazán never wrote, we have her succinct and suggestive statement about Huysmans's "conversion" as well as the intertextuality of *Dulce dueño*, whose complexity did not escape the expansive critical vision of Bieder. If male characters can travel the spiritual road from aesthetic decadence to mystic substitution's reliance on the faith and practice of contemplatives or other innocent sufferers and finally arrive at atonement for their own sins as well as those of others, a woman can do it too—in the space of just one novel.

NOTES

1. Maryellen Bieder, "Divina y perversa: La mujer decadente en *Dulce dueño* de Emilia Pardo Bazán," in *Perversas y divinas: La representación de la mujer en las literaturas hispánicas: El fin de siglo y/o el fin de milenio actual*, ed. Carme Riera et al. (Valencia: Ediciones ExCultura, 2002), 7–8.
2. Bieder, 8.
3. Bieder, 9.
4. Bieder, 9.
5. Bieder, 10.
6. Bieder, 10.
7. For an excellent summary of other readings of *Dulce dueño*, see Jennifer Smith, "Women, Mysticism and Alternative Technologies of the Self in Selected Writings of Emilia Pardo Bazán," *Revista de Estudios Hispánicos* 45, no. 1 (2011): 163–164.
8. Emilia Pardo Bazán, *Dulce dueño*, ed. and intro. by Marina Mayoral (Madrid: Castalia, 1989), 263.
9. Pardo Bazán, 264–266.
10. Pardo Bazán, 269.
11. Pardo Bazán, 269, 272.
12. Pardo Bazán, 273–274.
13. Pardo Bazán, 275.
14. Pardo Bazán, 275.
15. Pardo Bazán, 275.
16. Pardo Bazán, 276.
17. Pardo Bazán, 276.
18. Pardo Bazán, 276.
19. Helen Waddell, ed., *The Desert Fathers* (New York: Vintage, 1998), 13.
20. See chapter 12 of Joris-Karl Huysmans, *The Oblate* [*L'oblat*], trans. Edward Perceval (New York: E. P. Dutton, 1924). The Beguines, who engaged in manual labor (such as beekeeping), were "one of the rarest examples of a mystically inspired new form of life created by women for women . . . : [they] put into place new forms of common life and self-administered commonality that connected with the traditions of monastic life through the commitment to celibacy and poverty," yet "their new forms maintained a different relation to the world and a different independence in their lifestyle as female laypersons"

(Dorothee Soelle, *The Silent Cry: Mysticism and Resistance*, trans. Barbara and Martin Rumscheidt [Minneapolis: Fortress Press, 2001], 165).

21. Pardo Bazán, *Dulce dueño*, 277.

22. Pardo Bazán, 278.

23. Pardo Bazán, 279.

24. Pardo Bazán, 281.

25. Pardo Bazán, 282.

26. Pardo Bazán, 284–285.

27. Pardo Bazán, 285–286. Bieder perceptively labels the pursuit of "divinization" (i.e., theosis or deification) as one of Lina's goals, arguing that "una de las metas de Lina es la divinización" (one of Lina's goals is divinization). Bieder, "Divina y perversa," 15, in reference to Pardo Bazán, *Dulce dueño*, 131: "Mi íntima voluntad de elevarme, de divinizarme si cupiese" (My innermost will to raise myself up, to become divine if possible). The question Bieder points to is whether Lina sees divinization in the same way *after* having the experiences she narrates in the novel. One could certainly make the case that Lina's perception and goals change over the course of the novel, but it could also be argued that the very terminology the character employs even in this early stage taps into the patristic tradition of sanctification as divinization (deification) of the human person and anticipates her mystical turn. For patristic and Thomistic notions of deification, see Fergus Kerr, *After Aquinas: Versions of Thomism* (Malden, Mass.: Blackwell, 2002), ch. 9.

28. Joris-Karl Huysmans, *Against Nature* [*À rebours*], trans. Robert Baldick (New York: Penguin, 1959), 27.

29. Huysmans, 22.

30. Susan Kirkpatrick, "Gender and Modernist Discourse: Emilia Pardo Bazán's *Dulce Dueño*," in *Modernism and Its Margins*, ed. Anthony L. Geist and José B. Monleón (New York: Garland, 1999), 123–124; Carmen Pereira-Muro, "Mimetismo, misticismo y la cuestión de la escritura femenina *en Dulce Dueño* de Emilia Pardo Bazán," *La Tribuna* 4 (2006): 171; Bieder, "Divina y perversa," 13.

31. Robert Baldick, introduction to *Against Nature*, 12.

32. Huysmans, *Against Nature*, 50, 88.

33. Huysmans, 72.

34. Huysmans, 75.

35. Huysmans, 76.

36. Huysmans, 77.

37. Huysmans, 86.

38. Huysmans, 87.

39. Huysmans, 88.

40. Huysmans, 92.

41. Huysmans, 153.

42. John Kronik, "Emilia Pardo Bazán and the Phenomenon of French Decadentism," *PMLA* 81, no. 5 (1966): 425.

43. Kronik, 425. In reference to Emilia Pardo Bazán, see *La literatura francesa moderna*, vol. 3, *El naturalismo* (Madrid: Renacimiento, 1911), 202–205.

44. Huysmans, *Against Nature*, 114–115, 181.

45. Pardo Bazán, *La literatura francesa moderna*, 3:57.

46. Francisca González Arias, "Emilia Pardo Bazán and *La Tentation de saint Antoine*, or the Countess and the Chimera," *Hispania* 71, no. 2 (1988): 212–216.

47. Huysmans, *Against Nature*, 202.

48. Huysmans, 220.

49. Joris-Karl Huysmans, *En route*, trans. C. Kegan Paul (New York: E. P. Dutton, 1918), 313.

50. Robert Baldick, *The Life of J.-K. Huysmans* (Gardena, Calif.: Dedalus, 2006), 279.

51. Huysmans, *En route*, 313.

52. Baldick, *Life of J.-K. Huysmans*, 318.

53. For a discussion of this legislation and the orders' response, see Baldick, 395; Stephen Schloesser, *Jazz Age Catholicism: Mystic Modernism in Postwar Paris, 1919–1933* (Toronto: University of Toronto Press, 2005), ch. 1; and William J. Callahan, *The Catholic Church in Spain, 1875–1998* (Washington, D.C.: Catholic University of America Press, 2000), 68–69. See chapter 12 of Huysmans's *Oblate* for Durtal's vision of the oblature as a way to save monastic life from political and social resistance and aggression and as a vehicle for the vindication of artistic expression central to the Catholic faith. In this sense, Durtal anticipates writer monk Thomas Merton. For Merton's story, see Paul Elie, *The Life You Save May Be Your Own: An American Pilgrimage* (New York: Farrar, Straus and Giroux, 2003).

54. Huysmans, *Oblate*, 303.

55. Huysmans, 303–304.

56. Huysmans, 304.

57. Huysmans, 304.

58. Baldick, *Life of J.-K. Huysmans*, 267. Mystical substitution is a complicated and contested topic. For a helpful discussion of reversibility in Huysmans, see the prologue to Schloesser's *Jazz Age Catholicism*. I would urge to the reader to see in particular Brenna Moore's introduction to her *Sacred Dread: Raïssa Maritain, the Allure of Suffering, and the French Catholic Revival (1905–1944)* (Notre Dame, Ind.: University of Notre Dame Press, 2013), 1–13, in which the author critiques readings such as the one offered by Richard D. E. Burton, *Holy Tears, Holy Blood: Women, Catholicism, and the Culture of Suffering in France, 1840–1970* (Ithaca, N.Y.: Cornell University Press, 2004). As Moore explains, her own work "demonstrates the risks of our tendency to write off these suffering centered theologies as little more than examples of pathology," and I have found her search for "richer morphologies" that are "beyond the atavistic and pathological" (*Sacred Dread*, 7–8) to be illuminating with respect to *Dulce dueño*.

59. See Emilia Pardo Bazán, "Blanca de los Ríos de Lampérez," in *Catálogo de las obras de Blanca de los Ríos de Lampérez y algunos juicios de la crítica acerca de ellas* (Madrid: Sanz Calleja, 1927), 39. I discuss her comparison of Lydwine and de los Ríos in a bit more detail in what follows.

60. Huysmans, *En route*, 39. For more information on this holy woman, Caroline Walker Bynum includes an interesting treatment of Lydwine's case in chapter 4 of her *Holy Feast and Holy Fast: The Religious Significance of Food to Medieval Women* (Berkeley: University of California Press, 1987).

61. Huysmans, *En route*, 39.

62. Huysmans, 45.

63. Huysmans, 55. Baldick provides a more graceful translation of this passage: "How they must pity us, and how anxious they must be to expiate the imbecility of this world which dismisses them as hysterical lunatics, for it is incapable of understanding the agonizing joys of such souls as these!" (*Life of J.-K. Huysmans*, 299–300).

64. Huysmans, *En route*, 40–41.

65. Huysmans, 144.

66. Joris-Karl Huysmans, *Saint Lydwine of Schiedam* [*Sainte Lydwine de Schiedam*], trans. Agnes Hastings (New York: E. P. Dutton, 1923), 27–29.

67. Huysmans, 47.

68. Huysmans, 54–55.

69. Huysmans, 66.

70. Huysmans, 66.

71. Huysmans, 66.

72. Huysmans, 67.

73. Huysmans, 67.

74. Baldick, *Life of J.-K. Huysmans*, 428; also see Huysmans, *Oblate*, 241–245.

75. Huysmans, *Saint Lydwine*, 219–220.

76. Huysmans letter, quoted in Baldick, *Life of J.-K. Huysmans*, 343.

77. Huysmans, *Saint Lydwine*, 220.

78. Huysmans, 220.

79. Huysmans, 221–222.

80. Pardo Bazán, "Ríos de Lampérez," 39.

81. Bieder, "Divina y perversa," 11, in reference to Emilia Pardo Bazán, "Ojeada retrospectiva a varias obras francesas de Daudet, Loti, Bourget, Huysmans, Rod y Barrés," in *Obras completas*, vol. 3, ed. Harry L. Kirby (Madrid: Aguilar, 1973), 1069.

82. Emilia Pardo Bazán, *La literatura francesa moderna*, vol. 2, *La transición* (Madrid: V. Prieto y Compañía, 1911), 149–150.

83. Pardo Bazán, *La literatura francesa moderna*, 3:62.

84. Huysmans, *Saint Lydwine*, 196.

85. Pardo Bazán, *Dulce dueño*, 269.

86. Bieder, "Divina y perversa," 10.

87. Pardo Bazán, *Dulce dueño*, 282. Self-abandonment, annihilation, or abasement should be understood in the tradition of the Spanish Carmelites or the French school of spirituality, according to which "interior debasement [is] a way to incorporate oneself into the inner life of the suffering Christ" (Moore, *Sacred Dread*, 9). In other words, Lina seeks the erasure of her ego as productive strategy—to be achieved, of course, only through God's grace.

88. Pardo Bazán, *Dulce dueño*, 286. Along these lines, the theory of mystical substitution provides a plausible explanation for the disturbing ending of Pardo Bazán's *La sirena negra*: the child is sacrificed in order to effect the father's redemption. We could also relate mystical substitution to Clara Ayamonte's entrance into the Carmel as an expression or extension of her love for Silvio Lago in *La quimera*.

89. See Baldick, *Life of J.-K. Huysmans*, 391–395.

90. Baldick, 464–465.

91. Baldick, 460–478.

92. Quoted in Baldick, 468.

93. Baldick, 469.

94. Baldick, 470.

95. Baldick, 472–473.

96. Pardo Bazán, *Dulce dueño*, 291.

97. See, for example, Luke 22:42 and Matt. 26:39.

98. Writing of Jean de Caldain, April 1907, quoted in Baldick, *Life of J.-K. Huysmans*, 473.

99. Baldick, 474.

100. Writing of Jean de Caldain, quoted in Baldick, 474.

101. Baldick, 474.

102. Emilia Pardo Bazán, "La vida contemporánea," *La Ilustración Artística* 1807 (August 14, 1916), in *La vida contemporánea*, by Emilia Pardo Bazán, ed. Carlos Dorado (Madrid: Hemeroteca Municipal, 2005), 600.

103. See Baldick, *Life of J.-K. Huysmans*, 314.

104. Pardo Bazán, "La vida contemporánea," 600.

105. Pardo Bazán, "La vida contemporánea," 600.

CHAPTER 7

"A Most Promising Girl"

GENDER AND ARTISTIC FUTURE IN EMILIA PARDO BAZÁN'S "LA DAMA JOVEN"

Margot Versteeg

Fascination with the figure of the actress in the collective and literary imaginary of nineteenth-century Spain is related to a dual historical and social reality. Over the course of the century, the expansion of the theater industry led to an increased presence of women on the stage, and the figure of the female performance artist became a source of both attraction and anxiety. On the one hand, the stage actress was an aesthetic object and an instrument of pleasure. On the other hand, she was a self-sufficient subject and a threatening subversion of the idealized model of the wife and mother. Contrary to the traditional angel-prostitute binary, the professional performer embodied par excellence Spain's nineteenth-century efforts to redefine gender categories. While male authors constructed the actress as a dangerous force that needed to be contained, for women who pursued a literary career, such as Emilia Pardo Bazán, she was above all an example to emulate.[1]

Emilia Pardo Bazán's story "La dama joven" ("The Ingénue"; 1885) is one example from an extensive corpus of nineteenth-century texts in which the character of the stage actress represents this growing preoccupation/fascination with a female subject who defies stereotypical representations of gender. In this long short story, or *nouvelle*, Pardo confronts her readers with a young woman of great dramatic talents who turns down an offer to pursue a career as a professional actress and instead accepts the marriage proposal of a humble woodworker who proves to be extremely jealous and possessive.[2] This essay interprets the problematic decision of the young woman in light of the discourses on gender and dramatic arts that are constructed and deconstructed by the story and in dialogue with some of the text's most suggestive intertexts: the romantic *folletín* (serialized novel) of the virtuous woman, Adelardo López de Ayala's play *Consuelo*

(1878), and George Sand's novel by the same name, *Consuelo* (1842). As I intend to show, in "La dama joven," Pardo Bazán distances herself both from the female authors of the generation that preceded her and from her male realist colleagues by producing a text that expresses a distinct opinion about the future of the female artist and of women in general.[3]

Concha, the story's protagonist, is a nineteen-year-old orphan who, just like her older sister, Dolores, makes a poor but decent living by working as a seamstress. Concha is not only physically attractive; she also possesses great dramatic talent. Aware of this talent, an acquaintance encourages Concha to join an amateur theater group and even invites her to perform the role of the female protagonist in Adelardo López de Ayala's play *Consuelo* during a benefit show organized in the theater of Marineda's Casino de Industriales (Industrial Casino). During the performance, the girl stands out among all the other amateur actors, and Juan Estrella, a nationally renowned impresario, offers the talented Concha a position as a *dama joven* (ingénue) in his theater company. The possibility that the young woman could pursue a future on the stage is met with strong resistance from both her sister Dolores and her fiancé, Ramón, neither of whom understand anything of art or artistic vocation. In spite of the prospect of a brilliant future, the girl declines the offer and decides to marry.

In "La dama joven," Emilia Pardo Bazán establishes an intertextual dialogue with the romantic *folletín* of the virtuous woman. This *folletín*, meticulously studied by Alicia Andreu, is based on the stereotypical story of the beautiful orphan girl who lives poor but happily in her humble room and makes an honorable living as a seamstress.[4] There are many versions of this *folletín*, but all these stories have in common that although the female protagonist finds herself besieged by a series of devilish attempts against her female virtue, the story always ends happily with marriage. According to Jean-François Botrel, the popularity of the *folletín* peaked during the years 1850 to 1870.[5] In 1885, when Pardo Bazán published "La dama joven," the *folletín* was already in decline. A year earlier, Benito Pérez Galdós had parodied its artificial conventions and implausible arguments in his novel *Tormento* (*Torment*; 1884). The realist author despised the *folletín* and considered the genre to have had a disastrous effect on the development of art.[6] Stephanie Sieburth has analyzed how Galdós's parody of the conventions of the *folletín* simultaneously denounces the repressive socioeconomic structures that supported the society in which the genre flourished.[7]

Just like her admired Galdós, Emilia Pardo Bazán affiliated herself solidly with realist aesthetics, and in 1881, the Galician author wrote in the preface to *Un viaje de novios* (*A Honeymoon*) that the novel no longer was "mero entretenimiento, modo de engañar gratamente unas cuantas horas"[8] (mere entertainment, a way to pleasantly pass the time) but instead had been transformed into an "estudio social, psicológico, histórico, pero al cabo estudio"[9] (social, psychological, historical study, but ultimately a study).

In "La dama joven," Pardo Bazán turns to parodying the romantic *folletín* of the virtuous woman, a genre predominantly written and read by women,[10] in order to distance herself from the female authors of the previous (post-)Romantic generation, who exalted a model of femininity characterized by moral superiority, abnegation, and asexuality.[11] Pardo also dissociates herself from the realist production of her male colleagues by putting her narrative at the service of the emancipation of women and by reclaiming a voice for women that allows them to express their own (sexual) desires and defend their equal status.[12]

While in the literary world, the virtuous woman was an archetype of the Romantic *folletines*, in the real world, the concept of the virtuous woman took shape in the myth of the angel in the house, whose exemplary behavior was recommended to the nineteenth-century readers of conduct manuals. Indeed, often the terms *virtuous woman* and *angel in the house* are used as synonyms. The angel is a fragile, submissive, and pure being who is denied any corporeal integrity and form of desire.[13] She lives in a precarious situation of economic dependency and is limited by domesticity. In "La dama joven," Dolores, Concha's sister, and her fiancé, Ramón, defend the concept of the angel in the house and the ideal of domesticity.

Ever since the two girls became orphans, Dolores, Concha's elder by twelve years, has taken care of her sister as if she were her own daughter. The story suggests, however, that the excessive protection that Dolores offers Concha is not entirely selfless. On the contrary, this protection stems from Dolores's ambition to "borrar lo pasado"[14] (efface the past) and a desire to hide her loss of virtue, as her own sexual curiosity led her to be seduced. Abandoned by her lover, she gave birth to a son who died shortly afterward due to malnourishment. As a result, Dolores hates men, most of all the *señoritos* (rich young gentlemen), whom she considers to be a source of evil. Dolores is determined to protect her sister and to avoid at all costs the destiny that had been bestowed upon her: "Para desgracia bastaba ella: a Concha que no la tocase ni el aire: corría de su cuenta defenderla con dientes y uñas"[15] (Enough with disgrace: not even air should touch Concha: it was her responsibility to defend her tooth and nail). Dolores comes off badly in the narrative, which specifies that she has a "cerebro estrecho y femenino, pero tenaz y aferrado a las pocas ideas que, nacidas allí, o sugeridas, se aposentaban en él"[16] (narrow and feminine brain that stubbornly clings to the few ideas that, because they were born there or suggested to her, have become lodged in it). The text seems to suggest that it is because of Dolores's rigid ideas and her opposition to any form of change that she dreams to "casar a Concha, ante el cura, con un hombre de bien"[17] (marry Concha, in the presence of a priest, to a good man) and that she imagines the day of the wedding as "el día de la tranquilidad completa"[18] (a day of complete tranquility).

The "good man" to whom Dolores hopes to marry her sister is Ramón, a woodworker who wants to marry as soon as he has accumulated sufficient money to open his own workshop. Ramón, who is characterized by his speech acts, does not conceal what type of love he feels for Concha when he states that he loves her "tanto como a mi madre"[19] (as much as my mother). Neither is there any doubt that Ramón has planned out an exclusively domestic existence for his future wife: "Cuando nos casemos . . . yo no consiento que vuelvas a representar, aunque se empeñe Dios del cielo . . . ¿Te has enterado? . . . ve acostumbrándote a la idea, por si acaso"[20] (Once we are married . . . I will not allow you to return to the stage, not even if God in heaven insists . . . Do you get that? . . . Get used to the idea, just in case).

The discourse of domesticity that Dolores and Ramón reproduce relegates the woman to the private space of the home and, by extension, to the sewing workshop, where women execute the same tasks as those required of the angel in the house, but on a larger scale. Pardo Bazán's narrative debunks, however, the connotations of peace and tranquility normally associated with the private space. In the room that Concha and Dolores share, and that the text, not without a touch of irony, qualifies as a "palacio modistil"[21] (dressmaker's palace), it smells of petroleum, and chaos reigns supreme. Although the narrative specifies that the "elemento de desorden"[22] (element of disorder) is a result of the time constraints in which the girls have to sew the many wardrobe pieces of the actress-seamstress, it is inevitable that the reader gains a sense of the hard labor that takes place in this space where seamstresses are chained to their sewing machines. Chad Wright, following Roland Barthes, defines sewing as "arreglar, crear, reparar"[23] (fixing, creating, repairing) and suggests that this activity implies a desire to mend one's lost virtue and thus, adds Stephanie Sieburth, to maintain the status quo.[24] This seems to apply to Dolores's case. However, Sieburth also proposes that sewing can be a way to undermine the patriarchal system.[25] For Concha, who transforms a series of borrowed and used clothes into her wardrobe for the play's premiere, sewing becomes a form of "autocreación y esperanza social"[26] (self-creation and social hope): "Salió el famoso vestido de baile. Era de seda azul bajo, algo verdoso ya y por muchas partes salseado; pero merced a la buena idea de Concha, de velarlo con infinitos volantes de tarlatana del mismo color, parecería nuevecito de allí a poco . . . fue a ocupar su puesto en el sofá al lado de otros pingos también remozados y disfrazados hábilmente con recogidos, lazos y encajes"[27] (And there was the famous gown. It was made of light-blue silk, which had turned a little green and was marked with several stains; but thanks to Concha's fine idea to cover it with infinite flounces made of tarlatanes of the same color, it looked almost like new . . . the dress went to occupy its place on the sofa, next to other clothes that had also been rejuvenated and handily disguised with gathers, bows, and laces). Her eagerness to create herself causes Concha to distance herself from the feminine model of the virtuous woman. And it is not only in her wardrobe transformation that she distinguishes herself. Although the girl is pretty and virtuous, she is neither obedient nor submissive, and she shows a nascent sexual curiosity. In her narrative, Pardo Bazán describes Concha's body as somewhere between virginal and eroticized:

> Sus carnes tibias conservan aún la suave morbidez del sueño, y la breve camisa descubre mucha parte de su gallarda escultura. Los brazos blancos y puros, los pies rosados por la frialdad del piso, los senos recogidos y breves como capullos de flor, hacen honesta por extremo aquella semi-desnudez juvenil, que la claridad del amanecer baña con delicados matices opalinos. Remata el cuerpo una cara oval, sumamente pálida, algo pecosa hacia el contorno de las mejillas; el pelo, rubio como la harina tostada, nace copioso en la nuca y frente, y desciende en patillas ondeantes hasta cerca del lóbulo de la oreja: entre los labios gruesos y cortos brilla como un relámpago la nitidez de la dentadura. Los ojos, aunque hinchados de dormir, no encubren que son garzos y candorosos todavía.[28]

> Her warm flesh still has the soft morbidity of the dream, and the short shirt uncovers a great deal of her beautifully sculptured body. Her arms white and pure, her feet rosy because of the cold apartment, her breasts firm and small like flower buds, make this juvenile half-nudity that the clarity of daybreak saturates with delicate opalescent hues, extremely honest. The body is completed by an oval face, extremely pale, a little freckled near the contours of the cheeks; the blonde hair, like toasted wheat, starts copiously at the back of the neck and on the forehead, and descends in wavelike sideburns to the earlobe; between the thick and short lips the clearly defined teeth shine like lightning. The eyes, although swollen from sleeping, do not yet hide their bluishness and innocence.

Concha has been constructed as a woman "de carne y hueso" (flesh and blood) with the desires that correspond to such a designation. Just as Pardo Bazán would do a few years later in *Insolación* (*Sunstroke*; 1889), the author from A Coruña deconstructs the hegemonic patriarchal discourses that propagate the notion of women's inherent asexuality. It is important to also emphasize the interest that Concha has in the body of her suitor, whose presentation in the story is focalized through the young woman. Although she observes that Ramón is somewhat "tosco" (uncouth), the girl stresses the "varonil presencia" (manly presence) of this "mocetón arrogante y guapo" (arrogant and handsome young man) with his "ancho pecho, oscura barba, pelo rizoso y grandes y vigorosas manos" (broad chest, dark beard, curly hair, and large and vigorous hands). Contrary to Dolores's statement that Concha is "fácil de guardar"[29] (easy to watch over), the girl does not always obey her sister. In spite of Dolores's explicit orders to the contrary, Concha allows Ramón to accompany her to the theater. At first, she strictly refuses to give him the kiss he asks for, since the echoes of Dolores's voice reverberate in her head. Concha, however, is far from another example of the model of female asexuality propagated in the *folletines*, and a little later we read that "una invencible curiosidad de virgen"[30] (an invincible virginal curiosity) drives her to desire the caress she had previously turned down. When Ramón, in a sudden and determined outburst, puts his arm around her waist and kisses her on the cheek with all his strength, devouring her skin, Concha feels a wave of hot blood streaming through her veins.[31] Later, in the theater, as she remembers Ramón's kiss, the girl experiences once again the physical sensation, and a blush spreads over her face: "¡Qué poco había durado!"[32] (How short had it lasted!).

Concha's great dramatic talent opens the door to a life unrestricted by domestic confinement, to a brilliant artistic future that will enable her to give shape to her desire to create herself. In a time when women defined themselves spatially through domesticity, the profession of the stage actress challenged the neat divide between public and private spaces. Escaping from home to be a performer was an antidomestic decision, since the professional actress exhibited on stage a type of woman whose qualities differed radically from those that the middle classes considered essentially female: passivity, modesty, virtue, and a lack of interest in sexuality.[33] The opposite of the angel's negation of corporeality was the spectacle of the body displayed by the actress.

Pardo Bazán's story informs us that from an early age, Concha has had a great passion for theater, and she knows by heart fragments of poems and plays that she has seen represented on the stage.[34] Contrary to many other girls who dream about an acting career, Concha's merits are not limited to her "buen palmito"[35] (good looks), although the text specifies that the physical attraction of her beautiful figure was certainly no hindrance in the beginning of her career. During the performance of *Consuelo*, the young woman knows her part by heart and puts her best foot forward. Concha takes her acting seriously and tries to pronounce her dialogue with the appropriate inflections. Her candor and freshness draw the attention of all the spectators, as does her capacity to transmit emotions and passion. We read that she is cold and coquettish in the first act of *Consuelo*, while in the last act she is all "celos y furia"[36] (jealousy and fury). The last verse of the play, pronounced between "femenil y pérfido" (feminine and perfidious), unleashes applause in the audience: "Todo Marineda, la gente fina, el *señorío*"[37] (All of Marineda, the refined public, the *upper echelon*) devoured her with their eyes; with all binoculars directed toward her, Concha becomes the object of rumors and gossip.

Concha's success meets with resistance from Ramón, who disapproves of his fiancée dressing up and exhibiting herself on stage. Although Ramón has put on his own Sunday best because he sings in a choral group—the text specifies that this attire makes him look like a *señorito*—the young man insists, before Concha appears on the stage in the third act of the play, that if her dress is too low cut, he will break up with her forever.[38] Ramón considers the men in the audience as his rivals for Concha's love, and he cannot tolerate "esos brutos de señoritos" (these stupid *señoritos*) talking about his girlfriend. Most of all, he is annoyed by "las voces que penetraban como lancetas en todo lo que él más quería, en la reputación, en la garganta, en la carne de Concha"[39] (the voices that, like lances, penetrated everything that he most loved, Concha's reputation, her throat, her flesh), and he flees from the theater, leaving his girlfriend behind in a ridiculous situation. It never occurs to Ramón that the enthusiastic response of the audience could be explained by Concha's artistic abilities and not her physical appearance.[40]

It is most of all with her voice that Concha gains the admiration of the spectators. The text emphasizes repeatedly that the girl's voice is fresh and clear and has a very pleasant timber[41] that can also transmit "notas penetrantes y apasionadas"[42] (penetrating and passionate notes). But most important is Concha's clear enunciation, and the narrator notes that when she pronounces her dialogue, the audience hears and understands everything.[43] Joseba Gabilondo has pointed out that in the nineteenth century, through the *performance* of the actresses in the theater, the female voice reached new heights of presence and importance.[44] Concha is very conscious of the power she has over her audience and the opportunity that the theater gives her to affirm her subjectivity. She looks at the spectators with tranquility,[45] and instead of wearing a high-necked dress, as her boyfriend wants, she uses the provocative power of her body and appears on stage after having lowered "con un dedo impaciente"[46] (with an impatient finger) the tulle that surrounded the neckline of her gown.

The text undermines the angel in the house ideology even more by indicating that Concha, although far from being an angel at home, and in spite of her provocative body, becomes spiritualized on the stage, where she is transformed into an angelic being. The text mentions "su aparición blanca y rubia envuelta en tarlatana azul" (her white and blonde appearance wrapped in blue tarlatan) and the "brillo alabastrino de los hermosos brazos y desnudos hombros"[47] (alabaster shine of her beautiful arms and naked shoulders). Concha seems to have become fascinated with the term *ángeles* (angels), which the public used for actresses, and the old actor Gormaz advises her to "tener alma"[48] (to perform with heart and soul) during the performance. Concha's *performance* is so impressive that the text insists on the divine nature of the girl's talent by specifying that the abilities of the seamstress-actress "no permitían ni por un momento dudar que Dios la había destinado a la gloria escénica"[49] (did not allow for a moment that anyone doubt that God had destined her to theatrical glory). Concha is an actress to the core, and she too feels the extraordinary communication that takes place between her and the audience: "Embriagada y penetrada hasta lo más íntimo de su ser, sentía esas cosquillas indefinibles, esa corriente magnética que pone en comunicación, por un instante, el alma de un artista con muchos miles de almas; singular amor colectivo . . . que une al individuo con la multitud"[50] (Intoxicated and penetrated to the most intimate part of her being, she felt these indefinable tickles, this magnetic current that for a moment allows for communication between the soul of the artist and thousands of souls; a unique, collective love . . . that unites the individual with the multitude).

Her impresario compares Concha to the great Spanish actresses, including Bárbara and Teodora Lamadrid, Maltilde Díez, and most of all, Concepción Rodríguez, because the timber of the girl's voice somewhat resembles Rodríguez's voice, which "llegaba al alma"[51] (touched one's soul). The mentioned performers are not considered inferior to any of the great male actors of their time, and the director of the local newspaper foresees in Concha a distinguished artist, destined to bring the nation glorious days at a moment when the Spanish stage is plagued by decadence and a lack of prestigious actors and actresses.[52] Pardo Bazán has Juan Estrella, the impresario, explain the necessity of female performers who measure up to their male colleagues: "¿Qué hay en mujeres, qué hay? Cuatro gatitas, que sueltan unos mayidos, que sacan unas colas de raso y están pensando en ellas toda la noche"[53] (What do we have when it comes to the women? Four meowing kittens that move the tails of their satin skirts and don't think of anything else the entire night).

As Concha promises to become a great actress, she is offered a position as an ingénue. After consideration, the girl does not accept the offer but decides to marry her ill-mannered boyfriend. It seems surprising that "La dama joven," in which Pardo Bazán questions the model of abnegation and female asexuality that characterizes the virtuous woman, ends with a capitulation toward conventional morality. In spite of Concha's rejection of a *folletín*-like behavior, and although she distinguishes herself from the angel in the house by her wish to self-create and her sexual desire, the narrative concludes with marriage, just like any *folletín*. It is well known that Pardo Bazán did not have a particularly high opinion of marriage, an institution she considered to be "una de las cadenas más determinantes que tiene la mujer, pues la condena a la dependencia y a la subordinación"[54] (one of the most determining chains for a woman, since it condemns her to dependency and subordination); "el error fundamental que vicia el criterio común respecto de la criatura del sexo femenino . . . es el de atribuirle un destino de mera relación; de no considerarla en sí, ni por sí, ni para sí, sino en los otros, por los otros, y para los otros"[55] (the fundamental error that vitiates the common criterion of the essence of the feminine sex . . . is that of attributing to her a destiny of mere relativity; of not considering her in herself, by herself, nor for herself, but rather in others, by others, and for others).[56] An author who manifested a certain animosity against marriage her entire life now seemingly gives Concha a destiny of mere relativity. At first sight, this does not exactly seem a way to settle the score with the angel in the house paradigm.

Concha's decision to accept Ramón's marriage proposal has been interpreted as an act of submissiveness on the part of the girl and as the result of her internalization of patriarchal ideas and her wish to please her sister, confessor, and boyfriend.[57] It is true that Dolores, with her rigid ideas, cannot accept that her sister, whom she has looked after as if she were her own daughter, now shows an independent will and tries to outline her own future, wishing to "disponer de su persona, echarse a perder, ir a correr el mundo en busca de aventuras, con una compañía de cómicos"[58] (determine her own life, go off, travel the world in search of adventures, with a troupe of comedic actors). However, we have already observed that Concha does not always obey her older sister. Nor does she obey her boyfriend, as we have seen in the case of the neckline on her costume. Finally, the influence of her spiritual father is minimalized by the text, which informs us that Concha does not confess very often and at night prefers sleeping to praying. We might thus conclude that the girl has her own agenda. And indeed, if we follow the girl's interior monologue, Concha seems perfectly able to make her own decisions. Julia Biggane has emphasized the narratological sophistication of the story: while the narrator of "La dama joven" is extradiegetic and omniscient, the focalization is fundamentally unstable and lies alternatively with the narrator and the characters, at least partially implying a changing intradiegetic perspective.[59] What's more, the narration uses free indirect discourse to relate the characters' thoughts. In Concha's case, all fragments in free indirect discourse consist of the mental musings of the girl, who has to decide between a life on the stage or a marriage with Ramón. As readers, we witness how she carefully weighs the pros and cons of an artistic future.

In the beginning of the story, Concha does not seem to see any conflict between marrying and pursuing a career as an actress: "¡Casarse! ¡Bah! Claro que se casaría; pero ¿qué prisa corría eso?"[60] (To marry! Huh! Of course she would marry, but why would she hurry?). She is seduced by the glamour of the stage, but she also sees that acting is an arduous profession: "Cómo saldría ella de aquel apuro? ¿Se cortaría? ¿Se le olvidarían los versos?"[61] (How would she do in such a difficult situation? Would she lose her nerve? Would she forget her part?). The approaching premiere absorbs all her attention, and she even forgets about her boyfriend: "¡Bastante pensaba Concha en Ramón! Todo el día, en el taller, estuvo repasando su papel mentalmente. ¡Don Manuel Gormaz le había encargado tanto que 'se fijase' y que 'tuviese alma' en algunas escenas! Tener alma . . . ¿sería gritar mucho?"[62] (She thought about Ramón enough! The entire day, in the workshop, she was mentally rehearsing her part. Don Manuel Gormaz had told her insistently to focus and to represent certain scenes "with heart and soul"! With heart and soul . . . would that mean that she had to shout loudly?).

After her argument with Ramón, the young woman becomes more serious about her future: "Ella podría ser actriz . . . es decir, dominar aquel arte apenas entrevisto, ponerse en comunicación todas las noches con el público, volver a escuchar aquellos embriagadores aplausos, viajar a ciudades grandes, para ella nunca vistas . . . Un destino ancho, grande, hermoso"[63] (She could be an actress . . . that is to say, master this art of which she has caught a glimpse, get in touch every night with the audience, hear again this intoxicating applause, travel to cities she had never seen . . . a great, large, beautiful destiny). Compared to her subaltern condition in the sewing workshop, the idea of being an actress evokes in the girl the promise of climbing the social ladder: "¡Artista! ¡Qué bien le sonaba a Concha el nombre! Ser *artista* era pertenecer a una clase aristocrática, superior a la humilde condición de costurera"[64] (Artist! How well did that term sound! To be an *artist* was to belong to an aristocratic class, above her humble condition as a seamstress). In her mind, Concha rejects the objections formulated by Dolores as well as her fear that she would go astray, explicitly alluding to her sister's loss of honor: "¡No parece sino que en Marineda no se perdían a cada paso cientos de muchachas, de allí, del mismo taller, sin necesidad de salir a la tablas a representar!"[65] (It just seems that in Marineda, hundreds of girls go astray, from here, from this very sewing workshop, without the need to appear on the stage and to perform!). The narrative refers to Dolores's fear of the *señoritos* several times in order to emphasize that danger is everywhere, not only in the theater.[66] Neither is Concha inclined to adapt herself to her boyfriend's desires: "¿Qué diría su novio si ella se hiciese cómica? ¡Bah! ¿Y qué había de decir, después de su comportamiento de ayer? ¿No la había puesto allí en ridículo, delante de todo el mundo, dándola el desaire de marcharse y de no echarle la corona, precisamente el día que? . . . se alegraba ella de que viese aquel majadero que no le necesitaba y que podía arreglarse de otro modo y buscarse otra vida! ¡Que rabiase Ramón!"[67] (What would her boyfriend say if she would become an actress? Huh! What was there to say, after his bad behavior yesterday? Had he not made her look ridiculous, in front of everybody, disdaining her by walking away and not giving her the crown, precisely on the day that . . . it cheered her up that the fool would see that she did not need him and that she could solve her own problems and choose another life. Let Ramón rage!) Concha does not believe she will be blinded by the glory of the theater. Instead, she attentively observes the hardship and lack of comfort that Estrella and the members of his theater troupe suffer. The young woman recognizes that it can be very difficult to make a living as a stage actress. This unknown destiny fills her with fear. Concha has heard that stage actors pass days of terrible hardship and sometimes even have nothing to eat. She has also heard rumors that Estrella has problems paying his company. Concha remembers seeing the actors and actresses coming out of the theater one evening: the women looked like witches, wrapped in clouds of wool, wearing old raincoats, and men and women were all together.[68] The theater world is like the façade of the casino: brilliantly illuminated on the outside but dark on the inside.[69]

Besides, Concha never wanted to be more than an amateur: "Jamás se le pasaría por las mientes ser actriz *de veras*. Entre ambas categorías, la de aficionada y la de actriz de profesión, juzgaba ella que existía un abismo infranqueable, como si las tablas del teatro público fuesen de otra madera enteramente distinta de las del Casino"[70] (It would never have occurred to her to be a *real* actress. Between both categories, the amateur and the professional actress, there was in her opinion an impassable abyss, as if the stage of the public theater was made of a different type of wood than that of the Casino).

After having followed Concha's considerations, we have plenty of reason to suppose that the girl, who uses her voice so well in the theater, is able to make and defend her own decisions, something that all parties have emphasized, be it or not as a simple strategy: "Ella es la que debe hablar . . . al fin se trata de su porvenir"[71] (She is the one who has to talk . . . in the end, it is about her future). What, then, is the decisive element in her decision to marry? We find the answer in a short dialogue between Gormaz and Juan Estrella: "'Con el novio hemos tropezado, Juanillo.' 'No hay peor tropiezo . . . ,' afirmó Estrella"[72] ("We have bumped into the boyfriend, Juanillo." "There is no worse encounter," Estrella confirmed). The impresario Juan Estrella, accompanied by the old actor Gormaz, has just returned from the girl's room, where he, like a suitor asking for a woman's hand, had gone to receive her answer about becoming an ingénue for the company. By presenting the impresario and the suitor as rivals, the narrative foregrounds what they have in common: both the boyfriend and the impresario will condemn the woman to dependency and subordination—the first by subjugating her at home, the second by exploiting her in the theater. The impresario talks about Concha as if she were a commodity: "Esta será encantadora: se escribirán papeles para ella. Esa juventud, ese aire de candor, esa frescura, unidos al talento, ya verá usted *lo que dan de sí*"[73] (She will be enchanting; they will write parts for her. This youth, this candor, this freshness, combined with her talent, you will see *what that will bring*). It is with the idea to exploit Concha that Juan Estrella offers her a modest salary.[74] What, then, is it that the boyfriend possesses and is attractive to Concha that the theater, with all its charms, does not offer her? The only attractiveness of the uncouth Ramón is, as we have seen, his physical appearance. The nineteen-year-old girl who, like many young women, lives only in the present, or at least in the very near future,[75] sees a much more immediate gratification in her boyfriend's body than the theater could ever give her.

Dolores's confessor, a sharp and intelligent Jesuit, firmly understands what it is that makes Concha's heart beat faster. Consulted by Dolores, who wants to know how to keep Concha away from the "sumamente arriesgada"[76] (very risky) stage, the Jesuit suggests with gentle irony that if the girl would be a little more involved with her boyfriend, Satan would not tempt her to try her luck on the stage.[77] Dolores follows her spiritual father's advice to the letter and facilitates the relationship between Concha and Ramón, and when Gormaz and Juan Estrella arrive at Concha's room to receive an answer to Estrella's proposal, they surprise the girl in a tête-à-tête with her boyfriend: "En el sofá . . . una pareja se hablaba muy de cerca, casi al oído, en esa estrecha proximidad que sólo origina un estado del alma; actitud elocuente, que con ninguna otra se confunde.

Separáronse y levantáronse de pronto al ver entrar gente, ella *confusa, encendida y casi sin habla*, él serio y sorprendido"[78] (On the couch . . . a couple talked very closely, almost in each other's ears, in this close proximity that only comes from the heart; a telling attitude, that can't be confused with any other. They separated and stood up when they saw people enter, she *confused, on fire, and almost speechless*, he serious and surprised). Concha's initial answer to Estrella's proposal—"Lo que quiera mi hermana" (Whatever my sister wants)—is therefore not so much the result of the internalization of someone else's ideas but of the girl's state of confusion. In this embarrassing situation, Concha does not know what to say, and she stammers a thousand apologies. When she finally answers, first hesitating and later with a convincing voice, she states that she does not think of working in the theater because she cannot foresee more than her immediate future. For this lack of foresight, Pardo Bazán condemns her to marriage, a metaphorical death and "tranquilidad completa"[79] (complete tranquility).

In "La dama joven," the discourse of *folletines* and realism mutually deconstruct each other. Stephanie Sieburth, following Alicia Andreu, points out that the *folletín* of the virtuous woman ends in marriage to reward the poor heroine's chastity and abnegation. The realist novel, on the contrary, ends with the punishment of the individual who dares to challenge social norms.[80] Pardo Bazán punishes Concha, whom she has gifted with a voice and desires, because the girl does not think beyond her immediate future and because she turns out to be just as narrow-minded as her sister when, blinded by the immediate gratification of enjoying her future husband's body, she resigns herself to a routine life instead of liberation. Marriage in the story is not the happy ending of the *folletines* but an existence of sacrifice and resignation—in other words, a metaphorical death in life, as is once again illustrated by the dialogue between Gormaz and Juan Estrella:

> —¡Y que lástima de chica! . . . Ahí se queda para siempre, sepultada oscurecida . . .
>
> —¡Bah!—murmuró Gormaz—. ¡Y quién sabe si la acierta, hijo! A veces en la oscuridad se vive más sosegado. . . . Acaso ese novio, que parece un buen muchacho, le dará una felicidad que la gloria no le daría.
>
> —¿Ese?—exclamó Estrella. . . . Lo que le dará ese bárbaro será un chiquillo por año . . . y si se descuida, un pie de paliza.[81]
>
> "And how bad I feel for that girl! . . . She will stay there forever, buried, in the shadows . . ."
>
> "Huh!" murmured Gormaz. "And who knows if she did the right thing! Sometimes life is more peaceful in the shadows . . . Perhaps her boyfriend, who seems to be a good guy, will bring her the happiness that fame would not give her."

> "That guy?" exclaimed Estrella. "What that animal will give her is a kid per year . . . and if she lets herself go, a beating."

When she condemns her protagonist to a metaphorical death in life, Pardo Bazán anticipates what Virginia Woolf would describe in 1931: killing the angel—that is, eliminating one of the major obstacles when it comes to writing. Killing the angel, writes Barbara Zecchi, implies that the limitations previously imposed on women's work have been overcome, a necessary step in order to "defeminize" writing.[82]

In spite of what Pardo Bazán wrote in 1881, this "defeminization" of writing does not mean that the Galician author cuts all entertainment or literary playfulness out of her work. In "La dama joven," the author not only dialogues intertextually with the *folletín* of the virtuous woman; she also appeals to the literary competency of her readers when, in the narrative, she points to two other intertexts that can contribute to my interpretation of Concha's problematic decision. Although insinuation can be more powerful than explicit affirmation, this is only true for well-read and active readers, since a reading of such a text without effort will be superficial, and the reader will not understand its ironic play. Therefore, the text establishes an opposition between the "feminine" readers of the *folletines*, with their bad reading habits, and an educated, "masculinized" reader who, instead of passively consuming the story, intelligently coproduces its meaning by his interpretation of its different intertexts.[83]

There are obvious tensions between, on the one hand, Pardo Bazán's rejection of the *folletines* and their readers and, on the other hand, her (sophisticated) use of the genre, which is emphasized by the illustrations in the 1885 edition. M. Obiols Delgado's illustrations clearly underscore the story's relation with the *folletín*. We see Concha and her sister at night in the sewing workshop; Concha receiving a kiss from Ramón; Concha in her dressing room wearing a dress with a very low neckline; Concha and her sister in their room, receiving Gormaz; the sisters in the sewing workshop; Dolores during confession; Concha and Ramón in amorous conversation on the couch in Concha's room; and finally, Gormaz and Juan Estrella finishing up their conversation.[84] Pierre Bourdieu's literary field theory can help explain these tensions. Pardo Bazán, still a newcomer to the literary scene at the time of the publication of "La dama joven," aims to produce works of literary value that will bring her prestige and secure "symbolic capital" (capital that only later will result in economic benefits), whereas her publishers are interested in making money immediately, in obtaining "economic capital." The *folletín*-esque topic and the illustrations bring readers and money, while Pardo Bazán's sophisticated use of intertexts to undermine the *folletín*—apart from furthering her feminist agenda—bring her prestige and admiration in the literary community.[85]

One of the intertexts in "La dama joven" is the play that Concha performs in Marineda's Casino: *Consuelo*, a comedy in three acts and in verse by Adelardo López de Ayala. This play, which premiered in 1878, was the playwright's final and most successful play.[86] Pardo Bazán, in her *Nuevo Teatro Crítico*, considers the work a "modelo admirable"[87] (admirable model). In view of the great success of the play, we can suppose that the 1885 audience was familiar with its content, which presents obvious similarities with "La dama joven." Consuelo is her mother's spoiled and only child (just as Concha is spoiled by Dolores), and Consuelo has two suitors (just as Concha has Ramón and the theater), of which Consuelo chooses the one that can give her the most luxury. After a while, however, Consuelo realizes that her husband is cheating on her, but when she regrets her decision, it is too late, as she is already trapped in marriage. Consuelo's regret suggests that Concha too will regret her decision to marry and that she might have done better to choose a future on the stage.

In 1889, Pardo Bazán complained that many actresses, once they got married, left the profession. This happened, for instance, to Elisa Boldún, who is mentioned in the story as a talented actress who never made it any further than being a most talented and promising "dama joven."[88] In 1904, Francisco Flores García published an article in the journal *Nuestro Tiempo*, in which, among other things, he comments on the retirement of Elisa Boldún:

> Cuando estaba en la madurez de su talento, en la plenitud de sus facultades y en todo el vigor de su genio poderoso, se casó y se retiró de escena, dejando un vacío muy difícil de llenar y que no se llenó en mucho tiempo. No sé en verdad cómo pudo resignarse a trocar las fulgurantes glorias de la escena por los dulzuras del hogar doméstico . . . por dulces que fuesen. . . . Al desaparecer la actriz que todo lo llenaba, podía decirse con el poeta: "¡Qué espantosa soledad!"[89]

> When she had reached artistic maturity, at the summit of her abilities and in full vigor of her powerful talent, she got married and retired from the stage, leaving a vacuum that was very difficult to fill and that would not be filled for a long time. I do not really know how she could resign herself to exchanging the shining glory of the stage for the delights of the home . . . however sweet they were. . . . With the disappearance of this actress who filled everything, we could say with the poet: "What an atrocious solitude!"

This last quote is, perhaps not coincidentally, the last line of López de Ayala's *Consuelo*.

If the intertextual dialogue with López de Ayala's play emphasizes the fatal consequences of Concha's decision, another intertext, less obvious perhaps, provides a different example to follow. I am referring to George Sand's novel *Consuelo* (1842), a work that tends to be considered one of the best novels written by the French author. Just like Concha, Sand's Consuelo is an orphan searching for love, but although she is tempted to seek refuge in a domesticity that paralyzes art, the protagonist struggles to obtain a position as a female artist. The most important aspect in Sand's novel—and by using this novel as an intertext, we see Emilia Pardo Bazán sending out an implicit message to her readership and defending her feminism—is that the artist is eventually successful thanks to her divine talent,[90] her hard work, and her many sacrifices;[91] Consuelo finally encounters an almost perfect liberty both in art and in love,[92] an opportunity that Concha loses because of her lack of foresight.

George Sand was an accomplished artist and a model of a woman who dared to publish in a time unkind to female authors.[93] Denise DuPont writes that Pardo Bazán did not always demonstrate an unconditional admiration for the French author, although her reluctance might have been caused by strategic motives.[94] Besides Madame de Staël's *Corinne* (1807), *Consuelo* is one of the most successful female *Künstlerromane* (artists' novels). Both Madame de Staël in *Corinne* and George Sand in *Consuelo* had the courage to imagine female geniuses who did not fit in with the conventional artistic conventions.[95] Although Pardo Bazán seems to have preferred Madame de Staël over George Sand, it is certain that for many female authors, *Consuelo* is an example of a work that illuminated the way for the female artist.[96] At the time Pardo Bazán wrote "La dama joven," she had just passed through a growing series of difficulties to make her married life compatible with her literary career. These difficulties would, in 1883, lead to the author's separation from her husband in order to dedicate herself entirely to writing, so it is difficult not to suppose an autobiographical subtext here.

In 1885, the year of the publication of "La dama joven," Pardo Bazán found herself on the verge of an uncertain future. In the field of literature, the writer from A Coruña was still a "dama joven" who did not know if the future, which looked promising, would fulfill its promises. How different was Pardo Bazán's situation twenty years later, when the author had Celina, one of the protagonists of her play *Cuesta abajo* (*Downhill*; 1906), openly choose a career on the stage, although Celina expresses her knowledge that such a career "la separa de la sociedad en vez de integrarla en ella, aislándola sobre todo del mundo de las mujeres sin integrarla en el mundo del poder masculino y situándola en otra esfera marginada, la del teatro"[97] (separates her from society instead of integrating her in it, isolating her above all from the world of women without integrating her in the world of male power and situating her in another marginalized sphere, that of the theater). In 1906, when *Cuesta abajo* premiered, Pardo Bazán already had published an impressive number of novels. By then, the Galician author knew that in spite of all the sacrifices, her decision to choose a future as an artist and to dedicate herself to literature had been the right one.

NOTES

1. About Emilia Pardo Bazán's love for the theater, see Cristina Patiño Eirín, "Trashumancias de Talía: Actores y actrices según Pardo Bazán," in *Emilia Pardo Bazán y las artes del espectáculo*, ed. José Manuel González Herrán et al. (A Coruña: Casa Museo Pardo Bazán, 2008), 189–242.

2. "La dama joven" was published in a volume with other stories in 1885. Ezama Gil has been unable to fully document the publication in the press of the narrative. It is certain, however, that "La dama joven" was published in *La Época* between July 19 and 31, 1893, and later as a "novela original" (original novel) in the collection *Los Contemporáneos* 231 (July 13, 1914). See Ángeles Ezama Gil, "El lugar de la novela corta en la narrativa de Emilia Pardo Bazán," in *Emilia Pardo Bazán: Los cuentos*, ed. José Manuel González Herrán et al. (A Coruña: Casa Museo Pardo Bazán, 2006), 202, 218. In Darío Villanueva and José Manuel González Herrán's recent edition of Emilia Pardo Bazán's *Obras completas*, "La dama joven" has been included in volume 7 (Madrid: Fundación José Antonio de Castro, 1999), 11–58. Julia Biggane examines the text as one of Pardo's novellas. See Biggane, *In a Liminal Space: The Novellas of Emilia Pardo Bazán* (Durham, N.C.: Durham Modern Language Series, 2000). According to Ángeles Ezama Gil, "No existe una conciencia clara de género ni en la teoría ni en la práctica, ya que la extensión de los relatos que se acogen bajo el [epígrafo de novela corta] es muy diversa hasta 1907" (Ezama Gil, "El lugar de la novela," 198; neither in theory nor in practice is there any clear consciousness about the genre, since the extension of the stories collected under the [title of novella] is highly diverse until 1907).

3. Critics who have dedicated attention to "La dama joven" (Biggane, Bravo-Villasante, Charnon-Deutsch, Henn, Miller) have interpreted the story in different ways, but all have struggled with Concha's decision. See Biggane, *In a Liminal Space*; Carmen Bravo-Villasante, *Vida y obra de Emilia Pardo Bazán* (Madrid: Revista de Occidente, 1962); Lou Charnon-Deutsch, *The Nineteenth-Century Spanish Story: Textual Strategies of a Genre in Transition* (London: Tamesis, 1985); David Henn, *The Early Pardo Bazán: Theme and Narrative Technique in the Novels of 1879–89* (Liverpool: Francis Cairns, 1988); Stephen Miller, "Emilia Pardo Bazán," in *Sobre una teoría española de la novela femenina del siglo XIX*, Biblioteca Virtual Cervantes, http://www.cervantesvirtual.com/obra/sobre-una-teora-espaola-de-la-novela-femenina-del-siglo-xix-0/. None of these critics has explored the work's intertexts, although Ezama Gil, in "El lugar de la novela," refers to the *folletines* (219). Ángeles Quesada Novás briefly touches on the illustrations in the 1885 edition. See Quesada Novás, "'La dama joven' de Pardo Bazán: Una forma de ilustrar un texto," *Salina* 23 (2009): 79–98.

4. See Alicia Andreu, *Galdós y la literatura popular* (Madrid: Sociedad General Española de Librería, 1982).

5. Jean-François Botrel, "La novela por entregas: Unidad de creación y consumo," in *Creación y público en la literatura española*, ed. Jean-François Botrel and S. Salaün (Madrid: Editorial Castalia, 1974), 131.

6. Alicia Andreu, "El folletín como intertexto en *Tormento*," *Anales galdosianos* 17 (1982): 56. Catherine Jagoe, following Alicia Andreu, also explores how Pérez Galdós in *La desheredada* parodies the romantic *folletín* written by women. See Jagoe, "Disinheriting the Feminine: Galdós and the Rise of the Realist Novel in Spain," *Revista de Estudios Hispánicos* 27, no. 2 (1993): 225–248.

7. Stephanie Sieburth, *Inventing High and Low: Literature, Mass Culture, and Uneven Modernity in Spain* (Durham, N.C.: Duke University Press, 1994), 100–136.

8. Emilia Pardo Bazán, *Un viaje de novios*, intro. and notes by Marisa Sotelo Vázquez (Madrid: Alianza Editorial, 2003), 52.

9. Pardo Bazán, 52.

10. Barbara Zecchi, "*Insolación* de Emilia Pardo Bazán: Intertextualidades y parodias, hacia una escritura de la igualdad," *MLN* 122 (2007): 311.

11. Catherine Jagoe ("Disinheriting the Feminine," 228–229) points out that in reality, there are two generations of female authors. The first generation of romantic writers, who started to write in 1841, were followed in the 1850s by a new group of postromantic female authors, including Pilar Sinués, Faustina Sáez, Angela Grassi, Teresa Arróniz y Bosch, Joaquina Balsameda, María Mendoza, Catalina Macpherson, and Emilia Serrano. These predecessors of Pardo Bazán saved the novel from its reputation of immorality and promoted the bourgeois values personified in the Angel of the House. The feminist critics Concepción Arenal and Concepción Sáiz de Otero struggled to deny woman's mental inferiority and accepted that women were morally superior to men. In the same vein as Concepción Gimeno de Flaquer, Pardo Bazán questions the feminine model of abnegation and asexuality, in which she sees the origin of a situation of subordination (see Zecchi, "*Insolación* de Emilia Pardo Bazán," 296–297). The name of the protagonist of "La dama joven" is perhaps an ironic allusion to these three female writers. Maryellen Bieder qualifies Pardo Bazán's relation with her female predecessors as "uneasy" (Bieder, "Emilia Pardo Bazán and Literary Women: Women Reading Women's Writing in Late 19th-Century Spain," *Revista Hispánica Moderna* 46, no. 1 [1993]: 19).

12. Zecchi, "*Insolación* de Emilia Pardo Bazán," 294–297.

13. Bridget A. Aldaraca, *El ángel del hogar: Galdós and the Ideology of Domesticity in Spain* (Chapel Hill: North Carolina Studies in the Romance Languages and Literatures, 1991), 144.

14. Pardo Bazán, "La dama joven," in *Obras completas*, vol. 7, ed. Darío Villanueva and José Manuel González Herrán (Madrid: Fundación José Antonio de Castro, 1999), 16.

15. Pardo Bazán, 16.

16. Pardo Bazán, 54.

17. Pardo Bazán, 18.

18. Pardo Bazán, 19.

19. Pardo Bazán, 26.

20. Pardo Bazán, 25.

21. Pardo Bazán, 56.

22. Pardo Bazán, 18.

23. Chad Wright, "'La eterna mascarada hispanomatritense': Clothing and Society in *Tormento*," *Anales Galdosianos* 20, no. 2 (1985): 31.

24. Sieburth, *Inventing High and Low*, 110n13.

25. Sieburth, 110n13.

26. Wright, "La eterna mascarada," 25.

27. Pardo Bazán, "La dama joven," 21–22.

28. Pardo Bazán, 21.

29. Pardo Bazán, 24.

30. Pardo Bazán, 27.

31. Pardo Bazán, 27.

32. Pardo Bazán, 33.
33. Jagoe, "Disinheriting the Feminine," 229.
34. Pardo Bazán, "La dama joven," 17.
35. Pardo Bazán, 40.
36. Pardo Bazán, 41.
37. Pardo Bazán, 33, emphasis in the original.
38. Pardo Bazán, 41.
39. Pardo Bazán, 42.
40. Pardo Bazán, 38.
41. Pardo Bazán, 37.
42. Pardo Bazán, 32.
43. Pardo Bazán, 32.
44. Joseba Gabilondo, "The Subaltern Cannot Speak but Performs: Women's Public and Literary Cultures in Nineteenth-Century Spain," *Hispanic Research Journal* 5, no. 1 (2003): 88–89.
45. Pardo Bazán, "La dama joven," 33.
46. Pardo Bazán, 41.
47. Pardo Bazán, 41.
48. Pardo Bazán, 20.
49. Pardo Bazán, 45.
50. Pardo Bazán, 43.
51. Pardo Bazán, 40. Concepción Rodríguez (1802–1880), Bárbara Lamadrid (1812–1893), her younger sister Teodora Lamadrid (1820–1896), and Matilde Díez (1818–1883) were famous stage actresses in Spain's romantic period.
52. Pardo Bazán, 45.
53. Pardo Bazán, 39.
54. Pardo Bazán, quoted in Zecchi, "*Insolación* de Emilia Pardo Bazán," 297.
55. Pardo Bazán, "Una opinión sobre la mujer," in *La mujer en los discursos de género: Textos y contextos en el siglo XIX*, ed. Catherine Jagoe et al. (Barcelona: Icaria, 1998), 502.
56. The translation of the quote is based on a translation by Walter Borenstein, introduction to *The Tribune of the People*, by Emilia Pardo Bazán, trans. Walter Borenstein (Lewisburg, Pa.: Bucknell University Press, 1999), 29.
57. Bravo-Villasante, *Vida y obra*, 100; Charnon-Deutsch, *Nineteenth-Century Spanish Story*, 87.
58. Pardo Bazán, "La dama joven," 47.
59. Biggane, *In a Liminal Space*, 18, 19, 23.
60. Pardo Bazán, "La dama joven," 19.
61. Pardo Bazán, 20.
62. Pardo Bazán, 23.
63. Pardo Bazán, 49.
64. Pardo Bazán, 19–20. The seamstresses in the sewing workshop consider Concha's victory in the theater as a victory over representatives of other social classes (the tobacco dealer and the shopkeeper) who performed the other female roles in López de Ayala's play. The narrative suggests, moreover, that a career on the stage will allow Concha to climb higher on the social ladder than a marriage with the artisan Ramón (48–49).
65. Pardo Bazán, 49.
66. The narrative also establishes a comparison between the theater, harshly condemned by those who feared the stage, and Carnival, a totally accepted but perhaps equally or even

more dangerous institution. (We recall that Dolores's seduction is related to the dance parties that take place during Carnival.) See Pardo Bazán, 15.

67. Pardo Bazán, 50.

68. Pardo Bazán, 49. Patiño Eirín shows in several quotes that Pardo Bazán was very conscious of the actors' hard labor and the poor material conditions in which the performers had to carry out their profession ("Trashumancias de Talía," 192–193).

69. Pardo Bazán, "La dama joven," 27–28.

70. Pardo Bazán, 49, emphasis in the original.

71. Pardo Bazán, 47.

72. Pardo Bazán, 58.

73. Pardo Bazán, 40, emphasis mine.

74. Pardo Bazán might have felt the same regarding her editors.

75. Pardo Bazán, 19.

76. Pardo Bazán, 51.

77. Pardo Bazán, 53.

78. Pardo Bazán, 57, emphasis added.

79. Pardo Bazán, 19.

80. Sieburth, *Inventing High and Low*, 131.

81. Pardo Bazán, "La dama joven," 58.

82. Zecchi, "*Insolación* de Emilia Pardo Bazán," 312.

83. Jagoe, "Disinheriting the Feminine," 240. In the 1885 edition, Pardo Bazán refers to the Cervantine influence in her short stories. See Pardo Bazán, prologue to "La dama joven," by Emilia Pardo Bazán, illustrations by M. Obiols Delgado (Barcelona: Biblioteca Arte y Letras, 1885), vii–xv.

84. M. Obiols Delgado, illustrations for "La dama joven," by Emilia Pardo Bazán (Barcelona: Biblioteca Arte y Letras, 1885), 19, 37, 50, 69, 74, 79, 87, 90.

85. See Pierre Bourdieu, *The Field of Cultural Production*, ed. Randal Johnson (New York: Columbia University Press, 1993).

86. Edward Coughlin, *Adelardo López de Ayala* (Boston: Twayne, 1977), 94.

87. Pardo Bazán, *Nuevo Teatro Crítico* 2, no. 16 (April 1892): 53.

88. Biggane, *In a Liminal Space*, 16; Pardo Bazán, "La dama joven," 40.

89. Francisco Flores García, "Actrices españolas—Matilde Díez, Elisa Boldún," *Nuestro Tiempo: Revista Mensual Ilustrada* 4, no. 42 (June 1904): 370.

90. Pardo Bazán, "La dama joven," 50.

91. Pardo Bazán, 42.

92. Pardo Bazán, 55.

93. Linda M. Lewis, *Germaine de Staël, George Sand, and the Victorian Woman Artist* (Columbia: University of Missouri Press, 2003), 13.

94. Denise DuPont, "Masculinity, Femininity, Solidarity: Emilia Pardo Bazán's Construction of Madame de Staël and George Sand," *Comparative Literature Studies* 40, no. 4 (2003): 373, 383, 388.

95. Margaret Higonnet in Patiño Eirín, "Trashumancias de Talía," 196.

96. Linda M. Lewis, *Germaine de Staël*, 9.

97. Maryellen Bieder, "El teatro de Benito Pérez Galdós y Emilia Pardo Bazán: Estructura y visión dramática en *Mariucha* y *Cuesta abajo*," in *Actas del IX Congreso de la Asociación Internacional de Hispanistas*, vol. 2, ed. Sebastián Neumeister (Frankfurt am Main: Vervuert, 1989), 21.

PART III

Representations of Female Deviance

CHAPTER 8

A Woman's Search for a Space of Her Own in Gertrudis Gómez de Avellaneda's *Dos mujeres*

Rogelia Lily Ibarra

The criticism on Gertrudis Gómez de Avellaneda's *Dos mujeres* (*Two Women*; 1842–1843) has situated the novel in the context of social Romanticism and interpreted it as a denunciation of the social injustices facing middle-class Spanish women.[1] The experiences of her protagonist, Catalina de S., have been read as a fictional representation of Avellaneda's own life experiences as described in her autobiography and letters.[2] Furthermore, according to Brígida M. Pastor, through Avellaneda's extended reading of French literature and philosophy, such as works by Jean-Jacques Rousseau, Jacques-Henri Bernardin de Saint-Pierre, François-René de Chateaubriand, Madame de Staël, and George Sand, she found a tradition that supplied narrative language for a critique of marriage and the subjection of women.[3] Influenced by these writers, Susan Kirkpatrick affirms that Avellaneda felt emboldened to challenge more directly the inequities of Spanish women's social destiny.[4]

Building on the aforementioned scholarship, this study contends that in *Dos mujeres*, Avellaneda takes what appears to be a typical love-triangle story of a *folletín* (serialized novel) and transforms it into an allegory of the fragmented state of the Spanish nation in the nineteenth century and a feminist critique. Through her representations of space, the author first highlights the cultural and ideological tensions resulting from the conflict between the preservation of traditional, autochthonous customs and the progressive French cultural influences during the historical period that encompasses the restoration of Fernando VII to the throne in 1813, the Trienio Liberal (Liberal Three-Year Period; 1820–1823), and the Década Ominosa (Ominous Decade) of Fernando VII's ten-year rule as an absolute monarch (1823–1833). Avellaneda then challenges gender divisions embraced by liberals and conservatives alike, in which men were allowed to move freely in the public sphere while women were restricted to a domestic, private existence. Avellaneda does this by introducing female characters who blur the boundaries of these spaces and fail to fit into any of the roles available to the female subject at the time.

Avellaneda's *Dos mujeres* was published in four short volumes between 1842 and 1843 in Madrid. The action takes place between Seville and Madrid from 1817 to 1826. It tells the story of an arranged marriage between two young cousins (Carlos and Leonor) who are temporarily separated by a sudden business matter that calls Carlos to Madrid. While Carlos visits with a relative in Madrid, he meets the glamorous and intriguing Countess Catalina de S., with whom he gradually falls in love and begins a passionate affair. Carlos and Catalina struggle with their visceral attraction for one another and their conflicting desire to uphold societal norms: Carlos is torn by a social responsibility to his wife and Catalina by her public reputation. In the end, Catalina decides to take her life to allow Carlos to keep his sacred contract of marriage intact.

The novel's beginning focuses on the De Silva household, located in provincial Seville. The first chapter opens with a disagreement between siblings, Francisco and Leonor De Silva, and thereby establishes the first conflict of the novel. Leonor argues with her brother about his son's future and disagrees with his decision to send the young Carlos off to Madrid when he returns from France, where he has been at school for eight years. Leonor's position is based on her perception of Madrid as a negative and corrupting place for Carlos. She reacts to Francisco's idea ironically: "Porque arrojar a un pobre muchacho de veinte años, que sale de un colegio, en esa Babilonia de Madrid, para que lo perviertan y corrompan, es el mejor medio de prepararlo para ser un buen marido. A la verdad, hermano, que discurres con un acierto"[5] (Because to thrust a poor boy of twenty years, coming from school, into that Babylon of Madrid, so that he is perverted and corrupted, is the best way to prepare him to be a good husband. The truth, brother, is that you reason so wisely). Thus Leonor begins to define spatial divisions by distinguishing Madrid from Seville. Comparing Madrid to Babylon, she suggests that Carlos will stray from his rightful and moral path to marriage in the more provincial Seville and instead become lost in, or corrupted by, Madrid's cosmopolitan urban culture. She also criticizes Francisco's decision to send Carlos away to study in France, a place she compares to Madrid because it promotes revolution and heretical tendencies. Leonor's concealed interest in this argument is her ardent desire for an arranged marriage between her nephew, Carlos, and her only daughter, Luisa.

While Leonor defends the moral values of the De Silva household and the union between Carlos and Luisa, her brother Francisco constantly challenges her views with his more liberal opinions. Leonor exhibits a strong anti-French sentiment held by monarchists who not only rejected the liberal ideas associated with the French Revolution but remained resentful of France's invasion of Spain in 1808. While the War of Spanish Independence ended with the expulsion of the French in 1814, Spaniards' continued hatred of the French fed the rejection of the French-inspired Spanish constitution of 1812. This reaction to the French, and French liberalism, facilitated Fernand VII's dissolution of the Cortes de Cádiz (the first national assembly in Spain), abolition of the new constitution, censorship of the press and the theater, reinstatement of the Inquisition, and the persecution of liberals. Liberals who had supported the French invasion were disparagingly referred to as *afrancesados* (Francophiles) and were now the object of political persecution.[6] Thus Leonor is tied to both the provinces (in this case, Seville) and Spain's return to a Catholic monarchy, while her brother is portrayed as an advocate of Madrid (cosmopolitanism) and political liberalism.

Indeed, the narrator describes Leonor as "ultra" Spanish by emphasizing her loyalty to King Ferdinand VII: "El culto que daba a Fernando VII estaba como enlazado al que tributaba a Dios, y la desafección al Rey legítimo y absoluto era para ella un pecado de herejía. De tal modo se confundían en su cabeza el altar y el trono"[7] (The tribute she rendered to Fernando VII was intertwined with what she paid to God, and the disaffection toward the legitimate and absolute King was for her a sin of heresy. In this way she confused in her mind the altar and the throne). Through Leonor's fanaticism, the narrator defines the traditional Spanish values in which religious faith and support of the monarchy were often conflated. However, with Francisco's defense of liberalism and French culture, the narrator questions and challenges Spanish tradition. In fact, the narrator makes clear that Francisco thought the French brought some positive changes to Spain: "No pocas veces había exaltado la bilis de su hermana, asegurando, a fuer de hombre previsor y político, que . . . ellos [the Bonapartes] habían traído ventajas a la España que debían hacerse palpables más tarde"[8] (Often he had angered his sister, assuring, as a foresighted and political man, that . . . they [the Bonapartes] had brought improvements to Spain that would become obvious in the future). Leonor and Francisco represent the love/hate relationship Spanish tradition will have with French modernity throughout the nineteenth century. Rejecting France's political and cultural ideology, conservative Spaniards fought to maintain Spain's autochthonous traditions and unique national identity. Liberals, on the other hand, tried to make liberal views more palatable in Spain by disassociating Enlightenment ideas from the French. According to Jesús Torrecilla, proponents of liberalism argued that Spain needed to become modernized and that progressive or enlightened ideas, regardless of their origin, were universal.[9]

Despite her disagreements with her brother, Leonor imposes her conservative ideology on her family and is more successful in defining the space of the De Silva home. In the narrator's words,

> Es de suponer que su casa y su familia hubieran podido transportarse al siglo XVII, sin que desdijesen en nada. El aire que allí se respiraba tenía un olor antiguo y monacal; los muebles, el orden interior, todo en casa de Leonor de Silva era español puro, antiguo y acendrado. Comíase a la una del día, merendábase chocolate y dulces a las cinco de la tarde, cenábase a las nueve de la noche, y a las diez en punto, en verano o en invierno, todo el mundo estaba en la cama.[10]

> Presumably, her house and family could have been transported to the seventeenth century, without anything seeming out of place. The air breathed there had an ancient and monastic smell; the furniture, the interior design, everything in Leonor de Silva's home was thoroughly Spanish. One ate at one o'clock, chocolate and sweets were served at five in the afternoon, dinner at nine at night, and at ten on the dot, in summer or winter, everyone was in bed.

Sequestered from the modern world, Leonor's home is physically and symbolically anachronistic, as it emulates a lifestyle of the past. Not only is there no room here for change or foreign influence, but no disorder is allowed, suggesting Leonor's support for Fernando VII's authoritarianism. Leonor's home symbolizes what Noël Valis describes as "a national distinctiveness that became associated with a form of tradition seen as backward and often identified with Andalusian, or southern, culture."[11] This behavior is an example of what Torrecilla signals as some Spaniards' adoption of "una actitud conservadora [que proponía] mantener (o recuperar) los usos y costumbres característicos de la tradición española de los Siglos de Oro"[12] (a conservative attitude [that proposed] maintaining [or recuperating] the uses and customs characteristic of the Spanish Golden Age tradition).

The backward and sheltered environment of the De Silva home is the space in which Leonor's only daughter, Luisa, receives a domestic education free from supposedly corrupting outside influences. Leonor establishes for Luisa an education program primarily based on religion and the cultivation of Luisa's domestic skills:

> No tuvo maestros de música ni de baile, ni de ningún género de habilidad; en compensación conocía todos los secretos de la economía doméstica, era sobresaliente en el bastidor y la almohadilla, conocía los primeros rudimentos de la aritmética y la geografía, podía recitar de memoria la historia sagrada y estaba medianamente instruida en la profana, con lo cual nada le faltaba, según el criterio de su madre, para poder llamarse una mujer instruida.[13]

> She did not have music or dance instructors, nor teachers of any particular skill: in compensation she knew all of the secrets of domestic economy, she was outstanding in the art of needlepoint frames and pincushions (embroidery and sewing), she knew the basics of arithmetic and geography, she could recite

> Biblical history from memory and knew a bit of secular history, therefore she lacked nothing, according to her mother's criteria, to prevent her from being able to call herself a well-educated woman.

Leonor thus carefully supervises her daughter's education and protects Luisa against possible outside influences, especially those of the young modern girls her age.[14] Leonor also shelters Luisa from girls who are educated according to a more liberal French program, which she blames for Spain's becoming infected with bad habits.[15] What Leonor does not grasp, however, is that the convent-like walls she has built around her daughter are not completely impermeable. Luisa receives from her uncle Francisco novels, such as *Paul and Virginia* and *Robinson Crusoe*, forbidden by her mother. Bernardin de Saint-Pierre's novel in particular functions as a suggestive intertext to *Dos mujeres*, particularly in the similarity between Paul and Virginia's naive and innocent love and Luisa and Carlos's idyllic marriage in Seville. The contrast of a paradisiacal setting and a corrupt urban society is also exemplified in both novels. Leonor's censoring of Luisa's books reflects the increased anxiety over women's reading practices in eighteenth- and nineteenth-century Europe.[16] Reading not only provided women with a way of being connected with the outside world but could also—in the case of certain types of fiction, such as sentimental novels and French literature—incite dangerous desires in women, as noted by Jacqueline Pearson.[17] Yet even though Luisa reads the novels Francisco gives her, she is not an overtly rebellious girl and does not challenge her mother's plans for her future.

Carlos and Luisa cultivate their pure, familial relationship in the De Silva home, where the patio, with its fragrant floral decor, provides a *locus amoenus* for the young lovers, making it "la única atmósfera en que debía vivir aquel ángel"[18] (the only atmosphere in which that angel should live). This reference to Luisa as an angel, just one of several in the novel, is important not only because it describes Luisa's physical characteristics—blonde and almost ethereal—but also because it reflects the popular nineteenth-century social ideal of woman as the angel in the house.[19] Luisa incarnates this ideal of the pure, self-abnegating, domestic woman who Bridget A. Aldaraca explains is "not defined ontologically, not functionally, but territorially by the space that she occupies."[20] Once married, Luisa and Carlos live a period of domestic bliss in which neither feels the need to leave their home. Luisa becomes *la perfecta casada*[21] (the perfect married woman) and maintains absolute domestic order:

> La salud de doña Leonor, que decaía rápidamente, y el hábito de una vida recogida, hacían que Luisa no saliese casi nunca de su casa. Carlos, feliz con su vida doméstica, se había separado también de toda sociedad. ¿Qué necesidad hay de placeres cuando se tiene ventura? Luisa había sustituido a su madre en los cuidados domésticos, y asistía a la anciana con esmero y

> ternura verdaderamente filiales. Sabía cumplir estos deberes sin descuidar un momento a su marido.[22]
>
> Doña Leonor's health, which was in rapid decline, and the habit of cloistered life, caused Luisa never to leave her home. Carlos, delighted with his domestic life, had also separated himself from society. What need is there for pleasure when one has such good fortune? Luisa had assumed her mother's domestic routine, and she assisted the elderly woman with dutiful care and the tenderness of a loyal daughter. She knew how to meet these duties without ever neglecting her husband.

The narrator thereby implies that Luisa and Carlos's pure love is secure within the walls of their home, which serves as a sanctuary for their marriage. Both represent the bourgeois ideal of family life, protected by economic comfort and placed within a private sphere.

However, this private sphere was generally seen as feminine during the nineteenth century in Spain. Indeed, Mar Soria López posits that "the emerging bourgeois conceptualization of the female sex and the home was so successful in permeating the national psyche that it came to seem the only natural and universal mode of existence for women."[23] It is therefore not surprising that only a few months after their marriage, Carlos is called on to take care of a matter outside the home. The De Silvas receive word from Madrid about the death of a family member who has bequeathed his estate to Francisco and Leonor. Taking advantage of the opportunity to give his son the experience of court life, Francisco sends Carlos to make arrangements on his behalf. Carlos's trip from Seville to Madrid and his temporary separation from his wife, Luisa, mark his foray into the masculine public sphere and the modern cosmopolitan space of Madrid.

Immediately upon his arrival in Madrid and his exit from the Atocha train station, Madrid and Seville are set in opposition; the former is filled with continuous activity in contrast to the tranquility of the latter. A fellow train passenger of Carlos's, as he sets foot in Madrid again, exclaims, "Hela allí, a la Hermosa villa, con su brillante irregularidad, sus numerosos paseos, sus cuarenta y dos plazas . . . Madrid no es España: Madrid es Madrid; fuera de aquí no se vive"[24] (There it is, the beautiful city, with its brilliant irregularity, its numerous promenades, its forty-two plazas . . . Madrid is not Spain: Madrid is Madrid; one does not truly live outside of here). This comment highlights Madrid as a world set apart from the rest of Spain, a separate universe that can exist almost on its own.

After his arrival in Madrid, Carlos's cousin Elvira contacts him and has him brought to her house. When they first meet, Carlos distinguishes Elvira from his beloved Luisa and perceives a polarity between these two women. Unlike the quiet, prudent, provincial Luisa, Elvira is imposing, loquacious, and worldly. The extroverted Elvira is a widow who lives her life unconcerned with ideals of domesticity. Carlos's initial criticism of Elvira reflects his traditional understanding of women's roles, embodied by Leonor and Luisa. He negatively judges Elvira immediately and distinguishes her from his wife and aunt, thereby differentiating between the spaces these women inhabit. Leonor and Luisa are relegated mostly to the private domestic space and the province of Seville, while Elvira inhabits the public, cosmopolitan sphere of Madrid's salons and theaters. Furthermore, unlike Leonor, Elvira gives her daughters a well-rounded education, which includes sending them abroad, unlike the De Silva women, who were educated in the home. If Leonor and Luisa are the embodiment of traditional Spain and uphold its values and morals, then Elvira symbolizes the modern, progressive values associated with France. By crossing the frontier between his home and Madrid and between Luisa and Elvira, Carlos travels not only from a private, intimate space to a public one but also from a traditional yet backward Spain to a progressive and modernized one.

However, women's inhabitancy of the public sphere is problematized even in the capital, as the reader soon discovers through the character of Catalina de S. (the countess of S.). Catalina is also the antithesis of the domestic angel. Carlos first learns of Catalina at a social gathering where he overhears a conversation about Catalina's problematic public image as an independent coquette who is indiscreet about her affairs with men. One of the guests criticizes Catalina's failure to adhere to the social norms for women: "La condesa de S. no piensa y habla como debiera, y esta es una falta remarcable"[25] (The countess of S. does not think or speak as she should, and this is a remarkable defect). Catalina is also criticized for contravening societal expectations for women by showing off her talents and intelligence. After she is praised by some of the guests, another asserts, "Detesto a esas mujeres hombres que de todo hablan, que de todo entienden, que de nadie necesitan"[26] (I detest these manly women who speak of everything, who understand everything, who need no one). The pejorative term *mujeres hombres* (manly women) was commonly used in the nineteenth century to refer to a woman who was too much like a man in that she acted in ways that only men could, such as displaying her intelligence publicly, acting or speaking independently, or attempting to fill a public position reserved only for men.[27] This comment reflects the reactions that Catalina's unconventional behavior invites even in Madrid; while she receives admiration and praise for her unique character from some, she is also subjected to harsh criticism for her deviation from expected social roles from others. Thus even in the capital, women are reproached by society for being too iconoclastic in public. In this way, the reader also witnesses the price a woman must pay for defying gender norms, even in Madrid's upper-class society. In other words, the facile dichotomy between modern Madrid and traditional Seville is problematized in regard to women.

Catalina's use of her home for entertainment purposes also blurs the public and private spheres. Despite Catalina's being the subject of rumors in Madrid's high society, she opens her home to the very people who circulate the rumors. Unlike the insularity of Leonor's house in Seville, Catalina's home functions as a social space for the gathering of Madrid's upper echelons. Her *tertulia* (regular social gathering to discuss society, ideas, and the arts) is modeled after the seventeenth- and eighteenth-century French salons that Dena Goodman describes as often galvanized by the presence of beautiful and educated patronesses.[28] By making her home the very center of public society, Catalina undermines the idea of the home as an exclusively domestic space.

Furthermore, in contrast to Luisa, Catalina enjoys public attention and appears to pride herself on keeping her audience's eyes on her by entertaining them with her physical charms, her multiple talents (singing, dancing, etc.), and even her public love affairs. In this way, Catalina represents the enlightened women with whom Luisa is contrasted. A native of France, Catalina married a Spanish count and rose in wealth and status through marriage. Thus it is a combination of her French nationality and her status as a wealthy, aristocratic widow that allows her to flout convention despite continued public censure.

The second half of the novel, with its focus on Catalina and Carlos's battle between their newfound love and the moral implications of their adulterous affair, sets up another spatial dichotomy: nature versus society. Both Carlos and Catalina are aware of the social definition of their love as "sinful" and/or "criminal." Catalina summarizes their dilemma, invoking nature in defense of their love and questioning society's label of a natural instinct as "criminal": "¿Y por qué, por qué injuriar nuestros corazones creyéndolos incapaces de sentimientos nobles y santos? ¿Qué es el amor? ¿No es la más involuntaria y bella de las pasiones del hombre? El adulterio dicen que es un crimen, pero no hay adulterio para el corazón. El hombre puede ser responsable de sus acciones, no de sus sentimientos. ¿Por qué sería un crimen en usted amarme? ¿No podría sentir por mí más que un amor adúltero y criminal?"[29] (And why, why disrespect our hearts by believing that they are incapable of noble and virtuous sentiments? What is love? Is it not mankind's most involuntary and beautiful passion? They say adultery is a crime, but there is no adultery for the heart. Man can be responsible for his actions, but not his sentiments. Why would it be a crime for you to love me? Could you feel for me anything but an adulterous and criminal love?). Here Catalina begins to develop a central philosophy that informs the second part of the novel: the disparity between natural inclinations and the laws of society. She suggests a conflict by contrasting nature, which is manifested through the impulse of human emotion, with societal laws that forbid love outside the artificial institution of marriage and concludes that one is irrelevant to the other. Surprisingly, after meeting Catalina and seeing the deep affection she feels for Carlos, Luisa herself concludes that Catalina is Carlos's true wife based on natural laws: "Ella es realmente su esposa, pensaba. La naturaleza le ha concedido un derecho de que me ha privado"[30] (She is truly his wife, she thought. Nature has bestowed on her a right of which it has deprived me).

With these arguments, the novel represents Rousseauian thought by suggesting that societal institutions constrict benevolent, natural human instincts.[31] During her period of intellectual exploration, Catalina mentions reading Rousseau, among other writers.[32] However, here again, the social and natural spheres are conflated on the question of women's roles. A woman's "natural" role, as expressed to Sophie in Rousseau's *Émile or On Education* (1762), is to educate her children and foster her husband's happiness, independence, and security within the family.[33] Since Rousseau defines the family as the very basis of moral society, the happy man will be a good husband and, in turn, a good citizen.[34] Rousseau's view of the role of women as keeping the family together and in harmony is similar to the angel in the house discourses embodied by Luisa. Thus the social and the natural are blurred in the case of women. Perhaps for this reason, Catalina is unable to disregard completely what she sees as Carlos's social obligation to his family: "No es libre. Tiene una patria, una familia, una esposa . . . será forzoso que vuelva a ellas"[35] (He is not free. He has a nation, a family, a wife . . . he must return to them). Catalina relates his commitment to his family to his loyalty to his nation, suggesting, as Rousseau did, a connection between the private (family) and the public (nation) spheres. Thus by violating his marriage, he is not only a deviant husband but also a deviant citizen.

It is precisely Catalina's inability to reconcile societal laws with her love for Carlos, as well as her inability to find acceptance as an independent woman even in the more modern and cosmopolitan world of Madrid, that lead to her ultimate suicide. However, while the novel forecloses all these dichotomous spaces to Catalina—Madrid/Seville, tradition/modernity, nature/society—before her death, an alternative space is opened up to her, the space of female friendship and solidarity. Catalina and Luisa meet when Luisa travels to Madrid in search of her absent husband and learns of his affair. Avellaneda modifies the traditional outcome of the *folletín* love triangle in which two women (or two men) become rivals and instead brings her two female characters together through an empathetic bond. In their first encounter, Luisa recognizes the genuine suffering and love in Catalina's eyes and concludes that she rightfully deserves Carlos's love.[36] As a result, Catalina is awed by Luisa's humble abnegation, and the two women share a moment of trust and affection: "Dos corazones, ligados en aquel momento por sentimientos generosos, se confiaron el uno al otro. ¡Y eran dos corazones de mujer sin embargo!"[37] (Two hearts, bound in that moment by generous feelings, they trusted in one another. And they were two female hearts nevertheless!). It is shortly after this meeting that Catalina decides to take her own life out of love for both Carlos and Luisa. In a letter she leaves for Elvira and Luisa to read, she writes, "No llores por mí. No lamentes mi vida tronchada en flor. La muerte no se me presenta bajo un aspecto lúgubre. Véola como un ángel libertador que Dios envía al infortunio. . . . El designio de la providencia me ha cumplido. El amor salva mi alma, y mi muerte expía mi amor"[38] (Do not cry for me. Do not lament my life cut off in full flower. Death does not present itself to me under a mournful guise. I see it as a freeing angel that God has sent in my misfortune. . . . Providence's plan for me has been fulfilled. Love saves my soul, and my death expiates my love).

The bond between Luisa and Catalina reminds us of Virginia Woolf's assertion that women novelists of the nineteenth century began to add a new dimension to the relationships between women.[39] Avellaneda does indeed make her female character's relationships more complex, especially through her representation of the connection between Luisa and Catalina. Avellaneda emphasizes the rarity of this type of relationship by stating, as we saw earlier, that it was the hearts of two women, not of a man and woman, that became united. In creating this unique relationship, Avellaneda opens a space for female solidarity and criticizes the limited gender roles and social restrictions to which both women are subjected.

In fact, it is through these two women's encounter that each finds a wholeness that neither was able to attain before. By taking her own life to ensure the happiness of Carlos and Luisa, Catalina exhibits altruism and selflessness, characteristics unexpected from the femme fatale and usually associated with the angel in the house. In Kirkpatrick's words, in her final act, Catalina "in a sense subsumes and preserves the angelic goodness of her rival in a more heroic and complex gesture."[40] Similarly, Luisa, despite her initial innocence and her conventional behavior throughout most of the novel, takes on the psychological anguish of Catalina. Luisa follows a psychologically human trajectory through doubt, anguish, and despair until she reaches the moment of sublime compassion and solidarity with Catalina, a choice Luisa voluntarily makes. In this manner, each woman finds wholeness only through uniting with her alter image.

Catalina's suicide also opens up another space for liberation: death. Although Lucía Guerra has interpreted Catalina's suicide as her only escape from the patriarchal restrictions on women in her society, it can also be read as a symbolic act of empowerment.[41] This idea is further underscored by Catalina's reference to death as an "ángel libertador" (liberating angel); unlike the angel in the house that confines women to a domestic space, this angel of death frees Catalina. Thus I concur with Pastor, who interprets Catalina's suicide as personal transcendence over desire (her rejection of Carlos at the end) and sees her death as a regeneration, or a way of reconnecting with her true self and becoming divine.[42]

Although Catalina's death has strong spiritual-religious connotations, it also has implications for her physical body. Toward the end, the novel suggests that Catalina became pregnant during her affair with Carlos; therefore, by committing suicide, she also sacrifices the life of her unborn child.[43] Jennifer Patterson

Parrack has proposed that Catalina's suicide while pregnant represents a more radical rejection of "the ultimate traditional assignation of identity for women, maternity, in favor of sorority, putting the desire for the possible happiness of her supposed rival, Luisa, ahead of her own child's need to survive."[44] Thus Catalina's suicide is a rejection of positivist and materialist views of women that argued that a women's entire existence was necessarily shaped by her reproductive anatomy and its function.

Through female characters unable to find satisfactorily inhabitable spaces within the public/private, modern/traditional, masculine/feminine, social/natural binary spheres, Avellaneda underscores the inadequacy of such divisions and of the meaning given to these spaces. Avellaneda brings home this lesson at the end of the novel, after Catalina has committed suicide and Luisa lives embittered and ignored by her husband. Carlos's cousin Elvira tells her daughters, one coincidentally blonde and angelic and the other dark with fiery eyes, "Cuando tengáis algunos años más, hijas mías, os contaré una historia triste: la historia de dos mujeres, ambas muy generosas, muy bellas y muy desventuradas. Esa historia será para vosotras una lección provechosa"[45] (When you are a bit older, I will tell you a sad story: the story of two women, both very generous, very beautiful, and ill fated. That story will be a useful lesson for you). Thus the separate spheres that led both Catalina and Luisa to live limited and unfulfilled lives will likely come to haunt the two sisters who, symbolically, through their physique, represent the angel in the house / femme fatale, domestic/public, feminine/masculine, traditional/modern binaries that were the undoing of both Catalina and Luisa. The ending of the novel implies, therefore, that the future generations of Spanish women will have to overcome these binary oppositions in order to find true happiness. And as their respective repressive gendered spaces are initially tied to geographical areas—provincial and traditional Seville and the modern capital Madrid—women's struggles are also explicitly connected to the divisions within a fragmented Spanish nation, suggesting that integrity, both individual and national, will require transcending these spatial divisions altogether.

NOTES

1. See Elena Grau-Llevería, "El romanticismo social en *Dos mujeres* de Gertrudis Gómez de Avellaneda," *Bulletin of Spanish Studies* 87, no. 1 (2010): 31–49; Brígida M. Pastor, "A Romance Life in Novel Fiction: The Early Career and Works of Gertrudis Gómez de Avellaneda," *Bulletin of Hispanic Studies* 75, no. 1 (1998): 169–181; and Joan Torres-Pou, "La Avellaneda y *Dos mujeres*: Un insólito alegato femenino en la literatura decimonónica," *Ojáncano* 22 (2002): 21–32.

2. See María de los Ángeles Ayala, "Dos mujeres: Novela reinvindicativa de Gertrudis Gómez de Avellaneda," in *Del romanticismo a la Guerra Civil. Actas del XII Congreso de la Asociación Internacional de Hispanistas 22–26 de agosto de 1995*, vol. 4, ed. Derek Flitter (Birmingham: Birmingham University Press, 1998), 76–83; Nancy LaGreca, "Literatura

y conciencia: El suicidio femenino en el *Álbum cubano de lo bueno y lo bello* (1860) y *Dos mujeres* (1842–1843) de Gertrudis Gómez Avellaneda," *Revolución y Cultura* 47, no. 4 (2006): 12–16; Pastor, "Romance Life in Novel Fiction," 169–181; and Torres-Pou, "Avellaneda y *Dos mujeres*," 22–32.

3. Pastor, "Romance Life in Novel Fiction," 169–181.

4. Susan Kirkpatrick, *Las Románticas: Women Writers and Subjectivity in Spain, 1835–1850* (Berkeley: University of California Press, 1989).

5. Gertrudis Gómez de Avellaneda, *Dos mujeres* (La Habana: Letras Cubanas, 2000), 5.

6. "19th-Century Spain, Overview: Politics," Spain Then and Now, last modified July 6, 2009, http://www.spainthenandnow.com.

7. Gómez de Avellaneda, *Dos mujeres*, 12.

8. Gómez de Avellaneda, 13.

9. Jesús Torrecilla, *España exótica: La formación de la imagen española moderna* (Boulder, Colo.: Society of Spanish and Spanish-American Studies, 2004), 4.

10. Gómez de Avellaneda, *Dos mujeres*, 13.

11. Noël Valis, *The Culture of Cursilería: Bad Taste, Kitsch, and Class in Modern Spain* (Durham, N.C.: Duke University Press, 2002), 8.

12. Torrecilla, *España exótica*, 4.

13. Gómez de Avellaneda, *Dos mujeres*, 11.

14. Gómez de Avellaneda, 12.

15. Gómez de Avellaneda, 12.

16. Some possible explanations for the censorship of *Paul and Virginia* could be its strong Rousseauian influence, the French origin of its author (which Leonor would strongly oppose), and the novel's supposedly infamous negative effects on its readers, especially its female audience. See Jacques-Henri Bernardin de Saint-Pierre, *Paul and Virginia*, trans. Paul Donovan (London: Peter Owen, 1982).

17. Jacqueline Pearson, *Women's Reading in Britain, 1750–1835: A Dangerous Recreation* (Cambridge: Cambridge University Press, 1999), 2. Instead, women were told to read conduct books, magazines, and domestic novels that indoctrinated them in their ideal relationship to the family and home. See Lou Charnon-Deutsch, *Narratives of Desire: Nineteenth-Century Spanish Fiction by Women* (University Park: Pennsylvania State University Press, 1994), 17.

18. Gómez de Avellaneda, *Dos mujeres*, 35.

19. Although the term *ángel del hogar* (angel in the house) did not circulate widely in the press and popular literature until after the 1850s in Spain, a neo-Catholic religious language is used to discuss the "appropriate" role or mission of women throughout the nineteenth century. With the rise of the bourgeoisie and the separation of spheres, middle-class women especially are not only relegated to the private domestic sphere but made to represent the moral center of society and to function as virtuous guardians of the home. See Catherine Jagoe, "La misión de la mujer," in *La mujer en los discursos de género: Textos y contextos en el siglo XIX*, ed. Catherine Jagoe et al. (Barcelona: Icaria, 1998), 21–53. This figure, appearing in images in the bourgeois press of the late nineteenth century, reminded women of their natural inclination to sacrifice themselves for the good of their family (Charnon-Deutsch, *Narratives of Desire*, 56) and was used as a way of emphasizing their "passionlessness," or denial of sexual desire, in order to concentrate only on maternal tenderness (Kirkpatrick, *Románticas*, 7). The angel in the house also became a status symbol of the man who does not need a working wife; it ranked among the various decorations

and products of an elite consumer society that was still exploring which images best symbolized wealth and distinction (Charnon-Deutsch, *Narratives of Desire*, 54).

20. Bridget A. Aldaraca, *El ángel del hogar: Galdós and the Ideology of Domesticity in Spain* (Chapel Hill: University of North Carolina Press, 1991), 27.

21. The inscription of domesticity onto women's roles was not invented in nineteenth-century Spain. Already in the sixteenth century, we see two popular texts, Juan Luis Vives, *Instrucción de la mujer cristiana* (1524); and Fray Luis de León, *La perfecta casada* (1583), prescribing female behavior in the home (Jagoe, "Misión de la mujer," 26). These texts remained in circulation in the nineteenth century and were used alongside female conduct manuals, as we see in *Dos mujeres*, when Fray Luis de León is mentioned among Luisa's list of approved readings (Gómez de Avellaneda, *Dos mujeres*, 65).

22. Gómez de Avellaneda, *Dos mujeres*, 48.

23. Mar Soria López, "Homebound Workers and the Destabilization of Bourgeois Domestic Space in Benito Pérez Galdós's *Tormento* (1884) and Emilia Pardo Bazán's 'Casi artista' and 'El mundo' (1908)," *Revista de Estudios Hispánicos* 48, no. 3 (2014): 571–595.

24. Gómez de Avellaneda, *Dos mujeres*, 57.

25. Gómez de Avellaneda, 75.

26. Gómez de Avellaneda, 73.

27. Avellaneda also faced public criticism from her male detractors for not adhering to the traditional social roles for women. Male critics of the time often noted her delicate physical beauty and "womanly" attributes, which seemed to contrast disturbingly with her "manly" talent for writing. Even her literary admirers were unable to accept her intelligence. Bretón de los Herreros, who valued her good character and her literary work's spiritual and expressive force, spoke highly of her in terms men used: "¡Es mucho hombre esta mujer!" (José Servera, introduction to *Sab*, by Gertrudis Gómez de Avellaneda [Madrid: Cátedra, 1999], 19; This woman is quite a man!). José Zorrilla offered another famous description of Avellaneda in his *Recuerdos del tiempo viejo*: "Era una mujer; pero lo era, sin duda, por error de la naturaleza, que había metido por distracción un alma de hombre en aquella envoltura de carne femenina" (21; She was a woman; but she was, without a doubt, by nature's error, which had mistakenly placed by distraction a man's soul in that fleshy female wrapping). Zorrilla's quote again stresses the social values concerning women's nature and that those women who diverged from the traditional model of femininity were perceived as monstrous, ambiguous, or anomalous.

28. Dena Goodman, "Enlightenment Salons: The Convergence of Female and Philosophic Ambitions," *Eighteenth-Century Studies* 22, no. 3 (1989): 342.

29. Gómez de Avellaneda, *Dos mujeres*, 192.

30. Gómez de Avellaneda, 292.

31. Avellaneda shows her knowledge of Jean-Jacques Rousseau by using the image of the "savage" living in a state of nature for the construction of her epistolary self in her *Autobiografía* to underscore her impulsive and primitive tendencies as a young girl. This behavior prevented the young Avellaneda from meeting her family's expectations of a proper girl. See Gertrudis Gómez de Avellaneda, *Autobiografía y epistolarios de amor* (Newark, Del.: Juan de la Cuesta, 1999), 54.

32. Gómez de Avellaneda, *Dos mujeres*, 138.

33. Jean-Jacques Rousseau, *Emile or On Education*, trans. Allan Bloom (New York: Basic Books, 1979), 134.

34. Rousseau, 133.

35. Gómez de Avellaneda, *Dos mujeres*, 212.
36. Gómez de Avellaneda, 292.
37. Gómez de Avellaneda, 293.
38. Gómez de Avellaneda, 320.
39. Virginia Woolf, *A Room of One's Own* (London: Harcourt, 1981), 82.
40. Kirkpatrick, *Románticas*, 173.
41. Lucía Guerra, "Estrategias femeninas en la elaboración del sujeto romántico en la obra de Gertrudis Gómez de Avellaneda," *Revista Iberoamericana* 51, nos. 132/133 (1985): 722.
42. Brígida M. Pastor, *Fashioning Feminism in Cuba and Beyond* (New York: Peter Lang, 2003), 139.
43. Gómez de Avellaneda, *Dos mujeres*, 115.
44. Jennifer Patterson Parrack, "Masquerade and Women's Writing in Spain: Gertrudis Gómez de Avellaneda's *Dos mujeres*," *Philological Review* 29, no. 1 (2003): 41.
45. Gómez de Avellaneda, *Dos mujeres*, 327.

CHAPTER 9

Caterina Albert i Paradís

WRITING, SOLITUDE, AND WOMAN'S *JOUISSANCE*

Neus Carbonell
Translated by Lourdes Albuixech

Víctor Català, Caterina Albert i Paradís's masculine pseudonym, functioned as a mask for the public image of a woman who was born in the bosom of a traditional Catalan family and who maintained a position independent of the discourses of her day. It is perhaps the manner in which she protected her own heterogeneity vis-à-vis the reality in which she lived, without the need to overtly confront that reality, that constitutes what is most remarkable about the position she adopted. She dissociated herself from many of the feminist discourses that vindicated the figure of the woman writer as well as from the literary currents of her time. Furthermore, she distanced herself from reigning conventions of gender and class, she wrote whatever pleased her or what she deemed she needed to write, and she lived the way she wanted or the way she believed she ought to live. And despite all this, she managed to remain within the limits of her society and to savor literary success. She was never an outsider, nor did she seek to become one. Moreover, she never sacrificed what she called her independence. In fact, in response to the scandal caused by the discovery that her excessively daring texts had been penned by a woman, by 1926 she was already querying, "¿És que pot tenir limits l'obra de l'artista? No crec que unes normes morals puguin frenar-la. Crec elemental advocar por la independència de l'art. Gràcies a aquesta independència he pogut ser fidel a la meva vocació que tothom hauria volgut intervenir"[1] (Can there be limits to an artist's work? I don't think moral norms can rein it in. I think advocating for the independence of art is fundamental. Thanks to that independence I have been able to be faithful to my vocation, which everyone would have tried to censure). Indeed, independence and fidelity to herself describe the foundations of the desire inspiring Albert's literary production. Maria-Aurèlia Capmany summarizes this drive in a single sentence: "Pero és cert que a Caterina Albert li calia molta més energia i decisió para vèncer l'astorament que la seva obra produïa, que a la més agressiva defensora del *Women's Lib* per organitzar un mitting"[2] (But it is undeniable that Caterina Albert required much more energy and determination to overcome the astonishment that her work produced than the most aggressive defender of *Women's Lib* needed to organize a meeting). In the dedication Caterina Albert wrote in 1964 to her biographer, Josep Miracle, she refers to him as "ilustre iluminador de una *figura oscura*"[3] (illustrious illuminator of an *obscure figure*). Let us take a closer look at the curious way in which she characterizes herself, at age ninety-five, in this dedication as "an obscure figure." This metaphor may hold the key to the persona (in the classical sense of the term) that she created for others and, who knows, perhaps also for herself.

The future author Caterina Albert i Paradís was born in 1869 in L'Escala, a small fishing town on the Catalan coast. However, her well-off family lived with its back toward the sea, as was fitting for the upper classes. Fishing was an occupation only for the poorest individuals. Caterina Albert's father was a lawyer and a politician. Her mother was the daughter of rural landowners from L'Escala. Caterina's biography describes a lonely childhood, marked by the stories her grandmother told her, which revolved around the rural life of her surroundings and that, presumably, she used as literary material for her works. Despite the fact that her siblings studied and moved to Barcelona—even her youngest sister, at Caterina's own request—she remained in the family's household taking care of her mother and grandmother, especially after her father's premature death. It is worth mentioning that a girl from the moneyed class was not allowed to leave the house unaccompanied. Therefore, her sheltered existence was imposed by the rigorous social conventions of the day. Nonetheless, Albert managed to get her own room from very early on, and it is my hypothesis that throughout her life, she strived to keep this space, a room of her own protected from the gaze of the Other. I find almost funny her biographer's emphasis on the fact that what enabled Caterina Albert to become a writer was precisely her being a woman, a condition that exempted her from having to study and obtain a professional position that would have inevitably—he argues—distanced her from a writing career. Yet it is indeed of interest for the purpose of this article to elucidate in what way Albert's femininity intersects with her pen.

Of the biographical details confirmed by the writer, I want to emphasize the circumstances of her life experience that she herself highlighted, such as her precocious interest in both painting and writing. There is, however, a difference between the two. While her family was aware of, and encouraged, her pictorial bent, she began writing in absolute solitude. This signifier, solitude, which serves as the title of her most successful novel, *Solitud* (*Solitude*; 1905), and that critics have frequently underscored as a fundamental aspect of the author's own life, should not be overlooked.

To be sure, it is impossible to know what the woman Caterina Albert's experience of solitude was like. We can only hope to uncover its traces in her texts and only do so by proceeding in a cautious way. In this sense, my hypothesis in this article is that Caterina Albert's narrative is an incursion into a woman's solitude, linked to her *jouissance* of being, to put it in Lacanian terms.[4] I will examine in detail her best-known novel, *Solitud*. In addition, I will attempt to demonstrate the unique way the author used writing to *symptomatically* treat her experience of *jouissance*.[5]

We know of two testimonial episodes that took place at pivotal moments of Caterina Albert's relationship with the written word. In both cases, the act of writing is revealed as what ought to remain hidden from the Other's gaze.[6] I contend that the well-known division that Albert maintained throughout her existence between her public figure and her private life, together with her use of the same masculine pseudonym, were her way of solving the tension arising from an experience of intimate *jouissance* that at the same time included and excluded, in an impossible paradox, the Other's gaze.

The first episode, related by her biographer, narrates how her family discovered her literary interests but, above all, indicates how these interests depended on solitude and modesty. Indeed, it seems that writing was from the beginning the manifestation of a solitary enjoyment that made the Other's gaze unbearable. Thus her biographer tells how Caterina was writing in the attic of her house—seemingly her stronghold—when she heard her parents coming upstairs. When they saw her, she felt "com atrapada en un delicte i optà per amagar-se" (as if she were caught in a crime and chose to hide). Her father found her writings, read them, and finally stated, "Aquesta mosseta escriurà" (That little girl will write). To her, this was an experience of "por i vergonya" (fear and shame) that did not change the fact that she continued writing "d'amagat"[7] (secretly). What needs to be emphasized about this episode is that Albert did not hide her writings. On the contrary, it seems like she left them in plain sight of her parents and that she was the one who ran to hide. This episode summarizes what the life of the future author was like. She does not conceal her creations from the public gaze, but she zealously hides herself, first behind a masculine pseudonym, keeping her distance from public life, and even disappearing inside what have been dubbed "sus silencios" (her silences). Indeed, it is in this sense that later on I will reflect on the writer's "largos periodos de silencio" (long periods of silence) and their relationship to the impossibility of her hiding any longer behind a secret identity. Likewise, the transgressive aspect of the writing act deserves attention. Caterina felt like a criminal, according to her own words. In this context, it is perhaps not for nothing that the monologue that drove her to hide forever behind a pen name has as its protagonist a woman who kills her newborn daughter and who recounts the story from her cell in a mental hospital. As we will see, there seems to be a reason for this.

This brings us to the second noteworthy testimonial episode. It happened after Caterina Albert won a literary contest with her dramatic monologue *La infanticida* (*Infanticide*; 1898). Nela, the main character, is a young woman who has been seduced and abandoned by her lover. Her condition as a woman and a poor peasant seduced by a young, attractive, wealthy man has relegated her to utter solitude during both her pregnancy and childbirth. First, the monologue narrates the seduction and sexual desire. Then it describes her abandonment, her fear of the community's gossip, and the paternal threats she endures. The text confronts class and gender conventions. Young Nela relates her passion as openly as she does her resolve to reject any suitors her father likes. As a desiring subject, she contravenes the class and gender dictates of her time. Madness is the price paid for transgression. Nonetheless, there is nothing, not even the ax her father uses to threaten her, that can keep her from her desire. Nela remains loyal to her love and her desire even while delirious and imprisoned. How is this meant to be read? Are madness and confinement in a psychiatric hospital metaphors for a passion that is "incòmoda, excessiva, fora del temps"[8] (bothersome, excessive, inopportune)—to appropriate the terms Capmany uses to describe Albert herself? Nela's monologue is in no way that of a subjugated subject. Her madness keeps her freedom intact. For the spectator, what remains is the drama of a child-killing mother, a dishonored daughter, and a young woman locked up.

Nela's monologue opens with a reference to the gaze: "Aquí també, com allà dalt, me miren i em pregunten, perseguint-me sempre"[9] (Here also, as up there, they look at me and ask me questions, always pursuing me). It continues with her father's gaze: "Em mirà fit a fit" (He looks at me intently), immediately after which he moves toward the ax: "El pare s'alça i despenja la falç . . . i se la mira"[10] (Father stands and takes the ax off the hook . . . and looks at it). The persecutory object, the threatening Other's gaze located on the ax, pursues Nela.[11] For this reason, the object can exercise all its violence without even being used. And in the end, after having thrown her newborn daughter under the weight of the millstone, the gaze is there once again: "Tots me guaitaven, amb ulls més badats"[12] (They all spied on me with their eyes wide open). Nela has tried fruitlessly to keep her *jouissance* outside the Other's gaze: she escapes at night to meet her lover, she covers up her pregnant body, she lives childbirth in silence and solitude, and she tries to quiet her daughter. But once the latter starts weeping and bawling, Nela can no longer hide. At this moment, her only escape is derangement. The monologue ends with Nela's desire to flee to France, "lluny del pare . . . i la falç . . . i aquella . . . mola"[13] (far from father . . . and the ax . . . and that . . . millstone).

The very last sentence of the monologue warrants close attention: "Aquella mola . . . que no vull . . . que m'esclafi . . . cap més . . . nena"[14] (That millstone . . .

that I don't want . . . to flatten me . . . ever again . . . little girl). First, the *mola* (millstone) is the text's most prominent signifier. In effect, it occupies the place in the text that Jacques Lacan reserves for the master signifier, or S1.[15] It horrifies Nela: its incessant noise makes her lose her mind, men gather around it to work, her father uses it to sharpen his ax, Nela gives birth beside it, and lastly, she throws her newborn girl under its weight. Marta Pessarrodona, a poet and author of a recent biography of Caterina Albert, recounts an anecdote about how the writer herself paid a visit to the owners of a mill in order to ask them about the millstone and whether its weight could kill a newborn.[16] What does this signifier embody—a signifier whose movement returns unceasingly, a signifier that is repetitive, unstoppable, and responsible for Nela's tragic destiny and from whose terror she yearns to escape? The reading of the monologue's last sentence affords us different meanings depending on how we order its punctuation. In fact, for Jacques Lacan, how the signifying chain is punctuated is a way to interpret the unconscious, since it allows for the repressed signified to reveal itself. Following this idea, the ambiguity of the last sentence of the monologue reveals what is repressed in Nela's discourse: "That / millstone / that I don't want / to flatten me / ever again / little girl." There is, of course, a sense effect in the reading: "I don't want that millstone to flatten me a little girl ever," resulting from a reordering of what Nela has told us up to then. However, other punctuation would give us other meanings: "That millstone that I don't want," "I don't want to flatten me any female," "That flattens me," "Little girl." The divisions reveal the overdetermined value of the *mola*. Surely, it signals the S1[17] under which the subject falls: the *mola*'s weight suspended over Nela but also the character's desire to be located in a great beyond far from the crushing presence of the *mola*.

Mola is thus the S1, the master signifier that controls the meaning of the text. But a second signified, an S2,[18] is required in order to produce a signifying chain. As we know, Lacan reduced the signifying chain to the minimal pair S1-S2, the effect of which is the subject expressed as $. The subject remains from the outset under the weight of the S1 only if the S1 can be tied together with another signifier that emerges as its effect. This is what one can gather from Lacan's sentence: "A signifier represents a subject to another signifier."[19] Nela's solitude vis-à-vis the signifier *mola* is radical, and because of that, her being ends up crushed to the point of madness. Of course, in Lacanian psychoanalysis, madness is the isolated signifier outside of the discursive chain. Therefore, to conclude for the moment, Nela's tragedy is the tragedy of the subject unable to become represented by the signifier, a point we will return to again.[20]

It is difficult to determine whether it was an irony or a logical consequence that this tale about transgression and about the impossibility of withdrawing from the Other's gaze exposed its author to both situations. Indeed, she submitted this monologue to a literary contest and it received a prize. Consequently, she was summoned in the pages of the press (or at least, that is how she told it) by the contest's jury to appear before them to debate the difficulty of staging the text, given its contents.[21] The author herself wrote many years later, in 1948, that due to this event, "esfereïda d'aquella facecia, que podria fer pasar son nom per les boques" (terrified of that incident that could cause her name to circulate from mouth to mouth), she decided to "no donar, emparat pel mateix nom, mai mès res al públic"[22] (not ever again give the public anything connected with her own name). When the opportunity to publish arose once again, she did not hesitate to do it, but she chose a different name: Víctor Català.

Effectively, one cannot speak about woman herself without tarnishing her reputation. In her written comment, Caterina Albert notes how close a woman comes to being the object of defamation when one speaks of her. We will see later how she again addresses this issue in her novel *Solitud*. Virginia Woolf also pointed this out in *A Room of One's Own* in writing of the use of masculine pseudonyms by female writers: "The chief glory of a woman is not to be talked of, said Perciles, himself a much-talked of man."[23]

In Lacan's seminar 20, titled *Encore*, we find one of his famous quotes in reference to women. In it, he creates the following play on words: "On la dit-femme, on la diffâme"[24] (She is called woman and is defamed). All too often, to talk about women has meant to defame them. Even beyond this historical observation, with this signifying pun Lacan alludes to the impossibility of representing women. To represent her presupposes defaming her—that is, to not say the truth about her because one cannot say everything about her. We should not infer from this that women cannot find some representation in signifiers, which by definition always belong to the Other; insofar as they are symbolic, they precede the subject. It is obvious that women search for, and at times find, sites of representation in the signifiers within their reach. A good part of the studies devoted to gender consist of no more than a history, and a criticism, of the difficulties encountered by women to become accurately represented. In fact, gender studies highlight the very complexity of such representation. Aside from the fact that obviously not all representations are the same, nor do they have the same consequences in the social order, female existence makes clear, or at least has made clear throughout the history of humanity, the limits of representation itself. The feminine has made obvious the fact that beyond the logic of the universal—that is, of everyone—there is also the singular, and that will never be subsumable in the realm of the same.[25] I believe Caterina Albert's position can be effectively understood in light of this logic. As early as 1902, in a letter to the poet Joan Maragall regarding the scandal her works were causing due to having been penned by a woman, she bemoans, "En aquesta terra en què és mes deshonrós per una dona escriure que fer altres disbarats"[26] (In that land where it is more dishonorable for a woman to write than to commit other follies). What Caterina Albert maintains is that "in this land," it is worse for a woman to traffic in words than to transgress moral law. This comment is even more relevant if we consider the fact that her works are riddled with female characters who live their desires against the norms of their time. Is it possible, then, that these characters who struggle to live their desires on the fringes of the hegemonic are saying something about the author's own experience?

Finally, what does *La infanticida* tell that should not be told? It tells of a woman's *jouissance*, beautifully expressed metaphorically in the urgency to meet a desire that smells of "jessamí i mareselva i cent altres olors desconegudes"[27] (jasmine and honeysuckle and a hundred other unknown scents). But it is also expressed metaphorically through the very madness that preserves that desire intact—a *jouissance* that must withdraw from the Other's gaze, a *jouissance* that transgresses any discourse of order because it belongs to a woman. In other words, it cannot be represented in an S1 that would link itself to an S2. Víctor Català was the masculine identity that Caterina Albert availed herself of in order to be represented in language and to the Other. Furthermore, it was the S1 that enabled Caterina Albert to make her singularity speak as a *jouissance* of being, as an "artist," to use a term that was dear to her. Indeed, in order to protect her "independence," her use of a pseudonym played a crucial role. In a letter to poet Joan Maragall, dated October 1903, she avows her annoyance with the public's discovery of the identity she tried to mask with the name Víctor Català: "Abans jo era jo i podía escriure lo que em demanava el cor i l'enteniment; avui torno a ésser una noia, una noia de familia i d'estament determinat, que té unes determinades relacions socials, i aquestes plenes de prejudicis i cosetes, judiquen i fallen segons elles, no segons jo"[28] (Before, I was I and could write what my heart and my good sense demanded of me; today I am again a girl from a particular family and social class, who has specific social relationships, and those being filled with prejudices and nonsense, assess and pass judgment according to their own way of thinking, not mine). She lacked another name, a masculine one, in order to speak of a woman's *jouissance*. She needed a masculine countenance that would shield her from defamation. She was not shielded under the signifier *girl*, since that S1 already represented her to the Other in the conditions demanded by the Other's discourse—that is, with S2s pertaining to the Other's discourse. But Caterina Albert was not entirely that girl belonging to a "particular family and social class." Therefore, she was not wholly represented by the signifier *girl*, just as she was not represented either by the signifier *Víctor Català*, whose function was more accurately that of a countenance, or by a mask. There was something to her being, something supplementary that was represented in her identity as an artist, as we shall see.

To be sure, Caterina Albert's position is shaped by social conventions. This is why it is surprising to feminist critics that she distanced herself from a feminist movement she never sought to establish any ties with.[29] It is not difficult to read in her work a criticism of the situation of women. However, I hold fast to the idea that Albert's position goes well beyond the restrictive aspect of the social order for women. Behind her position, there is a call for a freedom and independence as a singular subject that she is unwilling to relinquish to the signifier *woman*, which would allegedly represent her. The woman signifier carries with it the proscriptions of its time and, therefore, is insufficient to speak her being, but she separates herself as well from the feminist ideas that aroused in her "una forta corrent d'antipatia"[30] (a strong current of antipathy). She chose the signifier of the artist. Certainly, the exaltation of the figure of the artist can be interpreted in accordance with the era's modernist ideology.[31] But even so, it is noteworthy that this was the only signifier that seems characteristic of Albert: an artist is always unique and unrepeatable, and her only limitation is art itself. She lived by and defended the idea of being original and of distancing herself from fads, which explains in part her "silences."[32] In fact, I find here some affinity to Isak Dinesen's *Babette's Feast*. The protagonist, a female cook, invests her whole fortune in her art, thus dedicating it entirely to pure loss: a feast that brings a community of strict believers face-to-face with ephemeral pleasure.

Ultimately, it seems as though Albert accepted the countenance of a woman of her time in order to live, quite comfortably one may add, among members of her class and culture and used that of Víctor Català to gain access to publishing—that is, to be able to submit her work as an artist to the public gaze. Surely these master signifiers allowed her a place in the Other. Far from letting herself get crushed by them, however, they afforded her the means to give voice to what it was impossible for her to say. I believe she made use of them because she was able to not become identified with them. This was necessary in order to safeguard what she called her "independence." The difference between the writer and her character Nela is that the former could do without the master signifiers (S1s—so long as she made use of them). To paraphrase one of Lacan's famous sayings in reference to the Name-of-the-Father: "One can do without the Name-of-the-Father on the condition that one makes use of it."[33] In contrast, Nela's fate is determined by abandonment and solitude. In a way, Nela showed Caterina the path she needed to avoid.

In *Solitud*, Caterina Albert seems to have taken a different perspective on the issue of a woman's solitude. It is no longer, as it was for Nela, the solitude of a forced confinement but that of a fully accepted fate that turns the isolation into a proud distancing, as indicated by Mila's upright body as she abandons the hermitage in the last paragraph of the novel. Despite the varied scholarly readings this novel has received, the detail of the protagonist's acceptance of the conditions of her own future is never called into question. The novel narrates the story of a young recently wed woman's ascent up a mountain to serve as caretaker of a hermitage together with her husband. After living there for just a few months, a time that brings not only disappointment but also the attainment of a certain wisdom, Mila leaves the mountain, the hermitage, and her husband.

Víctor Català received a commission from the editor of *Joventut* (*Youth*)—the most important cultural magazine of the time—to write a novel to be published in weekly installments. According to the author herself, it was a difficult task, and she found herself writing under the pressure of the commitment she had taken on.[34] The fragmented format of a work conceived to appear in weekly installments leaves its trace on the structure of the work. From the very first chapter, the events of the novel's plot are already foreshadowed in the protagonist's dream that occurs during her first night's stay at the hermitage. The novel thus consists of Mila's discovery of the meaning of the dream. This epiphany comes with a knowledge of herself that will change forever the nature of her being in the world.

The title of the novel, *Solitude*, is the signifier framing Mila's relationship with her surroundings, both upon her arrival and upon her departure. Indeed, the first chapter ends with the impression the new situation makes on the protagonist. The sight of the mountain she has just climbed with her husband seems to her "un desert blau" (a blue desert). The mountain, with no trace of human existence, anticipates what Mila's stay there will be like: "'Quina solitud!' murmurà, aterrada, i sentint que el cor li devenia, d'improvís, tant o més obac que aquelles pregoneses"[35] ("What solitude!" she murmured, terrified, and feeling her heart suddenly become as shadow filled, or even more shadow filled, than those depths). Sure enough, eighteen chapters later, the novel ends with the confirmation of this premonition. But by then, the solitude is not just that suggested by nature but also that inhabiting her own being: "Les filtracions de la solitude havien cristal.litzat amargament en son destí"[36] (The filtrations of solitude had bitterly crystallized into her destiny). Due to all this, external reality acts as a sort of stage set for the manifestation of the protagonist's interior solitude as Mila awaits the moment she will be able to come to terms with it. In his analysis of the novel, Jordi Castellanos emphasizes how the character follows a double itinerary: "El geogràfic, extern, que porta la protagonista al coneixement de la realitat, i el personal, intern, que la porta al coneixement d'ella mateixa"[37] (The external, geographic one that leads the protagonist to the knowledge of reality, and the internal, personal one that leads her to knowledge of herself). Unquestionably, the novel repeatedly resorts to the pathetic fallacy. This device further accentuates the duality between the exterior and the interior, indicating up to a certain degree that the nature of her existence is already evident; it is now only a question of Mila being willing to see it. The cards have been dealt from the outset: Mila's disillusionment with both her husband and the place where the couple is going to live, with her husband's unfaithfulness and impotence, and with the poverty and solitude she encounters. Ultimately there will be no Other to whom

Mila can entrust her own future. The only possibility left is for her to take charge of her own destiny. But this realization comes slowly, and Mila unsuccessfully looks for something she can hold on to.

What does the solitude the novel deals with stand for? I contend, as I did in Nela's case, that it stands for Mila's solitude vis-à-vis her own *jouissance*. It is not isolation caused by her lack of relations with others but rather a solitude rooted in her relationship to the most intimate part of herself. She will try to go through the different possibilities available to a woman of her time in order to find a pleasure that accommodates itself to the desire of the Other, which, if achieved, would afford her a sanctioned space in the social fabric. But Mila fails at each attempt. The rape at the end of the story, after her name has been defamed by all her neighbors, becomes the final cancelation of any hope.

The first two chapters are full of bad omens, of signs of violence and death: the incessant uproar of the "Torrent de Mala-Sang" ("Bad Blood Torrent"), the sight of the mountains enveloped in a fog that "las amortaja" (enshrouds them), and of course, the dream. It is worth reflecting on this dream as foreshadowing events to come in the novel and of everything Mila still needs to go through. Despite its length, I quote the key passage in its entirety:

> Somià que se n'anava de l'ermita per tornar cap a la seva terra, muntanyes en avall: sols que com més muntanyes deixava enrere, més n'hi sortien al davant i mai acabava de passar-les totes. Fins que, camina que caminaràs, veié una petita resplandor al lluny.—Gràcies a Déu!—pensà ella—. És la llum de ferro del pastor . . . I seguí baixant, tota animada. Mes, en ésser-hi a prop, s'adonà de que aquell pic lluminós, que de cop s'havia tornat doble, no era el llum del pastor, sinó els ulls de Sant Ponç; del Sant Ponç de la capella, que llaurava un olivar, amb una mà en l'ara, l'altra en l'aire, amb els dos dits enrampats i arrossegant de costat el peu, aquell gran peu disform, que semblava la bossa de tabac d'En Matias . . . La Mila, al veure el sant, tractà de fugir, però el sant l'aturà, tirant-li al cap boletes vermelles, que eren boletes de galleran; i ella, sentint-se baixar aquelles boles fins a la boca, va pensar, amb terror, si tindria la closca foradada. Mes no: les boles li passaven pel trenc de la cella, que era obert com una finestreta i al passar-li li feien un dolor tan viu que ella demanà per l'amor de Déu al sant que plegués de tirar-n'hi. I aleshores el sant es posà a riure amb unes grans rialles, sacsejant, el ventre de dona grossa, i dient-li amb mofa:—Ermitana, ermitana, ermitana! . . .—aquell nom que a ella li feia tanta malícia. Al veure allò, la Mila sentí que el cor se li trencava, i es posà a plorar desoladament; mes el pastor, amoixant-la com a una criatura li eixugava les llàgrimes fent-li dolçament:—Tingueu pas por . . . Hi posarem esca![38]
>
> She dreamt she was leaving the hermitage and returning home, but the more mountains she crossed, the more loomed up before her and she never finished

> crossing them. Finally, after walking and walking, she saw a point of light in the distance. "Thank God," she thought. "It's the shepherd's lamp . . ." She excitedly started toward it, but as she drew near, she realized that the lights, of which there were now two, weren't the shepherd's lamp but St. Pontius's eyes: the same St. Pontius she had seen in the chapel. He was plowing around an olive tree, holding one hand on the plow while the other raised two stiff fingers, and he dragged behind him that huge deformed foot that looked like Matías's tobacco pouch. Mila tried to run, but the saint blocked her path and pelted her head with scarlet berries; and, feeling them drop into her mouth, she thought in terror that her skull must have split open. But no: they entered through the gash in her forehead, causing her such acute pain that she begged the saint for the love of God to stop. The saint, laughing so hard his fat lady's belly shook, sneeringly called out: "Hermitess, hermitess, hermitess!" that name she so despised. Mila felt her heart breaking, and burst into sobs; but the shepherd, stroking her like a child, dried her eyes and gently murmured: "Don't worry . . . we'll fix it."[39]

One must not ignore the fact that upon arriving at the hermitage, a place where she has come to consolidate her life and her marriage, a dream warns her that she will abandon that place but that in order to do so, she will have to get over more mountains than those visible to the naked eye. It will be a long and trying road because of the different illusions that will deceive her along the way. There at the place she expected to find her salvation—in the figure of the shepherd—she is met by the repulsive and deformed presence of Sant Ponç (St. Pontius). The saint's menacing and pursuing gaze will be recurrent throughout Mila's stay at the hermitage. Her rape by Ànima will also happen under his gaze. Thus far from providing saintly protection, St. Pontius's gaze is a threat evocative of a malevolent and destructive pleasure. The deformed foot, confused in the dream with Matías's tobacco pouch, is reminiscent of a repugnant phallus. In fact, upon seeing the figure of St. Pontius for the first time, Mila feels "fàstic i angoixa"[40] (revulsion and anguish),[41] expressions of the protagonist's own pleasure at the sight of something sexually prohibited.

During the dream, the saint throws the red knee holly's fruit at Mila, who, upon feeling them in her throat, imagines her head being full of holes. She realizes, though, that the fruit is coming in through a crack in her eyebrow. This, on the one hand, is a clear sexual allusion to the female body and, on the other, emphasizes the eye as a drive object, something we have seen repeatedly. It is, unquestionably, an experience of having her body invaded that hints at the scene of the final rape right under the saint's statue in the hermitage. Here is, therefore, a saint who mocks her and who laughs with his "fat lady's belly,"[42] a possible insinuation of the pregnancy suggested at the novel's end as a result of the rape.

Mila arrives at the hermitage with a name issued by the Other, "hermitess," which she abhors. She rejects it because she does not feel she can, or wants, to represent herself under that name. It is worth noting that this is a rejection of a signifier that represents her to the others but not to herself, since at the very end, when she is about to abandon the hermitage and her husband, the narrator refers to her anonymously: "*La dona*, èrtica i greu, amb el cap dret i els ulls ombrívols, emprengué sola la davallada"[43] (*The woman*, erect and solemn, with her head high and her eyes somber, began the descent alone). She is no longer the hermitess to the others; now she is for herself only a woman. In ridding herself of the Other's insignias, she is closer to what she wants to be. This is not a minor detail.

Critics agree that the shepherd is a protective character throughout the novel. However, his action is insufficient, just as it was regarding his own wife, who died while pregnant. He is not able to protect Mila, who will have to come to terms with the rigors of her existence on her own. Indeed, the words uttered by the shepherd in the dream reveal that he treats her as a defenseless child. Certainly this is the role he plays in her life. During the time that she befriends the shepherd, Mila longs to feel desired, and she even thinks that he loves her. Once she discovers his age and realizes the gap separating them, her feeling of repulsion works to lift the veil of her own ignorance: "No hi ha res cert, al món. . . . Tot són mentides, faules engañadores"[44] (Nothing is certain in this world. . . . Everything is lies, deceptive tales). For this very reason, she immediately associates her disappointment regarding the shepherd with her disillusionment with her own husband. She identifies both with "l'eterna anomalia que la perseguia a ella sense parar, emmetzinant-li i destruint-li la vida"[45] (the eternal anomaly that ceaselessly pursued her, poisoning her and destroying her life). The term *anomaly* cannot be overlooked because it points to the impossibility of fitting in between "reality and desire," to use poet Luis Cernuda's words. It is precisely that *anomaly* she has to come to terms with at the end of the novel. In any event, the dream alerts her from the start to the fact that to the shepherd, she will never be a woman; she will merely be a bewildered girl in need of a guide.

The dream predicts what will happen in a baffling way. This is why I propose to read the novel as an interpretation of the dream. If we take it in a Freudian sense—that is, as a formulation of the unconscious—we have to admit that Mila knows right then what awaits her, although she does not want to accept this understanding. In this way, the novel becomes an analysis of the dream that leads Mila to another realization, one with consequences. Unlike the role dreams had in antiquity—as in Genesis 41:1–16, 25–37, where Pharaoh dreams of seven fat and thin cows first, then of seven plump and thin ears of grain, and Joseph interprets his dreams—Mila does not have an interpreter who can tell her the outcome. She will, literally, have to suffer it in her own flesh, as affirmed by the moral dimension of the tale and the image of the tragic heroine that Mila acquires at the end.

Finally, the dream anticipates an element that is crucial in the novel. I am referring to the treatment of the body and, more precisely, to Mila's body. In fact, the body appears repeatedly as a receptacle of *jouissance.* Thus Matías's broad body in the first chapter contrasts with the deteriorated image he exhibits at the end as a result of a dissipated life with Ánima. We have already seen the effects engendered by the vision of the saint's deformed body. Moreover, the shepherd's agile body plays a key role, as does Arnau's young, handsome, and desire-filled body. We should also highlight the comparison alluded to by the narrative voice when Mila sees the mountains for the first time. To be sure, she describes the mountains as having the shape of "un pit de dona, fent-li, per a major retirança, de mugró, una escreixença o menhir natural"[46] (a woman's breast, for which, for creating a greater likeness, a natural excrescence or menhir, made a nipple). But most of all, Mila's experiences are embodied. Mila possesses a body, and the fact of having it is neither obvious nor simple. In the dream, her body is punctured, invaded, penetrated by means of the Other's violent action. For starters, in the first chapter, during the ascent of the mountain, Matías requires her to make a much greater effort than he had told her to expect, and she has to carry their belongings. She arrives at the hermitage with a tired body. Further on, she will experience the effects of desire as awakenings of the body with Arnau, with the shepherd, and with Baldiret. Finally, at the very end, the novel describes her body as humiliated and marked forever by rape. During the final descent down the mountain, however, she walks erect, her body showing the dignity and pride of someone who has firmly grasped her destiny's reins and who knows that she has nothing to lose because she owns nothing she can lose. By then, Mila has ceased to have an aching body—unlike during the ascent—as a result of the Other's desire; instead, she has the upright body of a woman alone. Her experiences seem to have forever transformed her way of inhabiting her body.

In addition, the signifying identifications the protagonist explores throughout the narrative are also revealing. One must say that from the start, there is tension between Mila's desire and the limitations of her surroundings. The main character is described as a young woman who strives to locate her desire in one of the places made possible by the Other. Upon arriving at the hermitage and after her initial disappointment upon finding the place is isolated from human company, in bad shape, and extremely dirty, Mila starts working and cleaning. The entire chapter devoted to Mila's cleaning activities is noteworthy. Surely we find here an important aspect of a woman's position: how to transform an inhospitable place into a house she can call home. After an enormous amount of work, she only receives praise from the shepherd. Mila has proven herself to be a clean woman, itself a virtue, of course. However, she is unable to situate her desire in the place of the wife. Her stay in the hermitage cuts her off more and more from a husband who is weak and impotent, a man who will never take her as the source of his desire. On the other hand, she awakens the sexual interest of a young and handsome Arnau, although that passion is not possible for Mila, albeit tempting. She dreams of motherhood and fantasizes about the idea of having Baldiret fulfill for her the functions of a son. Still, the visit of a mother and her crippled son to the hermitage shows her motherhood's suffering and disillusion. With the shepherd, Mila allows herself to become seduced by the power of words. His narratives fill her existence. As a character who knows the surroundings and who has the means to protect her from evil, the shepherd also awakens in her a strong desire to be loved. But as we detailed earlier, the shepherd also fails her. Neither motherhood nor love is a way out for a desire whose manifestation is clear from the outset of the narrative.

Furthermore, Mila is defamed by her neighbors. She is accused of being the shepherd's lover, even of stealing his fortune. Finally, the rape leaves an imprint on her forever, on her very flesh, in the wound piercing her cheek. Mila thus remains a marked woman forever. Without femininity's attributes, without property, even without a name, empty-handed, she has to face her future alone. Mila leaves the mountain, the hermitage, and her husband in absolute and radical solitude. For her, definitely, there remains no possible representation in the place of the Other. She is no more than a woman alone. Surely she must start anew but with an acquired understanding that makes her the tragic heroine she is by the end of the novel.

In her writings, Caterina Albert dramatizes a radical quandary, either defamation or solitude. Undoubtedly, this is the dilemma that—as I demonstrated in *Solitud* and in the monologue *La infanticida*—Víctor Català lays out repeatedly for women. One may understand this alternative as a result of a historical context that afforded women limited roles restricted by patriarchal morality. However, I also propose that Albert brings to the foreground something else that transcends the cultural question in the strictest sense. To be sure, as I mentioned earlier, beyond the sociological and historical readings the text allows, the vicissitudes experienced by Mila, her clearly tragic character, lay bare the terms and conditions of the subject's representability. Without question, in order to represent oneself, the subject only has at hand the signifiers that, as such, always belong to the Other. For any subject, some part of his or her being remains always outside of this representation. What remains unrepresentable has to do with what is most fundamental to *jouissance*—that is, with that part of the drive that cannot be captured by any means in the signifier. The conditions of a woman's *jouissance* make this impossibility more obvious because the feminine makes present a nonphallic *jouissance* that escapes the signifier, a *jouissance* difficult to name and to explain, as feminine sexuality makes clear. Mila's tragedy shows us this impossibility of representation as well. A condition of *jouissance* exists in her that longs to represent itself phallically—that is, with what stands for woman in the phallic regime: the mother, the spouse, the housewife. But Mila does not agree to this; she cannot. Her being opposes it, even if that opposition leads her to the greatest humiliation, to defamation, and to being raped. It is the magnitude of this opposition that makes her, undeniably, a heroine.

Of course, one could imagine kinder representations—indeed, they exist for women; we know them and we experience them—just as there are nicer representations for men. More than two centuries of feminist struggle have not been in vain, at least for some (not all) of the women on earth. But what Lacanian psychoanalysis uncovers is the existence of a *jouissance* that does not let itself be trapped in representation. It is in that *jouissance* that the ultimate singularity of the subject resides—unyielding, antagonistic to any comparison or any regime of equality. Nonetheless, as such, it does not go without a considerable dose of solitude. In effect, *jouissance* cannot be solitary, nor share itself, since it is outside the relationship with the Other. That is why, with such a *jouissance*, the best thing to do is *sympthomatize*—written with an *h*—a neologism coined by Lacan to name the transformation of *jouissance* into an invention, into something new and unknown.[47] After all, *Solitud* leaves the reader with an open ending from which it is impossible to surmise how far Mila could go in her solitude and her silent rebellion. On the other hand, and judging by what we know, it seems that the author managed to do well in life, leaving at least the products of her creation for future generations. We enjoy them, each one of us, in our own *sympthomatic* way.

NOTES

1. Víctor Català, "Conversa amb Víctor Català: Entrevista amb Tomàs Garcés, publicada a *La Revista*," in *Obres completes*, by Víctor Català, ed. Tomàs Tebé (Barcelona: Editorial Selecta, 1972), 1748.

2. Maria-Aurèlia Capmany, epilogue to *Obres completes*, 1860.

3. Josep Miracle, *Caterina Albert i Paradís "Víctor Català"* (Barcelona: Dopesa, 1978), 13, emphasis mine.

4. The term *jouissance* includes not only the meaning of "satisfaction" but also that which goes beyond satisfaction; in other words, that which goes beyond Freud's "pleasure principle" to resemble Freud's "death instinct." For Jacques Lacan, *jouissance* leads the subject to want to transgress the limitations imposed on his or her pleasure by language and society, a transgression that paradoxically leads to pain rather than more pleasure. According to Madan Sarup, *jouissance* "is unconscious pleasure which becomes pain" (*Jacques Lacan* [Toronto: University of Toronto Press, 1992], 90).

5. I am referring here to the concept of symptom that Lacanian psychoanalysis understands as the treatment for drive: "El síntoma emerge como ofreciendo a la pulsión, yo diría en cortocircuito, otra satisfacción. . . . El término goce se justifica por la noción de que el síntoma está articulado a la pulsión y que a la vez hace que esta se desvíe. El síntoma es el resultado de una desviación de su curso normal pero que, al mismo tiempo, satisface su exigencia de alguna manera" (Jacques-Alain Miller, *El partenaire-síntoma*, trans. Dora Glayds Saroka [Buenos Aires: Editorial Paidós, 2008], 82; The symptom emerges as if offering to the drive, I would say in a short-circuit, another satisfaction. . . . The term *jouissance* is justified by the notion that the symptom is joined to the drive and at the

same time it makes the drive change course. The symptom is the result of a detour from its regular course which, at the same time, somehow satisfies its demand).

6. *Other*, when capitalized in Lacan, refers to other people or subjects as well as "language and the conventions of social life" (John David Zuern, "Lacan: Mirror Stage, Term," Critica Link, http://www.english.hawaii.edu/criticalink/lacan/terms/other.html). It is differentiated from *other*, in lowercase, which refers to the imaginary other in the form of an idealized self (Zuern, "Lacan").

7. Miracle, *Albert i Paradís*, 28–29.

8. Capmany, epilogue, 1861.

9. Víctor Català, *La infanticida*, in *Obres completes*, 1578.

10. Català, 1585.

11. *Persecutory object* is a psychoanalytical term first used by Melanie Klein to refer to those objects. According to Klein, the infant's world was threatened from the beginning by intolerable anxieties, whose source she believed to be the infant's own death instinct (whose central importance she forcefully affirmed, in opposition to many other contemporary theorists). "These 'persecutory' anxieties, which were felt in the infant's own bodily needs as well as from the external frustrations to those needs, were overwhelming to the infant, and in order to combat them the infant resorted to defenses whose aim was to isolate her from them. Through these primitive defenses—*projection, denial, splitting, withdrawal,* and '*omnipotent control*' of these objects—the infant put threatening, '*bad*' *objects,* outside herself and into the external world; simultaneously, she preserved the '*good*' *objects,* both within herself and externally, by splitting them off from their malevolent counterparts" ("Psychoanalysis—Melanie Klein and Object Relations," Science Encyclopedia, emphasis in the original, http://science.jrank.org/pages/10906/Psychoanalysis-Melanie-Klein-Object-Relations.html).

12. Català, *La infanticida*, 1590.

13. Català, 1590.

14. Català, 1590.

15. S1 is the term Lacan uses for the master signifier—that is, the signifier that is still not linked to another signifier. It is the one that identifies and fixes the subject. However, a second signifier (S2) is needed to produce the signifying chain. According to Matthew Sharp, Lacan assigns great importance in his theorization of the psychoanalytic process to what he calls "master signifiers." These are those signifiers that the subject most deeply identifies with and that, accordingly, have a key role in the way he or she gives meaning to the world. As was stressed, Lacan's idea about these signifiers is that their primary importance is less any positive content that they add to the subject's field of symbolic sense; it is rather the efficacy they have in reorienting the subject with respect to all the other signifiers which structure his or her sense of herself and the world. It is precisely this primarily structural or formal function that underlies the crucial Lacanian claim that master signifiers are actually "empty signifiers" or "signifiers without a signified" (Sharp, "Jacques Lacan, 1901–1981," Internet Encyclopedia of Philosophy, http://www.iep.utm.edu/lacweb/#SH4a).

16. Marta Pessarrodona, "Una soledad sonora," *El País*, October 6, 2007, http://elpais.com/diario/2007/10/06/babelia/1191627567_850215.html.

17. See the definition of S1 in Sharp, "Jacques Lacan."

18. The S2 is the signifier needed to complete the signifying chain with the S1 (Sharp).

19. Jacques Lacan, "Position of the Unconscious," in *Écrits*, trans. Bruce Fink (New York: Norton, 2006), 713.

20. For further explanation of Lacan's understanding of madness, see Jacques Lacan, *The Seminar*, vol. 3, trans. Russel Grigg (New York: Norton, 1997).

21. Her biographer, Josep Miracle, notes that he was unable to find in any journal of the time of the call mentioned by Víctor Català. This leads him to believe that she was summoned by other channels (*Albert i Paradís*, 87).

22. Víctor Català, "El cant els mesos," in *Obres completes*, 1427.

23. Virginia Woolf, *A Room of One's Own* (London: Harcourt, 1981), 52.

24. Jacques Lacan, *Encore. Le seminaire libre XX* (Paris: Seuil, 1975), 79.

25. Concerning the debate about the representability of the feminine and Lacanian psychoanalysis, please refer to Slavoj Žižek, "La femme n'existe pas," in *Todo lo que usted siempre quiso saber sobre Lacan y nunca se atrevió a preguntarle a Hitchcock*, ed. Slavoj Žižek, trans. Jorge Piatigorsky (Buenos Aires: Manantial, 1994), 113–117; Serge André, *Que veut une femme?* (Paris: Seuil, 1995); Joan Copjec, *Imagine There Is No Woman: Ethics and Sublimation* (Cambridge, Mass.: MIT Press, 2004); Jacques-Alain Miller, *De la naturaleza de los semblantes*, trans. Silvia Elena Tendlarz (Buenos Aires: Paidós, 2002).

26. Víctor Català, "Epistolari," in *Obres completes*, 1786.

27. Català, *La infanticida*, 1583.

28. Català, "Epistolari," 1797.

29. See Francesca Bartrina's study, *Víctor Català / Caterina Albert i Paradís: La voluptuositat de l'escriptura* (Vic: Eumo, 2001).

30. Víctor Català, "Discurs. Llegit a la reial acadèmia de bones lletres de Barcelona, en la solemne recepció pública de Vector Català (14 gener 1923)," in *Obres completes*, 1695.

31. See Jordi Castellanos, "Solitud, novella modernista," *Els marges* 25 (1982): 45–70.

32. Capmany, epilogue, 1858–1868.

33. "On peut aussi bien s'en passer à condition de s'en servir," in Jacques Lacan, *Le Séminaire*, book 23, *Le sinthome* (Paris: Seuil, 2005), 136.

34. A year after giving Albert the assignment, the editor had only received the first three chapters of a work yet to be titled and a rough draft of the chapters to follow. Years later, the writer remembered, "Va ésser terrible. Jo no sé com *Solitud* ha tingut èxit, ni com ningú no s'ha adonat de les presses amb què va esser escrita i d'allò que hi manca" (Miracle, *Albert i Paradís*, 150; It was terrible. I don't know how *Solitud* became successful, or how no one noticed the haste with which it was written and what is lacking in it).

35. Víctor Català, *Solitud* (Barcelona: Editorial Selecta, 1980), 57.

36. Català, 305.

37. Castellanos, "Solitud, novella modernista," 45.

38. Català, *Solitud*, 70.

39. For the translation of Catalan, see David Rosenthal, trans., *Solitude*, by Víctor Català (Columbia, La.: Readers International, 1992), 35–36.

40. Català, *Solitud*, 66.

41. Rosenthal, *Solitude*, 32.

42. Rosenthal, 36.

43. Català, *Solitud*, 305, emphasis in the original.

44. Català, 254.

45. Català, 255.

46. Català, 53.

47. The purpose of Seminar 23, which Lacan dedicated to James Joyce, is to show how the Irish writer managed to transform his *jouissance* into literature, a literature that was as new as it was illegible.

CHAPTER 10

The Obstinate Negativity of Ana Ozores

Jo Labanyi

This chapter is an attempt to explore alternative approaches to Leopoldo Alas's 1884–1885 novel *La Regenta*. It has become a commonplace to see the novel as an anticipation of psychoanalysis because of its synergies, not only with Freud's concept of the unconscious and attribution of neurosis to sexual repression, but also with his view of woman as lack. Feminist theorists have long had problems with Freud's notion of woman as defined by lack of a penis (castration), which equates agency with ownership of the (biological as well as symbolic) phallus. As a woman, I find such a notion illogical and untenable, though admittedly the equation of woman with lack works brilliantly for a novel whose protagonist, Ana Ozores, lacked a mother, lacks a child, lacks a sexual relationship with her husband, and has nothing to do. Worse still: Ana lacks an identity—she reflects more than once that her true self is the disintegration of the self that she feels within. Indeed, it is hard to write a character sketch of her apart from the adjective *egoísta* (self-centered) that the narrator regularly applies to her—a negative affect, not only because it is the reverse of the altruism or *reciprocidad* (reciprocity) proposed as the ethical basis of society by the Krausist thinkers with whom Alas was closely associated, but also because it is precisely Ana's intense focus on her inner self that produces in her a sense of dissolution.[1] I have always been puzzled by how *La Regenta* succeeds in interesting us when its protagonist not only has no identity but does not progress or learn anything in the course of the novel's seven hundred pages, in most of which nothing happens.

I would like to see if this can be explained by reading the novel through the theorization of negative affect that has emerged in the last decade as part of the "affective turn."[2] I am thinking particularly of Sianne Ngai's *Ugly Feelings*, which argues that negative affects have agency and critical productivity. I shall dialogue also with Sara Ahmed's *The Promise of Happiness* and Lauren Berlant's

Cruel Optimism, which analyze how we come to desire what makes us unhappy.[3] I have used the phrase *obstinate negativity* in my title because what I find striking about Ana Ozores is the obstinacy with which she clings to negativity. Stephanie Sieburth has chided the narrator of *La Regenta* for systematically cutting off Ana's options, but one can perhaps see negativity as a resource that enables Ana to endure.[4] In this respect, my argument, while rejecting the psychoanalytic focus on the individual subject, is compatible with Alison Sinclair's psychoanalytical reading of the novel, which draws on the work of female psychoanalysts to argue that Ana's hysteria is not so much a response to female lack as strategic.[5]

Ngai defines negative affects (what she calls "ugly feelings") as those that allow no catharsis, no transcendence—unlike tragic or "noble" forms of unhappiness such as grief or a sense of injustice or even anger. The "ugly feelings" she analyzes are intransitive—turning away from, rather than toward, their object—and related to inertia, suspended agency, and inaction: these are concepts applicable to *La Regenta* as a novel about an introspective protagonist with no options, in which very little happens.[6] When things do happen, in the second part of the twenty-ninth chapter and first part of the final, thirtieth, chapter, the narrator rushes through them as if trying to get back as soon as possible to the inertia, suspended agency, and inaction that have driven the rest of the novel. For Ana's inertia, suspended agency, and inaction are not a lack but what drives the novel. Ngai notes that negative affects are fundamentally nonnarrative because they are about being stuck: *La Regenta* is an extraordinary example of a nonnarrative novel whose seven hundred pages go nowhere.[7] The fifteen chapters of its first part cover three days at such a slow pace that we feel we are not moving, while the fifteen chapters of its second part cover three years through a series of temporal loops that undo the sense of time progressing.[8] The novel ends as it starts: with Ana unsuccessfully seeking confession from the magistral in the cathedral in October. In this chapter, rather than analyze the reasons for Ana's "stuckness" (which only get us back to the conclusion that she is stuck), I would like to consider what her negativity does—for her, for her fellow Vetustans, and for us as readers.

First, some introductory remarks on affect theory are in order. Affect theory departs from psychoanalysis in that it refuses a subject-centered view of the world, in which emotions are authentic expressions of the inner self. On the contrary, affect occurs at the interface of self and world: it is the result of an encounter. In its extreme form, propagated by Brian Massumi (2002, 2015), affect theory sees affect as a preconscious, subjectless force or energy produced through the encounter between self and world (including other selves and things, for the human and the nonhuman are not distinguished). According to this view, affect is a material process, distinct from the subjective experience of emotion, which occurs once the subject acquires consciousness of this energetic charge and gives it a name—fear, joy, anger, or pity, for example.[9] Berlant has criticized Massumi for stressing the preconscious impact of the world on the self to the point that despite his insistence that affect is the capacity to affect as well as to be affected, human agency becomes diminished. Berlant is interested primarily in the active process of affective investment; for this reason, she prefers not to make a firm distinction between affect and emotion—a practice followed also by Ahmed and Ngai.[10] They are able to align affect and emotion (though seeing affect as characterized by a particularly intense energetic charge) because they see emotion too as occurring at the interface between self and world—as theorized in Ahmed's earlier study *The Cultural Politics of Emotion*.[11] This redefinition of emotion radically decenters the Romantic notion of emotion as the seat of an authentic inner self. For the rest of this essay, I will follow Ahmed, Berlant, and Ngai in using the terms *affect* and *emotion* interchangeably and in regarding both as taking place at the point of contact between self and world.

Affect theory renders irrelevant the nineteenth-century debates around determinism—Can subjects impose themselves on the world or does the world determine them?—since affect, occurring at the interface between self and world, involves a two-way process in which self and world mutually constitute each other. For affect theory, self and world cannot be seen as separate entities, for they are inextricably entangled, and affect is what binds them together. The debate on determinism versus free will was, of course, the context of the polemic in Spain over realism versus naturalism, which Émile Zola had proclaimed as the literary equivalent of social medicine in its analysis of the material causes of human dysfunction.[12] Alas's ambivalence in this polemic, supporting naturalism but rejecting determinism, perhaps signals that affect theory offers an appropriate reading of his novel, in which the same ambivalence exists.[13] On the one hand, *La Regenta* places considerable stress on emotions as a response to the material world rather than as residing in the inner self. On the other hand, the novel is also fundamentally about Ana's emotional investments, which suppose an active engagement with the world.

Affect theory is part of what has become known as the "new materialism."[14] The narrator of *La Regenta* goes into some detail about the reading of mid-nineteenth-century materialist thinkers by the local Don Juan, Álvaro Mesía. These thinkers include Ludwig Büchner, Jakob Moleschott, Rudolf Virchow, and Karl Vogt, not to mention Lucretius.[15] One of the devastating things about *La Regenta* is that Mesía's materialist diagnosis of Ana is proved right despite the narrator's scathing depiction of him. Mesía sees himself as a "máquina eléctrica de amor" (electrical love machine) able to "echar chispas"[16] (emit sparks). Ana's hysterical attacks are marked by her seeing "chispas de fuegos artificiales"[17] (sparks like fireworks). Given the similar terminology, we are invited to ask whether there is any difference between Mesía's materialist reading of the self and Ana's spiritual reading. The materialist doctor Benítez's maxim "*Ubi irritatio ibi fluxus*" (Where the irritation, there the flow)[18] could be seen as an anticipation of affect theory, for it refers to an energetic process that takes place at the point of contact between self and world.[19]

There are many passages in *La Regenta* that depict emotions as resulting from the contact between self and world rather than originating in the self. For example, Ana's expansiveness toward Mesía at the Vegallanas' mansion is triggered by his masculine smell: "Un perfume . . . que debía de tener algo de tabaco bueno y otras cosas puramente masculinas"[20] (A perfume . . . that was no doubt a mix of good tobacco and other purely masculine things). Her receptivity to him can be triggered by the impact of physical objects, as when the sight of the uncleared table after lunch provokes the desolation that makes her welcome his subsequent appearance on horseback at her balcony: "La insignificancia de aquellos objetos que contemplaba le partía el alma; se le figuraba que eran símbolo del universo, que era así, ceniza, frialdad, un cigarro abandonado a la mitad por el hastío del fumador"[21] (The insignificance of those objects displayed before her eyes struck at the core of her soul; she saw them as a symbol of the universe, which was like that too, ash, things gone cold, a cigar left half smoked thanks to the smoker's lethargy). The symbolism that Ana projects onto the objects on the table—the leftover coffee, the dirty liqueur glass, the cigar—is trite, but their material effect on her is real. Ana and Mesía's communication as they talk at the balcony takes place not through their verbal exchange but "por efluvios"[22] (via emissions).

These examples involve emotional processes that originate in the physical imprint of the world on the self. But Ana is not just a recipient of external stimuli; so little happens in *La Regenta* because the novel is primarily concerned with her affective investments, and her affective investments are aimed at producing stasis. In my earlier *Gender and Modernization in the Spanish Realist Novel*, I read the late nineteenth-century Spanish novel as obsessed with the concept of blockage, which I there related to contemporary medical and economic anxieties.[23] Here I wish to read the concept of blockage in terms of the "stuckness" that is central to the theorization of negative affect. In her book on *La Regenta* (which has a wonderful section on mud as an image of being stuck), Alison Sinclair turns around Freud's reading of hysteria as being stuck in the past (viz. his maxim "Hysterics suffer mainly from reminiscences") to argue that Ana resorts strategically to hysteria (whose physical symptom is a choking feeling) as an obstruction that allows her to avoid "the reality of sexual life, sexual intercourse, and reproduction."[24] According to this argument, Ana's enjoyment of being the object of Mesía's desire is a way of not acknowledging her desire for him. Indeed, by resisting the sexual temptation he offers but refusing to give the temptation up, she convinces herself that she does not need to confess her attraction to him, since a passive object is not guilty: "La tentación era suya, su único placer. ¡Bastante hacía con no dejarse vencer, pero quería dejarse tentar!"[25] (The temptation was hers, her only pleasure. She was fulfilling her duty by not submitting, but she wanted to permit herself the temptation!). Sinclair additionally observes that Ana strategically opts for objecthood by imagining that her life may change because a savior will intervene without her having to abandon her object position.[26] The irony of Mesía's name—as a profane messiah—underscores Ana's view of love as the surrender of subjecthood to a savior. Ana explicitly describes her confessor, the magistral, as her "salvador"[27] (savior); this invites a reading of her flirtation with mysticism in terms of Simone de Beauvoir's criticism of the female mystic for turning herself into the passive object of divine attention.[28] In offering to be the magistral's "esclava"[29] (slave) by walking in the Holy Week procession as a penitent, Ana will discover that her willed self-objectification only turns her into a semipornographic object of the collective gaze. She similarly treats her doctor Benítez as her savior, becoming his "esclava"[30] in turn. By blindly following Benítez's instructions, she frees herself from guilt at her plunge into the pleasures of the natural life—Mesía's sexual charms included.

It can be productive to read Ana's strategic denial of her subjecthood through Ahmed's *The Promise of Happiness*. The result confirms Ana as a tragic figure—one whose tragedy results not from transgression but from conformism. Indeed, the principal obstruction to Ana's happiness is that despite her abnormal upbringing, she is the one "normal" character in the novel who desires what society expects her to desire: the role of selfless wife and mother—what Ahmed has called the "happiness script" proffered to women by society. As Ahmed notes, happiness is constituted by a "'happiness archive': a set of ideas, thoughts, narratives, images, impressions about what is happiness"—an archive that is historically specific. She notes also that "happiness is crucial to the energy or 'forward direction' of narrative"; the search for happiness drives *La Regenta*, but the failure to get anywhere in the search for it accounts for the novel's nonnarrative quality.[31] One of the novel's great ironies is that everyone else in Vetusta is ignoring the appropriate happiness script by desiring what they are not supposed to desire—and faring much better as a result. All the men in Ana's life want to "cure" her, but the problem is not her but the prescribed script that circumstances (her husband's lack of sexual interest in her and her resulting childlessness) make it impossible for her to follow. I would argue that Ana is following the prescribed female happiness script not only in trying to be the perfect wife but also in desiring Mesía as the lover supposed to give her transcendental bliss, by contrast with the rest of Vetusta's mundane recourse to sexual activity. The ingenuousness of this belief in love as a means to transcendence is shown when, transported by Zorrilla's Romantic depiction of love in *Don Juan Tenorio*, Ana fails to notice Mesía's attempt to play footsie with her in the theatre box.[32]

Berlant has also analyzed how we construct our own unhappiness by insisting on desiring what we are supposed to desire when that desire cannot be fulfilled—a process that she calls "cruel optimism." By this, she means the maintenance of an attachment to fantasies that hurt us because we have no hope of achieving them.[33] Berlant is referring primarily to the continued adherence in today's conditions of precarity to the post–World War II Western dream of the "good way of life." But as she notes, cruel optimism is endemic to history, since happiness scripts become obsolete over time and yet continue to be followed, inevitably producing an impasse or blockage. She sees the problem of historical obsolescence as one of genre.[34] The theatre scene in *La Regenta* illustrates this point forcefully: Ana is stuck because she ascribes to a Romantic genre of happiness script, embodied by Zorrilla's 1844 play *Don Juan Tenorio*, whose incommensurability with reality is aggravated by the fact that, as Mesía rightly notes, it is anachronistic in the late 1870s.[35] But the narrator is also right to show that the Romantic promise of transcendental love continued to endure long after its sell-by date (indeed, into the mid-twentieth century, if not beyond).

Ahmed notes that not getting what you want allows you to preserve the fantasy that it would make you happy.[36] Accordingly, Ana persists in her unhappiness, since the impossibility of obtaining what she wants confirms it as desirable; conversely, the confirmation of its desirability allows her to endure in her unhappiness. Berlant expresses the same idea in more negative terms, suggesting that happiness scripts are clung to when it is clear that they are hurtful because "the loss of what's not working is more unbearable than the having of it."[37] This seems a good explanation for why Ana, despite knowing that Mesía is a serial seducer and that the magistral's desire for her is carnal and not just spiritual, continues to oscillate between them in her search for transcendental love—to the point of going back to the magistral at the end.

La Regenta can, then, be read not as the tragedy of a woman whose possibilities of self-fulfillment were denied but as the tragedy of a woman who persisted in desiring what she was supposed to desire. That she should fall for a worthless Don Juan can be seen not as a flaw in the novel, as one might conclude from the narrator's imbalanced treatment of the two rivals for Ana's love (Mesía and the magistral), but as the point, allowing a critique of the happiness script that offers women fulfillment through romantic love. Ahmed suggests that unhappiness can function as a critical tool: "My suggestion is that we can read the negativity of such [unhappy female] figures in terms of the challenge that they offer to the assumption that happiness follows relative proximity to a social ideal."[38] Judging by Alas's disappointingly traditional views on women expressed in his journalism, it is unlikely that he intended *La Regenta* to be a critique of the female happiness script that the novel exposes.[39] Ana, tragically, learns nothing. However, I do not find it anachronistic to suggest that at least some of Alas's contemporary female readers may have learned the lesson. The novel's devastating end depicts Ana—rejected by Vetustan society and by the one person (the magistral) able to appreciate her romantic desires—as an inert body awakening to the slimy contact of the homosexual Celedonio's kiss. This (homophobia apart) can be read as the narrator's punishment of Ana for committing adultery with a worthless Don Juan. But it can also be read, whether Alas intended it that way or not, as a warning to female readers that the pursuit of fulfilment through romantic love leads to the loss of subjecthood: happiness scripts produce objects and not subjects. We do not know whether Ana will, after she returns to consciousness, have the strength to abandon her cruel optimism or cling to it as a lesser evil than having no optimism at all. Either way, the reader has been given a wake-up call about the cost of desiring what causes you damage.

Ngai's *Ugly Feelings* devotes a chapter to envy as a noncathartic affect that is intransitive in that it turns away from, rather than toward, its object. As is well known, envy is what drives most of the inhabitants of Vetusta: the clergy and the members of the casino, who envy those who enjoy higher social status, and the women who envy Ana's status as the object of male desire.[40] Ngai draws on Melanie Klein's essay "Envy and Gratitude" to argue that "the ideal or good object envied and phantasmatically attacked is attacked precisely because it is idealized and good—as if the real source of antagonism is less the object than the idealization itself."[41] The envy of Ana by Vetusta's females can thus be read as providing a critique of the ideal of female virtue to which she clings. Indeed, Vetusta's womenfolk do not want to be like Ana; they want to destroy her reputation, to make her *como todas* (like other women). Conversely, we can note that Ana's pleasure in being an object of envy suggests a measure of complicity with her objectification. Another reason her obstinate negativity cannot be seen simply in terms of lack is because it has agency—that is, it produces effects (affects)—in others. Her persistence in unhappiness allows male fantasies of possessing her and provokes the female envy that wishes to destroy the ideal she represents. It is in this sense, above all, that Ana's negativity can be said to drive the novel. Ngai, discussing Melville's character Bartleby, talks of his "powerful powerlessness"; we could say the same of Ana Ozores.

What fascinates Ngai about emotional negativity is what she calls its "affective gaps and illegibilities."[42] Ana's descriptions of her negative feelings are full of ellipses, as, for example, when she struggles to define her illness to the magistral: "A veces se me figura que soy por dentro un montón de arena que se desmorona . . . No sé cómo explicarlo . . . siento grietas en la vida . . . me divido dentro de mí . . . me achico, me anulo"[43] (At times I feel as if my inner self were a pile of sand collapsing . . . I don't know how to explain it . . . I feel cracks in my life . . . I splinter internally . . . I shrink, I disintegrate). This is a description of emotional states that cannot be pinned down, that consist of not being rather than being in an illustration of what Ngai calls "a meta-feeling in which one feels confused about *what* one is feeling."[44] Ngai notes that this leads to doubts about whether what one is feeling is subjective or objective, coming from within or from without. In her analysis of film noir, she notes that this is expressed in the confusion between subjective and objective point of view.[45] This seems a wonderful explanation of the extensive use of free indirect discourse in *La Regenta*. In one of the best examples, when Ana goes for a country walk after her first confession with the magistral, we move from the narrator's description of the wagtail (observed by the narrator and by Ana) to her brief first-person reflections on "estos animalitos"[46] (those little creatures), giving way to six pages of free indirect discourse (Ana's thoughts presented directly but in the past tense and third person), ending with a return to the first person and present tense as Ana returns to reality and spots the toad beside her.[47] The use of speech marks in the novel is erratic (including in the passage mentioned previously), since they may be used for both direct speech and free indirect discourse (which at other times occurs without speech marks); this compounds the blurring of inner and outer worlds. In this and other passages that resort to free indirect discourse, not only can readers not determine whether what they are reading is Ana's thoughts or the narrator's reporting, since it is both at the same time, but this blurring of subjective and objective points of view could be interpreted as suggesting the impossibility for Ana—and perhaps also for the narrator—to disentangle what is subjective and what is objective. In this sense, free indirect discourse is a perfect expression of affect theory's insistence that emotions are not properties of the self but occur at the interface of self and world. This confusion makes Ana illegible even unto herself.

Ana's illegibility is what makes everyone in the novel—and us as readers—want to read her. This illegibility, with its ellipses and confusions between the subjective and objective, adds to the nonnarrative quality of *La Regenta* as a text about a character who is stuck; the text gives the impression of being stuck too, particularly in part 2 as the narrative keeps looping back on itself. In insisting on Ana's negativity, I have wanted to argue for the agency of negative affect, seeing Ana not as a victim of lack but as strategically opting for objecthood. Perhaps the ultimate meaning of Ana's *egoísmo* (egoism) is her obstinate persistence in a negativity that turns back on the self—a self that she can never pin down because it does not exist within her but at the point of contact between self and world.

NOTES

1. For a detailed discussion of Alas's relation to Krausism, see Yvan Lissorgues, *El pensamiento filosófico y religioso de Leopoldo Alas "Clarín"* (Oviedo: Grupo Editorial Asturiano, 1996), 156–187. A briefer account, relating specifically to *La Regenta*, is given in Jo Labanyi, *Gender and Modernization in the Spanish Realist Novel* (Oxford: Oxford University Press, 2000), 219–224.

2. For the affective turn, see, in particular, Teresa Brennan, *The Transmission of Affect* (Ithaca, N.Y.: Cornell University Press, 2004); Patricia Ticineto Clough, ed., *The Affective Turn: Theorizing the Social* (Durham, N.C.: Duke University Press, 2007); Nigel Thrift, *Non-representational Theory* (Abingdon: Routledge, 2008). For a brief survey, see Jo Labanyi, "Doing Things: Emotion, Affect, Materiality," *Journal of Spanish Cultural Studies* 11, nos. 3/4 (2010): 223–233.

3. Sianne Ngai, *Ugly Feelings* (Cambridge, Mass.: Harvard University Press, 2007); Sara Ahmed, *The Promise of Happiness* (Durham, N.C.: Duke University Press, 2010); Lauren Berlant, *Cruel Optimism* (Durham, N.C.: Duke University Press, 2011).

4. Stephanie Sieburth, "La poética del sufrimiento en *La Regenta*," in *Leopoldo Alas, un clásico contemporáneo (1901–2001). Actas del congreso celebrado en Oviedo (12–16 de noviembre de 2001)*, vol. 2, ed. Araceli Iravedra Valea et al. (Oviedo: Universidad de Oviedo, 2002), 805–811.

5. Alison Sinclair, *Dislocations of Desire: Gender, Identity, and Strategy in "La Regenta"* (Chapel Hill: University of North Carolina Press, 1998), 33, 39, 219. For Sinclair, the novel shows all the characters to be in flight from a more fundamental lack—that of an ontological formlessness or void.

6. Ngai, *Ugly Feelings*, 1–14.

7. Ngai, 25–26.

8. A significant proportion of part 2 is narrated via Ana's memories, which fill the reader in on what has happened since the previous chapter. On several occasions, the temporal loops circle back over the same period of time.

9. See Brian Massumi, *Parables for the Virtual: Movement, Affect, Sensation* (Durham, N.C.: Duke University Press, 2002); and *Politics of Affect* (Cambridge: Polity, 2015). Massumi notes that there is a half-second time lag between the preconscious registration of an external stimulus on the body (affect) and the conscious recognition of the feeling generated (emotion; *Parables for the Virtual*, 23–28).

10. Berlant, *Cruel Optimism*, 14.

11. Sara Ahmed, *The Cultural Politics of Emotion* (New York: Routledge, 2004), 5–12. In this book, Ahmed argues that one does not "have" emotions as a property of the self, nor do emotions enter us from the outside, but "emotions create the very effect of an inside and an outside" (8–10)—that is, the illusion that self and world are separate.

12. Émile Zola, *Le Roman expérimental* (1880; Paris: Garnier-Flammarion, 1971).

13. Leopoldo Alas, "Del naturalismo (*La diana*, 1882)," and "Prólogo a *La cuestión palpitante* (Fragmento)," in *Leopoldo Alas: Teoría y crítica de la novela español*, ed. Sergio Beser (Barcelona: Laia, 1972), 108–149, 149–153.

14. The "new materialism" questions the binary oppositions between body and mind, self and world, human and animal, and animate and inanimate. The common inspiration is the monism of Baruch Spinoza, read via Gilles Deleuze, which sees all phenomena as part of a material continuum in which everything is bound to everything else. See Gilles Deleuze, *Spinoza: A Practical Philosophy*, trans. Robert Hurley (San Francisco: City Lights, 2001). For a clear exposition of the materialist reading of affect based on Spinoza's definition of *affect* as "the capacity to affect and be affected," see Massumi's collection of interviews, *Politics of Affect*. The ecological implications of the new materialism are explored in Jane Bennett, *Vibrant Matter: A Political Ecology of Things* (Durham, N.C.: Duke University Press, 2010).

15. See Leopoldo Alas (Clarín), *La Regenta*, 2 vols., ed. Gonzalo Sobejano (1884–1885; Madrid: Castalia, 1981), 360–361. All page references to *La Regenta* are to Gonzalo Sobejano's 1981 edition for Castalia. As Sobejano explains (1:360–361nn18–22, 361n24), the philosopher of science Ludwig Büchner's best-known work, *Kraft und Stoff* (*Force and Matter*; 1854), cited by the narrator of *La Regenta*, argued that everything is matter in motion. The other German-language scientists mentioned by the narrator—the physiologist Jakob Moleschott, the founder of social medicine Rudolf Virchow, and the zoologist

Karl Vogt—argued that thoughts and emotions are physiological processes. Mesía was too lazy to read beyond the first half of Lucretius's *De rerum natura* (1:360–361). As the narrator wryly comments, Mesía tries to instill the notion that everything is energy and matter in his lovers because "cuando la mujer se convencía de que no había metafísica, le iba mucho mejor a don Álvaro" (1:361; when women were persuaded that there was no such thing as metaphysics, things went much better for Don Álvaro).

16. Alas, *La Regenta*, 2:358.

17. Alas, 1:174.

18. Alas, 2:405.

19. For the medical history of this Latin phrase, see Sinclair, *Dislocations of Desire*, 166.

20. Alas, *La Regenta*, 2:489.

21. Alas, 2:10.

22. Alas, 2:10.

23. Labanyi, *Gender and Modernization*. In that book, I argued that the Spanish realist novel subscribes to the economic and medical idea of "free flow" that was fundamental to liberal political theory, and that it explores anxieties about what happens when "free flow" is either too free or when it is blocked. For discussion of blockage in relation to *La Regenta*, see 236–240, 242.

24. Sinclair, *Dislocations of Desire*, 151, and (for the discussion of mud) 45–58. For Freud's maxim, see Sigmund Freud, *Standard Edition of the Complete Psychological Works*, vol. 2 of *Studies on Hysteria*, trans. and ed. James Strachey (London: Hogarth Press and Institute of Psycho-Analysis, 1955), 7.

25. Alas, *La Regenta*, 1:363.

26. Sinclair, *Dislocations of Desire*, 219.

27. Alas, *La Regenta*, 1:509.

28. Simone de Beauvoir, "The Mystic," in *The Second Sex*, trans. H. M. Parshley (1949; Harmondsworth: Penguin Books, 1972), 679–687.

29. Alas, *La Regenta*, 2:345.

30. Alas, 2:378.

31. Ahmed, *Promise of Happiness*, 15, 32, 37.

32. Alas, *La Regenta*, 2:52.

33. Berlant, *Cruel Optimism*, 23–24, 51.

34. Berlant, 4, 6, 10.

35. Alas, *La Regenta*, 2:49.

36. Ahmed, *Promise of Happiness*, 31–33.

37. Berlant, *Cruel Optimism*, 27.

38. Ahmed, *Promise of Happiness*, 53, and more generally, 50–87, 216–223.

39. See in particular Leopoldo Alas's substantial article "La psicología del sexo," *La Ilustración Ibérica* 12, nos. 575, 577, 589, 591, 596 (1894): 3, 6, 38, 231, 259, 262, 343, published in seven installments, which sees the female as suffering from a deficit of energy (hence women's need to "hoard" energy, making them passive and egoistic) and the male as having a surplus of energy (allowing men to be active and outgoing). Thus, Alas concludes, women are congenitally "conservative" and men are congenitally "liberal"—a definition of woman that was deeply threatening to a politically progressive thinker like Alas himself. Like other Krausist thinkers of his day, Alas supported education for women to equip them to be good educators of their children, on the supposition that they would cease working on marriage, and regarded women as incapable of a sense of justice, and hence

unfit for civil rights, because they were able to think only in subjective terms (see Labanyi, *Gender and Modernization*, 221–222).

40. Sinclair notes that envy is “the most pervasive expression of desire in the novel” (*Dislocations of Desire*, 59).

41. Ngai, *Ugly Feelings*, 162.

42. Ngai, 1.

43. Alas, *La Regenta*, 2:107.

44. Ngai, *Ugly Feelings*, 14.

45. Ngai, 14–22.

46. Alas, *La Regenta*, 1:341.

47. Alas, 1:341–347. This passage was used by me in a graduate seminar on “Reading Spanish Culture through Raymond Williams,” inspired by Williams’s attempt to trace the social circumstances that made possible the appearance in Elizabethan drama of the soliloquy as a dramatic mode. See Raymond Williams, *The Sociology of Culture* (Chicago: University of Chicago Press, 1995), 139, 145–147. The idea was to see if we could work out what might be the social frame that allowed free indirect discourse to first appear in the Spanish realist novel of the 1880s. The students observed that this example of free indirect discourse began and ended with an observation of the outside material world; this led them to hypothesize that free indirect discourse may have been an expression of concerns at the time about the difficulty of establishing a boundary between the external and inner worlds, since free indirect discourse superimposes objective and subjective narration such that the two cannot be distinguished. I thank the students in the seminar for their acute observations, on which I have drawn here. The relationship between the self and the outside world is precisely what was at stake in the above-mentioned debates on naturalism in 1880s Spain. As previously noted, affect theory too is concerned with the relationship of the external to the internal, which it sees as mutually constitutive.

CHAPTER 11

Female Masculinity in *La Regenta*

Jennifer Smith

In her book *Female Masculinity* (1998), Judith Halberstam challenges the idea that masculinity must be tied to men. She argues that masculinity is actually most visible, and most threatening, when it leaves the male body and asserts that one of her aims is precisely to pry apart masculinity, maleness, power, and domination.[1] In order to deconstruct such linkages, she employs terms such as *hegemonic masculinity* and *heroic masculinities* to refer to conventional ideas that link masculinity to power, strength, and dominance. Hegemonic masculinity has generally been used to describe a model of behavior for men who seek positions of power within certain groups in society.[2] Traditionally hegemonic models of masculinity have required constant demonstrations of manhood enacted by social or physical dominance over other men, thereby creating a hierarchy in which certain males necessarily dominate others.[3] In his historical analysis of models of hegemonic masculinity in the United States, Michael S. Kimmel cites the rise of capitalism, starting in the late eighteenth century, as pivotal in strengthening a dynamic that placed competition with other men at center stage in the achievement of manliness.

This concept of hegemonic masculinity is particularly useful in analyzing Leopoldo Alas's 1884–1885 novel *La Regenta*, as the question of power and dominance in a decaying feudal and imperial society threatened by social and economic change is intimately intertwined with questions of gender or, more specifically, with the degree to which various characters perform or defy their respective gender roles. While the ruling elite of Restoration Spain was clearly reluctant to renounce its privilege and waning empire in order to embrace a social hierarchy determined solely by the marketplace, we see in the novel the beginnings of the replacement of ideals of aristocratic manhood with bourgeois models of masculinity, just as the nouveau riche—the *indianos*, Pepe Ronzal, and even Fermín De Pas himself, although within the hierarchy of the traditional institution of the church—vie for positions of power within the upper echelons of society. This dynamic is played out most overtly in the power struggle between the canon and Don Álvaro Mesía to seduce Ana Ozores. Despite Fermín's genuine feelings for Ana, the central importance of the homosocial love triangle converts the female protagonist into a conduit for the interaction and competition between two men: a wealthy, middle-aged member of the ruling elite, Álvaro Mesía, and a more youthful, virile, ascending bourgeois, Fermín De Pas. This symbolic battle for dominance engages with medical and scientific discourses on gender and degeneration as well as those of Spain's national and imperial decline. Yet as the novel progresses, both men's inability to perform masculinity comes to the fore, leaving a void that is ultimately filled by masculine women.

Consequently, my approach to the discussion of female masculinity in *La Regenta* is two-pronged. First, I deconstruct the connection between the male body and masculinity by examining how the male characters' inability to perform masculinity undermines their claim to it. Then I turn my attention to the masculine women who populate the text. However, in contradiction to Halberstam's assertion that "female masculinity seems to be at its most threatening when coupled with lesbian desire,"[4] it is not same-sex desire that poses the greatest threat to society. Rather, it is a masculine, heterosexual woman with raw ambition and a strong capitalist sense who turns Vetustan society on its head.

The novel opens, appropriately, with the juxtaposition of images of virility and androgyny. We meet the protagonist, the canon Fermín De Pas, through the eyes of two prepubescent altar boys, Bismark and Celedonio, who, before the canon's arrival, are enjoying the feelings of superiority they receive from being atop the cathedral tower and looking down at the rest of Vetustan society. However, Celedonio quickly finds himself humbled and Bismark frightened when Don Fermín De Pas ascends to the top of the tower. Through the boys' eyes, the first thing we notice about Fermín is his size: "¡Qué grande se mostraba!"[5] (How huge he appeared!),[6] an observation that is followed by the narrator's statement that Celedonio barely reaches Fermín's waist.[7] The canon's refinement and impeccable dress also inspire awe and respect: "¡Aquello era un señorío!"[8] (This was real class!),[9] and his muscles and well-built frame reveal his physical strength and athletic potential. With thick black hair and no signs of aging, this thirty-five-year-old man in the prime of his life lengthens and brandishes his spyglass, which Bismark initially mistakes for a small cannon and then a rifle, over the various neighborhoods of Vetusta that he wishes to not only conquer but stab with his carving knife and devour.[10] His fascination with ascending hierarchies is represented by his passion for climbing to the tops of mountains and cathedral towers and by the tower itself, a sheath of muscles that shoots up into the sky like a gracious pyramid that cannot be matched in proportion and size.[11] Such phallic descriptions of the tower both serve as synecdochal representations of masculinity itself and tie Fermín's capitalist and colonial ambitions to his insatiable sexual appetite, which we become more acquainted with as the novel progresses.

This description of Fermín contrasts markedly with that of the twelve- to thirteen-year-old Celedonio, whose toothless mouth and large dirty-brown eyes reveal the salacious gaze of a street prostitute. This, combined with his feminine gestures and movements, lead the narrator to underscore this character's perverted nature.[12] The small, prepubescent, and grotesque Celedonio represents marginalized masculinities associated with feminine males and same-sex desire between men. Indeed, the gender crossing that this character embodies is represented in the novel by his and other characters' association to amphibians, specifically toads.[13] These slimy creatures that inhabit two worlds allude to Darwinian theory, since they evolved from fish that lived solely in the water into creatures that inhabit both land and water. This link to evolution is also important, as it relates to anxieties about the blurring lines between the sexes, since evolutionary theorists were arguing that the more advanced a civilization, the more distinct were the appearance and behavior of its men and women. Thus amphibians serve as metaphors for sexual androgyny and evoke anxieties about degeneration that would entail a large-scale blurring of the sexes.[14]

Yet in many ways, Celedonio is nothing more than a parodic representation of Fermín himself. Forced to hide his virility under a priest's cassock that feminizes him in the same way that it does other men in the church, Fermín desperately tries to prove his masculinity to Ana through displays of his physical strength—for example, by rescuing Obdulia when she is trapped in the swing—and to himself by dressing in hunter's attire and admiring his own masculine physique in the mirror. Yet his ultimate inability to get Ana to see him as a man rather than as an asexual priest shows the male body's inability, no matter how strong and sexually potent, to automatically confer masculinity. This is exemplified best in the scene in which De Pas is looking at himself in the mirror with his shirt off as he shaves:

> Estaba desnudo de medio cuerpo arriba. El cuello robusto parecía más fuerte ahora por la tensión a que le obligaba la violencia de la postura, al inclinarse sobre el lavabo de mármol blanco. Los brazos cubiertos de vello negro ensortijado, lo mismo que el pecho alto y fuerte, parecían de un atleta. El Magistral miraba con tristeza sus músculos de acero, de una fuerza inútil. . . . el mozo fuerte y velludo que tenía enfrente, en el espejo, le parecía otro yo que se había perdido, que había quedado en los montes, desnudo, cubierto de pelo como el rey de Babilonia, pero libre, feliz . . . Le asustaba tal espectáculo, le llevaba muy lejos de sus pensamientos de ahora, y se apresuró a vestirse. En cuanto se abrochó el alzacuello, el Magistral volvió a ser la imagen de la mansedumbre cristiana, fuerte, pero espiritual, humilde: seguía siendo esbelto, pero no

> formidable. Se parecía un poco a su querida torre de la catedral, también robusta, también proporcionada, esbelta y bizarra, mística, pero de piedra.[15]

> He was naked from the waste up. His powerful neck seemed even more powerful now, because of the strain put upon it by his tense position as he leaned over the white marble wash-basin. His arms, like his broad, powerful chest, were covered with fine black curly hair; they were the arms of an athlete. The canon looked sadly at his muscles of steel, charged with useless power. . . . The brawny, hairy young fellow before him in the mirror somehow seemed like a lost alter ego which had stayed behind in those hills—naked, as hairy as the king of Babylon, yet free, happy. He was alarmed by this sight, which carried his thoughts far away, and he dressed hurriedly. As soon as the canon had buttoned up his collar he was once again the image of Christian meekness, strong, yet spiritual and humble, still well built, of course, but no longer formidable. He was a little like his beloved cathedral tower, also powerful, well proportioned, well built and elegant and mystical; but made of stone.[16]

Without his vestments, Fermín is a muscular Hercules and a hirsute king of Babylonia, but as soon as he is dressed, he is emasculated and desexualized by being compared to a cathedral tower made of stone.

Ana's view of Fermín as androgynous is seen when, considering the possibility that the canon might actually be in love with her, she shakes as if she had come into contact with a cold, viscous body.[17] And Celedonio as a representation of Fermín's androgyny is seen most clearly at the close of the novel by Celedonio's taking Fermín's place and planting a toad's kiss on Ana's lips. In the end, the most masculine man in Vetusta is emasculated by Ana's inability to see him as a man, by Ana's choosing the cowardly and aging Álvaro as a lover over him, by Fermín's being the eroticized object of gaze of women such as Obdulia, by a society that provides no acceptable means of climbing the social ladder other than through the unnatural and desexing institution of the church, and finally, as the reader learns, by the complete control his masculine and tyrannical mother exercises over him.[18]

We meet yet another male "amphibian" in the opening chapter, Don Saturnino Bermúdez, the town historian, whose fear of women leads to his suspicious nighttime activities that leave him physically depleted the next morning and cause his chronic indigestion. This indirect reference to medical discourses on masturbation and seminal depletion in men—indigestion being just one of the many ills it was said to bring on[19]—is important as a motif that reappears throughout the novel and serves as the other principal threat to a man's masculinity. The nineteenth century saw an explosion of discourses warning against the ills of seminal depletion, which included nervous disorders, paralysis, and even death.[20] According to the prominent nineteenth-century doctor and hygienist Felipe

Monlau, the loss of one ounce of semen was equivalent to the loss of forty ounces of blood.[21] A virile male body wisely economized its semen. While masturbation was considered the most wasteful form of spending this vital fluid, any and all sexual activity was said to weaken the male body. The importance of this theory is related not only to bourgeois capitalist discourses that warned against profligate spending of any kind but also to the emasculation of other male characters in the text. Don Álvaro's waning sexual stamina is put to the test when this forty-something Don Juan, upon finding himself in the unnatural position of having to satisfy the desires of two sexually ravenous women, Ana and Petra, is unable to perform—a situation, however, he admits to having experienced before.[22] Even the young son of the Marquis, Paco Vegallana, exhibits "carne blanda" (flabby flesh) and a lack of muscular strength because of his sexual conquests, or "lides de amor"[23] (battles of love).[24] Thus here and elsewhere, the male body proves itself unable to reproduce heroic ideals of masculinity, as it has finite reserve of semen, an essential vital fluid, and a "currency of masculinity."[25] As seminal depletion was said to lead to nervous disorders such as hysteria and spermatorrhea (a dubious but greatly feared disease at the time in which the male body started to involuntarily leak semen), it further feminized the male body, tying it to leakage (the female body was said to be inferior precisely because it was always leaking), excessive spending (a vice associated mostly with women), and feminine nervous diseases such as hysteria. The result was a masculinity precariously held in place by a male body under constant threat of emasculation. It is important to note that in the novel, seminal depletion and/or impotence only affects men of the ruling classes (Álvaro, Paco, Saturnino, and Víctor), indirectly critiquing the ruling elite's lack of wise capitalist investment into the economy, which leaves the nation too enervated to hold on to its empire. Don Fermín, on the other hand, the son of a "licenciado en artillería"[26] (artillery graduate),[27] has an excess of sexual desire and vital bodily fluids, since neither Petra nor Teresina—nor any of the other maids whom he appears to have impregnated—dampen his sexual appetite or ability to perform sexually. This connects his capitalist acumen and successful political conquests to the strength of his promiscuous, savage, and bestial, ascending, working-class male body that will inevitably replace the unproductive, effete, and lazy upper-class elite male.

While these hygienic discourses on seminal depletion tried to discredit the idea that masculinity was conferred through heterosexual conquest, they do so by acknowledging this idea's hold on the cultural imaginary of the time. For example, Ciro Bayo in his 1902 *Higiene sexual del soltero* (*Sexual Hygiene for Single People*) argues that while sexual conquest is the most valued symbol of masculinity within society, the truth is, such men are less masculine than men who practice moderation in their venereal activities.[28] It seems that in Vetusta, few heed the words of the hygienists, as Don Álvaro's claim to hegemonic masculinity is conferred precisely through his sexual conquests, which he acknowledges he carries out solely for political reasons.[29] His conquests are publicized, and he himself boasts about them—most tellingly in the scene at the casino, where he recounts stories of former conquests, even a brutal rape, to the delight of his male interlocutors.[30] The more virtuous the women and/or the more formidable the male rival, the more cultural capital a conquest conferred. Thus the fact that Fermín, one of the most powerful men in Vetusta, is his rival in his pursuit of Ana only makes the battle more potentially rewarding. The canon recognizes this early on: "Había adivinado en [Álvaro] un rival en el dominio de Vetusta"[31] (He had conjectured that he [Álvaro] was a rival for the control of Vetusta).[32] While De Pas publicly displays his physical superiority over Álvaro, it is of secondary importance, since only the seduction of Ana can confer the spot at the top of Vetusta's hierarchy of men.

The warnings of the hygienists, however, come back to haunt Álvaro. Finding himself "bankrupted" from the ravenous sexual appetite of his last lover, he spends months attempting to recover his vigor. He reads hygiene manuals, goes to the gym, goes horseback riding, and most important, abstains from sexual activity.[33] While Álvaro exercises to restore his supply of essential bodily fluids, the canon exercises to burn off excess sexual energy despite all the women at his disposal.[34] Fermín therefore has the upper hand not only in terms of youth and physical strength but also in terms of sexual stamina. Toward the end, Álvaro admits to faking both youth and virility in exchange for social status,[35] an idea that is brought home when he tries to flee the duel with Don Víctor and when, during the duel, he cowardly shoots the man who just spared his life.

Interestingly, as is the case with Fermín, Álvaro's other claim to masculinity is his physical attractiveness, refinement, and elegance. Indeed, Ana and other women are attracted precisely to Álvaro's good looks, impeccable dress, and sophistication. Yet in this instance, Álvaro actually defies bourgeois norms of masculinity that recommended downplaying one's attire and avoiding the eroticized gaze. He acknowledges that it is his good looks that women admire in him and puts much care into his clothes, making purchases in Paris at a time when French fashion was discouraged for men, since it was seen as too feminine. Thus the contradiction is clear: Álvaro acquires masculine status by willingly accepting the feminine role of the eroticized object of the gaze and of the *elegante*, or dandy, who was criticized in nineteenth-century Spain for being frivolous and effeminate. This makes Álvaro conform to Kimmel's description of the genteel patriarch as "an anachronistic feminized dandy" who was "ineffective and outmoded"[36] and who would come to be replaced by bourgeois capitalist models of masculinity better embodied by Fermín De Pas and his mother—that is, if Fermín were not a dignitary of the church and if Paula were not a woman.

Paradoxically, it is actually certain female characters in the text who better exhibit many of the masculine traits these men lack or are unable to embody. Halberstam ascertains that in the early nineteenth century, the mannish woman who actively desired other women would have been referred to as a "hermaphrodite," a "tribade," or a "female husband" rather than a "lesbian."[37] S/he also makes clear, however, that there were surely "many examples of masculine women in history who had no interest in same-sex sexuality."[38] Accordingly, I will first look at two female characters who exhibit same-sex desire, Visita and Obdulia, and how they conform to nineteenth-century discourses on tribadism. Then I turn my attention to the most masculine woman in the text, Doña Paula, who actually exhibits little sexual desire whatsoever.

Nineteenth-century Spanish hygiene manuals describe the tribade as a woman with an overly developed clitoris who would inadvertently, and/or intentionally, stimulate herself by rubbing her enlarged organ against foreign objects or other people. For example, Juan Cuesta y Ckerner states, "El clitoris puede encontrarse enormemente desarrollado, y semejante disposicion puede llegar a producir la ninfomania por el orgasmo constante que ocasione el roce de los vestidos"[39] (The clitoris can be overly developed, and such an arrangement can come to produce nymphomania due to the constant orgasm produced from the friction with clothes).[40]

These women's overdeveloped organ was believed to make them manly, sterile, and indifferent to men and heterosexual intercourse. Monlau refers to these women as "marimachos ó mujeres hombrunas *{viragines}*, de costumbres masculinas, voz ronca, barba poblada, clitoris muy abultado, etc."[41] (Tomboys or butch women *{viragines}* with masculine ways, a husky voice, a bushy beard, a bulky clitoris, etc.).[42] And Suarez Casañ states that "mari-machos ['viragines'] de los latinos, son casi siempre esteriles"[43] (butch women ["viragines"] in Latin, are almost always sterile).[44] Both Monlau and Amancio Peratoner emphasize not only the lesbian behaviors of such women but also their proclivity to nymphomania, thereby tying tribadism and nymphomania together. Peratoner, for example, writes, "El desarrollo excesivo de dicho órgano hacia las mujeres indiferentes á las caricias de los hombres y las arrastraba a apetecer asiduamente la sociedad de las personas de su sexo. La voluptuosidad clitoridea es para esta clase de mujeres, llamadas TRIBADAS entre los antiguos, una necesidad imperiosa que acrecenta incesantemente el delirio de sus imaginaciones"[45] (The overdevelopment of said organ made women indifferent to men's caresses and led them to frequently desire the company of members of their own sex. The clitorian voluptuousness is for this type of women, called TRIBADES by the ancients, an urgent need that incessantly increases the delirium of their imaginations).[46] Doctors' pathologization of the clitoris stems from anxieties about this organ's role in female sexuality. Its lack of purpose in reproduction and its similarity to the penis challenged nineteenth-century views on sexuality. It blurred gender dichotomies by undermining theories of the sexes that posited that woman was man's polar opposite. It "became the source of great anxiety because it represented another penis on the female body. . . . Anxieties arose about clitorides capable of penetration; because of these anxieties, the clitoris, its size and function, was immediately likened to same-sex desire."[47]

Visita and Obdulia are the two female characters who most clearly reveal same-sex desire. Visita is married to a petit-bourgeois, an employee at a bank, whose modest income leads her to look for entertainment outside of the home among her circle of friends, leaving her husband and children hungry and abandoned. Indeed, she spends most of her time engaged in helping Álvaro seduce Ana, who, as Cristina Mathews has argued, seems to be her real object of desire.[48] Her "perverted" gender identity is due to not only her extramarital affairs, cuckolded husband, and her failure to conform to bourgeois discourses on the separate spheres (it is her husband who occupies the private space of the home, while she occupies the public masculine sphere)[49] but also her dirty undergarments, which make Álvaro wince just at the thought of them, and her sticky fingers. Her constant consumption of sweets not only is a sublimation of her sexual desires, seen most obviously in the scene where she eats sweets as she watches over Ana in her bed,[50] but ties to the motif of the viscosity associated with amphibians, already explained as a metaphor for sexual androgyny. Indeed, her same-sex desire is seen most explicitly when she tries to excite Álvaro by describing what Ana looks like when she is in the midst of one of her hysterical attacks.[51] As James Mandrell asserts, "El torrente de palabras y los signos de exclamación nos dicen todo: la descripción de los ataques de la Regenta no sirve solo para informar a Álvaro, también estimula y hasta excita Visitación, como indican los puntos suspensivos"[52] (The outpouring of words and exclamation marks says it all; the description of La Regenta's attacks serve not only to inform Álvaro but also to stimulate and even sexually excite Visitación, as the ellipsis suggests).[53]

While Visita's same-sex desire for Ana implicitly associates her with the nineteenth-century tribade, it is Obdulia who more clearly exhibits a phallic sexuality. Beginning in chapter 1, her sexual behavior, like the canon's, is dominating and described in militaristic terms of conquest: she wears a breastplate of scarlet silk from which her bosom appears about to explode and imperial boots.[54] Obdulia, like the "masculine and possibly predatory woman" Halberstam describes, has extramarital affairs and exhibits "aggressive sexual tendencies."[55] Her status as a beautiful young widow ties her to nymphomaniacs and hysterics and partially explains her predatory, sexual pursuits that objectify both men and women. For example, she actively pursues men of all professions and social classes, from the bishop of Nauplia, to the coachman Diego, to Pedro, the cook.[56] As Lawrence Rich insightfully points out in the case of Pedro, it is Obdulia who puts a spoon in Pedro's mouth, "which she has just caressed with her lips to excite him sexually," forming a parallel with the scene in which Fermín puts a biscuit in his maid's mouth. According to Rich, "Obdulia's behavior inverts bourgeois class and gender expectations: whereas Fermín gives and Teresa receives (the biscuit), Obdulia is shown as sexually active rather than passive, as she gives (the spoon) to a lower-class male who docilely receives it from her."[57] Obdulia's objectification of Fermín is actively resisted by the canon himself, who seems to sense Obdulia's dominating role as the bearer of the gaze.[58] Obdulia's masculine sexuality is explicitly tied to same-sex desire when she lusts after Ana, who is about to appear barefoot in the Holy Week procession: "'¿Cuándo llegará?' preguntaba la viuda, lamiéndose los labios, invadida de una envidia admiradora, y sintiendo extraños dejos de una especie de lujuria bestial, disparatada, inexplicable por lo absurdo. Sentía Obdulia en aquel momento así . . . un deseo vago . . . de . . . de . . . ser hombre"[59] ("When is she coming?" asked the widow, licking her lips, possessed by admiring envy, and conscious of the strange promptings of a kind of crazy, brutal lust, so absurd as to be inexplicable. Obdulia felt a—vague desire—to—to—to be a man).[60] The fact that Obdulia already "plays the man" in her sexual relationships with men, particularly with men of lower socioeconomic status, suggests that Obdulia's gender crossing in this scene is more than just a whim.

Despite these displays of aggressive female sexuality and same-sex desire between women, the manliest woman in the text is Paula Raíces, the canon's mother. For Doña Paula, her own sexual desires are of secondary importance, as she puts her own sexuality to the service of her ambition and desire for money. Rather, Doña Paula's claim to masculinity is secured through physical and character traits. Physically she resembles a man: she is almost as tall as her son and appears to be wider in the shoulders.[61] Her large masculine frame is coupled with a physical strength superior to most men, demonstrated by her ability to break up brawls among the miners in her bar as well as successfully fight off these men's sexual advances on her own.[62] She has a narrow, bony forehead; cold blue eyes that hide all emotion; and like her son, a large nose, thin lips, and a pointy chin.[63] And unlike the dandy Don Álvaro, Doña Paula follows the fashion advice for men that recommended dark, discrete clothing, especially black, so as not to draw attention to oneself. Indeed, she wears a black habit and shawl that conceal everything but her wide shoulders and choppy frame.[64] Her cigarette smoking is also a decidedly masculine activity with imperial connotations, as tobacco was a source of wealth coming into Spain from its American colonies.

Doña Paula's masculinity is also conveyed by her complete control over the men in her life (the first priest she worked for; the second, who is now a bishop; and her son). Indeed, she believes in "la omnipotencia de la mujer. Ella era buen ejemplo"[65] (the omnipotence of woman. She herself was a good example).[66] We see Paula's dominance over men specifically in the positions she has occupied. Her job as *ama de llaves* (head housekeeper) dialogs with J. E. Hartzenbusch's sketch in *Los españoles pintados por sí mismos* (*Spaniards Painted by Themselves*; 1843–1844), in which we learn that the *ama de llaves* was generally understood to be an ugly, masculine, single or widowed, servant woman who lived with a bachelor or widower that she came to control completely.[67] Hartzenbusch underscores these women's virile appearance, describing one with a mustache and another with wide shoulders, a thick waist, and huge feet.[68] Doña Paula's character seems to have been lifted not only from these pages but also from José de Grijalva's description of the *cantinera* (barmaid), which appears in the same volume. Like Doña Paula as a canteen owner and barmaid, the *cantinera* is an ugly woman of manly appearance married to a man who lets her do all the work at the bar.[69]

Doña Paula's past positions also allow her to develop her business skills at a time when economic matters were strictly considered the domain of men. First she makes a pretty penny selling cheap food and wine that has been watered down to exhausted and famished miners and later saves the priest Fortunato Camoirán from bankruptcy twice. These experiences then translate into a brutal laissez-faire capitalism in which she creates a monopoly on the selling of religious items, illegally using her son's influence to ruin the business and life of their competitor. These profits are then secretly deposited in the bank and used to purchase properties outside of Vetusta. But her most lucrative capitalist venture is her own son, whom she refers to as "su capital" (investment) and "una fábrica de dinero" (mint) from whom she has the right to "cobrar los réditos" (charge interest):

> Fermo, además de su hijo era su capital, una fábrica de dinero. Ella le había hecho hombre, a costa de sacrificios, de vergüenzas de que él no sabía ni la mitad, de vigilias, de sudores, de cálculos, de paciencia, de astucia, de energía y de pecados sórdidos; por consiguiente no pedía mucho si pedía intereses al resultado de sus esfuerzos, al Provisor de Vetusta. El mundo era de su hijo, porque él era el de más talento, el más elocuente, el más sagaz, el más sabio, el más hermoso pero su hijo era de ella, debía cobrar los réditos de su capital, y si la fábrica se paraba o se descomponía, podía reclamar daños y perjuicios, tenía derecho a exigir que Fermo continuase produciendo.[70]

> Fermo, as well as being her son, was her investment, her mint. She had made a man of him through self sacrifice, shameful deeds, half of which he knew nothing about, sleepless nights, sweat, calculation, patience, astuteness, energy and sordid sins. She was not, then, asking for too much if she asked the result of all her efforts, the vicar-general of Vetusta, for her interest. The world belonged to her son, because he was the most talented man of them all, the most eloquent, the shrewdest, the wisest, the handsomest; but her son belonged to her, she had a right to charge interest on her capital. And if the mint stopped working or broke down it was her prerogative to claim for damages; she had a right to demand that Fermo should maintain production.[71]

Doña Paula's natural talent for marketplace competition is also tied to her rejection of women and all things associated with femininity. In contrast to her son, Paula is devoid of affection or compassion and can only understand love as tyrannical control: "Doña Paula no se enternecía, tenía esa ventaja. Llamaba mojigangas a las caricias, y quería a su hijo mucho a su manera, desde lejos. Era el suyo un cariño opresor, un tirano"[72] (Doña Paula had the advantage of never being moved by anything. She called caresses tomfoolery, but she was very fond of her son in her way, from a distance. Her love for him was an oppressive tyrannical love).[73] Along with her lack of empathy is her blatant misogyny. She insists that prostitutes are better than the average woman, who sucks the life and honor from a man: "Cien veces, mil veces peor, que es que le tiran de la levita a don Saturno, porque ésas cobran, y dejan en paz la que la ha buscado; pero las señoras, chupan la vida, la honra . . . deshacen en un mes lo que yo hice en veinte años"[74] (A hundred times, a thousand times worse than the ones who tickle Don Saturn's fancy, because they take their money and leave the man who came for them in peace. But these fine ladies suck away at your life, your honour, they destroy in a month what it took me twenty years to build).[75] She therefore tries to prevent her son from idealizing any woman by procuring mistresses for him. She even has sadistic fantasies about Ana that include slitting her throat, dragging her by her hair, turning her into her son's sex slave, pulling out her tongue, and killing her:

> Pensó en mil absurdos, en milagros de madre, en ir ella misma a buscar a la infame que tenía la culpa de aquello, y degollarla, o traerla arrastrando por los malditos cabellos, allí, al pie de aquella cama a velar como ella, a llorar como ella, a salvar a su hijo a toda costa, a costa de la fama, de la salvación de todo, a salvarle o morir con él. . . . De estas ideas absurdas, que rechazaba después el buen sentido, le quedaba a doña Paula una ira sorda reconcentrada, y una aspiración vaga a formar un proyecto extraño, una intriga para cazar a la Regenta y hacerla servir para lo que Fermo quisiera . . . y después matarla o arrancarle la lengua.[76]

> She thought of a thousand absurdities, of a mother's miracles, of going herself in search of the infamous woman who was to blame for it all, and cutting her throat, or dragging her back by her damned hair, back to the foot of that bed, to watch over him like her, to weep like her, to save her son at any cost, at the cost of reputation, of salvation, of everything to save him or die with him. . . . These absurd ideas, which Doña Paula's good sense dispelled, left her with a pent-up, concentrated anger and a vague notion of forming a strange plan, a plot to catch the judge's wife and make her submit to being used by Fermo for whatever he wanted—and then kill her or tear out her tongue.[77]

Thus in her exaggerated masculine appearance and behavior, Paula is both a consummate and a parodic portrayal of dominant forms of masculinity.

Paradoxically, gender hybridity is simultaneously portrayed in the novel as both natural and artificial. The church, because of its "unnatural" rules on celibacy, creates sexually perverted gender hybrids guilty of sexual aberrations and crimes such as homosexuality, pedophilia, and solicitation. Yet "naturally" occurring phenomena, such as male physical beauty, impotence, and seminal depletion, "naturally" emasculate the male body by converting it into an eroticized sex object and easily leaving it physically and sexually depleted. Similarly, society causes Ana's hysteria by placing her in a marriage in which her "natural" urges for intercourse and reproduction are stifled. Yet at the same time, those women who give free expression to their "natural" sexual desires, such as Visita and Obdulia, are portrayed as nymphomaniacs, predatory sexual vampires who "suck" the life force from males, and tribades who turn their sexual desire from men onto women. This contradictory representation of gender hybridity is echoed in the motifs of amphibians and Frígilis's grafting (*los injertos*). While the omnipresence of viscous amphibians suggests the constant "natural" threat of gender ambiguity, Frígilis's pseudoscientific grafting experiments create sterile and/or deformed hybrids that cannot survive.

The term *hybridity* has its roots in biology, where it refers to "the cross-breeding of two species by grafting or cross-pollination to form a third, 'hybrid' species."[78] However, it has more recently been incorporated into linguistics and racial theory to refer to the mixing of languages and races, respectively. Although hybridity has historically been a negatively charged term that reinforced racist beliefs of purity and authenticity, Homi Bhabha has stressed that it is also precisely the space in which categories of hierarchical purity are contested:

> The word hybridity has been most recently associated with the work of Homi K. Bhabha, whose analysis of colonizer/colonized relations stresses their interdependence and the unusual construction of their subjectivities. . . . Cultural identity always emerges in this contradictory and ambivalent space [of hybridity], which for Bhabha makes the claim to a hierarchical 'purity' of cultures untenable. For him, the recognition of this ambivalent space may help us overcome the *exoticism* of *cultural diversity* in favour of the recognition of an empowering hybridity within which cultural difference may operate."[79]

While Bhabha is speaking specifically of culture and race, the same can be said of gender, as nineteenth-century medical and social discourses were insisting on the equally untenable polarization of the sexes. Thus while gender hybridity is employed in the novel to critique social degeneration and Spain's national and imperial decline, at the same time it appears as a naturally occurring phenomenon that disrupts artificial gender hierarchies. Perhaps most disruptive is Doña Paula's performance of masculinity, which can be seen as an example of *mimicry*,[80] which actually reproduces and contests the proclaimed superiority of men. The strong, competitive, and ruthless Doña Paula represents both what Spain needs (strength and capitalist enterprise) and what it should avoid (greedy self-centeredness and corruption). Moreover, by projecting the most dominant form of masculinity onto a working-class female body, the novel grotesquely critiques precisely what it suggests the nation is lacking and portrays a supposedly "unnatural," gender hybridity as an inherent, "natural" threat that society must combat—an aporia that the novel does not, and cannot, resolve.

NOTES

1. Judith Halberstam, *Female Masculinity* (Durham, N.C.: Duke University Press, 1998), 2.

2. R. W. Connell and James W. Messerschmidt, "Hegemonic Masculinity: Rethinking the Concept," *Gender and Society* 19, no. 6 (2005): 832.

3. Michael S. Kimmel, "Masculinity as Homophobia: Fear, Shame, and Silence in the Construction of Gender Identity," in *The Masculinities Reader*, ed. Stephen M. Whitehead and Frank J. Barrett (Cambridge: Polity, 2001), 272–275.

4. Halberstam, *Female Masculinity*, 28.

5. Leopoldo Alas, *La Regenta*, 2 vols., ed. Juan Oleza (1884–1885; Madrid: Cátedra, 1989), 1:149.

6. John Rutherford, trans., *La Regenta*, by Leopoldo Alas (London: Penguin, 2005), 25. All English translations of *La Regenta* are taken from Rutherford.

7. Alas, *La Regenta*, 1:149.

8. Alas, 1:149.

9. Rutherford, *La Regenta*, 26.

10. Alas, *La Regenta*, 1:151–152.

11. Alas, 1:138.

12. Alas, 1:148.

13. Celedonio is most directly related to an amphibian in the last chapter, when the kiss he gives Ana resembles that of the belly of a toad.

14. In *Degeneration* (1892), Max Nordau argued that degeneration was associated with effeminacy as well as a blurring of the distinctions between the sexes. See Lawrence Rich, "Fear and Loathing in Vetusta: Coding Class and Gender in Clarín's *La Regenta*," *Revista Canadiense de Estudios Hispánicos* 25, no. 3 (2001): 513.

15. Alas, *La Regenta*, 1:494–495.

16. Rutherford, *La Regenta*, 232–233.

17. "Ana se estremeció como al contacto de un cuerpo viscoso y frío. Aquel sarcasmo de amor la hizo sonreír a ella misma con amargura que llegó hasta la boca desde las entrañas" (Alas, *La Regenta*, 2:391–92). See the translation in Rutherford, *La Regenta*: "Ana shuddered as she had felt the touch of something cold and slimy. That travesty of love made her smile to herself with a bitterness which came to her mouth from deep in her body" (563–564).

18. Fermín himself recognizes the complete control his mother has over him:

> Aquel era su tirano: un tirano consentido, amado, muy amado, pero formidable a veces. ¿Y cómo romper aquellas cadenas? A ella se lo debía todo. Sin la perseverancia de aquella mujer, sin su voluntad de acero que iba derecha a un fin rompiendo por todo ¿qué hubiera sido él? Un pastor en las montañas, o un cavador en las minas. Él valía más que todos, pero su madre valía más que él. El instinto de doña Paula era superior a todos los raciocinios. Sin ella hubiera sido él arrollado algunas veces en la lucha de la

vida. Sobre todo, cuando sus pies se enredaban en redes sutiles que le tendía un enemigo ¿quién le libraba de ellas? Su madre. Era su égida. Sí, ella primero que todo. Su despotismo era la salvación; aquel yugo saludable. Además, una voz interior le decía que lo mejor de su alma era su cariño y su respeto filial. (Alas, *La Regenta*, 1:505)

She was his tyrant: a dear, beloved, deeply beloved tyrant, but sometimes an overpowering one. And how could he break his chains? He owed everything to her. Without her perseverance, without her iron will-power, which went straight to its goal, breaking through everything in its path, what would he be now? A cowherd in the mountains or a hewer of coal in the mines. He was abler than all the rest of them, but his mother was abler still. Doña Paula's instincts were superior to all reasoning. Without her he would have been routed more than once in the struggle of life. In particular, when his feet were enmeshed in the fine nets put in his path by his enemies, who pulled them free? His mother. She was his aegis. Yes, mother before everything else. Her despotism was his salvation; her yoke was a beneficent yoke. And, furthermore, an inner voice told him that his filial affection and respect were the best part of his soul. (Rutherford, *La regenta*, 241)

19. Collin McKinney, "'Enemigos de la virilidad': Sex, Masturbation, and Celibacy in Nineteenth-Century Spain," *Prisma Social* 13 (2014–2015): 81.

20. McKinney, 82.

21. McKinney, 87.

22. "Decaer y decaer en presencia de Ana era horroroso; era ridículo y era infame. Sí; él faltaba a su juramento envejeciendo, perdiendo fuerzas. Recordaba con escalofríos épocas pasadas en que decadencias pasajeras, producidas por excesos de placer, le habían obligado a recurrir a expedientes bochornosos" (Alas, *La Regenta*, 2:514). And see the translation: "Declining, and declining in front of Ana, was horrible, it was ridiculous and it was infamous. He shuddered as he remembered past periods of his life when temporary shortcomings, produced by excesses of pleasure, had made him resort to embarrassing stratagems" (Rutherford, *La Regenta*, 652, translation slightly modified).

23. Alas, *La Regenta*, 1:604.

24. Rutherford, *La Regenta*, 307.

25. McKinney, "'Enemigos de la virilidad,'" 88.

26. Alas, *La Regenta*, 1:639.

27. Translation mine.

28. Mark Harpring, "Sexo, sexualidad e ideal masculino en *Higiene sexual del soltero*, de Ciro Bayo," in *Memoria histórica, género e interdisciplinariedad: Los estudios culturales hispánicos en el siglo XXI*, ed. Santiago Juan-Navarro and Joan Torres-Pou (Madrid: Biblioteca Nueva, 2008), 163.

29. Alas, *La Regenta*, 1:369.

30. Alas, 2:239–241.

31. Alas, 1:504.

32. Rutherford, *La Regenta*, 240.

33. Alas, *La Regenta*, 2:397–398.

34. Alas, 2:399.

35. Alas, 2:514–515.

36. Kimmel, "Masculinity as Homophobia," 270.

37. Halberstam, *Female Masculinity*, 50.

38. Halberstam, 57.

39. Juan Cuesta y Ckerner, *Enfermedades de las mujeres: Extracto de las asignaturas que tienen que estudiar los cirujanos de segunda clase que aspiran al título de Facultativo habilitados por medio de estudios privados* (Madrid: Tomás Alonso, 1868), 7.

40. Translation mine.

41. Pedro Felipe Monlau, *Higiene del matrimonio o el libro de los casados* (Madrid: M. Rivadeneyra, 1858), 108.

42. Translation mine.

43. V. Suárez Casañ, *Enciclopedia médica popular*, vol. 2 (Barcelona: M. Maucci, 1894), 476.

44. Translation mine.

45. Amancio Peratoner, *Fisiología de la noche de bodas: Misterios del lecho conyugal* (Barcelona: N. Curriols, 1892), 111.

46. Translation mine.

47. Halberstam, *Female Masculinity*, 60.

48. Cristina Mathews, "Making the Nuclear Family: Kinship, Homosexuality, and *La Regenta*," *Revista de Estudios Hispánicos* 37, no. 1 (2003): 83.

49. James Mandrell, "Estudios gay y lesbianos: La revelación del cuerpo masculino: Una mirada gay," in *El hispanismo en los Estados Unidos: Discursos críticos/prácticas textuales*, ed. José Manuel del Pino and Francisco La Rubia Prado (Madrid: Visor, 1999), 219; Rich, "Fear and Loathing," 509–510.

50. Rich, "Fear and Loathing," 509–510; Mathews, "Making the Nuclear Family," 83.

51. Alas, *La Regenta*, 1:412; Mathews, "Making the Nuclear Family," 83.

52. Mandrell, "Estudios gay y lesbianos," 217.

53. Translation mine.

54. Alas, *La Regenta*, 1:177.

55. Halberstam, *Female Masculinity*, 51.

56. Rich, "Fear and Loathing," 511.

57. Rich, 512; Alas, *La Regenta*, 1:403.

58. "Las miradas más ardientes, más negras de aquellos ojos negros, grandes y arasadores eran para De Pas; los adoradores de la viuda lo sabían y le envidiaban. Pero él maldecía de aquel bloqueo" (Alas, *La Regenta*, 1:178). And see the translation: "The most ardent, the darkest look of those large, dark, burning eyes were for De Pas; and the widow's worshippers knew it, and envied him. Yet he cursed her blockade" (Rutherford, *La Regenta*, 44).

59. Alas, *La Regenta*, 2:428.

60. Rutherford, *La Regenta*, 591.

61. Alas, *La Regenta*, 1:497.

62. Alas, 1:645.

63. Alas, 1:497.

64. Alas, 1:497.

65. Alas, 1:503.

66. Rutherford, *La Regenta*, 239.

67. J. E. Hartzenbusch, "El ama de llaves," in *Los españoles pintados por sí mismos*, ed. Ignacio Boix (Madrid: I. Boix Editor, 1843), 124.

68. Hartzenbusch, 126.

69. José de Grijalva, "La cantinera," in *Los españoles pintados*, 271–272. A word about Petra, a woman who seems destined to follow in Paula's footsteps, seems in order here.

While Petra is physically much more conventionally feminine than Doña Paula, both women willingly use their sexuality as an item of exchange, manipulation, and blackmail to improve their own economic standing, revealing a pragmatism and ambition more associated with bourgeois capitalistic ideals of manhood than with bourgeois femininity.

70. Alas, *La Regenta*, 1:636.

71. Rutherford, *La Regenta*, 330–331.

72. Alas, *La Regenta*, 1:635.

73. Rutherford, *La Regenta*, 330.

74. Alas, *La Regenta*, 1:633.

75. Rutherford, *La Regenta*, 328–329.

76. Alas, *La Regenta*, 2:412.

77. Rutherford, *La Regenta*, 578.

78. Bill Ashcroft, Gareth Griffiths, and Helen Tiffin, *Post-colonial Studies: The Key Concepts* (London: Routledge, 2000), 118.

79. Ashcroft, Griffiths, and Tiffin, 118, 120–121, emphasis in the original.

80. "Mimicry has come to describe the *ambivalent* relationship between colonizer and colonized. When colonial discourse encourages the colonized subject to 'mimic' the colonizer, by adopting the colonizer's cultural habits, assumptions, institutions and values, the result is never a simple reproduction of those traits. Rather the result is a 'blurred copy' of the colonizer that can be quite threatening. This is because mimicry is never far from mockery, since it can appear to parody whatever it mimics. Mimicry therefore locates a crack in the certainty of colonial dominance, an uncertainty in its control of the behaviour of the colonized" (Ashcroft, Griffiths, and Tiffin, 138, emphasis in the original). The same occurs in terms of gender in *La Regenta*: Doña Paula's "mimicry" of masculinity both imitates and mocks the supposedly essential characteristics of the dominant sex.

Afterword

A few concluding words seem in order, as a lot has transpired in terms of feminist politics since I penned the introduction a little less than a year ago. During that time, Merriam Webster named *feminism* as the word of the year because it was the most frequently looked-up word in 2017; their online dictionary experienced a 70 percent increase in searches for the term.[1] Summarizing what appear to be the reasons for this renewed interest in feminism, Kristine Phillips of the *Washington Post* cites the size and impact of both the Women's March and the #MeToo movement.[2] The latter was sparked off by high-profile women speaking out against the sexual abuse they had experienced and was followed by thousands more women coming forward and many of the accused resigning or being fired.[3] More than anything, the #MeToo movement revealed how endemic sexual harassment still is despite all the gains women had made in the last century.[4]

Another reason for the spike in searches for the meaning of *feminism* was a comment by Kellyanne Conway, counselor to president Trump, in which she sought to distance herself from the term: "It's difficult for me to call myself a feminist in the classic sense because it seems to be very anti-male and it certainly is very pro-abortion, and I'm neither anti-male or pro-abortion."[5] This statement alone sent many to their online dictionaries in search of an answer to the question, What is feminism?

The recent prominence of and controversy surrounding feminism take us full circle to the discussion in the introduction. In the Conway quote, we see the persistence of many women's rejection of feminism, a phenomenon Emilia Pardo Bazán herself cited as the biggest obstacle to women's obtaining equality. Moreover, the discursive ambiguity of the word *feminist*—which Conway's comment highlights—is one of the themes of Pardo Bazán 1909 story "Feminista" ("Feminist") about a young woman, Clotilde Peregales, who marries an older man, Nicolás Abreu, who is both an incorrigible womanizer and an outspoken defender of the traditional gender order. To ensure that Clotilde knows her place from day one, the morning after their wedding night, Nicolás orders Clotilde to put on his pants, explaining, "He querido que te pongas los pantalones en este momento señalado para que sepas, querida Clotilde, que en toda tu vida volverás a ponértelos. Que los he de llevar yo"[6] (I wanted you to put on my pants right now so that you know, dear Clotilde, that you will never put them on again. I am the one who will wear them).

Clotilde fulfills her role as submissive wife until Nicolás contracts a terminal illness and becomes physically dependent on her. During this time, the initial power dynamic of the marriage is inverted and given symbolic representation when every morning Clotilde gives her husband the following order: "¡Ponte mis enaguas, querido Nicolás! ¡Ponte aprisa mis enaguas! . . . Para que sepas que las llevas ya toda tu vida, mientras yo sea tu enfermerita, ¿entiendes?"[7] (Put on my petticoat, dear Nicolás! Put on my petticoat right now! . . . So that you know that you will now wear it for the rest of your life, as long as I am your nurse, do you understand?).

This story has baffled critics, since it remains unclear if the story is a defense of feminism or a reinforcement of the negative conception of feminists as domineering and "anti-male," to use Conway's term. This story and the questions it raises also relate to the cover image of the volume, which shows Emilia Pardo Bazán slipping on a pair of trousers. How are we to read this visual image? Are we to admire her brave defiance of gender conventions or is the image ridiculing her gender transgression? Or is it perhaps doing a little of both? While women wearing pants is now a common practice, even today to say that a woman "wears the pants" bears with it all the original negative connotations.[8] Thus just like the image, the term *feminism* remains polysemic, carrying equally powerful positive and negative meanings depending on who reads or hears the sign. The perseverance of this phenomenon over the last century suggests that it will continue long into the future.

NOTES

1. Kristine Phillips, "'Feminism' Is Merriam-Webster's Word of the Year, Thanks in Part to Kellyanne Conway," *Washington Post*, December 12, 2017, https://www.washingtonpost.com/news/arts-and-entertainment/wp/2017/12/12/feminism-is-merriam-websters-word-of-the-year-thanks-in-part-to-kellyanne-conway/?utm_term=.3eab51ff72f8.
2. Phillips.
3. Phillips.
4. Some of the victims were men, but the vast majority were women.
5. Phillips, "'Feminism.'"
6. Emilia Pardo Bazán, "Feminista," in *"El encaje roto" y otros cuentos*, ed. Joyce Tolliver (New York: MLA, 1996), 115.
7. Pardo Bazán, 116.
8. This connection between feminism and fashion dialogs with Roberta Johnson's treatment of the matter in chapter 3.

Bibliography

Ahmed, Sara. *The Cultural Politics of Emotion*. New York: Routledge, 2004.

———. *The Promise of Happiness*. Durham, N.C.: Duke University Press, 2010.

Alas, Leopoldo (Clarín). "Del naturalismo (*La diana*, 1882)." In *Leopoldo Alas: Teoría y crítica de la novela español*, edited by Sergio Beser, 108–149. Barcelona: Laia, 1972.

———. "Prólogo a *La cuestión palpitante* (fragmento)." In *Leopoldo Alas: Teoría y crítica de la novela español*, edited by Sergio Beser, 149–153. Barcelona: Laia, 1972.

———. "La psicología del sexo." *Ilustración Ibérica* 12, nos. 575, 577, 589, 591, 596 (1894): 3, 6, 38, 231, 259, 262, 343.

———. *La Regenta*. 1884–1885. Edited by Juan Oleza. 2 vols. Madrid: Cátedra, 1989.

———. *La Regenta*. 1884–1885. Edited by Gonzalo Sobejano. 2 vols. Madrid: Castalia, 1981.

Aldaraca, Bridget A. *El ángel del hogar: Galdós and the Ideology of Domesticity in Spain*. Chapel Hill: North Carolina Studies in the Romance Languages and Literatures, 1991.

André, Serge. *Que veut une femme?* Paris: Seuil, 1995.

Andreu, Alicia. "El folletín como intertexto en *Tormento*." *Anales Galdosianos* 17 (1982): 55–60.

———. *Galdós y la literatura popular*. Madrid: Sociedad General Española de Librería, 1982.

Arenal, Concepción. *La emancipación de la mujer en España*. 1868. Madrid: Júcar, 1974.

———. *La mujer del porvenir*. 1868. In *La emancipación de la mujer en España*, by Concepción Arenal, 97–188. Madrid: Júcar, 1974.

———. *La mujer de su casa*. 1883. In *La emancipación de la mujer en España*, by Concepción Arenal, 189–284. Madrid: Júcar, 1974.

Arkinstall, Christine. "A Feminist Press Gains Ground in Spain, 1822–1866." In *A New History of Iberian Feminisms*, edited by Silvia Bermúdez and Roberta Johnson, 112–125. Toronto: University of Toronto Press, 2018.

———. "Forging a Nation for the Female Sex: Equality, Natural Law, and Citizenship in Spanish Feminist Essays, 1883–1920." In *A New History of Iberian Feminisms*, edited by Silvia Bermúdez and Roberta Johnson, 147–157. Toronto: University of Toronto Press, 2018.

Ashcroft, Bill, Gareth Griffiths, and Helen Tiffin. *Post-colonial Studies: The Key Concepts*. London: Routledge, 2000.

Ayala, María de los Ángeles. "*Dos mujeres*: Novela reinvindicativa de Gertrudis Gómez de Avellaneda." In *Del romanticismo a la Guerra Civil. Actas del XII Congreso de la Asociación Internacional de Hispanistas 22–26 de agosto de 1995*, vol. 4, edited by Derek Flitter, 76–83. Birmingham: Birmingham University, 1998.

———. Introduction to *Los pazos de Ulloa*, by Emilia Pardo Bazán, 5–59. Madrid: Cátedra, 1997.

Bailley-Bailliere, Carlos, ed. *Anuario del comercio, de la industria, de la magistratura y de la administración*. Madrid: Bailley-Bailliere, 1883.

Baldick, Robert, trans. Introduction to *Against Nature* [*À rebours*], by J.-K. Huysmans, 5–14. New York: Penguin, 1959.

———. *The Life of J.-K. Huysmans*. Gardena, Calif.: Dedalus, 2006.

Ballarín, Pilar. "La construcción de un modelo educativo de 'utilidad doméstica.'" In *Historia de las mujeres en Occidente*, vol. 4, *El siglo XIX*, edited by Georges Duby and Michelle Perrot, 598–611. Madrid: Taurus, 1993.

———. Introduction to *La mujer moderna y sus derechos*, by Carmen de Burgos, 15–48. Madrid: Biblioteca Nueva, 2007.

Bartrina, Francesca. *Víctor Català / Caterina Albert i Paradís: La voluptuositat de l'escriptura*. Vic: Eumo, 2001.

Baudelaire, Charles. *The Painter of Modern Life, and Other Essays*. London: Phaidon, 1964.

Beauvoir, Simone de. *The Second Sex*. 1949. Translated and edited by H. M. Parshley. Harmondsworth: Penguin Books, 1972; New York: Vintage, 1989.

Bennett, Jane. *Vibrant Matter: A Political Ecology of Things*. Durham, N.C.: Duke University Press, 2010.

Berlant, Lauren. *Cruel Optimism*. Durham, N.C.: Duke University Press, 2011.

Bermúdez, Silvia, and Roberta Johnson, eds. *A New History of Iberian Feminisms*. Toronto: University of Toronto Press, 2018.

Bernardin de Saint-Pierre, Jacques-Henri. *Paul and Virginia*. Translated by Paul Donovan. London: Peter Owen, 1982.

Berquist, Emily. "Early Anti-slavery Sentiment in the Spanish Atlantic World, 1765–1817." *Slavery and Abolition* 31, no. 2 (2010): 181–205.

Bianco, Marcie. "What Sisterhood? White Women Voted for Trump in 2016 because They Still Believe White Men Are Their Saviors." *Quartz*, November 14, 2016. https://qz.com/835567/election-2016-white-women-voted-for-donald-trump-in-2016-because-they-still-believe-white-men-are-their-saviors/.

Bieder, Maryellen. "Ambigüedad narrativa y compromiso social en Marina Mayoral ¿Víctimas o asesinas?" In *Escritoras y compromiso: Literatura española e hispanoamericana de los siglos XX y XXI*, edited by Angeles Encinar and Carmen Valcárcel, 351–368. Madrid: Visor, 2009.

———. "Carmen de Burgos: Modern Spanish Woman." In *Recovering Spain's Feminist Tradition*, edited and introduced by Lisa Vollendorf, 241–259. New York: Modern Language Association of America, 2001.

———. "Carmen de Burgos: Una mujer española moderna." Translated by Giovanna Urdangarain. In *Literatura y feminismo en España (s. XV–XXI)*, edited by Lisa Vollendorf, 225–240. Barcelona: Icaria; 2005.

———. "Carme Riera and the Paradox of Recovering Historical Memory in *La meitat de L'ànima*." *Foro Hispánico* 31 (2007): 169–189.

———. "Cataclysm and Rebirth: Journey to the Edge of the Maelstrom: Mercè Rodoreda's *Quanta, quanta Guerra*." In *Actes del tercer colloqui d'estudis catalans a Nord-Amèrica: Toronto, 1982: Estudis en honor de Josep Roca-Pons*, edited by Patricia Boehne, Josep Massot i Muntaner, and Nathaniel Smith, 227–237. Barcelona: Pubs. de l'Abadia de Monserrat, 1983.

———. "Concepción Gimeno de Flaquer." In *Spanish Women Writers: A Bio-bibliographical Source Book*, edited by Linda Gould Levine, Ellen Engelson Marson, and Gloria Feiman Waldman, 219–229. Westport, Conn.: Greenwood, 1993.

———. "Cultural Capital: The Play of Language, Gender, and Nationality." *Catalan Review: International Journal of Catalan Culture* 14, nos. 1/2 (2000): 53–74.

———. "Divina y perversa: La mujer decadente en *Dulce dueño* de Emilia Pardo Bazán." In *Perversas y divinas: La representación de la mujer en las literaturas hispánicas: El fin de siglo y/o el fin de milenio actual*, edited by Carme Riera, Meri Torras, and Isabel Clúa, 7–19. Valencia: Ediciones ExCultura, 2002.

———. "Emilia Pardo Bazán: Veintiuna cartas a Gabriela Cunninghame Graham." *Siglo Diecinueve* 18 (2012): 29–64.

———. "Emilia Pardo Bazán and Gabriela Cunninghame Graham: A Literary and Personal Friendship." *Bulletin of Spanish Studies* 89, no. 5 (2012): 725–749.

———. "Emilia Pardo Bazán and Literary Women: Women Reading Women's Writing in Late 19th-Century Spain." *Revista Hispánica Moderna* 46, no. 1 (1993): 19–33.

———. "Emilia Pardo Bazán y la emergencia del discurso feminista." In *Breve historia feminista de la literatura española (en lengua castellana)*, edited by Iris M. Zazala, 75–110. Barcelona: Anthropos, 1998.

———. "Emilia Pardo Bazán y las literatas: Las escritoras del XIX y su literatura." In *Actas del X Congreso de la Asociación de Hispanistas*, vol. 2, edited by Antonio Vilanova, 1203–1212. Barcelona: Promociones y Pubs. Universitarias, 1992.

———. "En-gendering Strategies of Authority: Emilia Pardo Bazán and the Novel." In *Cultural and Historical Grounding for Hispanic and Luso-Brazilian Feminist Literary Criticism*, edited by Hernán Vidal, 473–495. Minneapolis: Institute for Study of Ideologies & Literature, 1989.

———. "El escalpelo anatómico en mano femenina: The Realist Novel and the Woman Writer." *Letras Peninsulares* 5, no. 2 (1992): 209–225.

———. "Feminine Discourse / Feminist Discourse: Concepción Gimeno de Flaquer." *Romance Quarterly* 37, no. 4 (1990): 459–477.

———. "Género y Mercado literario en la narrativa de Carme Riera." In *Género y géneros II: Escritura y escritoras iberoamericanas*, edited by Ángeles Encinar, Eva Löfquist, and Carmen Valcárcel, 167–175. Madrid: Universidad Autónoma de Madrid, 2006.

———. "Imágenes visuales de Emilia Pardo Bazán en la prensa periódica." In *Literatura hispánica y prensa periódica (1875–1931)*, edited by Javier Serrano Alonso and Amparo de Juan Bolufer, 221–235. Santiago de Compostela: Universidad de Santiago, 2009.

———. "Intertextualizing Genre: Ambiguity as Narrative Strategy in Emilia Pardo Bazán." In *Intertextual Pursuits: Literary Mediations in Modern Spanish Narrative*, edited by Jeanne P. Brownlow and John W. Kronik, 57–75. London: Associated University Press, 1998.

———. "Memory and Gender: Neus Carbonell's *Alguna cos més que tu*." *Revista de Estudios Hispánicos* 35, no. 1 (2001): 137–150.

———. "La mujer invisible: Lenguaje y silencio en dos cuentos de Mercèr Rodoreda." In *Homenatge a Josep Roca-Pons: Estudis de llengua i literatura*, edited by Jane White Albrecht, Janet Ann DeCesaris, Patricia V. Lunn, and Jospe Miquel Sobrer, 94–110. Barcelona: Abadia de Montserrat, 1991.

———. *Narrative Perspective in the Post–Civil War Novels of Francisco Ayala*. Chapel Hill: University of North Carolina Press, 1979.

———. "Negotiating Modernity in Multicultural Spain: Emilia Pardo Bazán's *Una Cristiana* and *La prueba*." *Siglo Diecinueve* 16 (2010): 137–169.

———. "Picturing the Author: The Private Woman Meets the Public Gaze." *Revista de Estudios Hispánicos* 39, no. 2 (2005): 301–329.

———. "Plotting Gender / Replotting the Reader: Strategies of Subversion in Stories by Emilia Pardo Bazán." *Indiana Journal of Hispanic Literature* 2, no. 1 (1993): 137–157.

———. "Racial Identity, Social Critique, and Class Dynamics in Pardo Bazán's *Una prueba-La Cristiana and El becerro de metal*." In *Intersections of Race, Class, Gender, and Nation in* Fin-de-Siècle *Spanish Literature and Culture*, edited by Jennifer Smith and Lisa Nalbone, 91–107. New York: Routledge, 2017.

———. "Reading the Sign of Spain: Negotiating Nationality, Language, and Gender." In *Mapping the Fiction of Cristina Fernández Cubas*, edited by Kathleen M. Glenn and Janet Pérez, 41–65. Newark: University of Delaware Press, 2005.

———. "Representaciones visuales en la vida y obras finiseculares de Emilia Pardo Bazán." In *La literatura de Emilia Pardo Bazán*, edited by José Manuel González Herrán, Crisitna Patiño Eirín, and Ermitas Penas Varela, 193–207. A Coruña: Real Academia Galega; Casa-Museo Emilia Pardo Bazán; Fundación Caixa Galicia, 2009.

———. "Self-Reflexive Fiction and the Discourses of Gender in Carmen de Burgos." *Bucknell Review: A Scholarly Journal of Letters, Arts and Sciences* 39, no. 2 (1996): 73–89.

———. "Sexo y lenguaje en Emilia Pardo Bazán: La deconstrucción de la diferencia." In *Actas del XII Congreso de la Asociación Internacional de Hispanistas, IV: Del Romanticismo a la Guerra Civil*, edited by Derek W. Flitter, 92–99. Birmingham: University of Birmingham, Department of Hispanic Studies, 1998.

———. "Silent Women: Language in Mercè Rodoreda." In *Voices and Visions: The Words and Works of Mercè Rodoreda*, edited by Kathleen McNerney, 80–97. Selinsgrove, Pa.: Susquehanna University Press, 1999.

———. "El teatro de Benito Pérez Galdós y Emilia Pardo Bazán. Estructura y visión dramática en *Mariucha* y *Cuesta abajo*." In *Actas del IX Congreso de la Asociación Internacional de Hispanistas*, vol. 2, edited by Sebastián Neumeister, 17–24. Frankfurt am Main: Vervuert, 1989.

———. "Woman and the Twentieth-Century Spanish Literary Canon: The Lady Vanishes." *Anales de la Literatura Española Contemporánea* 17, no. 3 (1992): 301–324.

———. "The Woman in the Garden: The Problem of Identity in the Novels of Mercè Rodoreda." In *Actes del segon colloqui d'estudis catalans a Nord-Amèrica: Yale, 1979*, edited by Manuel Durán, Albert Porqueras-Mayo, and Josep Roca-Pons, 353–364. Barcelona: l'Abadia de Montserrat, 1982.

———. "Women, Literature, and Society: The Essays of Emilia Pardo Bazán." In *Spanish Women Writers and the Essay: Gender, Politics, and the Self*, edited and introduced by Kathleen M. Glenn and Mercedes Mazquiarán de Rodríguez, 25–54. Columbia: University of Missouri Press, 1998.

Bieder, Maryellen, and Roberta Johnson, eds. *Spanish Women Writers and Spain's Civil War*. New York: Routledge, 2016.

Biggane, Julia. *In a Liminal Space: The Novellas of Emilia Pardo Bazán*. Durham, N.C.: Durham Modern Language Series, 2000.

Biss, Eula. "Layers of Time." *New York Times*, March 29, 2015.

Blanco, Alda. "Teóricas de la conciencia feminista." In *La mujer en los discursos de género: Textos y contextos en el siglo XIX*, edited by Catherine Jagoe, Alda Blanco, and Cristina Enríquez de Salamanca, 445–472. Barcelona: Icaria, 1998.

Booth, Wayne. *The Rhetoric of Fiction*. 2nd ed. Chicago: University of Chicago Press, 1983.

Borenstein, Walter. Introduction to *The Tribune of the People*, by Emilia Pardo Bazán, translated by Walter Borenstein, 9–34. Lewisburg, Pa.: Bucknell University Press, 1999.

Botrel, Jean-François. "La novela por entregas: Unidad de creación y consumo." In *Creación y público en la literatura española*, edited by Jean-François Botrel and S. Salaün, 111–155. Madrid: Editorial Castalia, 1974.

Bourdieu, Pierre. *The Field of Cultural Production*. Edited by Randal Johnson. New York: Columbia University Press, 1993.

Bravo-Villasante, Carmen. *Vida y obra de Emilia Pardo Bazán*. Madrid: Revista de Occidente, 1962.

Brennan, Teresa. *The Transmission of Affect*. Ithaca, N.Y.: Cornell University Press, 2004.

Bretz, Mary Lee. *Voices, Silences and Echoes: A Theory of the Essay and the Critical Reception of Naturalism in Spain*. London: Tamesis, 1992.

Brooks, Peter. *The Melodramatic Imagination: Balzac, Henry James, Melodrama, and the Mode of Excess*. New Haven, Conn.: Yale University Press, 1976.

Burgos, Carmen de. "Misión educadora de la mujer en el periodismo." *Unión Ibero Americana*, December 1905, 85–89.

———. *La mujer moderna y sus derechos*. Edited by Pilar Ballarín. Madrid: Biblioteca Nueva, 2007.

Burguera, Mónica. *Las damas del liberalismo respetable: Los imaginarios sociales del feminismo liberal en España (1834–1850)*. Madrid: Cátedra, 2012.

Burton, Richard D. E. *Holy Tears, Holy Blood: Women, Catholicism, and the Culture of Suffering in France, 1840–1970*. Ithaca, N.Y.: Cornell University Press, 2004.

Bynum, Caroline Walker. *Holy Feast and Holy Fast: The Religious Significance of Food to Medieval Women*. Berkeley: University of California Press, 1987.

Callahan, William J. *The Catholic Church in Spain, 1875–1998*. Washington, D.C.: Catholic University of America Press, 2000.

Capmany, Maria-Aurèlia. Epilogue to *Obres completes*, by Víctor Català, edited by Tomàs Tebé, 1853–1868. Barcelona: Editorial Selecta, 1972.

Carmona González, Ángeles. "Tartilán, Sofía." In *Escritoras andaluzas en la prensa de Andalucía del siglo XIX*, 253–256. Cádiz: Universidad de Cádiz, Instituto Andaluz de la Mujer, 1999.

Castellanos, Jordi. "Solitud, novella modernista." *Els marges* 25 (1982): 45–70.

Català, Víctor. "El cant els mesos." In *Obres completes*, edited by Tomàs Tebé, 1423–1427. Barcelona: Editorial Selecta, 1972.

———. "Conversa amb Víctor Català: entrevista amb Tomàs Garcés, publicada a *La Revista*." In *Obres completes*, edited by Tomàs Tebé, 1747–1755. Barcelona: Editorial Selecta, 1972.

———. "Discurs. Llegit a la reial acadèmia de bones lletres de Barcelona, en la solemne recepció pública de Vector Català (14 gener 1923)." In *Obres completes*, edited by Tomàs Tebé, 1695. Barcelona: Editorial Selecta, 1972.

———. "Epistolari." In *Obres completes*, edited by Tomàs Tebé, 1783–1850. Barcelona: Editorial Selecta, 1972.

———. *La infanticida*. In *Obres completes*, edited by Tomàs Tebé, 1577–1590. Barcelona: Editorial Selecta, 1972.

———. *Solitud*. Barcelona: Editorial Selecta, 1980.

Cervantes Saavedra, Miguel de. *El ingenioso hidalgo don Quijote de la Mancha*. 3 vols. Madrid: Clásicos Castalia, 1978.

Charnon-Deutsch, Lou. *Fictions of the Feminine in the Nineteenth-Century Spanish Press*. University Park: Pennsylvania State University Press, 2000.

———. *Narratives of Desire: Nineteenth-Century Spanish Fiction by Women*. University Park: Pennsylvania State University Press, 1994.

———. *The Nineteenth-Century Spanish Story: Textual Strategies of a Genre in Transition*. London: Tamesis, 1985.

Charques Gámez, Rocío. *Los artículos feministas en el* Nuevo teatro crítico *de Emilia Pardo Bazán*. Cuadernos de trabajos de investigación 5. Sant Vicente del Raspeig: Centro de Estudios sobre la Mujer, 2003. http://pmayobre.webs.uvigo.es/pdf/emilia_pardo_bazan/nuevoteatrocritico.pdf.

Clèmessy, Nelly. *Emilia Pardo Bazán como novelista*. Madrid: Fundación Universitaria Española, 1981.

Clough, Patricia Ticineteo, ed. *The Affective Turn: Theorizing the Social*. Durham, N.C.: Duke University Press, 2007.

Connell, R. W., and James W. Messerschmidt. "Hegemonic Masculinity: Rethinking the Concept." *Gender and Society* 19, no. 6 (2005): 829–859.

Copjec, Joan. *Imagine There Is No Woman: Ethics and Sublimation*. Cambridge, Mass.: MIT Press, 2004.

Coronado, Carolina. "A la abolición de la esclavitud en Cuba." In *Obra poética*, vol. 2, edited by Gregorio Torres Nebrera, 839. Mérida: Editora Regional de Extremadura, 1993.

———. "Oda a Lincoln." In *Obra poética*, vol. 2, edited by Gregorio Torres Nebrera, 731–733. Mérida: Editora Regional de Extremadura, 1993.

Coughlin, Edward. *Adelardo López de Ayala*. Boston: Twayne, 1977.

Criado Domínguez, Juan P. "Tartilán, Doña Sofía." In *Literatas españolas del siglo XIX: Apuntes bibliográficos*, 156–158. Madrid: Imprenta de Antonio Pérez Dubrull, 1889.

Cruz, Jacqueline, and Barbara Zecchi. *La mujer en la España actual*. Madrid: Icaria, 2004.

Cuesta y Ckerner, Juan. *Enfermedades de las mujeres: Extracto de las asignaturas que tienen que estudiar los cirujanos de segunda clase que aspiran al título de Facultativo habilitados por medio de estudios privados*. Madrid: Tomás Alonso, 1868.

Dale, Javier. "El voto femenino en España cumple 80 años." *La Vanguardia*, November 13, 2013. http://www.lavanguardia.com/vida/20131119/54393615758/voto-femenino-espana-cumple-80-anos.html.

Deleuze, Gilles. *Spinoza: Practical Philosophy*. Translated by Robert Hurley. San Francisco: City Lights, 2001.

Díez de los Ríos San Juan, María Teresa. "Catálogo de publicaciones periódicas masónicas (siglo XIX)." In *Fuentes y documentos para la historia de la educación en su relación con la masonería española*, edited by Pedro Álvarez Lázaro. https://dialnet.unirioja.es/descarga/articulo/1154999.pdf.

Dinesen, Isak. *Babette's Feast*. Translated by Karen Blixen. London: Penguin, 2011.

Dorado, Carlos, ed. *La vida contemporánea*. By Emilia Pardo Bazán. Madrid: Hemeroteca Municipal, 2005.

Duby, Georges, and Michelle Perrot, eds. *Historia de las mujeres en Occidente*. Vol. 4, *El siglo XIX*. Madrid: Taurus, 1993.

DuPont, Denise. "Masculinity, Femininity, Solidarity: Emilia Pardo Bazán's Construction of Madame de Staël and George Sand." *Comparative Literature Studies* 40, no. 4 (2003): 372–393.

Easley, Jason. "Women's March Is the Biggest Protest in US History as an Estimated 2.9 Million March." *Politicus USA*, February 17, 2017. http://www.politicususa.com/2017/01/21/womens-march-biggest-protest-history-estimated-2-4-million-march.html.

Elie, Paul. *The Life You Save May Be Your Own: An American Pilgrimage*. New York: Farrar, Straus and Giroux, 2003.

Enríquez de Salamanca, Cristina. "The Question of the Political Subject in Nineteenth-Century Spanish Domestic Discourse." In *Spain Today: Essays on Literature, Culture, Society*, edited by José Colmeiro, Christina Duplaa, Patricia Greene, and Juana Sabadell, 103–112. Hanover, N.H.: Dartmouth College, Department of Spanish and Portuguese, 1995.

Etxebarria, Lucía. *La Eva futura: Cómo seremos las mujeres del siglo XXI, y en qué mundo nos tocará vivir*. Barcelona: Destino, 2000.

———. "Me presenté al Nadal para suavizar la reacción de mis padres a mi novela." *El País*, January 8, 1998.

Ezama Gil, Ángeles. "El lugar de la novela corta en la narrativa de Emilia Pardo Bazán." In *Emilia Pardo Bazán: Los cuentos*, edited by José Manuel González Herrán, Cristina Patiño Eirín, and Ermitas Penas Varela, 197–223. A Coruña: Casa Museo Pardo Bazán, 2006.

Faus, Pilar. *Emilia Pardo Bazán: Su época, su vida, su obra*. 2 vols. A Coruña: Fundación Pedro Barrié de la Maza, Conde de Fenosa, 2003.

Flores García, Francisco. "Actrices españolas—Matilde Díez, Elisa Boldún." *Nuestro Tiempo: Revista Mensual Ilustrada* 4, no. 42 (June 1904): 359–371.

Freire Lopez, Ana María. "La primera redacción, autógrafa e inedita de los 'Apuntes autobiográficos' de Emilia Pardo Bazán." *Cuadernos para Investigación de la Literatura Hispánica* 26 (2001): 305–336. http://www.cervantesvirtual.com/obra-visor/la-primera-redaccin-autgrafa-e-indita-de-los-apuntes-autobiogrficos-de-emilia-pardo-bazn-0/html/ffbb8ec8-82b1-11df-acc7-002185ce6064_2.html#I_1_.

Freud, Sigmund. *Standard Edition of the Complete Psychological Works*. Vol. 2 of *Studies on Hysteria*. Translated and edited by James Strachey. London: Hogarth Press and Institute of Psycho-Analysis, 1955.

Friedman, Vanessa. "Changing the Rules of Power Dressing." *New York Times*, July 28, 2016.

———. "The Power That Comes from Clothes." *New York Times*, October 30, 2014.

———. "Ralph Lauren May Have Found a New Muse in Clinton." *New York Times*, October 11, 2016.

———. "What's Daring These Days? Try a Political Manifesto." *New York Times*, September 13, 2016.

Gabilondo, Joseba. "The Subaltern Cannot Speak but Performs: Women's Public and Literary Cultures in Nineteenth-Century Spain." *Hispanic Research Journal* 5, no. 1 (2003): 73–95.

Gálvez, María Rosa. *Zinda*. Biblioteca Virtual Miguel de Cervantes. http://www.cervantesvirtual.com/obra-visor/zinda--drama-tragico-en-tres-actos/html/dcd228aa-2dc6-11e2-b417-000475f5bda5_2.html#I_0_.

Gálvez de Cabrera, María Rosa. *Zinda*. In *Obras poéticas*, vol. 3, 100–168. Madrid: Imprenta Real, 1804.

García Balmaseda, Joaquina. "¡Caridad en favor del esclavo!" In *El cancionero del esclavo. Colección de poesías laureadas y recomendadas por el jurado en el certamen convocado por la Sociedad Abolicionista Española*, 77–85. Madrid: Publicaciones Populares de la Sociedad Abolicionista Española, 1866.

García Colmenares, Carmen, and José Luis Sánchez García. "Sofía Tartilán: Autobiografía de una educadora desconocida." In *Actas VI Coloquio de Historia de la Educación: Mujer y educación en España, 1868–1975*, 153–160. Santiago de Compostela: Universidad de Santiago, 1990.

Geier, Kathleen. "Inequality among Women Is Crucial to Understanding Hillary's Loss." *Nation*, November 11, 2016. https://www.thenation.com/article/inequality-between-women-is-crucial-to-understanding-hillarys-loss/.

Gies, David. "La mujer vista por la mujer: El personaje femenino en el teatro escrito por mujeres en la segunda mitad del siglo XIX." In *Lectora, heroína, autora (la mujer en la literatura española del siglo XIX)*, edited by Virginia Trueba Mira, Enrique Rubio Cremades, Pau Miret Puig, Luis F. Díaz Larios, Jean-François Botrel, and Laureano Bonet, 149–158. Barcelona: Promociones y Publicaciones Universitarias, 2005.

Gold, Hazel. "Del foro al fogón: Narrativas culturales en el discurso culinario de Emilia Pardo Bazán." In *La literatura de Emilia Pardo Bazán*, edited by José Manuel González Herrán, 313–323. A Coruña: Real Academia Galega, 2009.

———. *The Reframing of Realism: Galdós and the Discourses of the Nineteenth-Century Spanish Novel*. Durham, N.C.: Duke University Press, 1993.

Gómez de Avellaneda, Gertrudis. *Autobiografía y epistolarios de amor*. Newark, Del.: Juan de la Cuesta, 1999.

———. *Dos mujeres*. La Habana: Letras Cubanas, 2000.

———. *Sab*. Edited by José Servera. Madrid: Cátedra, 2004.

González Arias, Francisca. "Emilia Pardo Bazán and *La tentation de saint Antoine*, or the Countess and the Chimera." *Hispania* 71, no. 2 (1988): 212–216.

González Sanz, Alba. *Contra la destrucción teórica: Teorías feministas en la España de la Modernidad* (Oviedo: KRK, 2018).

Goodman, Dena. "Enlightenment Salons: The Convergence of Female and Philosophic Ambitions." *Eighteenth-Century Studies* 22, no. 3 (1989): 329–350.

Grau-Llevería, Elena. "El romanticismo social en *Dos mujeres* de Gertrudis Gómez de Avellaneda." *Bulletin of Spanish Studies* 87, no. 1 (2010): 31–49.

Grijalva, José de. "La cantinera." In *Los españoles pintados por sí mismos*, edited by Ignacio Boix, 271–281. Madrid: I. Boix Editor, 1843.

Grinstein, Julia Bordiga. "Nzinga-Nbandi / Zinda Njinga, heroína del nacionalismo africano." Biblioteca Virtual Miguel de Cervantes. http://www.cervantesvirtual.com/obra-visor-din/nzinga-nbandi-zinda-njinga-heroina-del-nacionalismo-africano/html/325122fe-1dd2-11e2-b1fb-00163ebf5e63_2.html#I_0_.

Guerra, Lucía. "Estrategias femeninas en la elaboración del sujeto romántico en la obra de Gertrudis Gómez de Avellaneda." *Revista Iberoamericana* 51, nos. 132/133 (1985): 707–722.

Guerrero y Pallarés, Teodoro, and Ricardo Sepúlveda. *Pleito del matrimonio entre T. Guerrero y R. Sepúlveda: Entendiendo en él como jueces, letrados y testigos, distinguidos escritores.* 1880. 4th ed. Madrid: M. Tello, 1880.

Halberstam, Judith. *Female Masculinity*. Durham, N.C.: Duke University Press, 1998.

Harpring, Mark. "Sexo, sexualidad e ideal masculino en *Higiene sexual del soltero*, de Ciro Bayo." In *Memoria histórica, género e interdisciplinariedad: Los estudios culturales hispánicos en el siglo XXI*, edited by Santiago Juan-Navarro and Joan Torres-Pou, 163–174. Madrid: Biblioteca Nueva, 2008.

Hartzenbusch, J. E. "El ama de llaves." In *Los españoles pintados por sí mismos*, edited by Ignacio Boix, 123–138. Madrid: I. Boix Editor, 1843.

Hays, Michael, and Anastasia Nikolopoulou. Introduction to *Melodrama: The Cultural Emergence of a Genre*, vii–xv. New York: St. Martin's Press, 1996.

Henn, David. *The Early Pardo Bazán: Theme and Narrative Technique in the Novels of 1879–89*. Liverpool: Francis Cairns, 1988.

Horyn, Cathy. "First in Fashion." *New York Times*, December 30, 2012.

———. "The First Lady Tells a Story with Fashion." *New York Times*, January 21, 2009.

Huysmans, Joris-Karl. *Against Nature* [*À rebours*]. Translated by Robert Baldick. New York: Penguin, 1959.

———. *En route*. Translated by C. Kegan Paul. New York: E. P. Dutton, 1918.

———. *The Oblate* [*L'oblat*]. Translated by Edward Perceval. New York: E. P. Dutton, 1924.

———. *Saint Lydwine of Schiedam* [*Sainte Lydwine de Schiedam*]. Translated by Agnes Hastings. New York: E. P. Dutton, 1923.

Jagoe, Catherine. *Ambiguous Angels: Gender in the Novels of Galdós*. Berkeley: University of California Press, 1994.

———. "Disinheriting the Feminine: Galdós and the Rise of the Realist Novel in Spain." *Revista de Estudios Hispánicos* 27, no. 2 (1993): 225–248.

———. "La misión de la mujer." In *La mujer en los discursos de género: Textos y contextos en el siglo XIX*, edited by Catherine Jagoe, Alda Blanco, and Cristina Enríquez de Salamanca, 21–53. Barcelona: Icaria, 1998.

Jagoe, Catherine, Alda Blanco, and Cristina Enríquez de Salamanca. *La mujer en los discursos de género: Textos y contextos en el siglo XIX*. Barcelona: Icaria, 1998.

Jiménez Morell, Inmaculada. *La prensa femenina en España (desde sus orígenes a 1868)*. Madrid: Ediciones de la Torre, 1992.

Kahn, Eve M. "Dressed to Kill, in Leopard Prints." *New York Times*, April 29, 2016.

Kerr, Fergus. *After Aquinas: Versions of Thomism*. Malden, Mass.: Blackwell, 2002.

Kimmel, Michael S. "Masculinity as Homophobia: Fear, Shame, and Silence in the Construction of Gender Identity." In *The Masculinities Reader*, edited by Stephen M. Whitehead and Frank J. Barrett, 266–287. Cambridge: Polity, 2001.

Kirkpatrick, Susan. "Gender and Modernist Discourse: Emilia Pardo Bazán's *Dulce Dueño*." In *Modernism and Its Margins*, edited by Anthony L. Geist and José B. Monleón, 117–139. New York: Garland, 1999.

———. *Las Románticas: Women Writers and Subjectivity in Spain, 1835–1850*. Berkeley: University of California Press, 1989.

Kronik, John. "Emilia Pardo Bazán and the Phenomenon of French Decadentism." *PMLA* 81, no. 5 (1966): 418–427.

Labanyi, Jo. "Doing Things: Emotion, Affect, Materiality." *Journal of Spanish Cultural Studies* 11, nos. 3/4 (2010): 223–233.

———. *Gender and Modernization in the Spanish Realist Novel*. Oxford: Oxford University Press, 2000.

Lacan, Jacques. *Encore. Le seminaire libre XX*. Paris: Seuil, 1975.

———. "Position of the Unconscious." In *Écrits*, translated by Bruce Fink, 703–721. New York: Norton, 2006.
———. *Le Séminaire*. Book 23, *Le sinthome*. Paris: Seuil, 2005.
———. *The Seminar*. Vol. 3, translated by Russel Grigg. New York: Norton, 1997.
Lafitte, María. *La mujer en España: Cien años de su historia, 1860–1960*. Madrid: Aguilar, 1964.
Laforet, Carmen, and Ramón Sender. *Puedo contar contigo: Correspondencia*. Edited by Israel Rolón Barada. Barcelona: Destino, 2003.
LaGreca, Nancy. "Literatura y conciencia: El suicidio femenino en el *Álbum cubano de lo bueno y lo bello* (1860) y *Dos mujeres* (1842–1843) de Gertrudis Gómez Avellaneda." *Revolución y Cultura* 47, no. 4 (2006): 12–16.
La Violeta. "Variedades." 3, no. 159 (December 17, 1865): n.p.
León, Rogelia. *Auras de la Alhambra*. Granada: Imprenta y Librería de D. José María Zamora, 1857.
Lewis, Elizabeth Franklin. "Breaking the Chains: Language and the Bonds of Slavery in María Rosa Gálvez's *Zinda*." Biblioteca Virtual Miguel de Cervantes. http://www.cervantesvirtual.com/obra-visor-din/breaking-the-chains-language-and-the-bonds-of-slavery-in-maria-rosa-galvezs-zinda-1804/html/b0e06e38-0bce-11e2-b1fb-00163ebf5e63_3.html#I_0_.
Lewis, Linda M. *Germaine de Staël, George Sand, and the Victorian Woman Artist*. Columbia: University of Missouri Press, 2003.
Lissorgues, Yvan. *El pensamiento filosófico y religioso de Leopoldo Alas "Clarín."* Oviedo: Grupo Editorial Asturiano, 1996.
Loomba, Ania. *Colonialism/Postcolonialism*. 3rd ed. New York: Routledge, 2015.
López de Ayala, Adelardo. *Consuelo: Comedia en tres actos y en verso*. Edited, introduced, and annotated by Aurelio M. Espinosa. New York: Henry Holt, 1930.
Los Angeles Times. "Dressed to Impress." January 18, 2009.
Mandrell, James. "Estudios gay y lesbianos: La revelación del cuerpo masculino: Una mirada gay." In *El hispanismo en los Estados Unidos: Discursos críticos/prácticas textuales*, edited by José Manuel del Pino and Francisco La Rubia Prado, 211–230. Madrid: Visor, 1999.
Martín, Elvira. *Tres mujeres gallegas del siglo XIX: Concepción Arenal, Rosalía de Castro, Emilia Pardo Bazán*. Biblioteca Biográfica. 2nd ed. Barcelona: Aedos, 1962.
Martín Gaite, Carmen. *El cuarto de atrás*. 3rd ed. Barcelona: Destino, 1980.
Massumi, Brian. *Parables of the Virtual: Movement, Affect, Sensation*. Durham, N.C.: Duke University Press, 2002.
———. *Politics of Affect*. Cambridge: Polity, 2015.
Mathews, Cristina. "Making the Nuclear Family: Kinship, Homosexuality, and *La Regenta*." *Revista de Estudios Hispánicos* 37, no. 1 (2003): 75–102.
Mayoral, Marina, ed. *Estudios sobre "Los pazos de Ulloa."* Madrid: Cátedra, 1989.
———. Introduction to *Dulce dueño*, by Emilia Pardo Bazán, 7–44. Madrid: Castalia, 1989.
McKenna, Susan. *Crafting the Female Subject: Narrative Innovations in the Short Fiction of Emilia Pardo Bazán*. Washington, D.C.: Catholic University of America Press, 2009.
———. "Images of Paternity in the *Quijote*." *Hispanófila* 132 (2001): 43–52.
McKinney, Collin. "'Enemigos de la virilidad': Sex, Masturbation, and Celibacy in Nineteenth-Century Spain." *Prisma Social* 13 (2014–2015): 72–108. http://www.isdfundacion.org/publicaciones/revista/numeros/13/secciones/tematica/pdf/t_03_enemigos_virilidad_72-108.pdf.
Merkin, Daphne. "The Politics of Appearance: In a Realm Where Simulation Is All Authenticity May Lie in the Details." *New York Times Style Magazine*, August 26, 2007.
Mesonero Romanos, Ramón de. "Carta prólogo de Ramón de Mesonero Romanos." In *Costumbres populares: Colección de cuadros tomados del natural*, by Sofía Tartilán, edited by José Luis Sánchez García, 29–30. Madrid: Miraguano, 2004.
Messager, Annette. "Body Politic." Excerpt from *Voluntary Tortures*, first published in 1972. Reprinted in *New York Times Style Magazine*, February 25, 2007.

Miller, Jacques-Alain. *De la naturaleza de los semblantes*. Translated by Silvia Elena Tendlarz. Buenos Aires: Paidós, 2002.

———. *El partenaire-síntoma*. Translated by Dora Gladys Saroka. Buenos Aires: Editorial Paidós, 2008.

Miller, Stephen. *Sobre una teoría española de la novela femenina del siglo XIX*. Alicante: Biblioteca Virtual Miguel de Cervantes, 2008. http://www.cervantesvirtual.com/obra/sobre-una-teora-espaola-de-la-novela-femenina-del-siglo-xix-0/.

Miracle, Josep. *Caterina Albert i Paradís "Víctor Català."* Barcelona: Dopesa, 1978.

Mohanty, Chandra Talpade. "Cartographies of Struggle: Third World Women and the Politics of Feminism." In *Third World Women and the Politics of Feminism*, edited by Chandra Talpade Mohanty, Ann Russo, and Lourdes Torres, 1–47. Bloomington: Indiana University Press, 1991.

Monlau, Pedro Felipe. *Higiene del matrimonio o el libro de los casados*. Madrid: M. Rivadeneyra, 1858.

Moore, Booth. "Can She Stay 'Everywoman'?" *Los Angeles Times*, January 18, 2009.

———. "A National Pastime: Ever since Martha Washington, We've Fixated on First Lady Fashion and the Messages It Conveys." *Los Angeles Times*, January 18, 2009.

Moore, Brenna. Introduction to *Sacred Dread: Raïssa Maritain, the Allure of Suffering, and the French Catholic Revival (1905–1944)*, by Brenna Moore, 1–23. Notre Dame, Ind.: University of Notre Dame Press, 2013.

Morgado García, Arturo. "*Zinda* (1804), de María Rosa Gálvez de Cabrera, y las reflexiones sobre la esclavitud en la España finidieciochesca." In *Mujeres esclavas y abolicionistas en la España de los siglos XVI al XIX*, edited by Aurelia Martín Casares and Rocío Periáñez Gómez, 187–209. Madrid: Iberoamericana-Vervuert, 2014.

Mortimer, Armine Kotin. "Fortifications of Desire: Reading the Second Story in Katherine Mansfield's 'Bliss.'" *Narrative* 2, no. 1 (1994): 41–52.

———. "Romantic Fever: The Second Story as Illegitimate Daughter in Warton's 'Roman Fever.'" *Narrative* 6, no. 2 (1998): 188–198.

———. "Second Stories." In *Short Story Theory at the Crossroads*, edited by Susan Lohafer and Jo Ellyn Clarey, 276–298. Baton Rouge: Louisiana State University Press, 1989.

———. "Second Stories: The Example of 'Mr. Know-All.'" *Studies in Short Fiction* 25 (1998): 307–314.

Mulvey, Laura. "Pandora: Topographies of the Mask and Curiosity." In *Sexuality and Space*, edited by Beatriz Colomina, 52–71. New York: Princeton Architectural Press, 1992.

Nash, Mary. "Identidad cultural de género, discurso de la domesticidad y la definición del trabajo de las mujeres en la España del siglo XIX." In *Historia de las mujeres en Occidente*, vol. 4, *El siglo XIX*, edited by Georges Duby and Michelle Perrot, 585–599. Madrid: Taurus, 1993.

Ngai, Sianne. *Ugly Feelings*. Cambridge, Mass.: Harvard University Press, 2007.

Nieto Bedoya, Margarita, and Carmen García Colmenares. "El pensamiento educativo de Sofía Tartilán." In *Actas VI Coloquio de Historia de la Educación: Mujer y educación en España, 1868–1975*, 254–260. Santiago de Compostela: Universidad de Santiago, 1990.

Obiols Delgado, M. Illustrations for "La dama joven," by Emilia Pardo Bazán. Barcelona: Biblioteca Arte y Letras, 1885.

Olson, Greta. "Reconsidering Unreliability: Fallible and Untrustworthy Narrators." *Narrative* 11, no. 1 (2003): 93–109.

Ordóñez, Elizabeth J. "Passing Notes: Theory and Self-Representation in Pardo Bazán's 'Apuntes autobiográficos.'" *Crítica Hispánica* 24, nos. 1/2 (2002): 145–156.

Ortiz Albear, Natividad. *Las mujeres en la masonería*. Málaga: Universidad de Málaga, 2005.

Osborne, Robert E. *Emilia Pardo Bazán: Su vida y sus obras*. Mexico City: Ediciones de Andrea, 1964.

Parada, Diego Ignacio. "Sofía Tartilán." In *Escritoras y eruditas espanolas*, vol. 1, pp. 265–266. Madrid: M. Minuesa, 1881.

Pardo Bazán, Emilia. "Apuntes autobiográficos." In *Obras completas*, vol. 7, edited by Dario Villanueva and José Manuel González Herrán, 5–59. Madrid: Fundación José Antonio de Castro, 1999.

———. "El baile del Querubín." In *Cuentos completos*, vol. 1, edited by Juan Paredes Núñez, 225–232. A Coruña: Fundación Pedro Barrié de la Maza, Conde de Fenosa, 1990.

———. "Blanca de los Ríos de Lampérez." In *Catálogo de las obras de Blanca de los Ríos de Lampérez y algunos juicios de la crítica acerca de ellas* (1910), 39–48. Madrid: Sanz Calleja, 1927.

———. "Confidencia." In *Cuentos completos*, vol. 1, edited by Juan Paredes Nuñez, 166–169. A Coruña: Fundación Pedro Barrié de la Maza, Conde de Fenosa, 1990.

———. *Cuentos nuevos*. In *Obras completas*, vol. 2, edited by Federico Carlos Sainz de Robles, 1387–1473. Zaragoza: Aguilar, 1964.

———. *La cuestión palpitante*. Edited by José Manuel González Herrán. Barcelona: Anthropos, 1989.

———. "La dama joven." In *Obras completas*, vol. 7, edited by Darío Villanueva and José Manuel González Herrán, 11–58. Madrid: Fundación José Antonio de Castro, 1999.

———. *Dulce dueño*. Edited and introduced by Marina Mayoral. Madrid: Castalia, 1989.

———. "La educación del hombre y de la mujer: Sus relaciones y diferencias." In *La mujer española y otros escritos*, edited by Guadalupe Gómez-Ferrer, 149–177. Madrid: Cátedra, 1999.

———. *"El encaje roto" y otros cuentos*. Edited by Joyce Tolliver. New York: MLA, 1996.

———. "En coche-cama." In *Cuentos completos*, vol. 4, edited by Juan Paredes Nuñez, 307–310. A Coruña: Fundación Pedro Barrié de la Maza, Conde de Fenosa, 1990.

———. "Feminista." In *"El encaje roto" y otros cuentos*, edited by Joyce Tolliver, 110–117. New York: MLA, 1996.

———. *La literatura francesa moderna*. Vol. 2, *La transición*. Madrid: V. Prieto y Compañía, 1911.

———. *La literatura francesa moderna*. Vol. 3, *El naturalismo*. Madrid: Renacimiento, 1911; 1914.

———. "Madre." In *Cuentos completos*, vol. 1, edited by Juan Paredes Nuñez, 190–193. A Coruña: Fundación Pedro Barrié de la Maza, Conde de Fenosa, 1990.

———. "La mujer española." In *La mujer española y otros escritos*, edited and introduced by Guadalupe Gómez Ferrer, 83–116. Madrid: Cátedra, 1999.

———. *Nuevo Teatro Crítico* 2, no. 16 (April 1892).

———. *La obra periodística completa en* La Nación *de Buenos Aires*. Vol. 2. Edited by Juliana Sínovas Maté. A Coruña: Diputación Provincial de A Coruña, 1999.

———. "Ojeada retrospectiva a varias obras francesas de Daudet, Loti, Bourget, Huysmans, Rod y Barrés." In *Obras completas*, vol. 3, edited by Harry L. Kirby, 1056–1072. Madrid: Aguilar, 1973.

———. "Una opinión sobre la mujer." In *La mujer en los discursos de género: Textos y contextos en el siglo XIX*, edited by Catherine Jagoe, Alda Blanco, and Cristina Enríquez de Salamanca, 500–504. Barcelona: Icaria, 1998.

———. *Pascual López: Autobiografía de un estudiante de medicina*. 3rd ed. Madrid: Librería de Fernando Fé, 1889.

———. "Presentido." In *Cuentos completos*, vol. 4, edited by Juan Paredes Nuñez, 104–106. A Coruña: Fundación Pedro Barrié de la Maza, Conde de Fenosa, 1990.

———. Prologue to "La dama joven," by Emilia Pardo Bazán, illustrations by M. Obiols Delgado, vii–xv. Barcelona: Biblioteca Arte y Letras, 1985.

———. *La quimera*. Madrid: Cátedra, 1991.

———. *San Francisco de Asís (siglo XIII)*. México: Editorial Porrúa, 1982.

———. *La sirena negra*. Madrid: Espasa-Calpe, 1963.

———. *Un viaje de novios*. Introduction and notes by Marisa Sotelo Vázquez. Madrid: Alianza Editorial, 2003.

———. "La vida contemporánea." *La Ilustración Artística* 1807 (August 14, 1916), edited by Carlos Dorado, 600. Madrid: Hemeroteca Municipal, 2005.

Paredes Nuñez, Juan, ed. *Cuentos completos*. 4 vols. A Coruña: Fundación Pedro Barrié de la Maza, Conde de Fenosa, 1990.

Parkins, Ilya. "Fashion." In *The Cambridge Companion to Modernist Culture*, edited by Celiz Marshik, 96–110. Cambridge: Cambridge University Press, 2015.

Parrack, Jennifer Patterson. "Masquerade and Women's Writing in Spain: Gertrudis Gómez de Avellaneda's *Dos mujeres*." *Philological Review* 29, no. 1 (2003): 27–45.

Pastor, Brígida M. *Fashioning Feminism in Cuba and Beyond*. New York: Peter Lang, 2003.

———. "A Romance Life in Novel Fiction: The Early Career and Works of Gertrudis Gómez de Avellaneda." *Bulletin of Hispanic Studies* 75, no. 1 (1998): 169–181.

Patiño Eirín, Cristina. "Aproximación a los prólogos de Emilia Pardo Bazán." *Boletin de la Biblioteca de Menendez Pelayo* 71 (1995): 137–167.

———. "Trashumancias de Talía: Actores y actrices según Pardo Bazán." In *Emilia Pardo Bazán y las artes del espectáculo*, edited by José Manuel González Herrán, Cristina Patiño Eirín, and Ermitas Penas, 189–242. A Coruña: Casa Museo Pardo Bazán, 2008.

Paton, Elizabeth. "More Than Pearls, a Bag and a Crown: A Peek inside the Wardrobe of Queen Elizabeth II." *New York Times*, August 11, 2016.

Pearson, Jacqueline. *Women's Reading in Britain, 1750–1835: A Dangerous Recreation*. Cambridge: Cambridge University Press, 1999.

Peratoner, Amancio. *Fisiología de la noche de bodas: Misterios del lecho conyugal*. Barcelona: N. Curriols, 1892.

Pereira-Muro, Carmen. "Maravillosas supercherías: Género sexual y nacionalismo en los 'Apuntes Autobiográficos' de Pardo Bazán y *Trafalgar* de Galdós." *Hispanic Review* 78, no. 1 (2010): 71–100.

———. "Mimetismo, misticismo y la cuestión de la escritura femenina en *Dulce dueño* de Emilia Pardo Bazán." *La Tribuna* 4 (2006): 153–180.

Pérez-Rasilla, Eduardo. Epilogue to *La cadena rota*, by Faustina Sáez de Melgar, 197–201. Madrid: Publicaciones de la Asociación de Directores de Escena de España, 1998.

———. Introduction to *La cadena rota*, by Faustina Sáez de Melgar, 5–51. Madrid: Publicaciones de la Asociación de Directores de Escena de España, 1998.

Perinat, Adolfo, and María Isabel Marrades. *Mujer, prensa y sociedad en España 1800–1939*. Madrid: Centro de Investigaciones Sociológicas, 1980.

Pessarrodona, Marta. "Una soledad sonora." *El País*, October 6, 2007. http://elpais.com/diario/2007/10/06/babelia/1191627567_850215.html.

Phelan, James. *Living to Tell about It: A Rhetoric and Ethics of Character Narration*. Ithaca, N.Y.: Cornell University Press, 2005.

———. "Narrative Judgments and the Rhetorical Theory of Narrative: Ian McEwen's *Atonement*." In *A Companion to Narrative Theory*, edited by James Phelan and Peter J. Rabinowitz, 322–336. Malden, Mass.: Blackwell, 2005.

Phillips, Kristine. "'Feminism' Is Merriam-Webster's Word of the Year, Thanks in Part to Kellyanne Conway." *Washington Post*, December 12, 2017. https://www.washingtonpost.com/news/arts-and-entertainment/wp/2017/12/12/feminism-is-merriam-websters-word-of-the-year-thanks-in-part-to-kellyanne-conway/?utm_term=.3eab51ff72f8.

Quesada Novás, Ángeles. *El amor en los cuentos de Emilia Pardo Bazán*. Alicante: Publicaciones de la Universidad de Alicante, 2005.

———. "'La dama joven' de Pardo Bazán: Una forma de ilustrar un texto." *Salina* 23 (2009): 79–98.

Rich, Lawrence. "Fear and Loathing in Vetusta: Coding Class and Gender in Clarín's *La Regenta*." *Revista Canadiense de Estudios Hispánicos* 25, no. 3 (2001): 505–518.

Rodríguez Sánchez, María de los Ángeles. "Matilde Cherner: Una voz femenina y crítica ante la prostitución en la España de 1880." In *Actas XIII Congreso Asociación Internacional de Hispanistas*, vol. 2, edited by Florencio Sevilla Arroyo and Carlos Alvar Ezquerra, 370–378. Barcelona: Castalia, 2000. http://cvc.cervantes.es/literatura/aih/pdf/13/aih_13_2_046.pdf.

Rosenthal, David, trans. *Solitude*. By Víctor Català. Columbia, La.: Readers International, 1992.

Rousseau, Jean-Jacques. *Emile or On Education*. Translated by Allan Bloom. New York: Basic Books, 1979.

Rubio Cremades, Enrique. "Costumbrismo: Definición, cronología y su relación con la novella." Biblioteca Virtual Miguel de Cervantes. http://www.cervantesvirtual.com/obra/costumbrismo-definicin-cronologa-y-su-relacin-con-la-novela-0/.

Rutherford, John, trans. *La Regenta*. By Leopoldo Alas. London: Penguin, 2005.

Sáez de Melgar, Faustina. *La cadena rota*. Edited by Eduardo Pérez-Rasilla. Madrid: Publicaciones de la Asociación de Directores de Escena de España, 1998.

———. *Páginas para las niñas*. Barcelona: Librería de Juan y Antonio Bastinos, 1881.

Sáinz de Robles, Federico. Introduction to *Obras completas de Emilia Pardo Bazán*, vol. 1, 4th ed., 9–37. Madrid: Gráficas Halas, 1973.

Sánchez Carrera, María del Carmen. "El pensamiento de Sofía Tartilán y el krausismo." In *Actas de las VII Jornadas de Investigación Interdisciplinaria: Mujeres y hombres en la formación del pensamiento occidental*, vol. 2, edited by Virginia Maquieira d'Angelo, 267–275. Madrid: Universidad Autónoma de Madrid, 1989.

Sánchez-Eppler, Karen. *Touching Liberty: Abolition, Feminism, and the Politics of the Body*. Berkeley: University of California Press, 1993.

Sánchez García, José Luis. *El ateneo científico, literario y artístico de Palencia (1876–1926)*. Palencia: Merino Artes Gráficas, 1989.

———. "Bibliografía." In *Costumbres populares: Colección de cuadros tomados del natural*, by Sofía Tartilán, edited by José Luis Sánchez García, 23–25. Madrid: Miraguano, 2004.

———. Prologue to *Costumbres populares: Colección de cuadros tomados del natural*, by Sofía Tartilán, edited by José Luis Sánchez García, 9–19. Madrid: Miraguano, 2004.

Sánchez Llama, Íñigo. *Galería de escritoras isabelinas: La prensa periódica entre 1833 y 1895*. Madrid: Cátedra, 2000.

Sanfeliu, Luz. "Del laicismo al sufragismo: Marcos conceptuales y estrategias de actuación del feminismo republicano entre los siglos XIX y XX." *Pasado y Memoria: Revista de Historia Contemporánea* 7 (2008): 59–78.

Sarap, Madan. *Jacques Lacan*. Toronto: University of Toronto Press, 1992.

Scanlon, Geraldine. *La polémica feminista en la España contemporánea (1868–1974)*. Madrid: Siglo XXI, 1976.

———. *La polémica feminista en la España contemporánea, 1868–1974*. Translated by Rafael Mazarrasa. Madrid: Akal, 1986.

Schloesser, Stephen. *Jazz Age Catholicism: Mystic Modernism in Postwar Paris, 1919–1933*. Toronto: University of Toronto Press, 2005.

Science Encyclopedia. "Psychoanalysis—Melanie Klein and Object Relations." http://science.jrank.org/pages/10906/Psychoanalysis-Melanie-Klein-Object-Relations.html.

Scott, Nina. Introduction to *Sab*, by Gertrudis Gómez de Avellaneda, xi–xxvii. Austin: University of Texas Press, 1993.

Servera, José. Introduction to *Sab*, by Gertrudis Gómez de Avellaneda, 9–83. Madrid: Cátedra, 1999.

Shapiro, Bee. "Malia Obama's Look, like Mom's, Sells Clothes." *New York Times*, August 27, 2015.

Sharp, Matthew. "Jacques Lacan, 1901–1981." Internet Encyclopedia of Philosophy. http://www.iep.utm.edu/lacweb/#SH4a.

Sieburth, Stephanie. *Inventing High and Low: Literature, Mass Culture, and Uneven Modernity in Spain.* Durham, N.C.: Duke University Press, 1994.

———. "La poética del sufrimiento en *La Regenta*." In *Leopoldo Alas, un clásico contemporáneo (1901–2001). Actas del congreso celebrado en Oviedo (12–16 de noviembre de 2001)*, vol. 2, edited by Araceli Iravedra Valea, Elena de Lorenzo Álvarez, and Álvaro Ruis de la Peña, 805–811. Oviedo: Universidad de Oviedo, 2002.

Simmel, Georg. "Fashion." *International Quarterly*, October 1, 1904. http://www.modetheorie.de/fileadmin/Texte/s/Simmel-Fashion_1904.pdf.

Simón Alegre, Ana I. "Diez cartas y una escritora: Concepción Gimeno." Universidad de Zaragoza. https://siem.unizar.es/sites/siem.unizar.es/files/users/siem/Premio/xiv_premio_investigacion-ana_simon.pdf.

Simón Palmer, Carmen. *Actividades públicas de las madrileñas en la I República.* Madrid: Artes Gráficas Municipales / Área de Régimen Interior y Patrimonio, 2002.

———. "Puntos de encuentro de las mujeres en el Madrid del siglo XIX." *RDTP* 56, no. 1 (2001): 183–201. http://rdtp.revistas.csic.es.

———. "Revistas españolas femeninas del siglo XIX." In *Homenaje a don Agustín Millares Carlo*, vol. 1, edited by Fondo para la Investigación Económica y Social de la Confederación Española de Cajas de Ahorros, 401–446. Las Palmas de Gran Canaria: Caja Insular de Ahorros de Gran Canaria, 1975.

Sinclair, Alison. *Dislocations of Desire: Gender, Identity, and Strategy in "La Regenta."* Chapel Hill: University of North Carolina Press, 1998.

Sinués, María del Pilar. *Premio y castigo.* Madrid: Julián Peña, 1857.

Smith, Jennifer. "Women, Mysticism and Alternative Technologies of the Self in Selected Writings of Emilia Pardo Bazán." *Revista de Estudios Hispánicos* 45, no. 1 (2011): 155–175.

Smith, Sidonie. *A Poetics of Women's Autobiography.* Bloomington: Indiana University Press, 1987.

Smith, Sidonie, and Julia Watson. Introduction to *Women, Autobiography, Theory: A Reader*, 3–52. Madison: University of Wisconsin Press, 1998.

———, eds. *Women, Autobiography, Theory: A Reader.* Madison: University of Wisconsin Press, 1998.

Smith, Theresa Ann. *The Emerging Female Citizen: Gender and Enlightenment in Spain.* 1993. Berkeley: University of California Press, 2006.

Sociedad Española de Historia de la Educación. *Actas VI Coloquio de Historia de la Educación: Mujer y educación en España, 1868–1975.* Santiago de Compostela: Universidad de Santiago, 1990.

Soelle, Dorothee. *The Silent Cry: Mysticism and Resistance.* Translated by Barbara and Martin Rumscheidt. Minneapolis: Fortress Press, 2001.

Soria López, Mar. "Homebound Workers and the Destabilization of Bourgeois Domestic Space in Benito Pérez Galdós's *Tormento* (1884) and Emilia Pardo Bazán's 'Casi artista' and 'El mundo' (1908)." *Revista de Estudios Hispánicos* 48, no. 3 (2014): 571–595.

Spain Then and Now. "19th-Century Spain, Overview: Politics." Last modified July 6, 2009. http://www.spainthenandnow.com.

Spear, Laura Susan. "Vanishing Vectors: Trains and Speed in Modern French Crime Fiction and Film." PhD diss., University of Illinois at Urbana-Champaign, 2007.

Spivak, Gayatri Chakravorty. "Can the Subaltern Speak?" In *Marxism and the Interpretation of Culture*, edited by Cary Nelson and Lawrence Grossberg, 271–313. Urbana: University of Illinois Press, 1988.

———. "Imperialism and Sexual Difference." *Oxford Literary Review* 8, nos. 1/2 (1986): 225–240.

Stein, Jeannine. "Arms and the Woman." *Los Angeles Times*, March 29, 2009.

Suárez Casañ, V. *Enciclopedia médica popular.* 2 vols. Barcelona: M. Maucci, 1894.

Surwillo, Lisa. "Poetic Diplomacy: Carolina Coronado and the American Civil War." *Comparative American Studies: An International Journal* 5, no. 4 (2007): 409–422.

Tartilán, Sofía. *Borrascas del corazón*. Madrid, 1884.

———. *La caja de hierro*. In *La lengua larga*, edited by José R. Seoane, 219–240. Madrid: Juan Iniesta, 1871.

———. "Cartas de Tartilán a Barbieri, 1877–1879." In *Apuntes biográficos de diversas personas, cartas y otros documentos*, edited by Francisco A. Barbieri. MSS/14045/70-77. National Library of Spain.

———. "Cartas 1875–1877, Madrid, a Juan Eugenio Hartzenbusch." In *Apuntes biográficos de diversas personas, cartas y otros documentos*, edited by Francisco A. Barbieri. MSS/20809/17-22. National Library of Spain.

———. *Costumbres populares: Colección de cuadros tomados del natural*. Edited by José Luis Sánchez García. Madrid: Miraguano, 2004.

———. *Una deuda de veinte años*. *El Correo de la Moda* 2 (January 10, 1875): 10; no. 3 (January 18, 1875): 18–19; no. 4 (January 26, 1875): 26–27.

———. "Estudio del natural." *Revista de Andalucía* 11 (January 1, 1878): 263–267.

———. *Historia de la crítica*. Seville: Salvador Acuña, 1875.

———. *Páginas para la educación popular*. Madrid: Enrique Vicente, 1877.

———. "La Roma del Imperio y la Francia moderna." *Revista de Andalucía* 7 (January 1, 1877): 230–238; no. 8 (January 2, 1877): 111–114; no. 9 (January 3, 1877): 71–77.

———. www.mcnbiografias.com.

Thrift, Nigel. *Non-representational Theory: Space/Politics/Affect*. Abingdon: Routledge, 2008.

Tolliver, Joyce. *Cigar Smoke and Violet Water: Gendered Discourse in the Stories of Emilia Pardo Bazán*. Lewisburg, Pa.: Bucknell University, 1998.

———, ed. *"El encaje roto" y otros cuentos*. By Emilia Pardo Bazán. New York: MLA, 1996.

Torrecilla, Jesús. *España exótica: La formación de la imagen española moderna*. Boulder, Colo.: Society of Spanish and Spanish-American Studies, 2004.

Torres-Pou, Joan. "La Avellaneda y *Dos mujeres*: Un insólito alegato femenino en la literatura decimonónica." *Ojáncano* 22 (2002): 21–32.

Trautenberg, Ezequiel. "The Yoke of the Hat: Consumption, Middle-Class Values, and Social Mobility in Carmen de Burgos's *La flor de la playa*." *Hispanic Review* 84, no. 1 (2016): 25–46.

Trueba Mira, Virginia. "Paradojas de la alteridad en *Zinda* de Rosa Gálvez." Biblioteca Virtual Miguel de Cervantes. http://www.cervantesvirtual.com/obra-visor-din/paradojas-de-la-alteridad-en-zinda-de-rosa-galvez/html/a36ef558-0bce-11e2-b1fb-00163ebf5e63_3.html#I_0_.

Valera, Juan. *Apuntes sobre el nuevo arte de escribir novelas*. Madrid: M. Tello, 1887.

Valis, Noël. *The Culture of Cursilería: Bad Taste, Kitsch, and Class in Modern Spain*. Durham, N.C.: Duke University Press, 2002.

Waddell, Helen, ed. *The Desert Fathers*. New York: Vintage, 1998.

Walter, Susan. *From the Outside Looking In: Narrative Frames and Narrative Spaces in the Short Stories of Emilia Pardo Bazán*. Newark, Del.: Juan de la Cuesta, 2010.

Wheaten, Sarah. "Latest Campaign Issue? One Candidate's Neckline." *New York Times*, July 28, 2007.

Willem, Linda M. "The Story Not Told: Sex and Marriage in Pardo Bazán's 'Los cirineos' and 'La argolla.'" *Hispania* 95, no. 4 (2012): 587–595.

Williams, Raymond. *The Sociology of Culture*. Chicago: University of Chicago Press, 1995.

Woolf, Virginia. *A Room of One's Own*. London: Harcourt, 1981; San Diego, Calif.: Harcourt Brace Jovanovich, 1984.

Wright, Chad. "'La eterna mascarada hispanomatritense': Clothing and Society in *Tormento*." *Anales Galdosianos* 20, no. 2 (1985): 24–34.

Zamora Juárez, Andrés. *El doble silencio del Eunuco: Poéticas sexuales de la novela realista según Clarín.* Madrid: Fundamentos, 1998.

Zecchi, Barbara. "*Insolación* de Emilia Pardo Bazán: Intertextualidades y parodias, hacia una escritura de la igualdad." *MLN* 122 (2007): 294–314.

Žižek, Slavoj. "La femme n'existe pas." In *Todo lo que usted siempre quiso saber sobre Lacan y nunca se atrevió a preguntare a Hitchcock,* edited by Slavoj Žižek, translated by Jorge Piatigorsky, 113–117. Buenos Aires: Manantial, 1994.

Zola, Émile. *Le Roman expérimental.* 1880. Paris: Garnier-Flammarion, 1971.

Zuern, John David. "Lacan: Mirror Stage, Term." Critica Link. http://www.english.hawaii.edu/criticalink/lacan/terms/other.html.

Index

About the Contributors

Lourdes Albuixech, a native of Spain, is an associate professor of Spanish in the Department of Languages, Cultures, and International Trade at Southern Illinois University Carbondale. Her research centers mainly on the areas of late medieval and early modern Spanish literature and culture. She has written extensively about Spanish sentimental romance, Spanish *comedia*, and Cervantes and published in journals such as *Celestinesca*, *Hispanófila*, *Anales Cervantinos*, and *Bulletin of the Comediantes*. Albuixech is also coauthor of an introductory study to Luis Vélez de Guevara's *La Serrana de la Vera* (Juan de la Cuesta, 2002). More recently, her areas of interest have expanded to include translation studies.

Christine Arkinstall is a professor of Spanish at the University of Auckland. Born in New Zealand, she obtained her master's degree from the University of Oviedo, Spain, and her PhD from the University of Auckland. A specialist in Spain's late nineteenth- and twentieth-century literatures and cultures, she has published widely on issues of gender, genre, and nation. Her 2014 book *Spanish Female Writers and the Freethinking Press, 1879–1926* (University of Toronto Press) foregrounds the exceptional contributions made by female freethinking writers in the fin de siècle to the beginnings of democracy in Spain. Previous books include *Histories, Cultures, and National Identities: Women Writing Spain, 1877–1984* (2009) and *Gender, Class, and Nation: Mercè Rodoreda and the Subjects of Modernism* (2004), both published by Bucknell University Press.

Neus Carbonell is a native of Catalonia and holds undergraduate degrees in Catalan philology and psychology, a master's degree in Spanish literature and comparative literature, and a PhD in comparative literature from Indiana University. A professor at the Universidad Oberta de Catalunya, she is a researcher for the Centre Dona i Literatura, specializing in feminist theory, comparative literature, and psychoanalytic theory. In addition to her numerous scholarly publications, she is the author of the prize-winning novel *Alguna cosa més que tu*. She is also a member of the Asociación Mundial de Psicoanálisis and works as a psychoanalyst in Barcelona. Her three most recent books are *La dona que no existeix. De la Il·lustracio a la Globalizació* (Eumo Editorial, 2003), *No todo sobre el autismo* (in collaboration with Iván Ruiz; Gredos, 2013), and *Cultura i Subjectivitat* (Edicions UOC, 2013).

DENISE DUPONT is a professor of Spanish at Southern Methodist University in Dallas, Texas. She has published *Realism as Resistance: Romanticism and Authorship in Galdós, Clarín, and Baroja* (Bucknell University Press, 2006), *Writing Teresa: The Saint from Ávila at the Fin-de-Siglo* (Bucknell University Press, 2012), and articles in *Romance Quarterly*, *Hispanic Journal*, *Bulletin of Spanish Studies*, *Revista de Estudios Hispánicos*, *Revista Canadiense de Estudios Hispánicos*, *Latin American Literary Review*, *Bulletin of Hispanic Studies*, *Comparative Literary Studies*, and *MLN*. Her recent work focuses on late nineteenth- and early twentieth-century Spanish prose, particularly short stories and essays, and on theological questions in Saint Teresa. DuPont is currently studying theology at the Perkins School of Theology (SMU) and working on a book manuscript on Catholicism in the writings of Emilia Pardo Bazán.

ROGELIA LILY IBARRA is an associate professor of Spanish at Dominican University. Her primary research focus is nineteenth-century Hispanic women's narratives and representations of nation. Ibarra's research questions the complex position of women writers in the production of cultural and national discourses. In her most recent essay, "Rewriting History and Reconciling Cultural Differences in *Guatimozín*," Ibarra argues that Avellaneda contests hegemonic discourses of civilization and barbarism and creates a critical subtext on contemporary issues of her time related to gender, race, and colonial relationships of power between Spain and the newly forming Latin American nations. Ibarra's work has been published in journals such as *Hispania*, *Fashion, Style and Popular Culture*, *Popular Culture Studies Journal*, and *Encyclopedia of Ethnic Clothing in the United States*.

ROBERTA JOHNSON is a professor emerita at the University of Kansas and an adjunct professor in the Department of Spanish and Portuguese at UCLA. She has authored five books, including the seminal *Gender and Nation in the Spanish Modernist Novel* (Vanderbilt University Press, 2003). Her some one hundred articles on a variety of subjects related to twentieth- and twenty-first-century Spanish literature and thought have appeared in journals such as *Revista Canadiense de Estudios Hispánicos*, *Revista Hispánica Moderna*, *Anales de la Literatura Española Contemporánea*, and *Revista de Estudios Hispánicos*. She recently coedited *Antología del pensamiento feminista español 1726–2011* (Cátedra, 2013) with Maite Zubiaurre and is currently completing a book on major concepts in Spanish feminist theory. Professor Johnson has won numerous awards and grants, including a Fulbright lectureship at the University of Valladolid, Spain, and a year-long NEH fellowship in residence at Duke University.

JO LABANYI is a professor of Spanish at New York University. She is the editor of the *Journal of Spanish Cultural Studies* and directs the book series Remapping Cultural History for Berghahn Books. A specialist in modern Spanish cultural history, her most recent publications are the volume on Spanish literature in Oxford University Press's Very Short Introduction series (2010) and the coedited volumes *Europe and Love in Cinema, A Companion to Spanish Cinema* (both 2012) and *Engaging the Emotions in Spanish Culture and History* (2016). She is currently coauthoring *Cultural History of Modern Spanish Literature* (Polity) and *An Oral History of Cinema-Going in 1940s and 50s Spain*. Her research interests include literature, film, photography, popular culture, gender, and memory studies (with particular reference to the Spanish Civil War).

SUSAN M. MCKENNA is an associate professor of Spanish at the University of Delaware, where she teaches courses in Spanish language, literature, and culture. She is the author of *Crafting the Female Subject: Narrative Innovation in the Short Fiction of Emilia Pardo Bazán* (Catholic University of America Press, 2009) as well as articles on Pardo Bazán, Juan Valera, Galdós, Sor Juana Inés de la Cruz, and Cervantes published in *Hispanic Review*, *Hispanófila*, *Letras Peninuslares*, and *Revista Hispánica Moderna*. Her current research focuses on the American playwright and author Barrie Stavis and his relationship to the Spanish Civil War. The study explores the dynamics of transatlantic cultural transfer in Stavis's modernism, especially in regard to his search for idioms and dramatic forms that could reengage the stage with political reform and social justice.

JENNIFER SMITH is an associate professor of Spanish and interim chair of the Department of Languages, Cultures, and International Trade at Southern Illinois University Carbondale. Her main area of research is late nineteenth- and early twentieth-century Spanish literature and culture. Her current book project focuses on the role of science and medicine in the construction of female gender identities and how, in certain contexts, women writers made use of Spain's rich mystical tradition to contest the scientific determinism of the day. In addition to a coedited volume titled *Intersections of Race, Class, Gender, and Nation in Fin-de-Siècle Spanish Literature and Culture* (Routledge, 2017) and a bilingual edition of Emilia Pardo Bazán's *Insolación* (Cervantes, 2011), Dr. Smith has articles published in journals such as *Revista Canadiense de Estudios Hispánicos*, *Revista de Estudios Hispánicos*, and *Anales de la Literatura Española Contemporánea*.

AKIKO TSUCHIYA is a professor of Spanish at Washington University in St Louis. Her areas of specialization include nineteenth- and twentieth-century Spanish literature and culture and gender studies. She is the author of a book on Galdós and has published extensively on nineteenth-century Spanish narrative and on women writers of contemporary Spain. Her most recent books include *Marginal Subjects: Gender and Deviance in Fin-de-siècle Spain* (University of Toronto Press, 2011) and the coedited volume *Empire's End: Transnational Connections in the Hispanic World* (Vanderbilt University Press, 2016). Tsuchiya previously served as the peninsular editor of the *Revista de Estudios Hispánicos* for twelve years. Most recently, she was elected president of the International Association of Galdós Scholars (2015–2017). Her current research on Spanish women of letters and the antislavery movement forms part of a collaborative project with researchers at the Consejo Superior de Investigaciones Científicas (Madrid, Spain).

MARGOT VERSTEEG is an associate professor of Spanish at the University of Kansas. A native of the Netherlands, Professor Versteeg has published numerous articles on nineteenth- and early twentieth-century literature and culture and is the author of *De fusiladores y morcilleros: El discurso cómico del género chico 1870–1910* (Rodopi, 2000) and *Jornaleros de la pluma: Hacia la (re)definición del papel del escritor-periodista en la revista Madrid Cómico* (Iberoamericana/Vervuert, 2011). Her current book project, *After Empire: Emilia Pardo Bazán's Theatrical Vision of a New Spain*, focuses on the theatrical production of Emilia Pardo Bazán. Versteeg also is coediting, with Susan Walter (University of Denver), a volume on Pardo Bazán in the MLA's Approaches to Teaching World Literatures series.

LINDA M. WILLEM is the Betty Blades Lofton Professor of Spanish at Butler University. She holds a PhD from UCLA. Her primary area of specialization is nineteenth-century Spanish literature, with a secondary research area in Spanish film. She currently is the president of the Asociación Internacional de Galdosistas and has served as its secretary treasurer (2007–2016) and executive board vocal (2002–2005). Her book-length publications include *Galdós's segunda manera* (University of North Carolina Press) and *Carlos Saura: Interviews* (University of Mississippi Press) as well as an edition of Galdós's *Doña Perfecta* (Cervantes, 2004) and a collection of Pardo Bazán's short stories (Cervantes, 2010). In addition, she has published more than thirty articles, has presented more than forty papers at national and international conferences, and has received three NEH Summer Seminar awards.